MIDDLE
ADULTHOOD

MIDDLE ADULTHOOD

A Lifespan Perspective

EDITORS

Sherry L. Willis
Pennsylvania State University, University Park

Mike Martin
University of Zurich, Switzerland

SAGE Publications
Thousand Oaks ▪ London ▪ New Delhi

For information:

Sage Publications, Inc.
2455 Teller Road
Thousand Oaks, California 91320
E-mail: order@sagepub.com

Sage Publications Ltd.
1 Oliver's Yard
55 City Road
London EC1Y 1SP
United Kingdom

Sage Publications India Pvt. Ltd.
B-42, Panchsheel Enclave
Post Box 4109
New Delhi 110-017 India

Printed in the United States of America.

Library of Congress Cataloging-in-Publication Data

Middle adulthood: a lifespan perspective / editors, Sherry L. Willis, Mike Martin.
    p. cm.
Includes bibliographical references and index.
ISBN 0-7619-8853-X (cloth)
    1. Middle age—Longitudinal studies. 2. Middle age—Social aspects.
3. Middle aged persons—Social conditions. I. Willis, Sherry L., 1947- II. Martin, Mike, 1965-
HQ1059.4.M52 2005
305.244—dc22   2005003173

This book is printed on acid-free paper.

05 06 07 08 09 10 9 8 7 6 5 4 3 2 1

Acquisitions Editor:	Jim Brace-Thompson
Editorial Assistant:	Karen Ehrmann
Production Editor:	Tracy Alpern
Copy Editor:	Colleen Brennan
Typesetter:	C&M Digitals (P) Ltd.
Indexer:	Pamela Van Huss
Cover Designer:	Glenn Vogel

Contents

Preface

The aim of this volume is to contribute to the literature on development in middle adulthood from a lifespan perspective and within a cultural context. We believe the volume has two unique features. First, most chapters are written by scholars associated with a major longitudinal study that has included the middle years. Depending on the scope of a particular longitudinal study, some authors have considered the impact of early life events on functioning in middle age. Other authors discuss the influence of midlife factors on successful aging in the later years. Such a lifespan perspective is particularly important given the centrality of this age period (approximately 35–65 years) within the life course.

A second distinctive feature of the volume is the focus on midlife from a multicultural perspective. The recent explosion of scholarly volumes on middle age has focused largely on midlife research conducted in the United States, in part due to the huge baby boom cohorts now in middle age. It is well established, however, that middle age is impacted to a greater extent by sociocultural factors (and less by biological determinants) than either the earlier or later periods in the life span, hence arguing for the need for diversity in sociocultural perspective. Furthermore, all Western societies are experiencing a rectangularization of the age distribution, such that there is a greater proportion of individuals in middle and old age than in childhood, as would be the case in the traditional pyramid age structure. Hence, the salience of middle age as a developmental period meriting study is a growing concern in many societies. Determining universal normative patterns of midlife development versus aspects of functioning unique to a given culture is crucial in a lifespan orientation.

The volume's scope can be viewed from three different perspectives. First, there is the lifespan perspective. Some chapters examine factors in adolescence and young adulthood that have an impact on functioning in midlife; other chapters examine the influence of development in middle age on individual functioning and coping in old age. Second, the scope of the volume can be considered with respect to the substantive focus of the chapters. Topics range from a historical perspective of the emergence of middle age as a normative developmental period in the life course during the 20th century, to genetic influences particularly salient in middle age, to stability and change in personality and identity, to cognitive development and decline, and to mental health issues in midlife. Third, the scope of the book can be considered from the range of prestigious longitudinal studies of development featured in the chapters, including the Swedish Adoption/Twin Study of Aging (SATSA), Pulkkinen's Jyväskylä Longitudinal Study of Personality and Social Development (JYLS), Deeg and colleagues' Longitudinal Aging Study Amsterdam (LASA), the work of Martin and colleagues with the Interdisciplinary Study on Adult Development (ILSE), and Schaie's Seattle Longitudinal Study (SLS).

In Part I of the book, historical and demographic perspectives of midlife are considered. In Chapter 1, Wahl and Kruse provide, we believe, one of the first historical overviews of the period of midlife. The conception of middle age is considered at various time periods and from various cultural perspectives. Middle-aged adults are not only in the central part of the life span, but also are typically middle generations within families. In Chapter 2, Kohli and Künemund provide a demographic perspective of the midlife generation, using data from the specific cultural context of Germany.

The chapters in Part II of the book focus on longitudinal studies documenting the impact of early life periods on middle age. SATSA has shown that there are age differences in heritability associated with phenomena such as cognition, personality, and health behaviors; heritability in middle age contrasted with earlier age periods is the focus of Chapter 3 by Pedersen, Spotts, and Kato. In Chapter 4, Pulkkinen, Feldt, and Kokko use JYLS data to examine issues such as continuity and accumulation of social functioning problems from young adulthood to middle age and also the influence of personality factors on social and work lives in midlife. In Chapter 5, Perrig-Chiello and Perren consider the implications of the pluralization of lifestyles and the destandardization of an age-graded society on lifelong development and future well-being. Using data from the Transitions and Life Perspectives in Middle Age study, Perrig-Chiello and Perren report on middle-aged persons' experience of past transitions early in the life span and how these specific experiences may affect current well-being and subsequent aging. In Chapter 6, Martin and Zimprich use ILSE study data to examine stability and change in cognitive functioning in early middle age for cohorts reared in the former East versus West Germany.

Whereas Part II considers the impact of early life experience on midlife, Part III focuses on longitudinal studies that explore the impact of midlife influences on the aging process. In Chapter 7, Deeg describes the transition from late middle age to early old age in terms of physical and mental health, from the vantage point of late midlife as a starting point for older age; the chapter is based on data from LASA. Willis and Schaie utilize data from the SLS, in Chapter 8, to illustrate differences in cognitive change trajectory patterns in midlife; they suggest that patterns of cognitive change in middle age have important and clinically meaningful implications for cognitive outcomes in old age. In Chapter 9, Dörner, Mickler, and Staudinger discuss individuals' self-development in midlife with an emphasis on growth rather than adaptation. Dittmann-Kohli draws on data from both European studies and anthropological data from non-Western societies, in Chapter 10, to discuss development of identity in midlife and the associated gains and losses. Hertzog and Dixon, in Chapter 11, focus on metacognition as an important aspect of self-regulation and how findings in middle age differ from those in other age groups. Finally, in Chapter 12, Martin and Willis highlight future directions for research on middle adulthood toward an integration of research on middle adulthood development in the lifespan developmental literature.

We wish to thank the many people and institutions that have made this volume a reality. We thank Jim Brace-Thompson and the staff at Sage Publications for their support throughout the development and publication of the volume. We thank our intellectual mentors in lifespan developmental psychology for their groundbreaking theoretical and empirical endeavors that laid the foundation for the study of midlife development, including K. Warner Schaie, Paul B. Baltes, and Hans Thomae. Sherry Willis acknowledges the financial and intellectual support of the National Institute on Aging, which has funded her research and the SLS for many years. Mike Martin acknowledges the support of the German Center for Research on Aging at The University of Heidelberg, Ursula Lehr, and the colleagues in Heidelberg for their support of the ILSE, the financial support of the Swiss National Science Foundation for ongoing longitudinal study projects, and Caroline Moor for her insightful comments on the manuscripts.

Finally, we thank our families for their support during the development of this book, but most importantly for their love and care during our own pilgrimage through the midlife years.

* * *

Sage Publications wishes to thank those who reviewed the book, including Rosemary Blieszner, Virginia Polytechnic Institute and State University; Bert Hayslip, University of North Texas, Denton; Michael Marsiske, University of Florida; and Daniel K. Mroczek, Fordham University.

PART I
The Study of Middle Age

*Historical and
Demographic Perspectives*

One

Historical Perspectives of Middle Age Within the Life Span

Hans-Werner Wahl and Andreas Kruse

To our knowledge, there has never been a historical treatise on the concept of middle age or middle adulthood (we will use these terms interchangeably throughout this chapter) within lifespan developmental psychology and lifespan developmental science. At most, the role of adult development in the middle of the life cycle has been touched on here and there in historical treatises such as Groffmann's essay, "Life-Span Developmental Psychology in Europe: Past and Present," which appeared in Goulet and Baltes' (1970) *Life-Span Developmental Psychology: Research and Theory*. Naturally, poets and philosophers have written much about the human life course, including middle age, over the centuries. Nonetheless, a systematic treatise on the history of middle age, how societies and cultures have interpreted the span of years that come after young adulthood and extend into later life, has never been undertaken. It seems as if the historical analysis of the concept of middle adulthood has not been of much interest, which contrasts with the extremes of the life span, childhood (e.g., Aries, 1981) and old age (e.g., Gruman, 1966).

Similarly, no additional "development" was expected after the completion of the adolescence and young adulthood period in traditional conceptions of developmental psychology, and efforts to counteract this tendency tended to jump to late life and old age. A famous example for this is *Senescence: The Last Half of Life*, published in 1922 by G. Stanley Hall (1844–1924), the best-known childhood and adolescence researcher of his time, as he approached his 80s. As expressed in the title, Hall regarded old age as "the last half of life" and reduced middle age, as the reader is informed in the preface of the book, to the adult years between 25 and 45 years of age. The remainder of the book focuses on "senescence," which begins thereafter and lasts until death. Senescence, according to Hall, thus covered part of what is now frequently considered as middle age, that is, ages 45 to 65.

Although developmental psychology and the study of the life course have long neglected middle age, there are promising signs of a sea change (e.g., Brim, Ryff, & Kessler, 2004; Lachman, 2004; Willis & Reid, 1999). The systematic "colonialization" of what Brim (1992) coined the "last uncharted territory in human development" (p. 171) has only recently taken clearer shape in aging and lifespan research. Still, many researchers of aging give middle adulthood slight or no serious attention, paying lip service to the issue without detailed conceptual and empirical consideration.

This book is the most recent attempt to accord middle age its rightful place in the study of human development, and we feel privileged to contribute to this endeavor by tracing the historical dimensions of middle age throughout the centuries. The aim of this chapter is to provide a comprehensive set of observations, analyses, and interpretations of the historical development of the concept of middle adulthood within the life span, with primary focus on social and behavioral science perspectives. "Comprehensive" means that we shall strive to open certain doors for understanding the historical development of the concept of middle adulthood. However, what is behind these doors can only be treated selectively, often by just highlighting names, studies, and approaches to illustrate more general trends. Given the focus of this volume on European research on middle age, and for the sake of brevity, we will consider predominantly Western European trends and perspectives in our historical argumentation. Moreover, we will be able to only briefly touch on intercultural variations in the historical understanding of the concept of middle adulthood. Finally, it should be said that we, the authors of this chapter, are developmental psychologists and gerontologists with deep interests in the historical origin of our field, not historians with interest in development and aging.

Descriptive and Evaluative Aspects, Four Perspectives, and a Working Definition of Middle Age

Descriptive and Evaluative Aspects of Middle Age

Coming to terms with the phenomenon of middle adulthood requires a set of basic categories. One helpful pair of categories in this regard seems to be the distinction between descriptive and evaluative components inherent in the concept of middle adulthood. A descriptive analysis involves studying middle age from perspectives such as chronological age or commonly held opinions on its position in the life span. An evaluative perspective focuses on the perceived quality of middle age and the perceived salience and importance of events and experiences in middle age for life-span development at large.

On the descriptive level, the easier task seems to be to approach the upper limit of middle adulthood by using common borders of when "old age" begins, such as retirement age. Formal retirement, however, is a rather young phenomenon in human history, dating back only to the late decades of the 19th century (Kohli, 1988). Although the idea that the life course could be separated into different stages has been prevalent for millennia, these notions—as will be shown in more detail later in the chapter—are quite diverse and do not allow one to narrow down the "exact" position of middle age during the human life span. Quite another approach to the issue of circumscribing middle age comes from Laslett (1989) in his sociohistorical account of the development of the ages of man. Laslett's conception of a "fresh map of life" defines middle age in a complex manner that cannot be reduced to simple calendar age limits. What others regard as middle age is, in his terminology, a mix of the "second" and "third ages." After a period of dependence, immaturity, socialization, and educational needs in the first age, the second age brings with it a measure of independence, maturity, responsibility, earning, and spending, followed by the third age, characterized by harvesting life achievements and personal fulfillment. The fourth age, according to Laslett, entails for the most part dependence, frailty, and dealing with approaching death.

At the evaluative level, there are also mixed connotations. Hall (1922) was not alone when he argued in the preface of his book on old age that middle age should be seen as "the prime, when we are at the apex of our aggregate of powers [. . .] commonly called our best" (p. vii). In Greek and Roman antiquity, middle age was viewed as the part of the life span "in blossom" (Nühlen-Graab, 1990). In contrast, Laslett (1989) maintained that the climax or "crown" of life is the third age, but argued that the climax sometimes occurs between the second and third age, or even between the first and second age, as may be the case with top-ranking athletes achieving their best physical performances quite early in their life course.

Introducing Four Perspectives to Reflect on Middle Age

It would seem then that middle age remains a slippery concept, regardless of whether one seeks to merely describe or evaluate it. Thus, we offer a classification of four major perspectives that address and differentiate middle age at both descriptive and evaluative levels. To wit, our plan of attack is to rely on a family of four historically framed perspectives on middle adulthood. Each of these perspectives will be treated in more detail in the following pages. We will attempt to delineate the multitude of ways middle adulthood has been understood throughout history. This could also be seen, to take the expression coined by Wittgenstein (1960), as describing the *Sprachspiel* (language usage) of the term *middle adulthood* in historical perspective.

The first perspective describes streams of events characteristic of particular historical eras. The common denominator to these streams of events is that they have fundamentally shaped the everyday world of people, how individuals planned their lives, and what society expected of the aging individual. In particular, we will address issues related to demography and the sociopolitical sphere. This perspective traces the origins of middle adulthood to the demographic and societal developments that naturally accompany the emergence of modern civilization.

In a second perspective, we consider how the genre of fiction over historical time is also able to add to the understanding of middle adulthood and its lifespan dynamics. This is, of course, a wide field, and we therefore only touch on some of the issues. For example, the German *Entwicklungsroman* (novel of development) is a classic form used to portray lifespan development. Middle age has been addressed in novels of development in endless variations.

A third perspective on middle adulthood illustrates how the ancients viewed the human life cycle. Philosophers have written a great deal about human development and the ethical conundrums appointed to various stages of the life cycle, and these classic notions of how life unfolds can be very illuminating.

A fourth perspective on middle adulthood discusses key theoretical conceptions and empirical approaches to the life cycle that stem from behavioral and social developmental science in historical view. We begin with forerunners during the 18th and 19th centuries, such as Tetens (1777/1979) and Quêtelet (1835), and then proceed to the present systematic research on the topic. One basic insight inherent in all of this work is that middle adulthood comprises a large portion of the "life map" and can be thought of as a "bridge of life" from which early lessons are conveyed to the later years. Another major message of this body of work is that pronounced interindividual variability in intraindividual developmental trajectories has been found in every period of the life span (Thomae, 1979) and, hence, also in middle adulthood.

A Working Definition of Middle Adulthood

When integrating various perspectives on middle age into a working definition of middle adulthood in terms of the essential *Familienähnlichkeiten* (family resemblance), to take another major concept of Wittgenstein's thinking (Wittgenstein, 1960), the distinction between descriptive and evaluative elements as introduced before is a helpful tool.

With respect to defining elements of middle age on the descriptive level, most approaches—be they scientific or lay conceptions of middle age—emphasize its unique position in the life course as turning point between the rise and decline of the flow of life. Because demographic, political, and cultural influences shape our lives, conceptions of middle adulthood should be seen as inherently dynamic. Furthermore, it seems that any attempt to identify middle adulthood in objective calendar age terms is problematic and preliminary, although traditionally the 40s, 50s, and early 60s of the human life span have often been identified as middle age, ending with retirement. Middle adulthood is also characterized by pronounced interindividual variation of intraindividual development, thus questioning any attempt to seek uniformity in this life period.

Regarding defining elements on the evaluative level, middle adulthood generally tends to be perceived positively, especially when compared to the period of old age. As has often been noted, middle age prepares individuals for the existential challenges of old age, which have been described as the struggle between despair and ego-integrity (Erikson, 1950). In addition, middle adulthood has been identified in many lifespan developmental conceptions, with the major exception of orthodox psychoanalysis, as the period of the life course with the most direct influence on the course and outcome of old age (Lachman, 2004).

We will use this working definition throughout the remainder of the chapter as a frame of reference, which will then be enriched and differentiated due to the content and findings of each of the chapter's major sections.

Perspective 1

Insights From Historical Demography

It may sound like a truism that the emergence of a circumscribed period of middle adulthood presumes that life expectancy allows for it. Thus, from a demographic perspective, middle age was created by the increase of life expectancy in modern society, which was—as is well-known—quite low until about two centuries ago. For example, while the ancient Greek and Roman empires (roughly from 1100 BC to 600 AD) saw a considerable number of old people, mean life expectancy at the time was about 30 to 35 years, after correcting for the high likelihood of death at birth and in early infancy (Gutsfeld & Schmitz, 2003). To take the example of Germany, life expectancy began to rise after the low mark of the Middle Ages and particularly after the Thirty Years' War (1618–1648). Nevertheless, reaching the age of 40 did not become a normative life event in Germany until the 17th and 18th centuries. Later, from the end of the 19th century until the present, life expectancy rose sharply: It was about 46 years at the beginning of the 20th century and about 79 years at the beginning of the 21st century (Lehr, 2000).

As a consequence of considering such demographic trajectories, people rarely considered what we would call middle age in their personal life planning until around the beginning of the 19th century. In all probability, residents of 18th-century Europe alternated fearing old age and denying that they would live long enough to see it. At the time, society did not regard old age as a distinct life period (a process which began in the early 20th century), but as the beginning of the end of life, a process that was expected to end abruptly. Only when the likelihood of survivorship beyond the age of 40 increased and became a normative event in objective demographic terms, but also in the everyday world experience, did people begin to anticipate a long and secure period following the completion of one's education and entry into marriage.

More recent demographic changes, starting in the 1970s, also helped usher in the notion of middle age. Middle age—as a separate and distinct life stage—somehow began to be characterized not only by the increase in life expectancy but also by a decrease in the end of childbearing. The first of these trends gives rise to a separation of middle adulthood from old age, while the latter implies a relative decrease in time spent rearing children and therefore a separation of middle adulthood from young adulthood (see also Moen & Wethington, 1999).

Sociopolitical Influences

In ancient times, an important aspect of the social construction of middle age was the fact that middle-aged men were considered too old for war service. Middle adulthood was a "safe port" for men in the life course, a welcome retreat from war service (Gutsfeld & Schmitz, 2003). However, in more recent history, this safe port role changed; particularly in World War II (1939–1945), middle-aged men until their 50s were recruited in the final phase, and men in their 40s were still drafted to serve in the Korean War (1950–1953).

In ancient Greece, entering middle adulthood was an important prerequisite for fulfilling major societal and legal duties. For instance, so-called Epheten, similarly to jurors in presence, had to be 50 years or older. Generally, those between the ages of 30 and 50 (i.e., those in the middle years, more or less) were the most powerful societal group in Greece as well as in ancient Rome. Furthermore, the upper limit of middle age in Greek antiquity was probably the calendar age of 60, roughly indicating the time in life when one's property was transferred to one's children (Gutsfeld & Schmitz, 2003).

Sociopolitical history redefined middle adulthood with the "institution-alization of the life course" (Kohli, 1986). According to the institutionaliza-tion thesis, since the late 19th century, modern life has been structured around a period of education and socialization toward career development and achievement, followed by a four- to five-decade long period of involve-ment in the labor force, and finally, mandatory retirement combined with a pension system. The latter provided the monetary basis for the remaining period of life and helped create a unique class of pensioners in society. Note in this context that European retirement legislation, specifically Bismarck's political efforts toward the introduction of a definite retirement age, only happened in the 1870s. Retirement was mandatory at the age of 70 for blue-collar workers and, although only about 20% actually did retire (Borscheid, 1992), it contributed substantially to the definition of middle adulthood by introducing its upper age limit. In 1916, retirement age in Europe was changed to 65. In contrast, mandatory retirement was out-lawed in the United States in 1970, which effectively erased the common upper limit of middle age, at least in the United States. It should be noted that retirement age is now rising in many European countries; this will have an impact on the understanding of middle age. Also, retirement age is a good example for the interaction of normative and nonnormative events (Baltes, Reese, & Lipsitt, 1980) in the societal and individual defini-tions of middle age. On the one hand, middle age may be prolonged to what before was frequently seen as early old age (or the young-old), when retirement age is rising. On the other hand, sharp health declines in per-sons in their 50s or 60s may serve on the individual level as a marker for the end of middle age and the beginning of old age.

As a consequence of the institutionalization of the life course, middle adulthood signaled the forthcoming end of the "working phase" of the life course. However, this probably was strongly shaped in terms of life quality by social class and job type. In the so-called working class, middle adulthood frequently was associated with the emergence of major ill-nesses due to work involvement, whereas middle adulthood in many middle-class jobs implied the right to reduce the number of heavy day-to-day job duties and prepare for the imminent retirement period.

One might argue that the institutionalization of the life course and its consequences apply predominantly to middle-aged men. However, given an ever-increasing portion of women in the labor force in the second half of the 20th century, the concept can be generalized to women as well.

Furthermore, historical periods of economic stagnation have probably had an impact on the understanding of middle adulthood in subjective as well as objective terms. For instance, being confronted with unemployment in middle adulthood, as was the case during the Great Depression in the United States and during the Weimarer Republik in Germany, would naturally alter older individuals' estimation of their "best years." Even in recent times, the natural experiment of German reunification in 1990 resulted in a loss of employment opportunities among many East German men and women "in the middle" of their careers. It remains to be seen how this will affect their experience of old age.

Most recently in historical-societal terms, dramatic changes in the culture of old age, specifically the introduction of what frequently is labeled as the "50+ generation" as well as the societal awareness of the baby boom generation, have had a lasting effect on the understanding of what middle age is or is not (Lachman, 2004). On the one hand, the baby boomers are often discussed in terms of who they will be rather than who they are: Around 2010 to 2015, this cohort will begin to retire, and their impact on societal and health expenditures is a major concern. At present, however, they constitute the largest middle-aged cohort ever alive and also the first to embrace aging with a proactive, "can do" attitude toward both their personal development and their emerging political agenda (Silverstone, 1996). Their vigor has seemingly stretched middle age toward something like the sixth or even the seventh decade. On the other hand, older people's organizations (such as the American Association of Retired Persons [AARP] in the United States), as well as the emergence of the "silver market," have extended their sphere of influence even below the magic border of age 50 and have thus appropriated a large section of middle adulthood. In Germany, the expectation is that the baby boomer generation will play an important role in the growth of the consumer market in decades to come and by this means even contribute to the reduction of the unemployment rate (Naegele, Gerling, & Scharfenorth, in press).

Perspective 2

From the Genres of Fiction, Film, and Music

The genre of fiction has addressed middle age in many variations, creating prototypes or stereotypes of this period of the life span. A few glances are illustrative: Wolfram von Eschenbach's *Parzival* (ca. 1200–1210), frequently regarded as the classic version of the German Entwicklungsroman (i.e., a novel showing the development of an individual's character), treats middle age as dealing with what has been achieved or not (in Parzival's case, searching for the grail) and what still is achievable or still has to be achieved. Shakespeare (1564–1616) addressed the ages of man in Act II, Scene 7 of his play *As You Like It*: "And then the justice, In fair round belly with good capon lin'd, With eyes severe, and beard of formal cut, Full of wise saws and modern instances; And so he plays his part." What then follows, according to Shakespeare's play, is the "sixth age," with a dramatic shift toward experiences of loss: "Sans teeth, sans eyes, sans taste, sans everything." Going further, consider Grimmelshausen's *Der Abentheuerliche Simplicissimus Teutsch* (The Adventurous Simplicissimus; 1668) and Goethe's *Wilhelm Meisters Wanderjahre* (Wilhelm Meister's Apprenticeship; 1821–1829) as additional classic versions of the German Entwicklungsroman. Here, middle age appears, specifically in the Grimmelshausen developmental novel, as a slippery terrain with the risk of failure, but also as the time of mastership and coming to terms with life's experiences, losses, and achievements, as in Goethe's novel.

The role of the middle-aged woman is not as evident as that of the middle-aged man in the genre of fiction. One example is Brecht's *Mutter Courage und ihre Kinder* (Mother Courage and Her Children; 1937), showing all the ambivalences of a woman as she enters middle adulthood, while caring for her children during Germany's Thirty Years' War (1618–1648). Variations of middle-aged protagonists found in post–World War II fiction in German-speaking countries are heavily influenced by the long-term consequences of the war as well as the ambivalences of the Wirtschaftswunder (German economic miracle) unfolding in the 1950s. For example, in Siegfried Lenz's novel *Der Mann am Strom* (Man at the River), published in 1957, the confrontation of a blue-collar worker in his 50s with the challenges of the modern industrial world is described. In the novel *Homo Faber* by Max Frisch, also published in 1957, a successful engineer in his 50s with a strong belief in rationality and the omnipotence of technological development has to accept that highly unlikely events (e.g., having intercourse with one's own daughter whose existence was not known to the father) can nevertheless happen and change one's whole life. A world-famous stereotype of middle age and its potential in terms of thoughtful and persistent analysis (not activism) is Commissaire Maigret in George Simenon's famous crime stories. Similarly, Raymond Chandler's protagonist Philippe Marlowe as the classic "cool" detective in the middle of his life may also come into the picture here, with work such as *The Big Sleep* (1939) and *The Long Goodbye* (1954). More recently, American writer John Updike has produced a strong stereotype of middle adulthood and, at the same time, of America in the 1970s and 1980s with his books featuring Harry Angstrom, called "Rabbit," as the "hero" (ending with *Rabbit at Rest*, published in 1990). Rabbit appears as the classic American middle-class man of that time struggling with his business (selling Toyota cars), the ups and downs in his marriage, his relationship to his children, and coming to terms with unfulfilled aspirations in his personal life.

When it comes to film and the role of middle age, actors as diverse as Humphrey Bogart (classic in *Casablanca*), Sean Connery (specifically in his James Bond roles), and Woody Allen (with all his potential to reveal right and wrong communications in "mature" relationships between men and women) may come to mind. Middle-aged men appear in these roles as being capable of taking decisions against their primary desires for the sake of higher political goals, such as supporting resistance to the Nazi regime (*Casablanca*), resisting all danger and even saving the whole world (James Bond), or surviving the day-to-day miscommunications in core personal relationships (as shown in many Woody Allen movies).

In the music business, particularly in rock music, among the classics of the "young wild" coming to middle age is Mick Jagger of the Rolling Stones, who has been on the stage for more than 40 years. The same holds for ex-Beatle Paul McCartney, although in contrast to Mick Jagger, he has developed in his middle age toward the mature composer and musician always searching for new musical frontiers.

In sum, the genre of fiction has produced many middle-aged prototypes and stereotypes, in which the tension between mastering a particular skill and running the risk of no longer being capable of coping with life appears in rich diversity. Differences between European and U.S. fiction can be found, for instance, in the role of World War II consequences (coping with the Nazi regime, coming to terms with the Wirtschaftswunder), which had a stronger impact on the course and outcome of middle age in European, and specifically German, fiction as compared to that of North America.

Perspective 3

Traditional Stages of the Life Course

Traditional scientific conceptions of the divisions of the human life span range from a simple two-stage conception of the human life course to a conception of 10 stages of human development (Nühlen-Graab, 1990, p. 21). Other metaphors and so-called life step rhymes helped a wider audience to better understand the flow of life. These historical divisions of the life span into distinct stages were not always pegged to calendar age and were typically loaded with evaluative connotations (Table 1.1).

As can be seen in Table 1.1, there is no single universally accepted definition of middle adulthood (Nühlen-Graab, 1990). While there was nothing such as middle age in the dichotomous view of the life course, all remaining conceptions address different facets of the phenomenon of middle age. "Middle" age tends to be included in the second half of life in conceptions involving four and five life stages, while inclusion of more life stages enhances the description of "middle," but also entails an increasingly limited definition of its lower and upper limits in terms of calendar age. The 10-stage conception places middle age roughly at the age range of 30 to 50 years. Gender differences always were important in these conceptions because it was tempting to use female menopause as a natural limit for the end of middle age and the beginning of old age. As a consequence, there always was a tendency to date the beginning of old age earlier in women, which also meant a shortened period of middle adulthood for women, compared with men.

Historical Metaphors of the Life Course

In addition to the historical partitioning of the life course, other metaphors have been used across the centuries to help understand the life flow and its expected and unexpected ups and downs. These metaphors were an important means of providing advice to others and handing down hearth-fire wisdom to one's children about how life unfolds. This is simply commonsense knowledge of what is "normal" at which periods of the life course as well as, from a society's perspective, what can be expected from societal members at which ages. The metaphor of a "life staircase" (*Lebenstreppe* in German, *Degrés des Ages* in French) with one part of the staircase going up while the other is going down, was a powerful metaphor that became quite popular across Europe in the 16th century (Schriften des Rheinischen Museumsamtes, 1983). The Renaissance and the Enlightenment nurtured such life course metaphors in the hopes of revealing a rational structure underlying the flow of life.

Life staircases came in many variations (e.g., separate variations for men and women) and depicted different life stages. Figure 1.1 shows a life staircase, drawn in 17th-century Germany (Augsburg), which includes both sexes. The writing under the life stairs refers to the most common

Table 1.1   Historical Stages of the Life Course at a Glance

Youth			Old Age		
Summer			Winter		
Two-stage conception according to the year's extreme seasons					

Child, Young Man		Adult		Old Age	
Sunrise		Sun summit		Sunset	
Three-stage conception according to the day course					

Child 0–20	Young Man 20–40	Man 40–60	Old Man 60–80
Morning/Spring	Noon/Summer	Afternoon/Fall	Evening/Winter
Four-stage conception according to the year's seasons			

0–15	15–30	30–45	45–60	60–Death
Five-stage conception according to Varro				

0–7	7–14	14–28	28–50	50–70	Death
Infantia	Pueritia	Adolescentia	Inventus, fermissima aetatum omnium	Aetas seniores, id est gravitas	Senectus
Six-stage conception according to Isidor of Sevilla					

0–7	7–14	14–21	21–28	28–35	35–42	42–49	49–56	56–63	63–70
Ten-stage conception according to the "Hebdomaden" separation of the life course									

0–10	10–20	20–30	30–40	40–50	50–60	60–70	70–80	80–90	90–100
A child	A young man	A man	Well-done	Standing still	Old age begins	A frail old person	No more wisdom	Children's mockery	Needs the mercy of god
Ten-stage conception based on astrological analogy (Also given is the content of a German so-called life step rhyme dating from the 16th century.)									

SOURCE: Adapted from Nühlen-Graab (1990).

Figure 1.1   Example of a Life Staircase ("Lebenstreppe"); Augsburg, Germany, circa 1660

SOURCE: Schriften des Rheinischen Museumsamtes. (1983). *Die Lebenstreppe* (S. 22). Köln, Germany: Rheinland-Verlag.

version of life step rhyme (see also Table 1.1, last row) and says (from left to right): 10 years—a child; 20 years—a young man; 30 years—a man; 40 years—well-done; 50 years—standing still; 60 years—old age begins, 70 years—a frail old person (*Greis*), 80 years—no more wisdom; 90 years— children's mockery. One hundred years of age is coming on a different level on the left-hand side beside the 90-year stage with the text: 100 years—needs the mercy of God.

The life staircase metaphor not only attracted much attention from the art world in ever-new variations (*Schriften des Rheinischen Museumsamts*, 1983), but also was frequently found cheaply produced in the living room of many private homes. The central element of this lay world metaphor was a two-dimensional image of human development with a balanced up-and-down movement as people age. In the majority of these depictions, middle adulthood clearly possessed a privileged position at the apex of the drawing, shown as occurring at the culmination of earlier life periods and before those characterized by decline. Middle adulthood was unique because it symbolized the pinnacle of human development and the turning point of the life course; thereafter, the dynamics toward decline and death were unavoidable. Again, the iconography for women was more pronounced toward decline, which was assumed to occur earlier in their lives compared with men and taking a more dramatic downward trajectory.

On Philosophical Treatises of Middle Adulthood

Human development has been an important subject of philosophical thought from the dawn of time. A recent book edited by German historians Gutsfeld and Schmitz (2003) affords an overview on how the aged were perceived in classical antiquity, pointing to important differences and similarities in Athens, Rome, and Sparta. The ideas of Aristotle, Plato, Seneca, and others are regularly recited in contributions to the history of contemporary gerontology. Perspectives on middle adulthood were, in a sense, indirectly addressed in classical Greek philosophy, given the Greeks' basic understanding of *old age*. In particular, Aristotle held a rather pessimistic view of old age, whereas middle adulthood was, in his conception, a period of life that still shared all the advantages of earlier life phases but not the disadvantages of old age. Plato had a much more positive attitude toward old age and thus did not consider the potential of middle adulthood as highly as Aristotle. Philosophical treatises of the life course generally posit the position that the ideals of full human maturity, autonomy, wisdom, responsibility, moral judgment, and identity can only be attained in later life, despite the fact that most bodily functions, by then, are on the wane.

Nonetheless, ancient philosophers rarely *explicitly* speculated in well-developed treatises about the nature of middle age. As a rule, classical treatises separate the old from the young. The period of middle age, as defined by contemporary research, is sometimes subsumed under old age in these treatises, sometimes under young adulthood. Because very few people reached what we would call "old age" and because societies were rarely able to provide prolonged freedom from societal obligations to what we would call "young adults," we argue that there was simply no need for a social construction of middle age as a separate and unique period of life. This seems to be particularly true for the female life course. In early societies, the main task for women was to raise children. Having fulfilled this life task, they were thought of as old. This statement seems to be valid even for European societies in the 19th and early 20th centuries (see Borscheid, 1992).

Perspective 4

Precursors of Lifespan Developmental Science

At the end of the 18th century, German scholar Tetens (1736–1807) was among the first to organize then-current theoretical conceptions on the human life span into a consistent picture. Tetens (1777/1979) embraced the classic dynamic of the rise and decline in human development, assuming that energy loss begins in the middle of the life span and accelerates across old age until death. Belgian mathematician and social statistician Quêtelet (1796–1874) added much to developmental science with his fundamental assumption that the flow of the human life course has its own laws that remained to be discovered by forthcoming lifespan-related research (Quêtelet, 1835). Quêtelet developed concrete ideas about the relations between calendar age and specific kinds of psychosocial development, thus supporting the notion that every period of human life should receive focused scientific attention. For example, Quêtelet assumed that mental illnesses were most likely to occur (and least likely to remit) between the ages of 30 and 50, that is, during middle adulthood. To transpose this to a more general argument, there was the assumption that what happens during middle adulthood is probably the most important determinant of the course, content, and outcomes of old age. Quêtelet also made a very important and convincing argument for interindividual differences in intraindividual variability, which should hold for any life period, including middle adulthood. Quêtelet mentioned sex, geographical, national, and social influences as important driving forces for such variation.

Motives for the Consideration of Middle Adulthood in Classic Life Course Conceptions in the 20th Century

In the preface to *Middle Age and Aging*, Bernice Neugarten (1968b) wrote about her pioneering efforts to teach a course on adulthood and old age in social sciences at the University of Chicago in the early 1940s. This field came to be called the "developmental behavioral sciences" by the end of the 1960s:

> In the first years of that curricular effort, the lack of published materials was a major handicap. Today the situation has drastically altered, for a wealth of studies has appeared, many being of considerable sophistication. The problem is now mainly one of organization, for the studies are scattered throughout a wide range of psychological and sociological books and articles. (p. vii)

According to Lehr (1978), the principal reasons why middle adulthood has long been neglected in developmental psychology are (a) the longtime predominance of biological theories of development, (b) the lack of research questions for a pedagogically oriented developmental psychology, (c) sampling problems and related methodological discussions, and (d) a research focus on social groups that are supposed to be disadvantaged or discriminated against.

However, some psychological approaches to the study of developmental processes in middle adulthood have been inspired by the results of gerontological research, showing that a substantial part of behavior in old age is determined by biographical factors: "Present behavior can only be completely understood if past behavior is known" (Shanas, 1975, p. 500). As an example, much research on intelligence, learning, and memory in middle adulthood was initiated to improve knowledge about how some older individuals maintain cognitive capacity while others experience cognitive decline. Other contributions to the developmental psychology of middle age were motivated by research interests in the long-term consequences of developmental paths that could be observed in childhood and adolescence. The progress of American longitudinal studies of child development, with origins in the 1920s and 1930s (Eichorn, Mussen, Clausen, Haan, & Honzik, 1981; Kagan & Moss, 1962; Maas & Kuypers, 1974; Terman & Oden, 1959; Vaillant, 1977), reflects these research interests.

Probably the oldest motive for research on middle age is apparent in early endeavors to discover the characteristic peaks and troughs, or laws, characterizing lifelong developmental processes (see also the perspectives described in previous sections). That is, middle age appears to be the major turning point in the life cycle. For example, a contribution by Neugarten (1968a) on the awareness of middle age focuses on this idea. Based on an extensive set of studies carried out in the Committee on Human Development at the University of Chicago (see also Achenbaum, 1995),

Neugarten argued that a then-recent issue of *Time* magazine, portraying 40- to 60-year-old Americans as "the command generation," corresponded very well with the self-perceptions of middle-aged Americans.

> Middle-aged men and women, while they by no means regard themselves as being in command of all they survey, nevertheless recognize that they constitute the powerful age-group vis-à-vis other age groups; that they are the norm-bearers and the decision-makers; and they live in a society which, while it may be oriented towards youth, is controlled by the middle-aged. (Neugarten, 1968a, p. 93)

According to research by Neugarten (1968a), middle age was perceived at that time as a distinctive period in the life cycle, that is, a period qualitatively different from other age periods. Individuals in the middle saw themselves as the bridge between the generations in family, work, and community. Moreover, time perspective changed from a focus on time-since-birth to a focus on time-left-to-live. Simultaneously, feelings of maximum capacity and ability to manage environmental demands as well as a highly differentiated self were expressed. Only very few expressed a wish to be young again.

A Glance at Selected Life Course Conceptions

Jung

Carl Gustav Jung (1928, 1933) has influenced the psychology of middle adulthood insofar as—similar to Hollingworth (1928)—he advocated the thesis that as a matter of principle, human beings are open to new experiences and able to realize potentials of development in this period of life. The thesis is reflected clearly in the formulation that middle-aged adults try to re-experience in their inner worlds what they previously found in the outer world. The general introversion of mental (or "psychic") energy is also seminal for increasing one's awareness of collective consciousness and symbols. According to Jung, acknowledging collective themes is an important developmental task as well as an important opportunity for inner growth in the second half of life. Jung's perspective on middle age (which is suggested to start at about age 40 and end at about age 65) proceeds from the assumption of major changes in physical and psychological life. People begin to experience decline in physical capacity and start to realize that they are no longer able to do things they used to do in younger years. From a psychological perspective, acquisition of new knowledge and skills becomes less important, and priority is given to questions of meaning and spirituality.

Bühler and Rothacker

The classic works of Charlotte Bühler, written in Vienna in the 1930s, have made a lasting contribution to our knowledge of middle adulthood. In her book *Der menschliche Lebenslauf als psychologisches Problem* (The Human Life Course as a Psychological Problem), Bühler (1933) elaborated a model of lifespan development that echoed the well-known dynamics of gains and losses. Middle adulthood again is seen as a transition period, before "regressive" tendencies take over. Bühler's attempts to empirically support her conceptions, using detailed reconstruction of the biographies of both well-known and ordinary persons, make her work all the more valuable. In contrast, German philosopher and psychologist Erich Rothacker (1938) argued that middle age is the stage of occurrence of a major crossing over of two fundamental trajectories in the human life span. According to Rothacker, while physiological functioning begins to decrease, psychological functioning continues to mature and grow until death (Kruse, 2000).

Erikson

In his well-known theory of ego development, Erik H. Erikson (1950) differentiated eight stages or "psychosocial crises" of the expanding ego. These crises are a consequence of both inner-world and outer-world demands, reflecting biological processes of maturation, personal experience, and aspirations as well as social norms and institutions. The theory states that the resolution of psychosocial crises determines future ego development; that is, failing to adapt successfully to the demands of a specific crisis prevents people from coping successfully with the demands of later psychosocial crises.

Each crisis is defined by a "positive" and a "negative" outcome. In early adulthood, the outcomes are intimacy and ego isolation, whereas in late adulthood, they are ego integrity and despair. Intimacy refers to the development of mutuality in a heterosexual partnership, while ego integrity refers to the acceptance of one's own life as inevitable, appropriate, and meaningful. In middle adulthood, building on the achievements of former ego development (i.e., a sense of basic trust, autonomy, initiative, industry, and intimacy), individuals have to manage the psychosocial crisis of generativity versus stagnation.

In his classic monograph, *Childhood and Society,* Erikson (1950) stated that generativity refers primarily to "the concern in establishing and guiding the next generation, although there are individuals who, through misfortune or because of special and genuine gifts in other directions, do not apply this drive to their own offspring" (p. 46). Moreover, generativity is said to include the more popular synonyms of productivity and creativity, which, however, cannot replace generativity. From a psychoanalytic perspective, Erikson argued that "the ability to lose oneself in the meeting of bodies and minds leads to a gradual expansion of ego-interests and to a libidinal investment in that which is being generated" (p. 47). As a consequence, Erikson's understanding of generativity implies advances in both psychosexual and psychosocial aspects of lifelong development (see also McAdams & Logan, 2004).

Marcia

Marcia (1980) expanded on the work of Erikson with respect to the development of identity. In Marcia's view, the status of identity development is determined by two dimensions: obligation and exploration. In contrast to the theoretical position of Erikson, further development of identity does not necessarily imply perceptions of crisis. Marcia (1980) differentiated between four developmental stages of identity, with some people passing through all and others passing through only some of the stages.

The first stage, "identity diffusion," is characterized by low levels of exploration and obligation. The second stage, "foreclosure," implies an adoption of norms and values from significant others. As such, foreclosure is simultaneously characterized by a low level of exploration and a high level of obligation. The third stage, "moratorium," corresponds to the crisis described by Erikson. Here, questions of identity involve a high level of exploration and a low level of obligation. Finally, "identity achievement" is characterized by high levels of exploration and obligation after people have extensively worked through alternative identities and established a preferred identity for themselves. Empirical evidence shows that this stage of identity achievement is not often reached before middle adulthood

(Kroger & Green, 1996). Moreover, a specific form of identity diffusion has been shown to result from failing to adapt successfully to critical life events or other developmental demands. As such, identity diffusion in middle adulthood might reflect a kind of regression due to unresolved tasks and challenges (Marcia, 1989; Whitbourne, 1986).

Peck

The contribution of Robert C. Peck to the understanding of psychological development in the second half of life proceeds from the perspective that Erikson's eighth crisis (ego integrity vs. despair) refers to a major issue of life after age 30. Specifically, Peck (1956) proposed to divide this crisis into several stages that represent "quite different kinds of psychological learning at different stages in the latter half of life" (p. 44). Concerning middle age, Peck distinguished between four stages that may occur in different sequences. The first stage, valuing wisdom versus valuing physical powers, refers to both inescapable decreases in physical strength, stamina, and attractiveness as well as to accumulated experiences and accomplishments. Peck defined wisdom as "the ability to make the most effective choices among the alternatives which intellectual perception and imagination present for one's decision" (p. 45). Successful adaptation to the demands of this stage of middle adulthood implies that self-definitions and behavior no longer rely primarily on physical aspects of the self. The resolution of the second stage, socializing versus sexualizing in human relationships, refers to a redefinition of partnership that accentuates aspects of individuality and companionship instead of sexual aspects. The third stage, cathectic flexibility versus cathectic impoverishment, refers to a time period during which most people are confronted with living with their children, experiencing the death of a parent, and seeing social relationships with peers diminish. Simultaneously, this is the time period during which maturity and status offer the best opportunities "to reinvest emotions in other people, other pursuits and other life settings" (p. 45). The fourth life stage, mental flexibility versus mental rigidity, refers to the risk of becoming more and more set in one's ways, inflexible, opinionated, and closed-minded. Successful adaptation to the demands of this developmental stage implies that "people learn to master their experiences, achieve a degree of detached perspective on them and make use of them as provisional guides to the solution of new issues" (p. 46).

Havighurst

Robert Havighurst (1948) introduced the concept of developmental tasks to refer to age-specific challenges that reflect biological changes, social roles, norms and expectations, and personal aspirations. Similar to the concept of crisis, successful development is conceptualized as the resolution of a conflict between the actual state of development and normative demands of the inner and outer world. However, Havighurst's concept of developmental task does not imply that individuals indeed experience a kind of crisis, as suggested by authors like Erikson and Peck. Early adulthood is described as a period during which people are well prepared for learning new things and numerous changes of behavior occur due to new experiences. By contrast, middle adulthood, particularly the period between the ages of 30 and 40, is characterized by a high degree of stability: "This is the period of least introspection and self-awareness. Doubts about oneself have been put to rest. The ego is in command, maturation introduces no new factors, and the situation is generally stable and satisfactory" (Havighurst, 1963, p. 31). For Havighurst, the decade from age 40 to age 50 is the prime time of life, a period of "expansion of power and influence," of "growing interest in civic and cultural study and activity" (p. 63). The following decade from age 50 to age 60 is characterized by interindividual variability, primarily nurtured by variables such as sex and membership in social groups. In sum, Havighurst claimed that in middle adulthood, that is, the period from age 30 to age 60, men and women reach the peak of their influence on society, and at the same time, society makes its maximum demands on them for social and civic responsibilities.

The Rise and Fall of the Concept of Midlife Crisis

The still most popular approach to crisis or developmental tasks in middle adulthood is the notion of midlife crisis (Levinson, Darrow, Klein, Levinson, & McKee, 1978). This concept emerged in the 1960s and 1970s, to some extent as a consequence of an overestimation of the importance of biological factors and to some extent as a consequence of the growing popularity of psychoanalysis. Even if the concept of midlife crisis might reflect "pure figment" or a kind of collective fantasy concocted by middle-aged white males for middle-aged white males (Whitbourne, 1986), the concept was originally (and sometimes still is) thought of as having fairly recognizable dimensions. As Rosenberg, Rosenberg, and Farrell (1999) noted,

> The midlife crisis was not a professional crisis, nor a marital crisis, nor an economic crisis, although these surface manifestations could certainly signal its presence. . . . Midlife crisis theory was less a paradigm than a set of beliefs or assumptions about the relation between the subject's experience of self . . . and correlative attitudes, symptoms and personality dimensions. The end of young adulthood and the beginning of middle age was thought to produce a reevaluation of the self, and (potentially) accompanying symptoms of depression, anxiety, and manic flight. (p. 49)

The notion of midlife crisis can be substantiated with reference to the work of Karin Horney, Erich Fromm, and, particularly Carl Gustav Jung. In *Neurosis and Human Growth* (1950), Horney argued that experience of crisis is a prerequisite for the realization of the universal need for self-fulfillment. Similarly, in *Escape from Freedom* (1945), Fromm argued that individuation, that is, the maturation of a unique and individual personality, implies a disengagement from former attachments. Freedom through disengagement is characterized as a risk because tolerating freedom always means to exchange trustworthiness in social relationships for uncertainty. According to Jung (1928, 1933), fulfillment of individuation is not possible without tension and disturbance of homeostasis. For the process of individuation, it is inevitable to experience crisis. Self-fulfillment through individuation is conceptualized as introversion, a tendency that might also lead to a growing awareness of singularity and isolation (see also Rank, 1945).

The concept of midlife crisis does not receive strong support from the current literature. In summarizing new thoughts and new directions of research on middle age, Reid and Willis (1999) concluded that the midlife crisis has been overdramatized.

> Some individuals, it is true, find the reality of faded youth and lost opportunities to be distressing. In addition, the growing realization of the inevitability of one's own mortality may lead to a sense of hopelessness and despair. However, for many individuals, the beauty of development during midlife involves an emerging sense of perspective regarding one's own place within the life cycle. (p. 277)

As early as 1978, Lehr noted that theoretical accounts of crises in midlife do not regularly rely on empirical data nor are they supported by them. Similarly, in a paper titled "Common Dimensions of Personality Development," Norma Haan (1981) concluded,

> Strictly speaking, most writers are not positing formal stages of personality development. Instead, they are describing circumstances arising from social or biological events that acquire the person to re-accommodate, for example an "empty nest" or menopause. Because we have no knowledge of adult structural changes, our best questions may concern the possibly more pervasive and invariant ways that people negotiate inevitable changes in their milieu during lifetimes. (p. 147; see also Eichorn, Clausen, et al., 1981)

Summary View on Life Course Conceptions and Middle Age

Summing up the aforementioned contributions from classic life course conceptions, we submit that although middle age was always considered as a period of transition, this must not be equated with the beginning of inevitable decline. Even if people are said to have reached a maximum of achievement and power (Neugarten), this does not mean that further development is to be equated with quantitative losses in social roles, physical abilities, and psychological functioning. Instead, transition in middle age is conceptualized as qualitative change, implying potentials for further development. Moreover, at least implicitly, descriptions of middle age always refer to a lifespan developmental perspective.

Historically, a good deal of research on development in middle age was motivated by an interest in further development of young adults, while other research was inspired by the insight that late-life development must be conceptualized as a continuation of former processes of development. The theories of Jung, Erikson, Havighurst, Marcia, and Peck all state that successful development in middle age requires the solution of specific developmental tasks. The long-standing interest in the concept of midlife crisis similarly reflects the assumption of lifetime specific requirements. The empirical evidence supporting the prevalence and developmental impact of a midlife crisis has, however, remained weak. In conclusion, it can be stated that most theoretical accounts reflect an overall positive evaluation of middle age; that is, middle age is seen as a period that offers substantial potentials for psychological growth.

Insights on Middle Adulthood
in Classic Empirical Work in
Developmental Science and Gerontology

Early cross-sectional studies that examined a wide range of individuals, from 18 to 60 years of age, such as the work on mental abilities provided by Yerkes (1921) or the study by Miles and Miles (1932), which covered the first until the eighth decade of the human life span, were not much interested in what happens during the rather "quiet" years of the human life span, that is, middle adulthood. By and large, the issue in developmental psychology in the 1930s and 1940s was to make a strong point that aging is worthy of study. Thus, it is no surprise that the classic handbook edited by Cowdry (1939) titled *Problems of Aging* hardly touched on middle adulthood in its 32 chapters.

Empirical work directly addressing middle adulthood has remained a rather rare enterprise. In Germany, for example, Lehr and Thomae (1958) conducted a study on middle adulthood with low-level white-collar workers aged 30 to 50. The rationale for the study was the high number of young men who died during World War II and the ensuing societal need to learn more about the potential of middle adulthood in the labor force. In addition, the Bonn Longitudinal Study on Aging (Lehr & Thomae, 1987) addressed middle age, at least indirectly, by the study's reconstruction of detailed biographies of its participants. The goal was to better understand the flow and outcome of aging as observed in seven measurement occasions from 1965 until 1983. Findings of the Bonn Longitudinal Study on Aging point not only to a high degree of inter-individual variability in physiological, psychological, and social dimensions of aging but also to the existence of different patterns of aging embedded in different biographical set-ups. More specifically, results of the Bonn Longitudinal Study on Aging show that although there was a trend toward higher life satisfaction among those who reported more activity in social roles, some people (especially women) might gain higher life satisfaction from low activity and social disengagement. Moreover, results showed a complex interaction of gender and stress exposure on the one hand and life satisfaction on the other hand, suggesting that the consequences of specific stressors cannot be understood without taking into account the individual ways people try to cope with the respective stressors.

Probably the best-known American study from a historical view of the development of this literature is the work of Henry S. Maas and Joseph A. Kuypers. In their book *From Thirty to Seventy*, Maas and Kuypers (1974) report results from a 40-year longitudinal study of adult lifestyles and personalities. Summarizing the evidence on continuity, constancies, and change, the authors noted that the most remarkable of their findings was that many of the parents found to be similar in lifestyle or personality in old age were also alike in their young adulthood. They continued that this general statement needed further qualification, because there was much variation in the strength of relationship between early and later adulthood for the different personality groups and lifestyle clusters. "For some groups, young-adult associations are very few, weak, and not particularly meaningful; for others the associations are many and strong" (p. 202). Moreover, findings indicate that even when people fail to realize developmental potentials or suffered from unfortunate developmental conditions in young adulthood, later years offer new opportunities. In sum, the results of Maas and Kuypers's study indicate that the "popular and literary myth of inescapable decline in old age" (p. 215) is not supported by empirical evidence. Moreover, results on the development of personality and lifestyles run contrary to the assumption of normative life crisis and universal sequences of stages in middle adulthood.

What has empirical work on middle age achieved up until the 1980s? Research on the subjectively perceived segmentation of the life course does not support the notion of normative stages or crises in adulthood. Biographical studies point to the importance of subjective perceptions and interpretations of individual experiences and episodes that, regardless of chronological, biological, or social age, challenge individual capacities to grasp the opportunities and cope with the demands of actual situations. The results of early longitudinal studies clearly disprove the hypothesis of a normative crisis as well as the hypotheses of a general continuity between the third and the fourth or the discontinuity between the fifth and the sixth decade of life (Lehr, 1969, 1978; Lehr & Thomae, 1965).

In their now classic book *Present and Past in Midlife*, Eichorn, Mussen, et al. (1981) distinguish between three major controversies in the developmental literature. The first is whether differences found in cross-sectional research designs reflect real age changes or simply cohort-specific sociohistorical contexts. The second controversy concerns the consistency of interindividual differences, that is, the question whether rank order within a given group remains stable when time and circumstances change. The third controversy is about appropriate models of change. The three longitudinal studies carried out at the Institute of Health and Development (IHD)—the Guidance Study, the Berkeley Growth Study, and the Oakland Growth Study—offer substantial insights into each of the three controversies. Moreover, the IHD's intergenerational studies demonstrate that sociohistorical events do not have an equal impact on all members of a cohort. Results on the consistency of interindividual differences, particularly on sex differences in paths to psychological health in the middle years (Livson, 1981), provide evidence that although self-reports reflect considerable long-term consistency, there is great situational variation in more specific behaviors (see also Eichorn, Clausen, et al., 1981). Furthermore, the now well-known work of Glen Elder on the effects of experiencing the Great Depression at different ages (Elder, 1974) extends the many former cohort studies that simply demonstrate differences without assessing possible reasons for cohort-specific development. Whether more recent empirical research on middle adulthood will add to these fundamental insights on middle adulthood remains to be seen (see Lachman, 2004; other contributions to this volume).

Summary and Conclusions

With this chapter, we hope to have shown that there are good reasons supporting the heuristic fruitfulness of a historical analysis of the concept of middle adulthood. First, current developmental science and empirical work in developmental psychology does not operate in a vacuum. Being aware of the history of the concept of middle adulthood illustrates the relativity of current approaches and allows one to identify each approach's intellectual roots. Second, review of the historical scope of treatments of middle adulthood may enrich current and future research on the issue by providing a collection of ideas and perspectives that are frequently forgotten in the day-to-day business of developmental science. Third, we argue that a historical treatise of middle age can directly add to the clarification of this period of the life span in conceptual and empirical terms.

That said, we have started this work with the insight that middle adulthood has long been neglected in the developmentally oriented research literature. We then outlined four historically framed perspectives on middle adulthood. Proceeding from the assumption that these perspectives could be a helpful starting point for a more systematic scientific approach to the characteristic features, tasks, and processes in middle age, we proposed a preliminary definition that differentiates between descriptive and evaluative elements inherent to the concept of middle age.

It is time to review our preliminary definition of middle adulthood, based on the insights afforded by the four perspectives on middle adulthood. As put forth in our definition, the four perspectives provide convergent support for the view that middle age possesses a unique position in the human life course. Middle age is, by most accounts, a turning point, that is, the bridge between the rise and fall dynamics of the life course. However, it also seems as if a detailed descriptive analysis of middle adulthood is, in a sense, similar to what Heisenberg (1969) coined an *Unschärferelation* (uncertainty relation): On the one hand, we all know what we mean when talking about middle age; on the other hand, any purposeful attempt to define the phenomenon of middle adulthood reveals its opacity, the fuzzy status of the concept. The concept of middle age seems to be quite dynamic and strongly subject to history-graded forces such as demographic, political, and cultural transitions. Thus, our discussion of the diverse perspectives on middle age supports our preliminary definition in yet another respect: Any attempt to identify middle adulthood in objective calendar age terms is problematic in principal terms, although traditionally, the fifth and sixth decades of the human life span have often been identified as the upper limits of middle age. Modern theoretical and empirical research on human development, however, emphasizes that any life period, including middle age, is characterized by pronounced interindividual variation of intraindividual trajectories. In that sense, middle-aged adults may provide fundamental insights into the heterogeneity of old age observed in current-day aging research (e.g., Nelson & Dannefer, 1992).

With regard to its evaluative notions, our discussion of the four perspectives of middle adulthood has found a preponderance of positive connotations. This is true not only compared with the period of old age, but also in relation to earlier ages; middle age entails taking over responsibility at both personal and societal levels. This process is strongly reflected in the classic use of the term *maturity*. At the same time, popular views on the crisis aspect of middle adulthood, although addressed here and there in a variety of spheres from the genre of fiction to empirical developmental science, seem to be problematic and should not be a substantial element of the evaluative component of the term *middle adulthood*.

References

Achenbaum, W. A. (1995). *Crossing frontiers: Gerontology emerges as a science.* New York: Cambridge University Press.

Aries, P. (1981). *Studien zur Geschichte des Todes im Abendland* [Studies on the history of death in the occident]. München, Germany: Deutscher Taschenbuchverlag.

Baltes, P. B., Reese, H., & Lipsitt, L. P. (1980). Lifespan developmental psychology. *Annual Review of Psychology, 31,* 65–110.

Borscheid, P. (1992). Der alte Mensch in der Vergangenheit [Old man in history]. In P. B. Baltes & J. Mittelstraß (Eds.), *Zukunft des Alterns und gesellschaftliche Entwicklung* (pp. 35–61). Berlin, Germany: Aldine de Gruyter.

Brim, G. (1992). *Ambition: How we manage success and failure throughout our lives.* New York: Basic Books.

Brim, O. G., Ryff, C. D., & Kessler, R. (Eds.). (2004). *How healthy are we: A national study of well-being in midlife.* Chicago: University of Chicago Press.

Bühler, C. (1933). *Der menschliche Lebenslauf als psychologisches Problem* [The human life course as a psychological problem]. Leipzig, Germany: Hirzel.

Cowdry, E. (Ed.). (1939). *Problems of aging. Biological and medical aspects.* Baltimore: Williams & Wilkins.

Eichorn, D. H., Clausen, J. A., Haan, N., Honzik, M. P., & Mussen, P. H. (Eds.). (1981). *Present and past in middle life.* New York: Academic Press.

Eichorn, D. H., Mussen, P. H., Clausen, J. A., Haan, N., & Honzik, M. P. (1981). Overview. In D. H. Eichorn, J. A. Clausen, N. Haan, M. P. Honzik, & P. H. Mussen (Eds.), *Present and past in middle life* (pp. 414–434). New York: Academic Press.

Elder, G. H., Jr. (1974). *Children of the Great Depression.* Chicago: University of Chicago Press.

Erikson, E. H. (1950). *Childhood and society.* New York: Norton.

Fromm, E. (1945). *Escape from freedom.* New York: Rinehart.

Goulet, L. R., & Baltes, P. B. (Eds.). (1970). *Life-span developmental psychology: Research and theory.* New York: Academic Press.

Gruman, G. J. (1966). *A history of ideas about the prolongation of life. The evolution of pro-longevity hypotheses to 1800.* Philadelphia: The American Philosophical Society.

Gutsfeld, A., & Schmitz, W. (2003). *Am schlimmen Rand des Lebens? Altersbilder in der Antike* [At the bad end of life? Images of age in ancient time]. Köln, Germany: Böhlau.

Haan, N. (1981). Common dimensions of personality development: Early adolescence to midlife. In D. H. Eichorn, J. A. Clausen, N. Haan, M. P. Honzik, & P. H. Mussen (Eds.), *Present and past in middle life* (pp. 117–153). New York: Academic Press.

Hall, G. S. (1922). *Senescence: The last half of life.* New York: Appleton.

Havighurst, R. J. (1948). *Developmental tasks and education.* New York: Longman.

Havighurst, R. J. (1963). Dominant concerns in the life cycle. In L. Schenk-Danzinger & H. Thomae (Eds.), *Gegenwartsprobleme der Entwicklungspsychologie* (pp. 27–37). Göttingen, Germany: Hogrefe.

Heisenberg, W. (1969). *Der Teil und das Ganze. Gespräche im Umkreis der Atomphysik* [The part and the whole]. München, Germany: Piper.

Hollingworth, L. S. (1928). *The psychology of the adolescent*. Englewood Cliffs, NJ: Prentice Hall.

Horney, K. (1950). *Neurosis and human growth*. New York: Norton.

Jung, C. G. (1928). *Die Beziehung zwischen dem Ich und dem Unbewussten* [Relation between the ego and the unconscious]. Zürich, Switzerland: Rascher.

Jung, C. G. (1933). *Modern man in search of a soul*. New York: Harcourt, Brace & World.

Kagan, J., & Moss, H. A. (1962). *Birth to maturity. A study in psychological development*. New York: Wiley.

Kohli, M. (1986). Gesellschaftszeit und Lebenszeit. Der Lebenslauf im Strukturwandel der Moderne [Societal time and life time. The life course in structural changes of modern time]. In J. Berger (Ed.), *Die Moderne. Kontinuitäten und Zäsuren* (pp. 183–208). Göttingen, Germany: Schwartz.

Kohli, M. (1988). Ageing as a challenge for sociological theory. *Ageing and Society, 8*, 367–394.

Kroger, J., & Green, K. E. (1996). Events associated with identity status change. *Journal of Adolescence, 19*, 477–490.

Kruse, A. (2000). Germany: Erich Rothacker 1888–1965. In J. E. Birren & J. J. F. Schroots (Eds.), *A history of geropsychology in autobiography* (pp. 330–331). Washington, DC: American Psychological Association.

Lachman, M. E. (2004). Development in midlife. *Annual Review of Psychology, 55*, 305–331.

Laslett, P. (1989). *A fresh map of life: The emergence of the Third Age*. London: Weidenfeld & Nicolson.

Lehr, U. M. (1969). *Die Frau im Beruf. Eine psychologische Analyse der weiblichen Berufsrolle* [Woman in the labor force. A psychological analysis of the female professional role]. Frankfurt, Germany: Athenäum.

Lehr, U. M. (1978). Das mittlere Erwachsenenalter—ein vernachlässigtes Gebiet der Entwicklungspsychologie [Middle age—A neglected area of developmental psychology]. In R. Oerter (Ed.), *Entwicklung als lebenslanger Prozess* (pp. 147–177). Hamburg, Germany: Hoffmann & Campe.

Lehr, U. M. (2000). *Psychologie des Alterns* [Psychology of aging]. Wiebelsheim, Germany: Quelle & Meyer Verlag.

Lehr, U. M., & Thomae, H. (1958). Eine Längsschnittstudie bei männlichen Angestellten [A longitudinal study with male blue-collar workers]. *Vita humana, 1*, 100–110.

Lehr, U. M., & Thomae, H. (1965). *Konflikt, seelische Belastung und Lebensalter* [Conflict, mental burden and age]. Köln, Germany: Westdeutscher Verlag.

Lehr, U. M., & Thomae, H. (Eds.). (1987). *Formen seelischen Alterns. Ergebnisse der Bonner Gerontologischen Längsschnittstudie (BOLSA)* [Forms of mental aging. Findings of the Bonn Longitudinal Study of Aging]. Stuttgart, Germany: Enke.

Levinson, D. J., Darrow, C. N., Klein, E. B., Levinson, M. H., & McKee, B. (Eds.). (1978). *The seasons of a man's life.* New York: Knopf.

Livson, F. B. (1981). Paths to psychological health in the middle years: Sex differences. In D. H. Eichorn, J. A. Clausen, N. Haan, M. P. Honzik, P. H. Mussen (Eds.), *Present and past in middle life* (pp. 195–222). New York: Academic Press.

Maas, H. S., & Kuypers, J. A. (1974). *From thirty to seventy: A forty-year longitudinal study of adult life styles and personality.* San Francisco: Jossey-Bass.

Marcia, J. E. (1980). Identity in adolescence. In J. Adelson (Ed.), *Handbook of adolescent psychology* (pp. 159–187). New York: Wiley.

Marcia, J. E. (1989). Identity diffusion differentiated. In M. A. Luszcz & T. Nettelbeck (Eds.), *Psychological development across the life-span* (pp. 289–295). Amsterdam: Elsevier.

McAdams, D. P., & Logan, R. L. (Eds.). (2004). *Generative society: Caring for future generations.* Washington, DC: American Psychological Association.

Miles, C. C., & Miles, W. R. (1932). The correlation of intelligence scores and chronological age from early to late maturity. *American Journal of Psychology, 44,* 44–78.

Moen, P., & Wethington, E. (1999). Midlife development in a life course context. In S. L. Willis & J. D. Reid (Eds.), *Life in the middle: Psychological and social development in middle age* (pp. 3–23). San Diego, CA: Academic Press.

Naegele, G., Gerling, V., & Scharfenorth, K. (in press). Productivity of old age in labour and consumption markets—The German case. In H.-W. Wahl, C. Tesch-Römer, & A. Hoff (Eds.), *New dynamics in old age: Individual, environmental, and societal perspectives.* Amityville, NY: Baywood.

Nelson, E. A., & Dannefer, D. (1992). Aged heterogeneity: Fact or fiction? The fate of diversity in gerontological research. *The Gerontologist, 32,* 17–23.

Neugarten, B. L. (1968a). The awareness of middle age. In B. L. Neugarten (Ed.), *Middle age and aging. A reader in social psychology* (pp. 93–98). Chicago: University of Chicago Press.

Neugarten, B. L. (Ed.). (1968b). *Middle age and aging. A reader in social psychology.* Chicago: University of Chicago Press.

Nühlen-Graab, M. (1990). *Philosophische Grundlagen der Gerontologie* [Philosophical basis of gerontology]. Wiesbaden, Germany: Quelle & Meyer.

Peck, R. C. (1956). Psychological developments in the second half of life. In J. E. Anderson (Ed.), *Psychological aspects of aging* (pp. 44–49). Washington, DC: American Psychological Association.

Quêtelet, A. (1835). *Sur l'homme et le développement de ses facultés* [On man and the development of his faculties]. Paris: Bachelier.

Rank, O. (1945). *Will therapy and truth and reality.* New York: Knopf.

Reid, J. D., & Willis, S. L. (1999). Middle age: New thoughts, new directions. In S. L. Willis & J. D. Reid (Eds.), *Life in the middle: Psychological and social development in middle age* (pp. 276–280). San Diego, CA: Academic Press.

Rosenberg, S. D., Rosenberg, H. J., & Farrell, M. P. (1999). The midlife crisis revisited. In S. L. Willis & J. D. Reid (Eds.), *Life in the middle: Psychological and social development in middle age* (pp. 47–74). San Diego, CA: Academic Press.

Rothacker, E. (1938). *Die Schichten der Persönlichkeit* [The layers of personality]. Leipzig, Germany: Johann Ambrosius Barth.

Schriften des Rheinischen Museumsamtes. (1983). *Die Lebenstreppe* [The life staircase]. Schrift Nr. 23. Köln, Germany: Rheinland-Verlag.

Shanas, E. (1975). Gerontology and the social and behavioral sciences: Where do we go from here? *Gerontologist, 15*(6), 499–502.

Silverstone, B. (1996). Older people of tomorrow: A psychosocial profile. *The Gerontologist, 36*(1), 27–32.

Terman, L. M., & Oden, M. H. (1959). *The gifted group at mid-life. Thirty-five years' follow-up of the superior child.* Stanford, CA: Stanford University Press.

Tetens, J. N. (1979). *Philosophische Versuche über die menschliche Natur und ihre Entwicklung* [Philosophical treatises on human nature and its development]. Hildesheim, Germany: Georg Olms Verlag. (Originally published 1777)

Thomae, H. (1979). The concept of development and life span developmental psychology. In P. B. Baltes & O. G. Brim (Eds.), *Life span developmental psychology* (Vol. 2, pp. 281–312). New York: Academic Press.

Vaillant, G. E. (1977). *Adaptation to life.* Boston: Little, Brown.

Whitbourne, S. K. (1986). *The me I know: A study of adult identity.* New York: Springer-Verlag.

Willis, S. L., & Reid, J. D. (Eds.). (1999). *Life in the middle: Psychological and social development in middle age.* San Diego, CA: Academic Press.

Wittgenstein, L. (1960). *Philosophische Untersuchungen* [Philosophical investigations]. Frankfurt, Germany: Suhrkamp.

Yerkes, R. M. (1921). *Psychological examining in the United States Army.* Washington, DC: National Academy of Science.

Two

The Midlife Generation in the Family

Patterns of Exchange and Support

Martin Kohli and Harald Künemund

M idlife is a unique period in life not only in terms of developmental trajectories but also in terms of bringing into focus some basic tensions of the life course rooted in its socioinstitutional patterns. Preoccupation with the "midlife crisis"—a prominent theme in the 1970s—has long ago ceased, but the problems and challenges that were behind it may still be present. It is in midlife that the discrepancy between potentials, aspirations, and goals on the one hand and realizations—attained or still attainable—on the other comes clearly to the fore (Kohli, 1977).

This is most obvious in the realm of work careers, but it also applies to the family, in terms of partner relationships and especially in terms of one's relations with other generations. For some, it is the life course window for childbearing that closes; for others, it is the realization of what is possible and legitimate to expect from one's growing children or the extent of autonomy vis-à-vis one's aging parents.

Current societal dynamics are putting intergenerational family relations squarely on the political and scientific agenda (cf. Kohli, 2004).

Contemporary aging societies are age-graded and, to a large extent, age-segregated societies. Their institutions tend to be age-homogeneous (Uhlenberg & Riley, 2000). Exchange and support among generations is critical for maintaining age integration. In this respect, the family plays a special role—it is the prototypical institution of age-heterogeneity. The family links live far beyond the coresiding nuclear unit, most prominently along the generational lineage. Moreover, the demographics of aging societies—especially the increasing longevity and proportions of elderly people—address new demands to the family and its functions, for example, in terms of support and care for the elderly. For societal welfare and welfare policy, it becomes vital to assess the current state of the family and its likely evolution.

Research on these themes is sometimes like fighting against windmills: raising empirical arguments against myths that seem to remain untouched by them. It is widely assumed that the modern welfare state has undermined family solidarity and the family itself. Increasing childlessness, decreasing marriage and birth rates, increasing numbers of singles and the decrease of multigenerational coresidence—to name just a few widely known facts—may indeed indicate a weakening of the family and its functions. But despite the high intuitive plausibility of such interpretations, in which large parts of the social sciences meet with common sense, it may turn out that the family has, in fact, changed but not diminished its role (cf. Kohli, 1999; Künemund & Rein, 1999).

Speculation about the future of the family has been a regular feature of modernization. At the end of the 19th century, Durkheim (1892/1975) predicted that the intergenerational horizon of the family—and by this, the family itself—would lose its salience. Half a century later, Parsons (1942) predicted an increasing structural isolation of the nuclear family, accompanied by a structural isolation of the elderly, after the exit of adult children from the household. Many others have taken up this discussion, mostly with the assumption of a general decline of family bonds (e.g., Berger & Berger, 1983). This restrictive view was first transcended by research on the emotional and support relations between adult family generations (e.g., Rossi & Rossi, 1990). But it is only during the last decade that sociology has discovered again the full extent of the family as a kinship and especially a generational system beyond the nuclear household (cf. Bengtson, 2001; Silverstein & Bengtson, 1997), which ranges across several different types of "solidarity": spatial and emotional closeness, frequent contact, personal and instrumental support, and massive flows of money and goods.

In this chapter, we will join the fight by presenting some of our research on the current state of the family as a generational system and of its middle-aged members. We will present empirical evidence on family constellations and proximity, selected dimensions of exchange and support between parents and adult children, and the problem of the so-called sandwich generation. We hope to provide some tangible evidence to help defuse the myth where it is unfounded, and to give it more substance where it is closer to reality.

The chapter is written from a European and, more specifically, German perspective. This applies to the data we analyze and to the social context in which the dynamics of midlife unfold: structural properties (e.g., those of demography), institutions (e.g., those of the labor market and welfare state), and normative expectations (e.g., those of solidarity or of what constitutes success in life). As an example, the position "in the middle" of the generational lineage—the often-addressed "sandwich" position—may turn out to be different depending on the prevailing family structure, labor market participation, available public support, and legitimate expectations of what the family is about—of how one can depend on family support.

The family may be less directly responsive to the institutional variation of welfare states and labor markets than work careers, but the indirect effects of these institutions may be no less salient (e.g., for the question, increasingly crucial for decisions about childbearing, of whether mothers are able to combine parenting and employment). Direct and indirect family policies as well as cultural conceptions of the good family may be seen as packaged together to form family regimes that can be ordered into nation-specific types (e.g., Kaufmann, Kuijsten, Schulze, & Strohmeier, 2002).

We base our arguments primarily on the German Aging Survey, a data set that offers some unique analytic possibilities concerning intergenerational transfers and support. It is a large representative survey of German nationals, aged 40 to 85 years old and living in private households, with the first wave collected in the first half of 1996. The sample ($n = 4,838$) is stratified according to age groups, gender, and East and West Germany. The survey program comprises sociological measures of the various dimensions of life situations and welfare—among them, intergenerational relations and transfers—as well as psychological measures of self and life concepts (cf. Dittmann-Kohli et al., 1997).[1] A second wave collected in 2002 (cf. Tesch-Römer, Wurm, Hoff, & Engstler, 2002) is not yet fully available; thus, our present analysis is limited to cross-sectional results. In addition, we sometimes refer to provisional findings from the Survey of Health, Aging, and Retirement in Europe (SHARE), a large survey with representative samples (of about $n = 1,500$ each) of the population over 50 years old in 10 Western and Southern European countries collected in the summer of 2004.[2]

What Is Middle Age?

Middle age is often defined in terms of chronological age boundaries, for example, as the life phase from age 40 to 60 or 70. As has been abundantly shown, these boundaries have little significance in terms of biology or functional capacities. However, with the modern institutionalization of the life course (Kohli, 1986), some of them have become highly significant as markers or even legal bases of institutional processes. This is especially the case for the transition to retirement, where in all European countries, the framework of labor market and welfare state provisions is based on specific chronological age thresholds (for Germany, see the overview by Igl, 2000). On the aggregate level of national populations, the transition to retirement has become longer and more diverse, with respect to amounts and types of employment and to the ages at which they change, but the broader chronological age boundaries of retirement are still far from having become empty and obsolete (see Kohli & Künemund, 2002, for a detailed discussion).

In the German Aging Survey, we have accordingly stratified our sample in three age groups, which we have retained through most of the analyses:

- The age group 40 to 54 is part of the core of the working population, with still high—and for women, increasing—employment activity rates. Most members of this group have reached, and in some cases passed, the high point of their occupational careers. They may be called the *younger midlifers*.

- The age group 55 to 69 is in the transitional period between work and retirement. At the starting point of this period, almost no one already benefits from an old age pension, and at the end point, almost everyone benefits. The length of this period corresponds to the time needed for the population to make the full transition. Members of this age group are often termed the *young old*, but *older midlifers* may be a more appropriate term.

- The age group 70 to 85 is fully retired and has established the pattern of life in retirement as a taken-for-granted reality. This group increasingly shows the typical demographic pattern of old age—unequal gender proportion, single household living—while mostly still conserving the potential for social activities and participation, with a small but quickly growing minority burdened by substantial disabilities.

It is debatable whether the upper chronological boundary of middle age, if we choose one, should be set at 65 or 70 (or any other age). The later boundary, however, is more in line with the currently observable trends toward a higher retirement age (both in institutional terms and in practice) and with the current extension of longevity and "active" life expectancy.

Interestingly, age 70 is also in line with widely shared popular conceptions. In the German Aging Survey, we have asked for a subjective age categorization: the starting point of being old ("From which age on would you say a person is old?"). The results show that this is considerably past the institutionalized retirement age (see Figure 2.1). The transition to

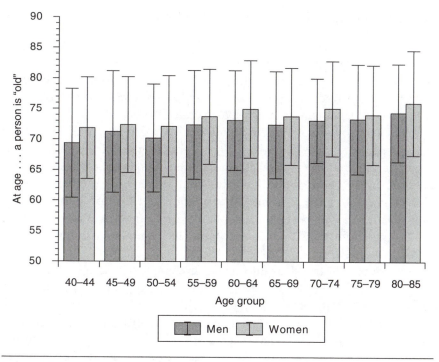

Figure 2.1   Subjective Age Categorization (Means and Standard Deviations)

SOURCE: Kohli and Künemund (2002).

retirement is no longer the defining event for being old. Being old now begins between 70 and 75—this seems to mark a new age boundary that does not (yet) have a clear sociostructural relevance but constitutes a sociocultural (and possibly psychological) cut.

With increasing age of the respondents, this boundary is located slightly later—the difference between the means of the 40- to 44-year-olds and the 80- to 85-year-olds is about 5 years. Thus, while other studies, albeit with rather selective samples, have maintained that there is a marked tendency with increasing age to delay the onset of subjective old age (Perrig-Chiello, 1998; Seccombe & Ishii-Kuntz, 1991), our representative sample shows only a very modest effect. On the whole, the age groups agree. Women set the beginning of old age (consistently across all age groups) about 2 years later than do men—possibly as a partial reflection of their higher longevity.

Family Constellations and Proximity

To what extent does the family still provide a potential for exchange and support? This question refers first to the extent of the kinship network. In the following description of the range of living kin, we focus on the generational lineage (including ascendants and descendants of current partners; see Kohli, Künemund, Motel, & Szydlik, 2000a).

Table 2.1 shows that even in a country like Germany, after more than three decades of very low fertility, most people in midlife and later still have a family that spans several generations. In younger midlife, only 2% have no other generation alive. This proportion rises to 10% in older midlife and 15% among the oldest age group, but the opposite tendency prevails for two-generation constellations: Eighty percent of our youngest, 72% of the middle, and 76% of the oldest age group live in a lineage of at least three generations.

How does this translate into actual exchange and support? The first question here is about coresidence with and geographical proximity to these other generations. For assessing residential proximity, there are two basic options: Ask for an objective measure of distance (kilometers/miles),[3] or ask for the time needed to reach a specific family member given the available means of transport, as we have done in the German Aging Survey. For the analysis, there are again two possibilities: Compute the mean distance to a given class of family members (e.g., all children), or

Table 2.1   Generational Constellations (Percentages)

	40-54 years	55-69 years	70-85 years	Total
No other generation existent:	2.3	10.2	14.8	7.3
Among them: no partner	1.5	5.7	9.1	4.3
Two-generation constellations:	17.6	17.7	9.7	16.2
With parents(-in-law)	9.8	3.6	0.5	6.0
With children	7.9	13.9	9.1	10.2
Three-generation constellations:	62.3	47.6	52.5	55.4
With parents(-in-law) and children	58.1	13.2	0.4	32.1
With children and grandchildren	3.3	34.2	51.7	22.7
More than three generations:	17.9	24.6	23.0	21.0
All constellations:				
With parents(-in-law)	85.9	37.3	3.2	53.6
With own parents	71.1	22.6	1.2	40.9
With children	87.2	86.6	84.9	86.8
With grandchildren	13.8	60.2	74.9	41.7

SOURCE: Kohli, Künemund, Motel, and Szydlik (2000a); data from German Aging Survey (1996), weighted.

focus on the most proximate one. We have opted for the latter because in the perspective of support, and especially of potential support, it is more important to have one family member living nearby than to have the whole family not too far away.

As mentioned earlier, the classic story of modernization, upheld and reinforced by Parsons (1942), held that as a consequence of the nuclearization of the family, the elderly would become isolated from their adult children. This myth has been hard to do away with, but the many empirical refutations, in the meantime, have been at least partially successful. There remains one piece of evidence that seems to support Parsons's claim: the development of coresidence among adult family generations. In all Western societies, it has decreased massively. Today, among the 70- to 85-year-old Germans who have at least one living child, only 9% live together with a child in the same household (Table 2.2). However, by extending the boundaries of "togetherness," the situation turns out to be very different. If one includes parents and children living not only in the same household but also in the same house, the proportion rises from 9% to 27%, and by

Table 2.2   Residential Proximity (Cumulative Percentages)

	40–54 years	55–69 years	70–85 years	Total
Distance to nearest parent:				
Same household	5.4	9.1	(10.2)	6.2
Same house or household	12.1	17.1	(14.7)	13.1
Neighborhood or closer	23.6	30.6	(20.9)	25.0
Same town or closer	48.2	53.1	(47.5)	49.2
Other town, closer than 2 hours	83.1	81.3	(59.8)	82.6
Larger distance	100.0	100.0	(100.0)	100.0
Distance to nearest child:				
Same household	77.4	25.4	8.8	46.4
Same house or household	79.1	36.0	26.7	54.2
Neighborhood or closer	83.6	50.9	44.5	64.8
Same town or closer	89.9	74.7	67.8	80.5
Other town, closer than 2 hours	97.6	93.6	90.6	94.9
Larger distance	100.0	100.0	100.0	100.0

SOURCE: Kohli, Künemund, Motel, and Szydlik (2000a); data from German Aging Survey (1996), weighted.

including the neighborhood, to 45%. Nine tenths have a child living not farther away than 2 hours. Thus, even the living arrangements are not very good evidence for the claim of a dissociation between parents and adult children.

From the perspective of the middle-aged children toward their elderly parents, the results are similar even though proximity is somewhat lower. Of the 40- to 54-year-olds with at least one living parent, 5% live together with a parent in the same household and 12% in the same house. Twenty-four percent have a parent at least in the same neighborhood, 48% at least in the same town, and 83% within 2 hours. Among the older midlifers, those aged 55 to 69, coresidence and living nearby is considerably more frequent. To the extent that this may be interpreted as a life course, and not cohort, effect, it indicates that with increasing age of parents and children, some of them move closer together. The fact that the most proximate child lives closer to parents than the most proximate parent to children is to be expected because both parents usually live together and often have several children. Another reason may be different perceptions of the parent-child relationship based on the different developmental stakes of the two sides—a well-established pattern with respect to feelings of closeness and solidarity (cf. Tables 2.3–2.5).

The large share of those living in separate households but under the same roof seems to indicate a preference for intimacy at some minimal distance. It is due less to large condominiums than to two-family homes—a German peculiarity reinforced by tax incentives for building or owning such homes.

At the European level, there is considerable variation between Scandinavia, Central and Western Continental countries, and those of the Mediterranean. The latter are often grouped together as "strong family countries" and contrasted with the "weak family countries" of the center and north of Europe and of North America (Reher, 1998). The strength or weakness refers not only to cultural patterns of family loyalties, allegiances, and authority but also to demographic patterns of coresidence with adult children and older family members and to organizing support for the latter. The strong family countries today, paradoxically, are also those with the lowest fertility—a state of affairs that has been explained by their cultural lag in gender equity, especially their marked gap between high gender equity in education and the labor market and low gender equity in the family and in public provisions for the family (McDonald, 2000).

As in Germany, this very low fertility of the past decades does not yet translate, for the midlifers, into lower numbers of children but does show up in the existence and number of grandchildren. On the other hand, coresidence with children and parents is much higher in the strong family countries of the South. For those aged 50 to 59 with at least one living parent, our data from SHARE show that 2% live under the same roof with a parent in Sweden and Denmark, 6% in Germany and Austria, but 13% in Spain and 14% in Italy. For coresidence with children, the differences are even larger as the Southern countries are characterized by very late (and increasing) ages of adult children leaving the parental home. Again of those aged 50 to 59 with at least one living child, 28% in Denmark and 36% in Sweden live together with a child in the same building, 48% in Germany and in Austria, but 79% in Spain and 82% in Italy. This is often interpreted solely as an effect of housing markets, but it may also plausibly be explained by a tendency toward closer intergenerational ties.

Dimensions of Exchange and Support Between Parents and Adult Children

A first dimension to be discussed here is emotional closeness between parents and children, assessed on the basis of asking respondents in the

German Aging Survey, "How close do you feel to ___?" If there are more than one living parent or children, we again focus on the closest one, not the mean quality of relationship to all of them. The pattern of results (Table 2.3) can be summarized in four points:

- Feelings of closeness among family generations are generally high, with 76% indicating that they feel close or very close to their parents, and 92% to their children.
- There are almost no differences between the age groups: Younger midlifers give the same pattern of responses as those in older midlife and in old age.
- Substantial differences exist between feelings toward one's parents and feelings toward one's children. These differences correspond to, and corroborate, the concept of the different developmental stakes of parents and children (Giarrusso, Stallings, & Bengtson, 1995).
- There are also systematic differences between the various parent-child dyads (not reported here; cf. Szydlik, 2000), with the mother-daughter relation being the closest, and the father-son relation the least close.

The midlifers also report frequent contact with both parents and children living outside their households (Table 2.4). For example, about three quarters have contact with a parent at least once a week, either face-to-face, by phone, or by mail. More than 50% report having contact more than once a week. Contact with children is even more frequent: Two

Table 2.3   Emotional Closeness (Cumulative Percentages)

	40–54 years	55–69 years	70–85 years	Total
To parent:				
Very close	35.2	38.6	/	35.9
Close	75.1	78.2	/	75.8
Medium	92.0	92.7	/	92.2
Less close	97.8	98.7	/	98.1
Not close at all	100.0	100.0	/	100.0
To child:				
Very close	59.6	60.8	60.1	60.3
Close	90.4	92.6	94.0	92.3
Medium	97.6	98.1	98.2	98.0
Less close	99.1	99.1	99.1	99.1
Not close at all	100.0	100.0	100.0	100.0

SOURCE: Kohli, Künemund, Motel, and Szydlik (2000a); data from German Aging Survey (1996), weighted.

/ = unweighted $n \leq 10$

Table 2.4   Frequency of Contact (Cumulative Percentages)

	40–54 years	55–69 years	70–85 years	Total
To parent:				
Daily	22.5	28.5	/	23.7
More than once a week	51.9	54.2	/	52.4
Once a week	74.8	76.8	/	75.1
One to three times a month	88.8	89.7	/	88.9
More than once a year	95.4	95.4	/	95.4
Less often	98.0	99.1	/	98.3
Never	100.0	100.0	/	100.0
To child:				
Daily	35.7	38.0	42.2	38.4
More than once a week	67.4	68.0	69.2	68.1
Once a week	85.4	83.5	86.2	84.7
One to three times a month	94.3	93.9	93.3	93.9
More than once a year	97.3	97.9	97.8	97.7
Less often	98.8	99.0	98.9	98.9
Never	100.0	100.0	100.0	100.0

SOURCE: Kohli, Künemund, Motel, and Szydlik (2000a); data from German Aging Survey (1996), weighted.

/ = unweighted $n \leq 10$

thirds report having contact with a child living outside their household more than once a week, 85%% at least once a week. Families with infrequent contact or without contact at all are a very small minority.

A long neglected dimension of family solidarity is material transfers among the generations. Until recently, sociologists left these lowly concerns to economists, as if the family were only about feelings and unpaid help, and not also about money and goods. Today this neglect is in the process of being redressed, aided by the increasing availability of appropriate data (cf. Kohli, 1999, 2004).

The study of family transfers among adult generations is important for at least four main fields of sociological inquiry:

- For *life course research,* where it follows the balance of giving and receiving across the life course and highlights the position of the elderly as net givers
- For *research on social security,* where it complements our understanding of the family as a pillar of the contemporary welfare mix
- For *stratification research,* where it draws attention to the fact that the transfer of social status is not over at the beginning of adulthood but continues by other means

- For *research on social inclusion,* where it shows that even in contemporary societies, the family remains one of the key providers of social bonds or "social capital"

Family transfers are of two kinds: between living family members (*inter vivos*) or as bequests. *Inter vivos* transfers are more interesting than bequests for two reasons. First, they reach their recipients earlier in life when needs (e.g., of starting a family and getting started in work, or of special crises such as divorce or unemployment) are more acute, and they are part of an ongoing relation that includes other dimensions of solidarity and exchange. Second, bequests present an interest of their own, not only because they are a quantitatively more important component of wealth acquisition—their relation to *inter vivos* transfers in Germany on a yearly basis is about 4:1 (Schupp & Szydlik, 2004)—but also because they are more prominent as a field of institutional regulation and political discourse. We will first go into *inter vivos* transfers and then briefly touch on bequests where the midlifers are now the prime beneficiaries.

To what extent do transfers to and from other persons occur, to what extent do they remain in the family, and which direction do they take? Figure 2.2 presents some of the answers. The first key result is that transfers

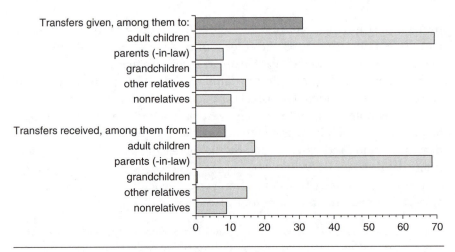

Figure 2.2   Private Transfers Given and Received by the 40- to 85-Year-Olds (Percentages)

SOURCE: Kohli, Künemund, Motel, and Szydlik (2000a); data from German Aging Survey (1996), weighted.

among the 40- to 85-year-olds are highly asymmetrical: Thirty-one percent have made larger gifts of money or commodities, or given regular financial assistance to at least one other person during the 12 months before the survey, whereas only 8% have received such material transfers.[4]

Figure 2.2 also shows that the transfer process is concentrated in the family lineage. The transfers go mainly downward, from the older to the younger generations. Among the transfer givers, almost 70% give to their adult children.[5] In 7% of the cases, transfers go to grandchildren, and in 8%, to parents(-in-law). Other relatives are the beneficiaries for 15% of all transfer givers, and nonrelatives for 10%. The sources of transfers to our respondents corroborate this pattern. Among the 8% who have received transfers, almost 70% have benefited from their parents(-in-law), and 17% from their adult children. Grandchildren do not play a role here: Only one of our respondents received a transfer from a grandchild.

In Figure 2.3, the lineage transfers are examined more closely, anchored on the 40- to 54-year-old respondents, and supplemented by the flows of instrumental support among generations. The basis of the calculations is different from that of Figure 2.2: The proportions of transfers and support are based only on those who have at least one living kin in the respective group.[6] In this perspective, the proportion of those giving transfers to their adult children (36%) is even larger.[7] The overwhelmingly downward direction of material transfers is again evident. With regard to instrumental support (e.g., help with household tasks, caregiving not included), the situation is different. Between the respondents and their children, the flow of support is balanced, whereas between respondents and their parents(-in-law), the net direction of flow is clearly upward.

Germany presents an interesting internal comparison: that between East and West (see Kohli et al., 2000b, for a broader discussion). In many respects, East and West Germany in 1996 were still two distinct societies. Differences observed at this point can be attributed either to the four decades of the socialist system or to the transformation period since 1990. Taking both sides into account, we expect that there are more intergenerational transfers in East than in West Germany, at least among those groups that still have resources for transfers. On the aggregate level, there are still important income differences between East and West, and even more important wealth differences. For home ownership, the relation between East and West in 1993 was about 1 to 1.8, and for mean household wealth, 1 to 3.6.[8] Within this aggregate picture, we can identify groups that have been relative winners and losers of the transformation process. With

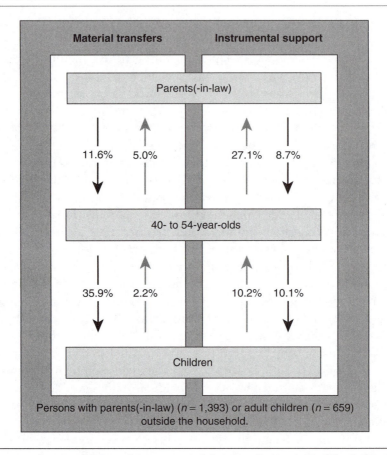

Figure 2.3   Transfers and Instrumental Support Between Family Generations
                    (Aged 40–54 Years)

SOURCE: Kohli, Künemund, Motel, and Szydlik (2000a); data from German Aging Survey
(1996), weighted.

regard to age groups and cohorts, the losers are those in midlife, and the
winners are the pensioners. In our data, the oldest age group (70–85) is
the one with the lowest equivalence income in the West and the highest in
the East. All three age groups have lower incomes in the East than in the
West, but the difference is smallest for the 70- to 85-year-olds. This group
is also the one with the highest proportion stating that their living standard has (much or somewhat) improved over the last 10 years. This distribution of resources accounts for the fact that the difference in transfer

behavior between East and West Germany is reversed for our oldest age group. The latter is closest to the "true value" expected under equal resource constraints.

The results from bivariate analyses can, of course, be misleading. In Table 2.5, the correlates of transfer giving to adult children are modeled by multivariate logistic regressions. The basis here is dyads of parents (among our respondents) and their adult children not living in the same household. The models for the three age groups turn out to be rather similar—while the effects are not uniformly significant across the three age groups, they mostly go into the same direction—with the one clear exception of the East-West difference, where the pattern found in the bivariate description holds in the multivariate analysis as well.

The strongest effects are those of the material resources of the parents and those of the labor force status of the children. Income position is a highly significant predictor of transfer giving, with those in the highest two quintiles being more likely to give than those in the lowest two quintiles. The availability of wealth also has a high positive effect. In addition, the number of adult children is inversely related to transfer giving. On the other hand, living together with a (married or unmarried) partner does not have a significant effect, and parents' level of education is only marginally significant.

With regard to the labor force status of the child, the significant criterion is those who are in need because they are in school or out of work. Of all the adult children in either of these conditions in our sample, 41% receive transfers from their parents, compared to 22% for those actively working, and 20% for homemakers and others. The targeting of *inter vivos* transfers to those children who are in a poorer economic position is strongly confirmed for France and the United States as well, and can be interpreted as an indicator of altruistic parental motivation.

This brief data overview has shown that transfers between adult generations in the family are sizable. The net direction of transfer giving is downward, from the older to the younger generations, and thus in the opposite direction of the public social security transfers. With regard to different types of resources and services, the overview has shown that there is some "reciprocity" in the aggregate: Net downward material transfer giving between parents and children is to some extent (although not completely) "balanced" by net instrumental support in the upward direction. It would be useful to link this up with qualitative studies demonstrating how expectations of reciprocity are formed and negotiated

Table 2.5 Transfers Given by the 40- to 85-Year-Old Germans to Their Adult Children Outside the Household (Logistic Regressions, Odds Ratios)

Age groups		Younger age group (40–54 y.) n = 836	Middle age group (55–69 y.) n = 2418	Older age group (70–85 y.) n = 1922
Attributes of parent [respondent]	Equivalence income (Reference: 1st + 2nd quintile) 3rd quintile	1.99***	1.25	1.70***
	4th and 5th quintile	2.63***	2.58***	2.08***
	Wealth (1 = yes)	2.14***	2.17***	1.58**
	Education (Reference: low) Middle	1.10	1.02	1.01
	High	1.91*	1.28	1.34
	Number of adult children in the family (Reference: one child) two adult children	1.00	0.98	0.90
	three or more children	0.79	0.41***	0.63***
	Living with partner (1 = yes)	1.22	1.77	1.12
	Gender (1 = female)	1.09	0.92	0.85
	West/East Germany (1 = West)	1.30	1.22	0.71***

Attributes of child	Labor force status (Reference: employed)			
	in school or unemployed	1.98***	1.72***	1.92***
	homemaker + other	0.72	0.90	1.05
	Marital status (1 = married)	0.71	0.90	0.80
	Has child(ren) [respondent's grandchild(ren)] (1 = yes)	1.36	1.16	1.15
	Gender (1 = female)	0.80	0.92	0.96
	Age up to 45 years	—	—	0.76**
	up to 30 years	0.97	0.84	—
Attributes of the parent-child relationship	Frequency of contact (Reference: daily) several times a week	1.34	1.20	1.13
	one to four times a month	0.82	0.79*	0.89
	less than once a month	0.58*	0.80	0.41***
	Emotional closeness (Reference: very close) close	0.89	0.99	0.87
	medium to not at all close	0.87	0.52	0.99
	ρ^2 (McFadden)	0.11	0.11	0.07

SOURCE: Kohli (1999).

NOTES: Units of analysis: Dyads of parents and their adult children not living in the same household.

$* = p < 0.1; ** = p < 0.5; *** = p < 0.01$.

(e.g., Finch & Mason, 1993), and how a specific child is "designated" as a future caregiver (e.g., Hareven & Adams, 1996). Another interesting point (developed by Kohli, 1999) is the relation between the private and the public transfers. On the aggregate level, it forms a clear and surprising pattern: Some of the public transfers from the employed population to the elderly are handed back by them to their family descendants.

Almost one half of our respondents have already received an inheritance; for about one fourth of these, the amount inherited has been above 50,000 Euro. The young midlifers (40–54 years) have inherited most often, which demonstrates a strong cohort effect that overcompensates the expected life course effect. There are massive differences between East and West Germany (more in the amount than in the rate of inheritance) but again no gender differences.

The "Sandwich Generation"

The metaphor of the "sandwich generation," along with similar formulas such as "women in the middle" or "being caught in the middle," is commonly used to describe a specific burden placed on midlifers, especially women, by competing demands from work and both older and younger family members.[9] The consequences of being sandwiched have often been described and illustrated through qualitative data and methods (e.g., Brody, 1990), or through small samples of women in the sandwich situation (e.g., Nichols & Junk, 1997). These studies, as well as a growing body of advisory literature (e.g., Roots, 1998; Zal, 1992), illuminate the relevance of the sandwich position and the often-dramatic burden it imposes at the individual level. However, this literature does not provide reliable information on the proportion of sandwiched adults nor on how many of them feel burdened. Speaking of a "generation" implies that the pattern should be valid for large groups—ideally, most or all members of the respective cohorts or lineage positions. Furthermore, because many studies focus solely on a few cases (or even a single case) in extreme situations (e.g., Chisholm, 1999), it is unclear whether the sandwich position is consistently negatively related to well-being and life satisfaction; there is some evidence that children may also be a source of help (e.g., Raphael & Schlesinger, 1994).

Studies based on quantitative data, on the other hand, report highly divergent and sometimes contradictory results. Between 1% and 80% of the population have been identified as sandwiched adults. Furthermore, many studies do not find a negative relationship to well-being (AARP, 2001; Loomis & Booth, 1995; Penning, 1998; Spitze, Logan, Joseph, & Lee, 1994; Ward & Spitze, 1998). There is already a tradition of calling the metaphor of the sandwich generation a modern myth (Höpflinger & Baumgärtner, 1999; Hörl & Kytir, 1998; Loomis & Booth, 1995; Putney & Bengtson, 2001; Rosenthal, Martins-Matthews, & Matthews, 1996). However, the surprisingly large differences among these studies are a consequence of different concepts used in the analyses. Some studies do not cover information on all relevant relationships; others lack information on concrete caring activities or on labor force participation. In general, it is possible to identify three different concepts in the literature (see also the recent overviews by Künemund, 2002; Putney & Bengtson, 2001):

1. A broad definition of the sandwich position takes into account only the generational constellation, for example, the existence of older and younger generations of kin. Depending on the available data, these studies sometimes also include relatives of the partner's side (e.g., parents-in-law, grandparents-in-law, children of the partner), which obviously increases the prevalence of the sandwich position. Studies using such an approach report up to 80% of sandwiched adults, depending on the age group in view.

2. Narrower definitions build on factual support exchange between these generations (e.g., caring for parents or grandchildren). The proportions obtained through this approach are much lower, although there is, again, great variation depending on the definitions of care and having children. Some studies focus on persons that care for an aged parent and simply have children (sometimes adult, sometimes coresiding), whereas others take into account whether there is indeed care for (grand)children.

3. Finally, strict definitions additionally take into account labor force participation. These studies usually report very low percentages of sandwiched adults.

Our data from Germany allow us to differentiate between these three concepts of sandwiched adults. At the first level, focusing on the generational constellation (including lineage relatives of the partner and both younger and older generations) seems to justify the term *sandwich generation* as a very common situation. More than 80% of the men and women aged 40 to 44 have at least one relative of both younger and older generations. The proportion of sandwiched adults declines rapidly in higher age groups because of a lower percentage of individuals with living parents; for example, less than 50% in the age group 55 to 59 are sandwiched. The majority of people aged 40 to 59 may therefore find themselves in a situation of competing demands from both older and younger relatives (and the labor market). However, most of the parents of these sandwiched adults are not in actual need of personal care. On the contrary, they may even be of help, for example, with child care. Therefore, based on these generational constellations, there does not seem to be a specific burden of the sandwich generation.

The narrower definitions of the sandwich generation result in considerably lower proportions of sandwiched adults. Ignoring the labor force participation and also the existence of children, the simple fact of caring for an elderly family member peaks at age 50 to 54 with roughly 15%. Therefore, any definition of a sandwich generation that includes elder care results in proportions of sandwiched adults under 15%.

Distinguishing women who care for a parent or parent-in-law (or grandparent or grandparent-in-law) from those who additionally care for grandchildren or have children at home, and from those who additionally participate in the labor force, reveals a completely different picture (Figure 2.4).[10] Only 4% of the women aged 40 to 44, 5% of those aged 45 to 49, and 4% of those aged 50 to 54 are caring for an elderly family member, have children at home or care for grandchildren, and participate in the labor force simultaneously. The strict definition of the sandwich generation, therefore, results in a small minority of women that are sandwiched. If we were able to distinguish children who are burdensome from those who are helpful, the proportion would be even lower.

The expression "women in the middle" aptly describes the generational constellation in midlife and is valid for more than 80% of men and women; however, it is not warranted to infer a specific burden from this constellation. Being burdened by multiple demands (the common connotation of the term sandwich generation and the expression "being caught in the middle") is a rather rare phenomenon. This conclusion is also supported both by the evaluations of the respondents themselves and by multivariate analysis. For example, only a minority of 1.4% of the women aged 40 to 54 say that they are overburdened due to health care activities (including caring for a partner or any other relative, regardless of the sandwich position) and demands from work and family. Controlling for

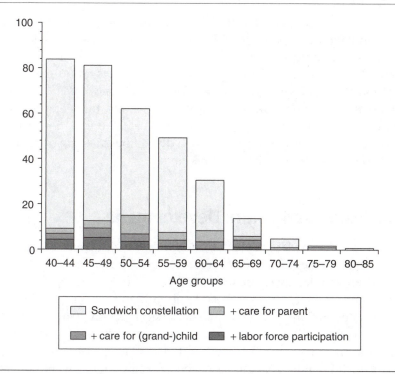

Figure 2.4   Sandwich Situations (Percentages)

SOURCE: Künemund (2002).

age, region, health, equivalence income, and the existence of a partner, none of these definitions of the sandwich position has a significant effect on life satisfaction or positive and negative affect (cf. Künemund, 2002). This does not mean that elder care is seldom burdensome, but it shows that, on average, being sandwiched does not make that situation any worse or better.

These results from Germany are in line with other recent international literature on the subject. A narrow or strict definition of the sandwich generation leads to the conclusion that the sandwich situation is a rather rare phenomenon, and there is no indication that it is necessarily associated with a specific burden. A possible explanation may be the fact that many younger family members are a source of help in case of elder care, not an additional burden. The same applies for many older members with respect to child care. There is no doubt that the competing demands from work and family, especially with regard to caring for disabled family members, may induce a heavy burden on some women. Many qualitative studies have illustrated this fact very well. But there is no systematic deterioration of well-being simply because of the existence of younger generations within the family. In the light of these results, the metaphor of the sandwich generation is not a valid description at the population level, and the connotation of a specific overburden due to the existence of both older and younger generations has to be rejected.

Conclusion and Future Developments

On the whole, our data provide evidence that the intergenerational relations within the family are intact and multifaceted. Aged parents and their adult children often live close to each other, and they keep regular and frequent contact, offer various types of support, and usually describe their relationships as close. The prediction of classical modernization theory that a nuclearization of the family would be the central outcome of the change to industrial society is not what we find today. Our results show that links between adult family generations beyond the nuclear household remain a core feature of private and public life in contemporary societies.

But where do we go from here? Based on demographic predictions, being sandwiched may increase in salience with regard not only to the elder care burden but also to demands from the younger generation: Grandparenting is often critical for the labor force participation of young mothers, even to the point where decisions about childbearing may be a function of the availability of grandparents. On the other hand, the beanpole family structure may lighten the burden: For the present baby bust generation of young women, there are often four competing grandparents for a dwindling number of children. Having fewer siblings may increase the burden of elder care (cf. Künemund & Rein, 2002).

In the long run, however, there can be no assurance that the present levels of family solidarity will remain intact. Although European families have proved to be remarkably resilient and have shown considerable long-term continuity (e.g., Reher, 1998), current tensions may weaken their capacity to maintain the strong bonds of intergenerational exchange and support. In addition to the massive demographic changes engendered by below-reproduction fertility, decreasing nuptiality, and increasing rates of divorce, there is also the cultural shift toward individualization, which makes considerations of autonomy increasingly legitimate. Finally, there is the current retrenchment of welfare state provisions. Given the now well-established fact that family solidarity depends on and is "crowded in" by public support (Künemund & Rein, 1999), many proponents of retrenchment who hope that the family will take over may be in for a disappointment.

Notes

1. The German Aging Survey has been designed and analyzed jointly by the Research Group on Aging and the Life Course at the Free University of Berlin and the Research Group on Psychogerontology at the University of Nijmegen (Netherlands) together with infas Sozialforschung, Bonn, and financed by the Federal Ministry of Families, the Elderly, Women, and Youth. A full report of the sociological results is given by Kohli and Künemund (2000). The responsibility for the content of this paper lies with the authors.

2. SHARE is a collaborative effort of several European teams directed by Axel Börsch-Supan (Mannheim); it is closely modeled after the U.S. Health and Retirement Study (HRS).

3. An elegant way of doing this has been devised in the Netherlands Kinship Panel Study (NKPS). Respondents are asked to give the postal codes of their family and network members, which are then used to derive distances in kilometers (see Mulder & Kalmijn, 2004). This additionally allows researchers to identify proximity among network members other than the respondent.

4. A breakdown by age (not given in Figure 2.2) shows that the asymmetry grows with age: Twenty-nine percent of the 40- to 54-year-olds, but 33% of the 55- to 69-year-olds and 32% of the 70- to 84-year-olds have given transfers, whereas the receivers amount to 13%, 5%, and 3%, respectively.

5. "Adult children" are defined as biological children as well as stepchildren and adopted children of at least age 18.

6. See Kohli, Künemund, Motel, and Szydlik (1997) for an account of family demographics and household constellations.

7. In addition to transfers in the last 12 months, we also asked about "major gifts of money or commodities" at any time before. By including these transfers, the proportion of givers rises again: More than 40% of parents have made transfers to their adult children.

8. With big wealth, not usually picked up by surveys, the contrast is even more dramatic. In important ways, East Germany now has capitalism without capitalists—owners as well as controlling elites.

9. In the discussion of the sandwich generation, the term *generation* is used solely with respect to the generational position within the family. This generational

membership changes over the life course (e.g., from grandchild to grandparent), as older generations disappear and younger ones are born. See Kohli (1996), Kohli and Szydlik (2000), and Lüscher and Liegle (2003) for discussions of the concept of generation and of the systematic links between societal and family generations.

10. All this information has been used in a conservative manner; for example, one hour of labor force participation or care a month, as well as irregular work, has been regarded as sufficient to indicate the respective activity.

References

American Association of Retired Persons (AARP). (2001). *In the middle: A report on multicultural boomers coping with family and aging issues.* Washington, DC: Author.

Bengtson, V. L. (2001). Beyond the nuclear family: The increasing importance of multigenerational bonds. *Journal of Marriage and Family, 63,* 1–16.

Berger, B., & Berger, P. L. (1983). *The war over the family.* Garden City, NJ: Doubleday.

Brody, E. M. (1990). *Women in the middle: Their parent-care years.* New York: Springer.

Chisholm, J. F. (1999). The sandwich generation. *Journal of Social Distress and the Homeless, 8,* 177–191.

Dittmann-Kohli, F., Kohli, M., Künemund, H., Motel, A., Steinleitner, C., & Westerhof, G. (1997). Lebenszusammenhänge, Selbst- und Lebenskonzeptionen— Erhebungsdesign und Instrumente des Alters-Survey [Life contexts and concepts of self and life—Design and instruments of the Aging Survey]. *Forschungsgruppe Altern und Lebenslauf (FALL).* Berlin, Germany: Freie Universität.

Durkheim, É. (1975). Cours de sociologie de la famille: la famille conjugale [Lectures on family sociology: The united family]. In É. Durkheim (Ed.), *Textes 3* (pp. 35–49). Paris: Minuit (Original work published 1892)

Finch, J., & Mason, J. (1993). *Negotiating family responsibilities.* London: Routledge.

Giarrusso, R., Stallings, M., & Bengtson, V. L. (1995). The "intergenerational stake" hypothesis revisited: Parent-child differences in perceptions of relationships 20 years later. In V. L. Bengtson, K. W. Schaie, & L. M. Burton (Eds.), *Adult intergenerational relations: Effects of societal change* (pp. 227–263). New York: Springer.

Hareven, T. K., & Adams, K. J. (1996). The generation in the middle: Cohort comparisons in assistance to aging parents in an American community. In T. K. Hareven (Ed.), *Aging and generational relations* (pp. 3–29). New York: Aldine de Gruyter.

Höpflinger, F., & Baumgärtner, D. (1999). "Sandwich-Generation": Metapher oder soziale Realität? [Sandwich generation: Metaphor or social reality?]. *Zeitschrift für Familienforschung, 11,* 102–111.

Hörl, J., & Kytir, J. (1998). Die "Sandwich-Generation": Soziale Realität oder gerontologischer Mythos? Basisdaten zur Generationenstruktur der Frauen mittleren Alters in Österreich [The sandwich generation: Social reality or gerontological myth? Basic data on the generational structure of middle-aged women in Austria]. *Kölner Zeitschrift für Soziologie und Sozialpsychologie, 50,* 730–741.

Igl, G. (2000). Zur Problematik der Altersgrenzen aus juristischer Perspektive [On the problem of age limits from the legal perspective]. *Zeitschrift für Gerontologie und Geriatrie, 33*(Suppl. 1), I57–I70.

Kaufmann, F.-X., Kuijsten, A., Schulze, H.-J., & Strohmeier, K. P. (Eds.). (2002). *Family life and family policies in Europe: Problems and issues in comparative perspective.* Oxford, UK: Oxford University Press.

Kohli, M. (1977). Lebenslauf und Lebensmitte [Personal biography and midlife]. *Kölner Zeitschrift für Soziologie und Sozialpsychologie, 29,* 625–656.

Kohli, M. (1986). The world we forgot: An historical review of the life course. In Victor W. Marshall (Ed.), *Later life: The social psychology of aging* (pp. 271–303). Beverly Hills, CA: Sage.

Kohli, M. (1996). *The problem of generations: Family, economy, politics* (Collegium Budapest, Public Lecture Series No. 14). Budapest, Hungary: Collegium Budapest.

Kohli, M. (1999). Private and public transfers between generations: Linking the family and the state. *European Societies, 1,* 81–104.

Kohli, M. (2004). Intergenerational transfers and inheritance: A comparative view. In M. Silverstein, R. Giarrusso, & V. L. Bengtson (Eds.), *Intergenerational relations across time and place* (Springer Annual Review of Gerontology and Geriatrics, Vol. 24, 266–289). New York: Springer.

Kohli, M., & Künemund, H. (Eds.). (2000). *Die zweite Lebenshälfte. Gesellschaftliche Lage und Partizipation im Spiegel des Alters-Survey* [The second half of life: The state of society and participation as reflected in the Aging Survey]. Opladen, Germany: Leske + Budrich.

Kohli, M., & Künemund, H. (2002). La fin de carrière et la transition vers la retraite. Les limites d' âge chronologiques sont-elles un anachronisme? [The end of a career and the transition into retirement. Are chronological age limits an anachronism?]. *Retraite et Société, 36,* 84–107.

Kohli, M., Künemund, H., Motel, A., & Szydlik, M. (1997). Generationenkonstellationen, Haushaltsstrukturen und Wohnentfernungen in der zweiten Lebenshälfte. Erste Befunde des Alters-Survey [Generational constellations, household structures, and housing distances in the second half of life]. In R. Becker (Ed.), *Generationen und sozialer Wandel. Generationendynamik, Generationenbeziehungen und Differenzierung von Generationen* (pp. 157–175). Opladen, Germany: Leske + Budrich.

Kohli, M., Künemund, H., Motel, A., & Szydlik, M. (2000a). Generationenbeziehungen [Generational relations]. In M. Kohli & H. Künemund (Eds.),

Die zweite Lebenshälfte. Gesellschaftliche Lage und Partizipation im Spiegel des Alters-Survey (pp. 176–211). Opladen, Germany: Leske + Budrich.

Kohli, M., Künemund, H., Motel, A., & Szydlik, M. (2000b). Families apart? Intergenerational transfers in East and West Germany. In S. Arber & C. Attias-Donfut (Eds.), *The myth of generational conflict: Family and state in ageing societies* (pp. 88–99). London: Routledge.

Kohli, M., & Szydlik, M. (2000). Einleitung [Introduction]. In M. Kohli & M. Szydlik (Eds.), *Generationen in Familie und Gesellschaft* (pp. 7–18). Opladen, Germany: Leske + Budrich.

Künemund, H. (2002). Die "Sandwich-Generation"—typische Belastungs-konstellation oder nur gelegentliche Kumulation von Erwerbstätigkeit, Pflege und Kinderbetreuung? [The sandwich generation—Typical care constellation or occasional accumulation of job, nursing care, and child care?]. *Zeitschrift für Soziologie der Erziehung und Sozialisation, 22,* 344–361.

Künemund, H., & Rein, M. (1999). There is more to receiving than needing: Theoretical arguments and empirical explorations of crowding in and crowding out. *Ageing and Society, 19,* 93–121.

Künemund, H., & Rein, M. (2002). Intergenerational relations and family size: Do siblings matter? In G. Burkart & J. Wolf (Eds.), *Lebenszeiten. Erkundungen zur Soziologie der Generationen* (pp. 161–174). Opladen, Germany: Leske + Budrich.

Loomis, L. S., & Booth, A. (1995). Multigenerational caregiving and well-being: The myth of the beleaguered sandwich generation. *Journal of Family Issues, 16,* 131–148.

Lüscher, K., & Liegle, L. (Eds.). (2003). *Generationenbeziehungen in Familie und Gesellschaft* [Generational relationships in family and society]. Konstanz, Germany: UVK.

McDonald, P. F. (2000). Gender equity, social institutions and the future of fertility. *Journal of Population Research, 17,* 1–16.

Mulder, C. H., & Kalmijn, M. (2004). *Geographical distances between family members.* Den Haag: Netherlands Kinship Panel Study.

Nichols, L. S., & Junk, V. W. (1997). The sandwich generation: Dependency, proximity, and task assistance needs of parents. *Journal of Family and Economic Issues, 18,* 299–326.

Parsons, T. (1942). Age and sex in the social structure of the United States. *American Sociological Review, 7,* 604–616.

Penning, M. J. (1998). In the middle: Parental caregiving in the context of other roles. *Journal of Gerontology: Social Sciences, 53B,* S188–S197.

Perrig-Chiello, P. (1998). *Geschlechtstypisierende und geschlechtstypische Aspekte des Alterns* [Gender-typing and gender-typical aspects of aging]. Unpublished manuscript.

Putney, N. M., & Bengtson, V. L. (2001). Families, intergenerational relations, and kinkeeping in midlife. In M. E. Lachman (Ed.), *Handbook of midlife development* (pp. 528–570). New York: Wiley.

Raphael, D., & Schlesinger, B. (1994). Women in the sandwich generation: Do adult children living at home help? *Journal of Women and Aging, 6*, 21–45.

Reher, D. S. (1998). Family ties in Western Europe: Persistent contrasts. *Population and Development Review, 24*, 203–234.

Roots, C. R. (1998). *The sandwich generation: Adult children caring for aging parents.* New York: Garland.

Rosenthal, C. J., Martin-Matthews, A., & Matthews, S. H. (1996). Caught in the middle? Occupancy in multiple roles and help to parents in a national probability sample of Canadian adults. *Journal of Gerontology: Social Sciences, 51B*, S274–S283.

Rossi, A. S., & Rossi, P. H. (1990). *Of human bonding: Parent-child relations across the life course.* New York: Aldine de Gruyter.

Schupp, J., & Szydlik, M. (2004). Inheritance and gifts in Germany: The growing fiscal importance of inheritance tax for the federal states. *DIW Economic Bulletin, 41*, 95–102.

Seccombe, K., & Ishii-Kuntz, M. (1991). Perceptions of problems associated with aging. *The Gerontologist, 31*, 527–533.

Silverstein, M., & Bengtson, V. L. (1997). Intergenerational solidarity and the structure of adult child-parent relationships in American families. *American Journal of Sociology, 103*, 429–460.

Spitze, G., Logan, J. R., Joseph, G., & Lee, E. (1994). Middle generation roles and the well-being of men and women. *Journal of Gerontology: Social Sciences, 49*, S107–S116.

Szydlik, M. (2000). *Lebenslange Solidarität? Generationenbeziehungen zwischen erwachsenen Kindern und Eltern* [Lifelong solidarity? Generational relationships between adult children and their parents]. Opladen, Germany: Leske + Budrich.

Tesch-Römer, C., Wurm, S., Hoff, A., & Engstler, H. (2002). *Die zweite Welle des Alterssurveys: Erhebungsdesign und Instrumente* [The second wave of the Aging Survey: Design and instruments]. Berlin, Germany: Deutsches Zentrum für Altersfragen (Diskussionspapier Nr. 35).

Uhlenberg, P., & Riley, M. W. (Eds.). (2000). Essays on age integration. *The Gerontologist, 40*, 261–308.

Ward, R. A., & Spitze, G. (1998). Sandwiched marriages: The implications of child and parent relations for marital quality at midlife. *Social Forces, 77*, 647–666.

Zal, M. H. (1992). *The sandwich generation: Caught between growing children and aging parents.* New York: Plenum Press.

PART II

Early Life Influences on Middle Age

Three

Genetic Influences on Midlife Functioning

Nancy L. Pedersen, Erica L. Spotts, and Kenji Kato

Regardless of the definition of "midlife," most of the research in this area is typically normative. Behavioral genetic designs, on the other hand, focus on individual differences, on partitioning genetic and environmental sources. Our goal in this chapter is to provide a review of behavioral genetic studies of midlife, focusing, when possible, on longitudinal findings. Surprisingly little research of this nature has been explicitly devoted to the adult years (between 30 and 65 years of age), although several twin and family studies either are maturing into midlife, have included individuals in midlife because they were parents of adolescents, or have included participants under the age of 65 in studies of aging.

Behavioral Genetic Designs and What They Can Tell Us

Before beginning our review of the research on genetic and environmental influences in midlife, we felt that we should provide some background on behavioral genetics in general. Specifically, we wanted to define some key terms, discuss basic aspects of the methodology involved, and present several different study designs.

Key Terms

Behavioral genetic studies are designed to partition variance into genetic and environmental components. Estimates of genetic influences are referred to as *heritability* estimates and are the proportion of total variation that can be attributed to genetic differences among individuals in the population. It is important to remember that heritability, as well as estimates of environmental influences, are statistics based on variability in a population, not on mean or group differences.

Environmental variance can be partitioned into two types: shared and nonshared. *Shared environmental influences* are those nongenetic factors that make family members similar, and *nonshared environmental influences* are those nongenetic factors that make family members different.

Genetic and environmental influences may not always have direct effects; rather, there might be interplay of some sort between genetic and environmental factors. This interplay might take the form of a *genotype-environment (GE) correlation,* simply a correlation between a genotype and the environment to which the genotype is exposed. There are three ways that a genotype and an environment can be correlated: passively, evocatively, and actively (Plomin, DeFries, & Loehlin, 1977; Scarr & McCartney, 1983). Passive GE correlation refers to the transmission of both genes and environment from parents to their children. For example, parents who have a very loving and warm marriage may pass on to their children those genetically influenced characteristics that have both helped to create their good marriage and also provided an environment for their child that teaches the skills needed for a warm and loving marriage. Evocative GE correlation refers to environments that are elicited by an individual's genotype. To again use the example of marriage, an adult who is warm and loving is likely to elicit warm, positive responses from his or her spouse, resulting in a satisfying marriage. Finally, active GE correlation occurs when individuals actively select environments that are correlated with their genotype. A caring adult is more likely to seek out other people who are also warm, rather than befriend those who tend toward more negative behaviors.

Genes and environments might also have moderating effects on each other. Genotype-environment (GxE) interactions refer to the sensitivity of one's genotype to the environment, such that genetic propensities might be modified by environmental circumstances. Searching for GxE interactions has been more successful in nonhuman primates than in humans because researchers can breed strains of animals uniform for the genes that influence particular behaviors and then randomly assign these strains to different environments. Regardless, there has been some recent evidence in human populations for GxE interaction (Caspi et al., 2003; Heath, Eaves, & Martin, 1998; Turkheimer, Haley, Waldron, D'Onofrio, & Gottesman, 2003).

Methodology and Designs

Behavioral genetic studies are based on quantitative genetic theory, which means that the model fitting that is done is based on expectations about familial similarity. For example, monozygotic (MZ) twins share all of their segregating genes, whereas dizygotic (DZ) twins share, on average, 50% of their genetic makeup, just as full siblings do. Half siblings share 25% of their genetic makeup. Unrelated siblings (either adopted siblings, or unrelated step siblings) share none of their genetic makeup, but they are excellent indicators of the shared environment because their similarity can only be explained by experiences that they have shared. By including these expectations in the model fitting, we can arrive at estimates of genetic and environmental influences for a given population.

There are a number of different study designs that behavioral geneticists use. One is the family design. Here a proband is selected, usually matched with a nonaffected control. Researchers then examine the incidence of a disease (or other phenomenon) in the proband's and control's relatives. Finding a higher incidence in relatives of the proband than in relatives of the nonaffected control suggests that the disease is familial in origin. By familial, we mean that genetic and\or shared environmental factors are influencing the disease. This design does not allow us to distinguish between the two types of factors.

Twin and sibling designs do allow us to distinguish between genetic, shared environmental, and nonshared environmental influences. If genetic factors were influencing a particular trait, we would expect correlations between each member of a sibling pair to follow this pattern:

MZ > DZ = full sibling > half sibling > unrelated sibling. If shared environmental influences played a role, we would expect correlations between each sibling of a pair to be of the same magnitude across sibling types. Nonshared environmental influences are indicated by an MZ sibling correlation that is not equal to one because any differences between MZ twins can only be due to different environmental influences as they share the same genotype.

Finally, adoption studies provide a unique way of disentangling genetic and environmental effects by using two different "types" of parents, so to speak. The biological parents of the adopted-away child serve as a marker of genetic influence, while the adoptive parents serve as a marker of environmental influences. Any correlation between the adopted child and his biological parents for a given trait is assumed to be due to genetic influences since the biological parent has had little if any contact with the child. Conversely, any association between the adoptive parent and the adopted child suggests an environmental contribution to the parent-child resemblance. For example, if antisocial behavior were largely heritable, we would expect to see similarities between birth parents and adopted children, but no similarity between adopting parents and adopted children.

What Behavioral Genetic Studies Can Tell Us

Behavioral genetic studies allow us access to very crucial information about development over the life course that other types of studies are not able to provide. Namely, behavioral genetic studies are able to estimate genetic and environmental influences rather than assume their presence. Using these studies, we can get a better handle on the etiology of a wide range of phenomena, as well as better understand why different traits, disorders, and other constructs are interrelated. We have been able to clarify the links between interpersonal factors and mental and physical health. Genetically sensitive designs also allow us to identify influences on developmental processes. Not only have we been able to highlight the role of genes in individual development, but we have also been able to elucidate the role of the environment by searching for sources of shared and nonshared environmental influences. Genetically sensitive studies are necessary to gain the most complete understanding of development.

Behavioral Genetic Studies of Midlife

To our knowledge, the Twin Offspring Study in Sweden (TOSS) is the only behavioral genetic study specifically designed to capture information about adjustment in midlife. In this study, female and male twin pairs who have adolescent children are the heart of the study design. At the present time, the study is not longitudinal. The numerous studies based on the Virginia Twin Registry and the "Virginia 30,000," based at the Virginia Institute of Psychiatric and Behavioral Genetics, have provided a wealth of information about psychiatric phenotypes in twins who were born between 1915 and 1971. Only some studies from these cohorts are longitudinal. Other twin registries, such as those in the Netherlands and Australia, have cohorts of twins, some of whom are currently in midlife, although most efforts for the former have focused on development of children and adolescents (Boomsma et al., 2002; Croft, Read, de Klerk, Hansen, & Kurunczuk, 2002). The Scandinavian twin registries have the largest cohorts of twins in midlife at the time of data collection (Bergem, 2002; Kaprio & Koskenvuo, 2002; Pedersen, Lichtenstein, & Svedberg, 2002; Skytthe, Kyvik, Holm, Vaupel, & Christensen, 2002), but most of the analyses from these cohorts are cross-sectional and primarily on medical end points. Two studies of aging, the Minnesota Twin Study of Adult Development and Aging (MTSADA; Finkel & McGue, 1993) and the Swedish Adoption/Twin Study of Aging (SATSA; Pedersen et al., 1991; see also Finkel & Pedersen, 2004) have sufficient numbers of pairs in midlife to provide comparisons of younger and older cohorts within the studies. All told, these studies with genetically informative populations have covered a broad array of behavioral and biomedical phenotypes and numerous environmental exposures. Among the many domains of relevance were social aspects (including education and occupation, environmental impingement by stress and life events), interpersonal relationships (parenting, marriage, social support), cognition, personality and adjustment, psychopathology and substance abuse, and health. In the following, we will focus on a limited number of traits that we believe are highly pertinent to understanding individual differences in midlife: interpersonal relationships, social aspects, self-rated health, and cognitive abilities. When possible, we will highlight longitudinal findings and multivariate analyses that go beyond the relatively simplistic characterization of heritabilities.

Interpersonal Relationships and Adjustment

Interpersonal relationships are of great importance in midlife. Marital relationships and parent-child relationships can become a primary focus for many people during this time. Support from friends and family is also an important factor in coping with life changes, such as aging of parents and one's own aging. This section describes the behavioral genetic research that has considered interpersonal relationships in midlife. Most studies included in this section have used samples not specifically geared toward studying midlife, but rather have used samples that happen to include subjects who are in that stage of development. The exception might be the Twin Moms study (Reiss, Cederblad, et al., 2001; Reiss, Pedersen, et al., 2001), which by default focused on parents in midlife because selection criteria required their children be between the ages of 10 and 18 years. We will first discuss behavioral genetic studies of parenting; then, we will move on to social support and then marriage. We will then discuss studies that have tried to account for genetic influences on interpersonal relationships, ending with studies that have examined underlying genetic and environmental influences on links between interpersonal relationships and outcomes.

Parenting

To date, the field of parenting research has probably been the area most affected by behavioral genetic inquiry. Traditional psychosocial research has long posited that parenting styles directly affect child outcome (e.g., Baumrind, 1973). Genetically informed studies do not necessarily support those claims. Both child-based (genetic information comes from the children) and parent-based (genetic information comes from the parents) studies support the notion that children influence how parents parent. Rowe was the first to examine the genetic and environmental influences on parenting using samples of adolescents (Rowe, 1981, 1983). He found that the adolescents' genetic influences contributed to their reports of their parents' warmth, and shared environmental influences contributed to parental control, with nonshared environmental influences contributing to about half of the variance of each. These findings have been replicated in several other studies (Braungart, 1994; Elkins, McGue, & Iacono, 1997; Goodman & Stevenson, 1989; Plomin, McClearn, Pedersen, Nesselroade, & Bergeman, 1989).

These findings come from child-based designs, so they only tell us about the influences of the child's genes. What about the parents' genes? Findings from the Twin Moms study—a sample of Swedish female twins, their spouses, and their adolescent child—tell us that the parents' own genetic factors also contribute to their parenting, for all aspects except for attempted and actual control (Neiderhiser et al., 2004).

Through what processes do these genetic factors influence parenting? There are several possibilities, all of which fall under the rubric of GE correlations. GE correlations are correlations between genetic factors of an individual and the environment. There are three types: passive, active, and evocative. Passive GE correlations refer to the fact that each parent provides 50% of their child's genetic makeup. So parents who exhibit warm parenting styles pass along the genes that influence their warmth, resulting in a child who also tends to be warm and caring, thereby contributing to the already pleasant family environment. In a case like this, it is difficult to untangle how much the children are influencing their parents' parenting or are reflecting shared genes. However, genetic characteristics of children might influence their tendency to be caring and, as a result, lead them to seek out positive environments. This is called an active GE correlation. Finally, genetic characteristics of the child might elicit warm parenting; this is referred to as an evocative GE correlation. Here, the child influences parenting by evoking particular reactions from his or her parents. Much could be said on this topic, but space considerations limit us to a brief summary of findings from a study that attempted to tease apart these different processes. A comparison of the child-based Nonshared Environment and Adolescent Development study (Reiss et al., 1994; Reiss, Neiderhiser, Hetherington, & Plomin, 2000) and the parent-based Twin Moms study suggested that passive GE correlations may be important for parental negativity and positivity but not for parental control (Neiderhiser et al., 2004). The implications of these findings contradict traditional socialization research suggesting that parents have a direct influence on their child's outcome.

Remembered Parenting

Several studies have addressed genetic and environmental influences on how adults remember their childhood family environment and parenting. MZ twins report their rearing environment as being more similar than the rearing environments of DZ twins, suggesting genetic influences on remembered parenting (Hur & Bouchard, 1995). A study using the Twin Moms sample found genetic influences on all subscales of remembered parenting, as well as shared environmental and nonshared environmental influences (Lichtenstein et al., 2003). Parental warmth was most strongly influenced by genetic influences, which could be accounted for by personality characteristics. Shared environmental influences were explained as an increasing importance of family-level experiences over time.

Social Support

High-quality social support is robustly associated with improved health and well-being, whereas a lack of social support is linked with poorer health (Ganster & Victor, 1988; Kessler, Kendler, Heath, Neale, & Eaves, 1992; Wade & Kendler, 2000). A number of genetically sensitive studies have begun to examine genetic and environmental factors involved in social support.

The first study to examine genetic and environmental influences on social support came from SATSA. This sample included men and women with an average age of 65.6, 62% of whom were female. Because this sample includes twins separated at birth and reared apart, not only could estimates of genetic and nonshared environmental effects be computed, but also shared environmental variance could be separated into shared rearing environment and correlated environment (similarity of twins beyond that accounted for by genetic influences or shared rearing environments). Findings differed for availability and adequacy of support. The availability of social support was influenced entirely by environmental factors: Primarily nonshared environments, but also shared rearing environments and correlated environments, played a substantial role. Adequacy of support was influenced by genetic and, predominantly, nonshared environmental influences.

A series of studies using a sample of twins drawn from the Virginia Twin Registry (now the Mid-Atlantic Twin Registry) have examined more detailed aspects of social support. In the first study, Kessler and colleagues (1992) examined more specific aspects of social support (perceived support from spouse, from other relatives, and from friends; access to a confidant; frequency of interaction with relatives and with friends; frequency of church attendance and of club attendance) in a sample of same-sex female twins aged 11 to 53 years. The aim was to examine the homogeneity versus heterogeneity of social support as a construct. Genetic factors played a role in perceived relative support, perceived friend support, having a confidant, frequency of church attendance, and frequency of club attendance. Shared environmental influences were important for perceived spouse support, perceived relative support, frequency of interaction with relatives, frequency of interaction with friends, and frequency of attending church. Nonshared environmental factors accounted for at least 50% of the variance for all aspects of social support, with the exception of frequency of church attendance (20%) and club attendance (48%). Given the differing patterns of influence across different types of social support, it seemed clear that social support is a heterogeneous construct.

A second study was conducted after an additional wave of data was collected on the female twins. Here, the reliable components of different aspects of social support were examined in a genetically informed way (Kendler, 1997). Using six slightly different categories than the first study (i.e., relative problems and support, friend problems and support, confidants, and social integration), this study found that relative problems and support were influenced by genetic, shared, and nonshared environmental influences, whereas the remaining four categories were influenced by only genetic and nonshared environmental influences. Findings of shared environmental influences on the relative problems and support were explained by the fact that twins share the same relatives.

A sample of same-sex male twins and opposite-sex twins was collected to correspond with the first wave of same-sex female twins. This sample was used to examine sex differences in social support, using the same constructs described in the previous paragraph (Agrawal, Jacobson, Prescott, & Kendler, 2002). Findings indicated no qualitative gender differences for any of the factors. In other words, there were no differences in the sources of genetic influences for men and women. On the other hand, quantitative differences in genetic influences between men and women were found for relative support and confidants. Consistent with previous studies, shared environmental influences were only found for relative support and problems.

Marital Relationships

Most genetically informed studies of marriage focus on marital *status* rather than marital *quality*, so those studies will be reviewed first. The first study to examine a component of marital status was a study of the genetic and environmental influences on divorce, using a sample drawn from the Minnesota Twins Registry (McGue & Lykken, 1992). Participants were between the ages of 34 and 53 years. Both male and female MZ twins were more similar for divorce status than DZ twins, indicating genetic influences. Having a divorced MZ co-twin increased one's odds of getting a divorce nearly sixfold, whereas having a divorced parent or DZ co-twin only increased risk by less than twofold. Heritability estimates for divorce were nearly equally divided between genetic and nonshared environmental influences, for both men and women.

The question has also been asked about whether people who have never married and people who have divorced can both be categorized as having "failed to marry successfully." If they are two sides of the same coin, MZ co-twins of those who have never married should have higher rates of divorce than DZ co-twins, and the MZ co-twins of those who have divorced should have a higher rate of never marrying than DZ co-twins. This question was addressed using the National Academy of Sciences–National Research Council (NAS–NRC) sample of World War II veterans (Trumbetta & Gottesman, 1997). These males were born between 1917 and 1927 and were surveyed in 1972 and 1985, when the men were 45 to 55 and 58 to 68 years old, respectively. Never marrying and divorcing were not co-heritable, though there was a nonsignificant trend for more co-twins of those who had divorced to have never married. The authors suggest that this indicates the possibility of a continuum of pair bondedness. The same authors later explored marital status in the evolutionary terms of pair bondedness and mate diversification, saying that being married resembles the former and divorce maps onto the latter (Trumbetta & Gottesman, 2000). Again using the sample of World War II veterans, they found that pair bonding seemed to be more genetically influenced than mate diversification, though the heritability declined over time.

The Vietnam Era Twin Registry was used to examine the heritability of marital status, so again the sample was composed only of males. These men served in the U.S. military between the years of 1965 and 1975 and were assessed in 1987. This study examined never marrying versus getting divorced, and whether the same factors that influenced never marrying also influenced divorce (Jerskey et al., 2001). Jerskey and colleagues found that there were no genetic influences on never marrying, but that if one was to marry, there were genetic influences on getting divorced, replicating previous work (McGue & Lykken, 1992). In other words, one twin's being married was independent of his co-twin's likelihood of divorce.

The propensity to marry seems to be a different story. A study using a sample from the Minnesota Twin Registry examined the genetic and environmental influences on getting married (Johnson, McGue, Krueger, & Bouchard, 2004). The total heritability, including additive and dominant effects, was .70. Gender differences were examined, and it was found that the heritability for men and women were similar, but the genetic components of variance were not the same for men and women. In other words, different genetic factors influence men's propensity to marry than influence women's.

Only recently have the genetic and environmental influences on marital *quality* been explored. One of the aims of the Twin Moms study described above was to examine how marital satisfaction impacted maternal mental health. Toward this aim, the Dyadic Adjustment Scale (DAS; Spanier, 1976) and the Marital Adjustment Test (Locke & Wallace, 1987), both often-used measures of marital quality, were administered to both the twin women and their spouses. Most measures of wife's marital quality were at least moderately influenced by genetic factors (standardized parameter estimates of .24–.33) and primarily influenced by nonshared environmental influences (standardized parameter estimates of .67–.85; Spotts, Neiderhiser, Towers, et al., 2004). One exception was DAS Affectional Expression, which showed negligible amounts of genetic influence. Shared environmental influences played no role in the twin women's reports of their marital quality. Genetic influences on husbands' reports of their marital quality were also examined, with results similar to those of wives' reports. It needs to be noted that influences on husband reports were those of the *wife's* genetically and environmentally influenced characteristics, so these findings of genetic influences represent the effects of the wife's genetically influenced characteristics on her husband's perceptions of their marriage. This could be the result of either active GE correlations, whereby the wife actively selects a husband that fits with her genetically influenced characteristics, or evocative GE correlation, whereby the wife's genetically influenced characteristics elicit a particular response from her husband.

Accounting for Genetic
Influences on Social Relationships

This section will discuss studies that have set about trying to identify what accounts for genetic and/or environmental influences on social relationships. These studies use multivariate analyses to examine the covariance among variables.

What accounts for the genetic influences on aspects of marriage? It appears that personality plays a large role. Using a sample drawn from the Minnesota Twin Registry, Jockin and colleagues extended McGue and Lykken's (1992) study of divorce to examine the extent to which personality accounted for the genetic influences on divorce (Jockin, McGue, & Lykken, 1996). They found that 30% and 42% of the genetic influences on divorce could be accounted for by personality for women and men, respectively. The authors suggested that the genetic influences on divorce actually influence personality, which in turn influences divorce risk. They also found that the environmental factors influencing personality and divorce were almost entirely independent of each other.

Another study using the same sample examined the extent to which personality characteristics accounted for the genetic influences (Johnson et al., 2004). Using composite scales of the Multidimensional Personality Questionnaire, they found that genetic influences accounted for 68% and 83% of the covariance between personality and the propensity to marry for men and women, respectively.

Another study using the Twin Moms sample tried to account for the genetic influences on marital quality and found that the personality characteristics aggression and optimism accounted for all of the genetic influences on wives' reports of marital quality (Spotts, Lichtenstein, Hensson, et al., in press). It had also been hypothesized that husbands' personality characteristics would account for a substantial portion of the nonshared environmental influences on wives' reports of marital quality, but this was not supported.

Associations Between Relationships and Adjustment

There is a large literature linking interpersonal relationships with various forms of adjustment. Behavioral geneticists are beginning to explore the underlying mechanisms of these associations by examining what types of influences account for the links.

Parenting is usually discussed in conjunction with child outcome. Because the focus of this book is on midlife, a discussion of these studies will be omitted. However, one study used causal modeling to examine the link between remembered parenting and psychological distress in adulthood (Gillespie, Zue, Neale, Heath, & Martin, 2003). The sample of females was drawn from the Australian National Health and Medical Research Council Twin Registry and ranged in age from 18 to 45 years.

Genetic and nonshared environmental factors were found to account for the association between remembered parenting and depressive and anxious symptoms. The best fitting causal model suggested that remembered parenting influenced psychological distress rather than the opposite.

Levels of social support are robustly associated with positive and negative outcomes. What is less clear are the mechanisms underlying this association. In addition to the possibility of high-quality social support leading to better health, there might also be genetic factors that influence both social support and adjustment. Behavioral genetic studies are uniquely equipped to test these possibilities.

Bergeman and colleagues used the SATSA sample to examine the links between social support and well-being, as measured by self-reports of depressive symptoms and life satisfaction (Bergeman, Plomin, Pedersen, & McClearn, 1991). Genetic and nonshared environmental influences were found to contribute to the associations between social support and each of the two outcome measures. This suggests underlying genetically influenced factors influence both social support and mental health, while factors that make the twins different affect both their relationships and their mental health. Such nonshared factors might include husbands, jobs, or children.

Studies using the Twin Moms sample expanded on this research by including both marital quality and adequacy of social support in examinations of associations among interpersonal relationships and both depressive symptoms and well-being in women. This was done to see if marital quality and social support made independent contributions to mental health. When looking at depressive symptoms, genetic influences were shared among marital quality, social support, and depressive symptoms (Spotts, Neiderhiser, Ganiban, et al., 2004). Social support shared genetic and nonshared environmental variance with depressive symptoms beyond that common to all three variables. Two aspects of positive mental health were examined: well-being and global self-worth (Spotts, Neiderhiser, Ganiban, et al., 2004); different patterns of genetic and environmental influences were found for each. For well-being, marital quality and social support accounted for the same genetic and nonshared environmental variance, with no additional variance explained by social support. On the other hand, social support was independently associated with global self-worth by genetic and nonshared environmental factors after taking marital quality into account. Several conclusions can be drawn from these findings. First, there are genetic factors that are common to relationships and mental health. Second, these findings suggest that marital quality is not the only source of social support influential to a sense of self-worth, though other aspects of marriage may be important. Third, it seems that influences on global self-worth may be wider ranging than those on well-being, as indicated by social support being independently associated with global self-worth. Finally, we can speculate on the findings of nonshared environmental influences. For each of these analyses, husbands' reports of marital quality were substituted for the wives' reports, and in all cases, nonshared environmental influences were shared among marital quality, social support, and the measure of mental health (Spotts, Neiderhiser, Towers, et al., 2004; Spotts, Pedersen, Neiderhiser, et al., in press). These findings suggest that the husband is an important source of nonshared environmental influence on his wife's feelings about her interpersonal relationships and her mental health.

Kessler and colleagues (1992) used the female twin sample drawn from the Virginia Twin Registry to examine the processes by which perceived social support and adjustment to stress, as indicated by onset of major depression (MD), were linked. Among the models tested was one hypothesizing that the link could be explained by a common genetic cause; the model was not supported. At first glance, these results seem to contradict the findings from the Twin Moms study reported above. However, the two studies used very different outcome measures: depressive symptomatology versus acute onset of MD. Also, the nature of the variables used in the analyses resulted in very different sample sizes, with the Virginia sample being reduced to 22 cases.

Wade and Kendler (2000) tested several possibilities explaining associations between lifetime MD (as indicated by an onset of MD within the past 12 months at either Time 1 or Time 2) and social support using the Virginia female twin sample. Three hypotheses were tested, but the one discussed here postulates that social support and the risk for MD may be linked by common, genetically influenced traits. To test this hypothesis, the level of social support in one twin was predicted by MD in her co-twin. A significant association was found, and it was stronger for MZ than DZ twins, indicating genetic influences on the association.

Measures of the Environment and Health

Education and Occupation

Not only family and social relationships but also socioeconomic status characterize midlife. Of several ways to operationalize socioeconomic status, education and occupation are referred to and examined most frequently. A great deal of research has demonstrated that socioeconomic status relates to health and well-being as well as financial success in life. It is therefore of interest to discuss here why there are individual differences in socioeconomic status and how genes and familial environment contribute to that variation.

One of the early attempts in this area was from studies using twins born in Norway between 1915 and 1960. Heath and colleagues revealed that the relative contributions from genetic and environmental sources varied across cohorts for education (Heath et al., 1985). Heritability was greatest (74% and 45% of the variance in men and women, respectively) for subjects born between 1940 and 1949, slightly lower for the younger subjects born after 1950, and lowest for those born before 1939. Similarly, Tambs and colleagues also reported secular change in the importance of genetic influences on education using part of the same cohorts of Norwegian twins (Tambs, Sundet, Magnus, & Berg, 1989).

Behavioral genetic research with a more powerful study design was conducted using Swedish twins including those who were reared apart. Lichtenstein and colleagues first used this study design to explore the sources of individual differences in educational achievement (Lichtenstein, Pedersen, & McClearn, 1992). Having divided the sample at the age of 60 years, they found that younger and older groups showed significant differences in the relative importance of genetic and environmental effects. Their findings suggested that genetic influences seem to have a greater impact on education for the younger age group than the older group, which was in accord with the Norwegian studies mentioned in the previous paragraph. By using a similar sample, Lichtenstein and Pedersen then investigated genetic and environmental contributions to educational achievement as part of multivariate analyses (Lichtenstein & Pedersen, 1997). Genetic factors for educational achievement were estimated as more important in this study than in the earlier study.

A large sample of Australian twins has provided longitudinal data to study genetic and environmental effects on educational achievement (Baker, Treloar, Reynolds, Heath, & Martin, 1996). Baker and colleagues evaluated the heritability of self-reported educational achievement using twins from older (born between 1893 and 1950) and younger (born after 1950) cohorts. Based on self-reports in 1981 and 1989, they estimated genetic variance in the longitudinal correlation of educational achievement measured at these two occasions as 57%. In contrast to the

Norwegian studies, there were no differences in the estimates for the younger and older cohorts in this Australian study. Baker and colleagues pointed out that the discrepancy in findings could be attributable to cultural differences, sampling differences, or statistical power.

Occupational status and work environment have also been studied, using twins primarily from socioeconomic status points of view. Arvey and colleagues assessed genetic component to job satisfaction based on the Minnesota Study of Twins Reared Apart, another unique resource for studying twins reared apart (Arvey, Bouchard, Segal, & Abraham, 1989). Having administered the Minnesota Job Satisfaction Questionnaire to reared-apart twins whose mean age was 42 years, they reported that approximately 30% of the variance in general job satisfaction was due to genetic factors, based on intraclass correlations. Keller and colleagues extended this study to evaluate the heritability of work values (Keller, Arvey, Dawis, Bouchard, & Segal, 1992). With the Minnesota Importance Questionnaire, they estimated genetic effects on the total variance as approximately 40%.

In the aforementioned study in SATSA (Lichtenstein et al., 1992), the authors investigated relative importance of genetic and environmental effects on occupational status as well as educational achievement. Substantial sex differences in the estimates were observed for this measure, although differences between younger and older groups were not tested. Based on the same sample, Hershberger and colleagues examined genetic and environmental influences on perceptions of organizational climate, using the Work Environment Scale and another measure of job satisfaction (Hershberger, Lichtenstein, & Knox, 1994). Genetic effects were significant for Supportive Climate (22% of the variance) but not for Time Pressure, implying difference in genetic effects on controllable and uncontrollable environment. Unlike Arvey et al. (1989), genetic effects were not significant for job satisfaction. Lichtenstein and colleagues then analyzed the dimensions of occupation and distances between occupational categories, by using intrapair differences in adult occupational position (Lichtenstein, Hershberger, & Pedersen, 1995). Genetic factors showed substantial influences (60% of the variance) on occupational status for men, while shared and nonshared environmental factors were of about equal importance. For women, genetic effects were less important (12% of the variance), and shared and nonshared environmental effects accounted for more of the variation. The results pointed to the importance of genetic effects for sources of familial resemblance in occupational status for men.

Lichtenstein and Pedersen further extended the previous SATSA studies of occupational and educational achievements in a multivariate study design with a measure of general cognitive ability (Lichtenstein & Pedersen, 1997). They found that educational achievement and occupational status showed significant genetic variance both in common with and independent of genetic variance for cognitive ability. The findings indicated that, although genetic influences for cognitive ability were important for socioeconomic status, a substantial portion of the genetic variance in socioeconomic status was independent of that for cognitive ability. These results were in agreement with the aforementioned Norwegian study (Tambs et al., 1989), in which the variance in occupational status was accounted for more by specific genetic effects than by those in common with educational achievement and general cognitive ability. In contrast, Lichtenstein and Pedersen also found that rearing environmental effects for educational achievement and occupational status were completely overlapping, which implied that the same factors in the rearing home made family members similar to each other for both education and occupation.

Taken together, there is evidence that genetic effects are responsible for a substantial part of individual differences in educational achievement and occupational status. However, estimates for the relative importance of genetic and environmental effects often differ between younger and older cohorts, a difference that is likely to be attributable to cohort differences. There also may be cultural differences that vary the estimates from study to study.

Stressful Life Events

In general, individuals experience a number of major life changes as they grow older. It is reasonable to think that such events significantly correlate with psychological development and health in later life. Since Holmes and Rahe introduced the Social Readjustment Rating Scale (Holmes & Rahe, 1967), stressful life events have been an important topic among developmental psychologists and behavioral geneticists, due to their potential function in the etiology of various mental disorders.

A SATSA study first explored genetic influence on perceptions of major events later in life (Plomin, Lichtenstein, Pedersen, McClearn, & Nesselroade, 1990). By using twins reared apart and reared together, whose ages ranged from 27 to older than 80, Plomin et al. estimated genetic influence on the occurrence of life events as 40% of the variance of the total life events score. Saudino and colleagues then assessed sex differences in genetic and environmental contributions to life events and genetic influences of personality on its association with life events (Saudino, Pedersen, Lichtenstein, McClearn, & Plomin, 1997). Significant genetic variance was observed only for women in controllable, desirable, and undesirable life events, and no sex differences were found for uncontrollable events. Multivariate analyses of personality (as indexed by Neuroticism, Extraversion, and Openness to Experience) and life events suggested that all of the genetic variance on controllable, desirable, and undesirable life events for women is common to personality. Saudino et al. thus concluded that genetic influences on life events appeared to be entirely mediated by personality in middle-aged and older women.

Besides the SATSA, a number of studies have been conducted to examine the relative contribution of genetic and environmental influences to stressful life events using the Virginia Twin Registry. Kendler and colleagues (Foley, Neale, & Kendler, 1996; Kendler, Neale, Kessler, Heath, & Eaves, 1993) reported that genetic factors and familial environment each accounted for around 20% of the variance of total life events in twins aged from 17 to 55 years. They suggested that stressful life events be classified into "network" events (those which occur within an individual's social network), where twin resemblance was due solely to the familial environment, and "personal" events (those in which the individual is directly involved), where most twin resemblance was the result of genetic factors. Their findings indicated that stable individual differences were more important determinants of personal stressful life events than random (occasion-specific) factors. Bolinskey and colleagues provided additional support for the previous findings with a sex limitation model (Bolinskey, Neale, Jacobson, Prescott, & Kendler, 2004). Unlike Saudino et al. (1997), they found that many of the same genetic factors were acting within both sexes.

Overall, genetic influences have been consistently demonstrated in adult samples on the probability of experiencing stressful life events. On the other hand, the importance of shared environment and sex remains unclear. In addition, longitudinal studies that address age differences are necessary to assessing changes in genetic and environmental effects across age.

Stress Coping

As we have seen significant genetic influences on stressful life events thus far, it is reasonable to question whether variation in the way adult individuals cope with stress is also influenced by genetic factors. Stress coping is, therefore, a potentially important area that could shed light on the mechanisms of stress-induced health problems, a major issue in later life.

Kendler and colleagues first investigated genetic and environmental influences on stress coping in young adults (Kendler, Kessler, Heath, Neale, & Eaves, 1991). Data were collected by self-report coping behavior based on 14 items of the Ways of Coping Checklist (WCC; Folkman & Lazarus, 1980) from female twin pairs (mean age, 29 years) in the Virginia Twin Registry. Using factor analysis, three coping factors were identified: Turning to Others, Problem Solving, and Denial. The authors reported that twin resemblance in Turning to Others and Problem Solving could be explained entirely by genetic factors with heritability of approximately 30%. For denial, shared environmental factors accounted for 19% of the total variation.

Busjahn and colleagues also attempted to evaluate genetic effects on stress coping by using 19 coping styles as well as four secondary coping factors, based on a German coping questionnaire with twin pairs aged 34 years on average (Busjahn, Faulhaber, Freier, & Luft, 1999). All the four coping factors (Defense, Emotional Coping, Substitution, and Active Coping) showed genetic influences, whereas shared environment had no significant influence. For more specific coping styles, genetic influences were found for 17 of the 19 coping styles, most of which were solely under genetic influences. On the other hand, there was no single genetic factor common to all the specific coping styles.

Whereas the two studies mentioned in the previous paragraphs used relatively young samples, a recent SATSA study explored the relative contribution of genetic and environmental influences to stress coping in middle-aged and older adults (Kato & Pedersen, 2005). The subjects were twins reared apart and reared together of both sexes, aged from 26 to 89 years. Three coping scales (Problem Solving, Turning to Others, and Avoidance) were derived by factor analysis based on the Billing and Moos coping measure (Billings & Moos, 1984). The results indicated not only genetic influences on all three coping styles, a result in line with the previous studies, but also significant sex differences in variance estimates for all of them. Shared rearing environmental influences were observed only for Turning to Others and Avoidance in women. Kato and Pedersen further examined the basis of covariation between coping styles and personality traits (as indexed by Neuroticism, Extraversion, and Openness to Experience) and revealed that genetic influences on adults' coping differentially reflected genetic factors in common with personality traits. The sources of covariation also showed significant sex differences.

As yet, little is known about the origin of individual variation in coping styles with middle-aged adult samples, despite the vast amount of coping studies at phenotypic levels. As with stressful life events, longitudinal data are warranted in order to distinguish cohort effects from aging effects on stress coping in adults.

Self-Rated Health

Self-rated (or self-reported) health is a global measure of an individual's physical and mental health, as a summary of his or her own perception from different aspects. Self-rated health is often measured by using three items based on Duke University's Older Americans Resources Survey (Duke University, 1978). Although it is a relatively simple measure, this subjective health assessment is often superior to clinical assessments for predicting outcomes such as mortality (Idler & Benyamini, 1997). As change in health is another important feature that characterizes midlife, it is rational to discuss behavioral genetic studies of self-rated health in this section.

A series of studies using Swedish twins have demonstrated the importance of genetic factors for individual differences in self-rated health. Harris and colleagues first analyzed cross-sectional data from twins reared apart and reared together, aged 26 to 86 years (Harris, Pedersen, McClearn, Plomin, & Nesselroade, 1992). There were significant age differences in the genetic and environmental influences on self-rated health in the sample: Genetic effects were important for subjects aged 60 years or older, whereas the total variance was accounted for entirely by environmental influences in the younger subgroup.

Using a computer-assisted telephone interview with twin pairs aged 17 to 85 years, Svedberg and colleagues tested age and sex differences in genetic and environmental sources of variation for self-rated health (Svedberg, Lichtenstein, & Pedersen, 2001). Having divided the sample into four age groups, they found that increase in total variance was primarily due to genetic influences in the two middle age groups (45–74 years), whereas no genetic influences were observed in either the youngest or the oldest age group, which was similar to what Harris et al. (1992) reported. In contrast, no sex differences were shown in variance components in the sample. Svedberg et al. further investigated longitudinal data in SATSA over a 9-year time period (Svedberg, Lichtenstein, Gatz, Sandin, & Pedersen, in press). They revealed that changes in means and variance of self-rated health were largely influenced by cohort differences, although socioeconomic status in childhood did not account for these cohort differences. The results also indicated that correlations between measurement occasions were explained almost equally by genetic and environmental factors.

In another SATSA study, Lichtenstein and Pedersen examined how the associations between self-rated health, stressful life events, and social relationships were mediated by genetic and environmental influences (Lichtenstein & Pedersen, 1995). For men, environmental influences were solely important for variation in the psychosocial measures and were the primary mediators of the relationship with health. For women, however, a substantial portion of the variance in the psychosocial factors was due to genetic influences, and these influences also contributed to the bulk of the correlations with health. Although inconsistent with the previous results from univariate analyses of self-rated health, these findings suggested the importance of sex differences for the relationships and mediation with the psychosocial factors.

In conclusion, it seems that individual variation in the way of assessing one's own health reflects complex effects of sex, psychosocial factors, and changes in society, as well as genetic predisposition to diseases. Given that the variance of individuals' health status increases with increased age, it can be said that lifestyle in middle age deserves more attention for the betterment of prevention and intervention that will lead to successful aging.

Cognitive Abilities

Until relatively recently, the greatest amount of longitudinal behavioral genetic research has been on cognitive abilities, both general and specific. Again, most studies concern childhood and adolescence, although currently there are a growing number of programs in "gerontological genetics," which include information on cognitive abilities in midlife. As has been the case historically with most efforts at characterizing the genetic and environmental sources of individual differences, the first analyses comprised cross-sectional estimates of heritability for specific cognitive abilities and composite measures of general abilities or IQ. As these studies were performed at a time when demonstrating that genetic variation could be of at least *some* importance for behavioral traits, there was little attention paid to hypothesis testing. The first heritability studies of cognitive abilities were based on twin infants, children, and adolescents, followed by adoption studies of the same part of the life span. As the results from these early developmental behavioral genetic studies emerged, Robert Plomin (1986) ventured a number of expectations about genetic influences across the life span. Among the expectations, he predicted that heritability would increase with increasing age, possibly as a result of amplification of genetic effects existing early in development. This proved to be the case for general cognitive abilities, at least from childhood through midlife (McCartney, Harris, & Bernieri, 1990; Pedersen & Lichtenstein, 1997), predominantly due to a concomitant decrease in shared environmental influences.

SATSA provided some of the first evidence for the relative importance of genetic and environmental influences on cognitive abilities in adults older than 50 years of age. Eighty percent of the individual differences seen for general cognitive ability are due to genetic differences (Pedersen, Plomin, Nesselroade, & McClearn, 1992). This value is somewhat higher than those found in adolescence and early adulthood but is consistent with two reports from middle-aged adults (Bouchard, Lykken, McGue, Segal, & Tellegen, 1990; Tambs, Sundet, & Magnus, 1984). The SATSA results were based on the first wave of in-person testing data, where the sample was treated as one age group, ranging from 50 to 85 years. However, a further exploration into age differences in heritability estimates found some differences across age groups (Finkel, Pedersen, McGue, & McClearn, 1995). Older Swedish twins (over 65 years) demonstrated a significantly lower heritability for general cognitive abilities, suggesting a possible inverted L-shaped function for the relationship between heritability and IQ later in life. Thus, genetic influences are substantial and stable through midlife but appear to decrease in importance after age 65, at least cross-sectionally.

Aging Trajectories for Cognitive Abilities

Any exploration of longitudinal changes in genetic and environmental influences on individual differences should first characterize normative (mean) and variance trajectories. If sufficient occasions of measurement are available, latent growth models are ideal for describing such patterns. Latent growth models incorporating two linear slopes were recently applied to cognitive data from SATSA in order to address several phenotypic issues (Finkel, Reynolds, McArdle, Gatz, & Pedersen, 2003). Results indicated stability or even improvement up to age 70 for measures of crystallized ability, followed by significant decline. Linear age changes were found for many cognitive abilities. For those measures with a large speed component, a growth curve model incorporating two separate slopes was indicated, suggesting stability prior to age 65 but a significant acceleration in linear decline thereafter. Accelerating decline in cognitive performance at age 65 may reflect true aging changes, or it may be a consequence of the transition from an active (presumably stimulating) work life to retirement. Furthermore, it is possible that a more accurate model of cognitive aging includes not one but two transition periods when the rate of decline changes.

Longitudinal Changes in Heritability of Specific Cognitive Abilities

Early longitudinal analyses of SATSA were cohort-sequential such that sliding-interval-based cohorts and longitudinal information were used to examine changes in genetic and environmental components of variance. Inspection of the longitudinal trends for the separate cohorts clearly demonstrates that heritability is relatively stable longitudinally at approximately 80% in midlife cohorts (50–65 years at first testing) but decreases longitudinally from approximately 80% at Time 1 to 60% at Time 3 in the older cohorts.

Subsequent research has taken advantage of expansions of the latent growth curve models to include twin data to examine genetic and environmental influences on mean level of cognitive ability, as well as rates of change over a 13-year span. Various models have been applied, including a two-slope model with centering based on time rather than age (Reynolds, Finkel, Gatz, & Pedersen, 2002) and most recently, a model with linear change prior to age 65 and a quadratic term for accelerated decline after age 65 (Reynolds et al., in press). In all cases, genetic influences were of greater importance for ability level than for linear change. Furthermore, genetic variance was often of greater importance for quadratic (accelerated) change than for linear change. Regardless of the model or time span, the period of midlife (in this case, 50–65 years) was characterized by relative stability, not only in total variation, but also in sources of individual differences. After age 65, decreasing genetic variance, but increasing nonshared environmental variance, was the most typical pattern across cognitive domains. Genetic variance decreases were most apparent for perceptual speed measures, fluid abilities, and general cognitive ability late in life; however, one verbal measure and two memory-related measures showed evidence of both increasing genetic and nonshared environmental variance after age 65. These results demonstrate clearly that the relative influence of genetic factors will change as the dynamic combination of genetic and environmental factors changes over the life span. Furthermore, each component of cognitive aging needs to be examined independently; we will not find a single aging trajectory, nor will we find a single explanation for cognitive aging. Relevant to students of midlife will be explorations of turning points (i.e., when relative stability changes to growth or decline) and the predictors of these events.

The Role of Speed in Cognition

In the previous descriptions of individual differences and cognition, we have focused on individual abilities and domains, but not at the associations within or among domains. Within cognition, some of the strongest evidence for age-related associations comes from studies of perceptual speed and cognitive performance. The processing-speed theory (Birren, 1964; Salthouse, 1996) posits that cognitive aging results from generalized slowing of perceptual and cognitive processes. Several lines of evidence support this theory (Salthouse, 2004), although relatively little work has been done to explore the role of genetic influences in these processes. Cross-sectional analyses of SATSA indicate that the heritability of cognitive ability in adulthood results, at least in part, from genetic influences associated with perceptual speed instead of genes for cognitive functioning, per se (Finkel & Pedersen, 2000). Additional longitudinal analyses were pursued in which latent growth curve models were applied to cognitive data from which the speed had been partialed out (Finkel & Pedersen, 2004). When variance components for original and speed-corrected measures were compared, two patterns of results were found. For Information and Thurstone's Picture Memory, greater nonshared environmental variance and less genetic variance were evident for the speed-corrected measures. In contrast, removing the speed variance from Block Design and General Cognitive Ability resulted in a marked difference in the shape of the age trajectory in genetic influence. For both variables, estimates of genetic variance began at comparable levels at age 50, but they declined at a much faster rate for the speed-corrected measure. This suggests that already during midlife, speed is an important source of genetic variation for fluid and general cognitive abilities.

Associations Between Cognitive and Physical Functioning

It is not unlikely that if perceptual speed is important for cognitive functioning in adulthood, motor speed is also important. A multivariate analysis incorporating measures of motor speed, perceptual speed, and cognitive ability was conducted on the middle-aged and young-old cohorts of SATSA (Finkel, Pedersen, & Harris, 2000) to examine possible age differences in the relationship between speed and cognition. Results indicated qualitative differences between cohorts in the nature of the genetic and environmental variance common to motor speed, perceptual speed, and cognitive abilities. The genetic variance in cognitive functioning in the middle-aged cohort was defined primarily by motor speed, whereas genetic variance in the older cohort was defined by perceptual speed.

Recent analyses of SATSA data have focused on the aging trajectory for variables that serve as markers of aging and on the genetic and environmental influences on the rates of decline. Growth curve analysis of five markers of aging indicated a steeper rate of decline for men than women in forced expiratory volume and grip strength and a moderate rate of increase in mean arterial pressure for both men and women (Finkel, Pedersen, et al., 2003). For two variables, motor functioning and well-being, growth curve analysis identified a turning point (age 70) at which functioning changed from stability to decline. Quantitative genetic growth curve analysis indicated genetic influences on the mean level of performance on all five markers of aging (Finkel, Pedersen, et al., 2003). The same was not true for the rates of change with age. Genetic influences on the slope were found for three of the variables: motor functioning, mean arterial pressure, and forced expiratory volume.

Summary of Cognitive Abilities in Midlife

Even though most of the longitudinal results concerning cognitive abilities in midlife have emanated from longitudinal studies of aging, we are able to discern clear patterns. Throughout the period of midlife, there are few dramatic changes in means and variances. In other words, midlife is a period of relative stability, at least with regard to cognitive abilities. Not only do mean levels remain stable until age 65, but individual differences also appear to be stable throughout this period. Similarly, sources of individual differences, both genetic and environmental, appear to be quite stable during this period. The exceptions appear to be related to the role that genes have in mediating the speed-cognition relationship. The reasons for this apparent stability, and at the same time considerable variability, may seem somewhat enigmatic. Perhaps our measures are not sensitive enough to pick up the sensitive changes that may reflect progression into dementia. If this is the case, we may not be able to detect whether there are changes in the genetic or environmental mechanisms for these changes. Furthermore, almost none of these studies have examined cognitive trajectories as a function of measured changes in the environment (such as lifestyle transitions) or biological processes (such as menopause or disease onset). It may be that there are myriad GxE interactions that can only be detected in stratified groups. Nevertheless, for the population as a whole, this is a period of relative phenotypic, genotypic, and environmental stability.

Conclusion

At the outset of this endeavor, we were skeptical as to whether there were sufficient empirical data available not only based, but also in particular focused, on behaviors and outcomes relevant to midlife. Our preconceptions were in part fulfilled: All too few studies focus on midlife, in particular those that are concerned with individual differences rather than normative characterizations. We found that most studies of developmental behavioral genetics included subjects in midlife only by default, as in the case of family studies (parents in midlife); by accident, as in the case of twin cohorts; or as a secondary baseline (aging studies). The lack of focus on midlife is perhaps understandable, as the sine qua non of behavioral genetic analysis is variability. For many outcomes, such as health, there is indeed little variability in midlife, as most individuals can be classified as fitting within a fairly narrow band of "normality." For other characteristics, such as behavior, the few results available indicate relative stability in variation throughout midlife. Furthermore, both theoretical and empirical emphasis has been placed almost exclusively on early and late development. As a result, there is a dearth of systematic information on sources of individual differences in midlife.

Fortunately, the era of demonstrating that genetic influences *may* be of importance for behavioral characteristics is at an end. The efforts of behavioral geneticists in the 1980s and 1990s, as well as public acceptance of the results from the human genome project, have redirected research inquiry toward understanding mechanisms and multivariate relationships, with the implicit understanding that both genes and environments are important for individual differences. There are enormous gains to be made by approaches that evaluate the mechanisms contributing to associations among characteristics, rather than isolating behaviors as independent entities. The associations between social support and adjustment, psychosocial factors and self-rated health, and cognition and physical functioning described earlier in this chapter exemplify the value of multivariate approaches, and further applications are to be encouraged.

Although little effort has been made to understand associations and mechanisms in midlife, there are notable exceptions, such as the study of interpersonal relationships described earlier in this chapter. These studies exemplify three important aspects that should be encouraged:

1. The behaviors and outcomes of interests are relevant to the ageband of interest (marital relationships, parenting, stress coping).

2. There are identifiable exposures (stressful life events, occupational stressors).

3. It is possible to test hypotheses regarding mechanisms because relevant genetically informative constellations of individuals are available (twin-family designs to test GE correlation).

Nonetheless, there are a number of areas in which improvement can be made. At the very least, greater attention should be paid to phenotypes of relevance in midlife. The study of interpersonal relationships is one good example, but far more can be done to understand other relevant responses, including responses to relevant stressors (e.g., work environment, familial demands, health-related behaviors, medically unexplained disorders such as "burnout"). Despite advancements in methodological techniques to incorporate measured environments in behavioral genetic designs, far too little effort has been placed on identifying and measuring relevant environmental exposures and incorporating these into the models. It is also quite likely that there are considerable gender and cultural differences in the multitude of genetic and environmental interactions that influence individual differences in midlife. What is the importance of genetic susceptibility to stress for women's and men's ability to adapt to rigidity in occupational structure, or to infectious agents? Finally, the study of variation in midlife must be approached from a longitudinal point of view rather than as a series of cross-sectional snapshots in time.

References

Agrawal, A., Jacobson, K. C., Prescott, C. A., & Kendler, K. S. (2002). A twin study of sex differences in social support. *Psychological Medicine, 32*(7), 1155–1164.

Arvey, R. D., Bouchard, T. J., Segal, N. L., & Abraham, L. M. (1989). Job satisfaction: Environmental and genetic components. *Journal of Applied Psychology, 74*(2), 187–192.

Baker, L. A., Treloar, S. A., Reynolds, C. A., Heath, A. C., & Martin, N. G. (1996). Genetics of educational attainment in Australian twins: Sex differences and secular changes. *Behavior Genetics, 26*(2), 89–102.

Baumrind, D. (1973). The development of instrumental competence through socialization. In A. D. Pick (Ed.), *Minnesota symposium on child psychology* (Vol. 7, pp. 3–46). Minneapolis: University of Minnesota Press.

Bergem, A. L. M. (2002). Norwegian twin registers and Norwegian twin studies—An overview. *Twin Research, 5*(5), 407–414.

Bergeman, C. S., Plomin, R., Pedersen, N. L., & McClearn, G. E. (1991). Genetic mediation of the relationship between social support and psychological well-being. *Psychology and Aging, 6*(4), 640–646.

Billings, A. G., & Moos, R. H. (1984). Coping, stress, and social resources among adults with unipolar depression. *Journal of Personality and Social Psychology, 46*(4), 877–891.

Birren, J. E. (1964). *The psychology of aging.* Englewood Cliffs, NJ: Prentice Hall.

Bolinskey, P. K., Neale, M. C., Jacobson, K. C., Prescott, C. A., & Kendler, K. S. (2004). Sources of individual differences in stressful life event exposure in male and female twins. *Twin Research, 7*(1), 33–38.

Boomsma, D., Vink, J., van Beijsterveldt, T., De Geus, E. J., Beem, A. L., Mulder, E. J., et al. (2002). Netherlands Twin Register: A focus on longitudinal research. *Twin Research, 5*(5), 401–406.

Bouchard, T. J., Jr., Lykken, D. T., McGue, M., Segal, N. L., & Tellegen, A. (1990). Sources of human psychological differences: The Minnesota Study of Twins Reared Apart. *Science, 250*(6), 223–228.

Braungart, J. M. (1994). Genetic influence on "environmental" measures. In J. C. DeFries, R. Plomin, & D. W. Fulker (Eds.), *Nature and nurture during middle childhood* (pp. 233–248). Cambridge, UK: Blackwell.

Busjahn, A., Faulhaber, H. D., Freier, K., & Luft, F. C. (1999). Genetic and environmental influences on coping styles: A twin study. *Psychosomatic Medicine, 61*(4), 469–475.

Caspi, A., Sugden, K., Moffitt, T. E., Taylor, A., Craig, I. W., Harrington, H., et al. (2003). Influence of life stress on depression: Moderation by a polymorphism in the 5-HTT gene. *Science, 301*(5631), 386–389.

Croft, M., Read, A. W., de Klerk, N., Hansen, J., & Kurunczuk, J. (2002). Population based ascertainment of twins and their siblings, born in Western Australia 1980 to 1992, through the construction and validation of maternally linked database of siblings. *Twin Research, 5*(5), 317–323.

Duke University Center for the Study of Aging and Human Development. (1978). *Multidimensional functional assessment: The OARS Methodology.* Durham, NC: Duke University Press.

Elkins, I. J., McGue, M., & Iacono, W. G. (1997). Genetic and environmental influences on parent-son relationships: Evidence for increasing genetic influence during adolescence. *Developmental Psychology, 32*(2), 351–363.

Finkel, D., & McGue, M. (1993). The origins of individual differences in memory among the elderly: A behavior genetic analysis. *Psychology and Aging, 8*(4), 527–537.

Finkel, D., & Pedersen, N. L. (2000). Contribution of age, genes, and environment to the relationship between perceptual speed and cognitive ability. *Psychology and Aging, 15*(1), 56–64.

Finkel, D., & Pedersen, N. L. (2004). Processing speed and longitudinal trajectories of change for cognitive abilities: The Swedish Adoption/Twin Study of Aging. *Aging, Neuropsychology, and Cognition, 11*(2–3), 325–345.

Finkel, D., Pedersen, N. L., & Harris, J. R. (2000). Genetic mediation of the associations among motor and perceptual speed and adult cognitive abilities. *Aging, Neuropsychology, and Cognition, 7*(2), 141–155.

Finkel, D., Pedersen, N. L., McGue, M., & McClearn, G. E. (1995). Heritability of cognitive abilities in adult twins: Comparison of Minnesota and Swedish data. *Behavior Genetics, 25*(5), 421–431.

Finkel, D., Pedersen, N. L., Reynolds, C. A., Berg, S., deFaire, U., & Svartengren, M. (2003). Genetic and environmental influences on decline in biobehavioral markers of aging. *Behavior Genetics, 33*(2), 107–123.

Finkel, D., Reynolds, C. A., McArdle, J. J., Gatz, M., & Pedersen, N. L. (2003). Latent growth curve analyses of accelerating decline in cognitive abilities in late adulthood. *Developmental Psychology, 39*(3), 535–550.

Foley, D. L., Neale, M. C., & Kendler, K. S. (1996). A longitudinal study of stressful life events assessed at interview with an epidemiological sample of adult twins: The basis of individual variation in event exposure. *Psychological Medicine, 26*(6), 1239–1252.

Folkman, S., & Lazarus, R. S. (1980). An analysis of coping in a middle-aged community sample. *Journal of Health and Social Behavior, 21*(3), 219–239.

Ganster, D. C., & Victor, B. (1988). The impact of social support on mental and physical health. *British Journal of Medical Psychology, 61*(1), 17–36.

Gillespie, N. A., Zue, G., Neale, M., Heath, A. C., & Martin, N. G. (2003). Direction of causation modeling between cross-sectional measures of parenting and psychological distress in female twins. *Behavior Genetics, 33*(4), 383–396.

Goodman, R., & Stevenson, J. (1989). A twin study of hyperactivity—II. The aetiological role of genes, family relationships and perinatal adversity. *Journal of Child Psychiatry and Psychology and Allied Disciplines, 30*(5), 691–709.

Harris, J. R., Pedersen, N. L., McClearn, G. E., Plomin, R., & Nesselroade, J. R. (1992). Age differences in genetic and environmental influences for health from the Swedish Adoption/Twin Study of Aging. *Journal of Gerontology: Psychological Sciences, 47*(3), 213–220.

Heath, A. C., Berg, K., Eaves, L. J., Solaas, M. H., Corey, L. A., Sundet, J., et al. (1985). Education policy and the heritability of educational attainment. *Nature, 314*(6013), 734–736.

Heath, A. C., Eaves, L. J., & Martin, N. G. (1998). Interaction of marital status and genetic risk for symptoms of depression. *Twin Research, 1*(3), 119–122.

Hershberger, S. L., Lichtenstein, P., & Knox, S. S. (1994). Genetic and environmental influences on perceptions of organizational climate. *Journal of Applied Psychology, 79*(1), 24–33.

Holmes, T. H., & Rahe, R. H. (1967). The Social Readjustment Rating Scale. *Journal of Pyschosomatic Research, 11*(2), 213–218.

Hur, Y. M., & Bouchard, T. J. (1995). Genetic influences on perceptions of childhood family environment: A reared apart twin study. *Child Development, 66*(2), 330–345.

Idler, E. L., & Benyamini, Y. (1997). Self-rated health and mortality: A review of twenty-seven community studies. *Journal of Health and Social Behavior, 38*(1), 21–37.

Jerskey, B. A., Lyons, M. J., Lynch, C. E., Hines, D. A., Ascher, S., Nir, T., et al. (2001). *Genetic influence on marital status.* Paper presented at the Tenth International Congress of Twin Studies, Kensington, London, UK.

Jockin, V., McGue, M., & Lykken, D. T. (1996). Personality and divorce: A genetic analysis. *Journal of Personality and Social Psychology, 71*(2), 288–299.

Johnson, W., McGue, M., Krueger, R. F., & Bouchard, T. J. (2004). Marriage and personality: A genetic analysis. *Journal of Personality and Social Psychology, 86*(2), 285–294.

Kaprio, J., & Koskenvuo, M. (2002). Genetic and environmental factors on complex diseases: The older Finnish twin cohort. *Twin Research, 5*(5), 358–371.

Kato, K., & Pedersen, N. L. (2005). Personality and coping: A study of twins reared apart and twins reared together. *Behavior Genetics, 35*(2), 147–158.

Keller, L. M., Arvey, R. D., Dawis, R. V., Bouchard, T. J., & Segal, N. L. (1992). Work values: Genetic and environmental influences. *Journal of Applied Psychology, 77*(1), 79–88.

Kendler, K. S. (1997). Social support: A genetic-epidemiologic analysis. *American Journal of Psychiatry, 154*(10), 1398–1404.

Kendler, K. S., Kessler, R. C., Heath, A. C., Neale, M. C., & Eaves, L. J. (1991). Coping—A genetic epidemiologic investigation. *Psychological Medicine, 21*(2), 337–346.

Kendler, K. S., Neale, M., Kessler, R., Heath, A., & Eaves, L. (1993). A twin study of recent life events and difficulties. *Archives of General Psychiatry, 50*(10), 789–796.

Kessler, R. C., Kendler, K. S., Heath, A. C., Neale, M. C., & Eaves, L. J. (1992). Social support, depressed mood, and adjustment to stress: A genetic epidemiologic investigation. *Journal of Personality and Social Psychology, 62*(2), 257–272.

Lichtenstein, P., Ganiban, J., Neiderhiser, J. M., Pedersen, N. L., Hansson, K., Cederblad, M., et al. (2003). Remembered parental bonding in adult twins: Genetic and environmental influences. *Behavior Genetics, 33*(4), 397–408.

Lichtenstein, P., Hershberger, S. L., & Pedersen, N. L. (1995). Dimensions of occupations: Genetic and environmental influences. *Journal of Biosocial Science, 27*(2), 193–206.

Lichtenstein, P., & Pedersen, N. L. (1995). Social relationships, stressful life events, and self-reported physical health: Genetic and environmental influences. *Psychology and Health, 10*(4), 295–319.

Lichtenstein, P., & Pedersen, N. L. (1997). Does genetic variance for cognitive abilities account for genetic variance in educational achievement and occupational status? A study of twins reared apart and twins reared together. *Social Biology, 44*(1–2), 77–90.

Lichtenstein, P., Pedersen, N. L., & McClearn, G. E. (1992). The origins of individual differences in occupational status and educational level: A study of twins reared apart and together. *Acta Sociologica, 35*(1), 13–31.

Locke, H., & Wallace, K. (1987). Marital Adjustment Test. In N. Fredman & R. Sherman (Eds.), *Handbook of measurements for marriage and family therapy* (pp. 46–50). New York: Brunner/Mazel.

McCartney, K., Harris, M. J., & Bernieri, F. (1990). Growing up and growing apart: A developmental meta-analysis of twin studies. *Psychological Bulletin, 107*(2), 226–237.

McGue, M., & Lykken, D. T. (1992). Genetic influence on the risk of divorce. *Psychological Science, 3*(6), 368–373.

Neiderhiser, J. M., Reiss, D., Pedersen, N. L., Lichtenstein, P., Spotts, E., Hansson, K., et al. (2004). Genetic and environmental influences on mothering of adolescents: A comparison of two samples. *Developmental Psychology, 40*(3), 335–351.

Pedersen, N. L., & Lichtenstein, P. (1997). Biometric analyses of human abilities. In C. Cooper & V. Varma (Eds.), *Processes in individual differences* (pp. 125–147). London: Routledge.

Pedersen, N. L., Lichtenstein, P., & Svedberg, P. (2002). The Swedish Twin Registry in the Third Millennium. *Twin Research, 5*(5), 427–432.

Pedersen, N. L., McClearn, G. E., Plomin, R., Nesselroade, J. R., Berg, S., & DeFaire, U. (1991). The Swedish Adoption Twin Study of Aging: An update. *Acta Geneticae Medicae et Gemellologiae, 40*(1), 7–20.

Pedersen, N. L., Plomin, R., Nesselroade, J. R., & McClearn, G. E. (1992). A quantitative genetic analysis of cognitive abilities during the second half of the life span. *Psychological Science, 3*(6), 346–353.

Plomin, R. (1986). *Development, genetics, and psychology.* Hillsdale, NJ: Erlbaum.

Plomin, R., DeFries, J. C., & Loehlin, J. C. (1977). Genotype-Environment interaction and correlation in the analysis of human behavior. *Psychological Bulletin, 84*(2), 309–322.

Plomin, R., Lichtenstein, P., Pedersen, N. L., McClearn, G. E., & Nesselroade, J. R. (1990). Genetic influence on life events during the last half of the life span. *Psychology and Aging, 5*(1), 25–30.

Plomin, R., McClearn, G. E., Pedersen, N. L., Nesselroade, J. R., & Bergeman, C. S. (1989). Genetic influence on adults' ratings of their current family environment. *Journal of Marriage and the Family, 51*(3), 791–803.

Reiss, D., Cederblad, M., Pedersen, N. L., Lichtenstein, P., Elthammar, O., Neiderhiser, J. M., et al. (2001). Genetic probes of three theories of maternal adjustment: II. Genetic and environmental influences. *Family Process, 40*(3), 261–272.

Reiss, D., Neiderhiser, J. M., Hetherington, E. M., & Plomin, R. (2000). *The Relationship Code: Deciphering genetic and social influences on adolescent development.* Cambridge, MA: Harvard University Press.

Reiss, D., Pedersen, N. L., Cederblad, M., Lichtenstein, P., Hansson, K., Neiderhiser, J. M., et al. (2001). Genetic probes of three theories of maternal adjustment: I. Recent evidence and a model. *Family Process, 40*(3), 247–259.

Reiss, D., Plomin, R., Hetherington, E. M., Howe, G., Rovine, M., Tyron, A., et al. (1994). The separate social worlds of teenage siblings: An introduction to the study of the nonshared environment and adolescent development. In E. M. Hetherington, D. Reiss, & R. Plomin (Eds.), *Separate social worlds of siblings: Impact of the nonshared environment on development* (pp. 63–110). Hillsdale, NJ: Erlbaum.

Reynolds, C. A., Finkel, D., Gatz, M., & Pedersen, N. L. (2002). Sources of influence on rate of cognitive change over time in Swedish twins: An application of latent growth models. *Experimental Aging Research, 28*(4), 407–433.

Reynolds, C. A., Finkel, D., McArdle, J. J., Gatz, M., Berg, S., & Pedersen, N. L. (in press). Quantitative genetic analysis of latent growth curve models of cognitive abilities in adulthood. *Developmental Psychology.*

Rowe, D. C. (1981). Environmental and genetic influences on dimensions of perceived parenting: A twin study. *Developmental Psychology, 17*(2), 203–208.

Rowe, D. C. (1983). A biometrical analysis of perceptions of family environment: A study of twins and singleton sibling kinships. *Child Development, 54*(2), 416–423.

Salthouse, T. A. (1996). The processing-speed theory of adult age differences in cognition. *Psychological Review, 103*(3), 403–428.

Salthouse, T. A. (2004). What and when of cognitive aging. *Current Directions in Psychological Science, 13*(4), 140–144.

Saudino, K. J., Pedersen, N. L., Lichtenstein, P., McClearn, G. E., & Plomin, R. (1997). Can personality explain genetic influences on life events? *Journal of Personality and Social Psychology, 72*(1), 196–206.

Scarr, S., & McCartney, K. (1983). How people make their own environments: A theory of genotype greater than environment effects. *Child Development, 54*(2), 424–435.

Skytthe, A., Kyvik, K., Holm, N. V., Vaupel, J. W., & Christensen, K. (2002). The Danish twin registry: 127 birth cohorts of twins. *Twin Research, 5*(5), 352–357.

Spanier, G. B. (1976). Measuring dyadic adjustment: New scales for assessing quality of marriage and similar dyads. *Journal of Marriage and the Family, 38*(1), 15–28.

Spotts, E. L., Lichtenstein, P., Pedersen, N. L., Neiderhiser, J. M., Hansson, K., Cederblad, M., et al. (in press). Personality and marital satisfaction: A behavioral genetic analysis. *European Journal of Personality*.

Spotts, E. L., Neiderhiser, J. M., Ganiban, J., Reiss, D., Lichtenstein, P., Hansson, K., et al. (2004). Accounting for depressive symptoms in women: A twin study of associations with interpersonal relationships. *Journal of Affective Disorders, 82*(1), 101–111.

Spotts, E. L., Neiderhiser, J. M., Towers, H., Hansson, K., Lichtenstein, P., Pedersen, N. L., et al. (2004). Genetic and environmental influences on marital relationships. *Journal of Family Psychology, 18*(1), 107–119.

Spotts, E. L., Pedersen, N. L., Neiderhiser, J. M., Reiss, D., Lichtenstein, P., Hansson, K., et al. (in press). Genetic effects on women's positive mental health: Do marital relationships and social support matter? *Journal of Family Psychology*.

Svedberg, P., Lichtenstein, P., Gatz, M., Sandin, S., & Pedersen, N. L. (in press). Self-rated health in a longitudinal perspective: A 9-year follow-up twin study. *Journals of Gerontology: Social Sciences*.

Svedberg, P., Lichtenstein, P., & Pedersen, N. L. (2001). Age and sex differences in genetic and environmental factors for self-rated health: A twin study. *Journal of Gerontology: Social Sciences, 56*(3), 171–178.

Tambs, K., Sundet, J. M., & Magnus, P. (1984). Heritability analysis of the WAIS subtests: A study of twins. *Intelligence, 8*(4), 283–293.

Tambs, K., Sundet, J. M., Magnus, P., & Berg, K. (1989). Genetic and environmental contributions to the covariance between occupational status, educational attainment, and IQ: A study of twins. *Behavior Genetics, 19*(2), 209–222.

Trumbetta, S., & Gottesman, I. (1997). Pair-bonding deconstructed by twin studies of marital status: What is normative? In N. Segal, G. E. Weisfeld, & C. C. Weisfeld (Eds.), *Uniting psychology and biology: Integrative perspectives on human development*. Washington, DC: American Psychological Association.

Trumbetta, S., & Gottesman, I. (2000). Endophenotypes for marital status in the NAS-NRC twin registry. In J. L. Rogers & D. C. Rowe (Eds.), *Genetic influences on human fertility and sexuality* (pp. 253–269). Boston: Kluwer Academic.

Turkheimer, E., Haley, A., Waldron, M., D'Onofrio, B., & Gottesman, I. (2003). Socioeconomic status modifies heritability of IQ in young children. *Psychological Science, 14*(6), 623–628.

Wade, T. D., & Kendler, K. S. (2000). The relationship between social support and major depression: Cross-sectional, longitudinal, and genetic perspectives. *Journal of Nervous and Mental Disease, 188*(5), 251–258.

Four

Personality in Young Adulthood and Functioning in Middle Age

Lea Pulkkinen, Taru Feldt, and Katja Kokko

Framework for the Study of Adult Personality Development

The development of adult personality can be viewed from many perspectives. The most dominant theoretical approaches to personality development across the entire life span specify the temporal order of life stages such as childhood, adolescence, adulthood, and old age, and stress an

This paper was funded by the Academy of Finland, prepared as a part of the project (44858) "Human Development and Its Risk Factors," financed by the Academy of Finland (Finnish Centre of Excellence Programme, 2000–2005).

individual's potential for positive growth. Implicit in the *stage approach* is a dynamic change in personality throughout the life course (e.g., Lachman & Bertrand, 2001). Erik H. Erikson (1950) analyzed an individual's growth through age stages in terms of ego within the psychoanalytical framework, and Havighurst (1948) in terms of developmental tasks referring to social-role demands in individuals' lives. Levinson (1978, 1986), on the other hand, conceptualized developmental stages of adult personality as a fluctuation between relatively stable phases and phases of transition during which the existing life structure is reappraised.

Another approach to personality development makes a distinction between functionally different aspects of personality and describes development in each of them or in their interaction. This *functional approach* has become popular in empirical psychology. Examples of it include trait models that are taxonomies of personality traits developed to facilitate the communication of interindividual differences in enduring characteristics. The number of traits that researchers have used in the description of personality has varied substantially. The taxonomies also vary in the extent to which they are theory bound or data bound. Over the past decades, a reasonable consensus has been reached on five factors: Extraversion, Conscientiousness, Neuroticism, Agreeableness, and Openness to Experience. The number of factors that adequately describes personality is still debated, as reviewed by Pulkkinen (2000). Eysenck (1997), for instance, argued that Agreeableness and Conscientiousness are primary rather than higher-order factors, and Digman (1997) demonstrated how different personality factors could be merged into two higher-level superfactors termed as Factor alpha, which describes socialization (Neuroticism, Conscientiousness, and Agreeableness), and Factor beta, which represents personal growth (Extraversion, Openness to Experience).

In the Jyväskylä Longitudinal Study of Personality and Social Development (JYLS), the functional approach has been extended from personality traits to the analysis of individuals' life courses in terms of social trajectories (Elder, 1998). One of the main goals of the JYLS has been to investigate to what extent psychological functioning plays a role in the development of social functioning. The following trajectories or functions were investigated: (a) psychological functioning, including personality traits, characteristics of socioemotional behavior, and well-being; (b) work, including education and work career; (c) family, including the family of origin, one's own family, and intergenerational relations; (d) health, including health behavior; and (e) social integration, including socialization and crime. Although these trajectories are intertwined, they can be separated for research purposes and their intersections analyzed.

In empirical research, the functional approach to development utilizes nomothetic methodology. It is based on an assumption that individuals can be quantitatively compared in measurable variables. The functional or variable-oriented approach has been criticized for studying personality traits or functions in isolation. Consequently, a *person-centered approach* has been advocated by Block (1971). Its application to the study of personality has resulted in typological models that focus on the total constellation of traits that define each person and the way these traits work together as an integrated system (Asendorpf & van Aken, 1999; Hart, Atkins, & Fegley, 2003). A central goal of the person-centered approach is to identify groups of individuals (types) who share the same basic personality structure (Block, 1971). Advanced person-centered procedures can be used to identify types empirically (Bergman, Magnusson, & El-Khouri, 2003).

Increasing attention has recently been paid to the replicability and generalizability of personality types across age, sex, and culture "with the ultimate goal being to construct a universally applicable personality taxonomy" (Robins & Tracy, 2003, p. 112). Also, the close dependency of individual functioning and individual development on the social, cultural, and physical characteristics of the environment has been emphasized and a more holistic approach to personality called for (Magnusson & Stattin, 1998). Except for Block (1971), few other researchers have studied or speculated the possible function of personality taxonomies in the understanding of human development. This article adds to the scarce literature by demonstrating, using the JYLS data, that personality types formulated in a holistic way may function as significant moderators of adult development.

The Jyväskylä Longitudinal Study of Personality and Social Development

The ongoing JYLS was originally a cross-sectional study, as were many other older longitudinal studies. In this case, Lea Pulkkinen's doctoral dissertation (Pitkänen, 1969) transitioned into a long-term longitudinal study in which the same individuals were studied from age 8 to age 42. Strengths of the JYLS are that socioemotional behavior in childhood was investigated from a broad perspective covering both adaptive and non-adaptive behavior, which has allowed for the study of diverse life paths, and that the sample studied represents an entire age cohort born in Finland in 1959. In many other studies on adult development, the sample is limited to females or males and, for instance, college graduates (Helson & Srivastava, 2001) or clinical patients (Vaillant & Milofsky, 1980).

Sample

In the JYLS, data from childhood to adulthood (from age 8 to at least one of the adult ages: 27, 36, or 42 years) are available for 94% of the original sample, which consisted of 12 complete second-grade school classes, randomly selected for the study in 1968 (Pulkkinen, 2004; Pulkkinen et al., 2003). Half of the classes were located in downtown Jyväskylä, a university and industrial town in central Finland with about 80,000 inhabitants, and half in the suburban areas of Jyväskylä. The sample included 196 boys and 173 girls aged 8 years (born in 1959). There was no initial attrition, because teacher ratings and peer nominations used for data collection on children's socioemotional behavior concerned all pupils in these classes. All participants were native Finns. Data on socioemotional behavior were also collected at age 14 (in 1974) using teacher ratings and peer nominations; the retention rate was 97%.

At ages 27, 36, and 42 (in 1986, 1995, and 2001), the participants were traced for a follow-up study. In adulthood, data were collected using questionnaires, inventories, and semistructured interviews and concerned different areas of adult psychological and social functioning; also, medical examination was conducted at age 42. Retention rates calculated from the original sample were 85% for men and 90% for women at age 27; 82% for men and 87% for women at age 36; and 81% for men and 85% for women at age 42. By age 42, five men and one woman had died, and 5 men and 15 women had withdrawn completely from the study. Consequently, the available sample size was 7% smaller than the original sample; at age 42, the retention rates were calculated from this sample. Two thirds of the original sample participated in all major data waves (at ages 8, 14, 27, 36, and 42).

No systematic reason for attrition was found, when the participants studied at age 42 were compared with nonparticipants, in the ratings of socioemotional behavior made by teachers and peers at age 8 or in school success. Neither did the participants differ from nonparticipants regarding smoking, use of drugs, drinking, or criminal recidivism, as measured at an earlier age. The only significant finding for attrition was that, among the individuals who had died by age 42 (five men and one woman) and among the two additional deaths since 2001 (two women), six participants had been heavy drinkers or alcoholics and died of accidents or intoxication; two participants died of disease.

Representativeness of the Sample

The sample studied at age 42 turned out to be representative of the age cohort born in 1959 when data on marital status, number of children, employment, and unemployment provided by Statistics Finland were used as criteria at ages 36 and 42 (Pulkkinen et al., 2003). Most participants (60.2%; 57.7% in the age cohort group) were married at age 42. The average number of children was 1.85 (1.87 in the age cohort group). Divorce rate has steadily increased in Finland since the 1960s in spite of the decrease in contracted marriages due to cohabitation; it is estimated that 50% of the marriages contracted in 2001 will end in divorce (Statistics Finland, 2002, p. 134). In our sample, almost one third (30.2%) of the participants had experienced a divorce by age 42. Cohabitation was common at some point in life (74%); at age 42, 19% of the participants were cohabiting.

In length of education, the male participants did not differ from their age cohort group, but female participants had a slightly longer education than women in their age cohort group; compared to the former, female participants more often had higher secondary education (e.g., a nurse, graduation from a Finnish commercial institute). Most participants (76.7% of women and 68.9% of men) were wage earners in 2001 (6.8% of women and 13.6% of men were private enterprisers, and 2% of men were freelancers); men were more often in blue-collar occupations than women, and women were more often in lower white-collar occupations. This gender difference in the socioeconomic status corresponded to that in the age cohort group. No gender difference existed in higher white-collar occupations.

At age 42, the unemployment rate in the sample (6.0% of women and 10.9% of men) corresponded to the rate in the age cohort group (8.2% of women and 8.6% of men). The rest of the women and men were students (2.3 and 2.0%) or pensioners (2.2 and 2.6%, respectively); some women were at home for child care (3.0%) or on sickness or other leave (3.0%). Finland experienced a sudden economic recession in the 1990s, resulting in, among other things, an increase in the national unemployment rate from 5% to approximately 20%. In the JYLS, we collected data for our 36-year-old participants in 1995—in the midst of the recession. At that time, about 19% of our participants were unemployed, well representing the national rate.

Measures in Adulthood

At each adult age, the participants were first approached by a mailed life situation questionnaire including questions on family, education, work, leisure activities, and health behavior, as well as a series of questions on life satisfaction, optimism, and trust in life. The interview included an Identity Status Interview (Marcia, 1966), and covered, for instance, family relationships, work conditions, and health. In the context of the interview at age 27, the participants were presented with two personality inventories standardized in Finland: the Eysenck Personality Questionnaire (EPQ; Eysenck & Eysenck, 1975) and the Sensation Seeking Scale (SSS; Zuckerman, 1979). In the context of the interview at age 36 and age 42, the participants were presented with the following inventories used in this article: the Karolinska Scales of Personality (KSP; af Klinteberg, Schalling, & Magnusson, 1990); Self-Esteem Scale (Rosenberg, 1965); Scales of Psychological Well-Being (Ryff, 1989); Depression scale of the General Behavior Inventory (Depue, 1987); a 12-item General Health Questionnaire (GHQ-12; Goldberg, 1972); a Psychosomatic Symptom Checklist (Aro, 1988); the Aggression Questionnaire (Buss & Perry, 1992); Strategic Attribution Questionnaire (Nurmi, Salmela-Aro, & Haavisto, 1995); the CAGE (Cutting down, Annoyance by criticism, Guilty feeling, and Eye-openers) questionnaire for alcoholism (Ewing, 1984); and the Malmö modification of the brief Michigan Alcoholism Screening Test (Kristenson & Trell, 1982; Selzer, 1971). At age 42, the 13-item Orientation to Life Questionnaire for measuring Sense of Coherence (Antonovsky, 1987) was also administered.

In addition, a Big Five Personality Inventory—an authorized adaptation of the Neuroticism, Extraversion, and Openness Personality Inventory (NEO-PI; Costa & McCrae, 1985) in which about one quarter of the items are substitutes for the original American items—was mailed to the original sample in the context of the standardization of the instrument in Finland and Estonia (Pulver, Allik, Pulkkinen, & Hämäläinen, 1995) when the participants were 33 years of age. At age 42, a 60-item version of the Big Five Personality Inventory was administered to the participants in the context of a personal interview.

The reliabilities of the composite variables used in this article were satisfactory as shown by Cronbach's alpha coefficients calculated for the whole sample ranging from 0.72 to 0.93.

Emotional and Behavioral Regulation

A Two-Dimensional Model

From the beginning of the JYLS, the framework for the study of individual differences in personality functioning has been a two-dimensional impulse control model developed by Pulkkinen (Pitkänen, 1969; Pulkkinen, 1982) and later modified and relabeled as a model of emotional and behavioral regulation (Pulkkinen, 1995, 1996). Its starting point was in the analysis of aggressive and alternative, nonaggressive behaviors. The model is described here because it is relevant for the interpretation of adult personality styles.

Pulkkinen's early studies of aggression (Pitkänen, 1969, Part I) generated questions about how children can avoid aggressive responses. In a stimulus-response learning theoretical framework (Hull, 1943; Miller, 1959), Pulkkinen postulated individual differences, first, in individuals' characteristic ways of expressing aggression and, then, in their characteristic ways of coping with thwarting stimuli; the latter term refers to antecedents of aggression, such as frustration, attack, and other noxious stimuli. She defined two main dimensions describing overt behavior in thwarting stimulus situations with the following basic assumptions (Pitkänen, 1969): (a) "An individual's habitual responses to thwarting situations are closely connected with his or her entire personality," and (b) "inhibition of impulses to aggression is possible in two ways: by suppressing the behavioral or extrinsic aspect, or by neutralizing the emotional or intrinsic aspect" (p. 102). The hypothesized main dimensions for the description of individual differences were the number of overt responses in a stimulus situation and the strength of control of behavior.

Furthermore, Pulkkinen (Pitkänen, 1969) postulated that the primary effect of a thwarting stimulus is to activate an organism, which is revealed as both emotional and behavioral reactions. Two alternative response tendencies were known from animal studies: approach and avoidance. She observed, however, that in human beings, the development of habits is complicated by cognitive processes, as a consequence of which certain emotional responses (e.g., anger and anxiety) are not necessarily conditioned to thwarting stimulus situations. "An individual may be able to appraise the stimulus situations he encounters and to decide between alternatives; i.e., the emotional aspect can be neutralized by cognitive control" (Pitkänen, 1969, p. 103).

It is challenging in a longitudinal study to find framework constructs that maintain their relevance across the years; Pulkkinen was fortunate in this respect. In the 1960s, her insight in that human emotional behavior could be cognitively controlled was a novel idea; today, emotion regulation is one of the most popular topics in the psychological literature. As reviewed by Pulkkinen (2004), certain philosophical questions pertaining to emotions were first formulated in the works of Plato and Aristotle (Knuuttila & Sihvola, 1998). Aristotle believed that it was usually better to act on a rational desire. He thought that a good human life depended on active participation in the myriad social activities that constitute a civilized society. Such a life is based on a complicated system of socially learned emotions. Aristotle emphasized that, just as in other virtues of character, the moderation of emotionality—between the extremes of too much and too little—is the goal.

The model of emotional and behavioral regulation (Figure 4.1) integrates the views on impulse control in a thwarting stimulus situation into a more general view on individual differences in the regulation of emotions. The model explicates that both socially active and passive behavior may be emotionally regulated or dysregulated. Emotion regulation helps maintain internal arousal within a manageable, performance-optimizing range to enable an individual to function adaptively in emotionally arousing situations, whereas behavioral regulation helps adjust reactions to external circumstances.

The inhibitory and enhancing processes included in the model are the neutralization and intensification of emotion and the suppression and activation of behavior (Pulkkinen, 1995). In the neutralization of emotion, an individual focuses attention on those aspects of the situation that help to regulate emotional arousal and its interpretation or intensification of emotion, whereas in the intensification of emotion, an individual's attention in a situation focuses on cues that intensify emotion, particularly, anger or fear. In the suppression of behavior, an impulse to act is inhibited, and in the activation of behavior, the threshold and latency of behavior are lowered. The idea of self-control is that anger and fear can be modulated toward friendliness or calmness through the socialization process and situational evaluation and processing. The four basic social emotions—anger, fear, friendliness, and calmness—can be found in Aristotle's writings (Sihvola, 1996).

The model can be used for the analysis of an individual's situational and habitual behavior. The combinations of the inhibitory and enhancing

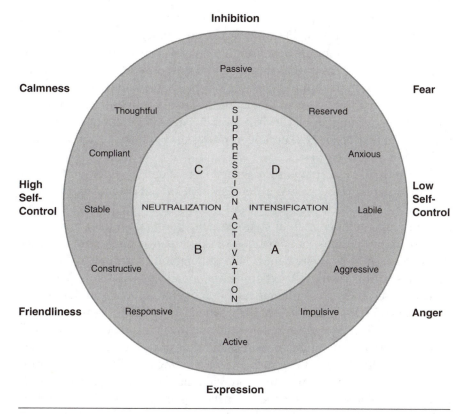

Figure 4.1   Model of Emotional and Behavioral Regulation

SOURCE: Adapted from Pulkkinen (1995).

processes define different behavioral strategies, Types A to D, that are not categorical concepts, but ends of dimensions. For instance, if both enhancing processes (intensification and activation) are active, the likelihood of an individual's reactivity to stimuli and emotional expression increases. This pattern is labeled Type A behavior, and it may be manifested in impulsive and aggressive behavior. (Note: Type A does not refer to the Type A behavioral pattern that is related to cardiovascular disease risk factors; Friedman & Rosenman, 1974.) In the opposite strategy, Type C, both inhibitory processes are active at the same time. An individual tends to block awareness of his or her emotion by a cognitive appraisal of the situation. Avoidance may occur either as a concrete withdrawal from the situation or as the use of rationalization and other defense mechanisms. The pattern labeled Type B results from simultaneous neutralization of emotion and activation of behavior, leading to constructive behavior in which the needs of the parties involved and the consequences of behavior are considered. In the opposite strategy, Type D, a simultaneous suppression and intensification mean that an individual perceives the situation as emotionally exciting, but overt behavior is blocked. Emotional activation is bound to fear of the threatening stimulus and anxiety regarding one's inability to defend oneself.

Each individual displays somewhat inconsistent behavior from situation to situation. However, the development of self-control of emotions is assumed to be facilitated by several factors, such as high regulation of reactivity as a temperamental characteristic, parental socialization, accurate social perceptions, anticipations of successful coping, and maturity (Pulkkinen, 1995). Temperament is here understood as defined by Rothbart and Bates (1998) according to whom temperament can be seen as "constitutionally based individual differences in emotional, motor, and attentional reactivity and self-regulation" (p. 109). Genetic inheritance, maturation, and experience influence temperament. Reactivity, which is modulated by self-regulatory processes, can be measured in terms of the onset, duration, and intensity of affective reactions such as fear and anger. Pulkkinen's assumption was that if a child learns emotion regulation at an early age, the likelihood for developing adaptive social functioning in adulthood is higher than if the child's socioemotional behavior is dysregulated. This assumption was consistent with the conception by Rothbart and Putnam (2002).

Low Self-Control as a Risk Factor for Social Functioning

The framework model presented above has turned out to be valid for the study of individual differences in socioemotional behavior (Pitkänen, 1969) and both homotypic and heterotypic continuity of behavior. Homotypic continuity refers to the continuity of "similar behaviours or phenotypic attributes over time" (Caspi & Roberts, 1999, p. 307). Kagan (1971) distinguishes it from heterotypic continuity, by which he refers to the situation where a particular attribute is predictive of a phenotypically different but theoretically reasonably related attribute at a later age. Caspi (1998) uses the term *coherence* to refer to heterotypic continuity, that is, continuity of an inferred genotypic attribute underlying diverse phenotypic behaviors. The broadest view of continuity was presented by Rutter (1984). For him, the concept of continuity implies meaningful links over the course of development—not a lack of change. This view embraces such cases where the observed continuity of behavior is more—or merely—a reflection of environmental continuity.

Our analyses on the continuity of aggression from middle childhood to middle age (Kokko & Pulkkinen, in press) show that when latent indices of aggression for childhood and adulthood (instead of single measurement points at ages 8 and 14, and ages 36 and 42, respectively) are used and, thus, the variance of the continuous aggression captured, then there is, in both women and men, significant differential continuity in aggression (estimate .42; Structural Equation Modeling [SEM]) from childhood to adulthood. In adulthood, aggression scores at ages 36 and 42 correlated by 0.53 in women and by 0.74 in men. Age 8 aggression has a stronger main effect on adult aggression in males than in females; for females, the effect of childhood aggression on adult aggression increases from age 8 to 14.

In case of heterotypic continuity, we have been interested in children's low self-control as a risk factor for later problems in social functioning, such as alcohol abuse (Pulkkinen & Pitkänen, 1994) and criminal arrests (Pulkkinen & Hämäläinen, 1995). For marital stability, a study by Kinnunen and Pulkkinen (2003) showed that both women and men who were divorced at age 36 had been more aggressive (Type A) at age 8 than those in an intact marriage; also, marriage at a young age in women, as well as an unstable working career and childlessness in men, were related to divorce. As for marital quality, it was found that in men, aggression and other indicators of low self-control of emotions, such as anxiety (Type D) and lability, at age 8 were related to poor marital quality at age 36. In women, the respective childhood antecedents were anxious and passive behaviors.

In addition to direct associations, indirect (mediator) relations have been observed between early socioemotional characteristics and later social and psychological functioning. One of our aims has been to identify developmental processes and risk mechanisms through which early personality explains later adjustment or maladjustment. Studies by Rönkä and her colleagues have shown that the effects of child aggression (Type A) on social functioning in adulthood can be seen as its accumulation with other early risk factors, such as family problems, poor peer relations, and school maladjustment (Rönkä & Pulkkinen, 1995). The accumulation of these risk factors in childhood was related to career instability and a sense of failure at age 27 in both women and men, and there was significant continuity in both career instability and sense of failure from age 27 to 36

(Rönkä, Kinnunen, & Pulkkinen, 2000). In men, the higher number of risk factors was additionally linked to other problems of social functioning, such as a poor financial situation, poor social relationships, poor intimate relationships, drinking problems, and criminality. In both genders, accumulated child risk factors preceded early timing of parenthood, which was further linked to the stability of career line; however, whereas early motherhood was related to an unstable career line, early fatherhood was associated with a stable career line.

In both men and women, problems in social functioning at ages 27 and 36 were accounted for by the outer strand of risk factors, which refers to the continuity and linking of poor environments or life events in the lives of multiproblem persons. In addition, the inner strand of risk factors explained problems in the social functioning in women (Rönkä et al., 2000). The inner strand refers to the increase of inner vulnerability to adversity due to repeated failure to gain acceptance and support in different contexts. Sense of failure correlated with career instability and problems of social functioning in women, but not in men. The harmful effects associated with early risk factors were significantly lowered if a person was faced with a turning point, particularly, warm interpersonal relationships in his or her life (Rönkä, Oravala, & Pulkkinen, 2002).

Our analysis of the early antecedents of later problems in the domain of work showed that a factor for low self-control of emotions at age 8, loaded by aggressive behavior and lability, was linked to long-term unemployment assessed at age 36 (Kokko, Pulkkinen, & Puustinen, 2000). Long-term unemployment refers to unemployment that has lasted for more than a total of 2 years between ages 27 and 36. The association of early aggression with later long-term unemployment is in line with the few previous prospective longitudinal studies existing on this topic: Both Caspi and his colleagues (1998) and Fergusson and his colleagues (1997) have shown, using New Zealand longitudinal samples, that early externalizing behavioral problems, such as a difficult temperament and conduct problems, are risk factors for frequent experiences of unemployment. Long-term unemployment increases vulnerability to psychological distress (Hanisch, 1999), but not directly; our results have shown for both women and men that the link is indirect via a lowered self-esteem and increased financial difficulties (Kokko & Pulkkinen, 1998).

Early aggression and its accompanying cycle of maladaptation involving school maladjustment and subsequent lack of occupational alternatives and alcohol abuse explained 25% of the variance of the subsequent long-term unemployment (Kokko & Pulkkinen, 2000). However, some aggressive children were protected against getting into this cycle of difficulties by their prosocial abilities and by their parents' child-centered parenting practices. It is also noted that at age 27 unemployment was not linked to early individual characteristics, such as aggression, but rather was explained by low education by age 27 (Kokko, Bergman, & Pulkkinen, 2003). Low education was, in part, explained by behavioral problems in childhood. This finding was obtained using both the JYLS sample and a sample drawn from the Swedish Individual Development and Adaptation study.

High Self-Control as a
Resource Factor for Social Functioning

The analysis of childhood antecedents of adult functioning has shown that high emotion regulation, indicated by constructive (Type B) and compliant (Type C) behavior in childhood, is an antecedent of adaptive social functioning in adulthood, more so in men than in women (Pulkkinen, Nygren, & Kokko, 2002). The SEM analysis revealed that in men, a broad second-order latent factor for favorable developmental background, comprising three first-order latent factors, such as high self-control over emotions (compliant and also constructive behavior) in childhood, school success in early adolescence, and supportive upbringing environment, explained 75% of the variance of social functioning in adulthood. Social functioning was one of the latent factors for successful development, indicated by the KSP socialization scale, the controlled use of alcohol, and stability of career line.

In women, supportive upbringing environment alone explained 52% of the variance of social functioning (Pulkkinen et al., 2002). School success, containing both cognitive-motivational orientation and constructive behavior, explained one aspect of social functioning: stability of career line for females. For women and men, the developmental background in childhood and adolescence did not explain the variance in the other latent factor for successful development in adulthood, called Psychological Functioning and indicated by satisfaction with life, self-esteem (Rosenberg, 1965), and psychological well-being (Ryff, 1989), but Psychological Functioning correlated with Social Functioning.

The previous analysis showed that compliant, Type C behavior together with constructive, Type B behavior were part of a male childhood latent factor for high self-control of emotions; in women, only constructive behavior was loaded on this factor (Pulkkinen et al., 2002). This role of compliant behavior in male adaptive social functioning was in accordance with the findings by Pulkkinen, Ohranen, and Tolvanen (1999) on early personality characteristics as antecedents of later career orientation. It was shown that in men, compliant behavior at age 8 was linked to compliance at age 14 and agreeableness at age 27, which were further associated with a high career orientation at age 36. In women, social activity at ages 8 and 14 and extraversion at age 27 played a more important role in explaining high career orientation than compliant behavior.

Personality Styles as Modes of Adjustment Across Years

In order to increase a more holistic understanding of individual differences in adult personality, the functional approach was complemented by a person-centered approach considering various aspects of psychological and social functioning. We have applied typological approaches to both child and adult behavior and followed the significance of the configuration from childhood to adult age, or through adulthood. The emphasis of this article is in the latter, but the former is found in the study by Laursen, Pulkkinen, and Adams (2002) in which profile analysis methods (i.e., discriminant analysis and configural frequency analysis) were used for the extraction of different behavioral types in childhood and adulthood. In that study, teacher and peer report of compliance (Type C), high self-control, and aggression (Type A) at age 8 and personality inventories for Agreeableness (for Type C) at age 33 and Socialization (for self-control) and Impulsivity (Type A) at age 36 were analyzed. Profile analyses revealed two behavioral types in childhood and two personality types in adulthood, with considerable continuity in the composition of these high- and low-agreeable types over time. Compared to low-agreeable childhood types, high-agreeable childhood types had fewer disobedience and concentration problems at age 8 and better school grades and fewer behavioral problems at age 14. High-agreeable adulthood types reported at age 36 less alcoholism and depression, fewer arrests, and more career stability than did low-agreeable adulthood types.

Personality Styles at Age 27

According to Adler (1929/1969), each individual has a somewhat unique style of life that develops in childhood and reflects life goals and ways to strive for them. A person's lifestyle can be inferred from three sources: character traits, physical movements, and early recollections. Lifestyle is here defined analogously as an organized whole of an individual's personality characteristics, social behavior, and life orientation, reminiscent to affective, behavioral, and cognitive components of human action. In this three-component triangular model of personality styles developed by Pulkkinen (1992, 1996), personality characteristics manifest interindividual differences in personality traits and emotional and behavioral regulation; social behavior concerns the ways in which an individual performs life tasks of family, work, leisure time, and health; life orientation refers to an individual's view of self and life. Since the concept of personality type is commonly used to refer to the configuration of personality traits (e.g., Asendorpf & van Aken, 1999), the concept of personality style is used here to refer to a holistic view of personality in which contextual factors are also considered.

Clustering Variables

Variables assessed at age 27 were grouped, accordingly, into the three components of personality style: personality characteristics, life orientation, and social functioning (or behavioral activities; Pulkkinen, 1996). The reduction of the number of variables out of several tens was made using a factor analysis. Four factors, Extraversion, Agreeableness, Neuroticism, and Nonconscientiousness, for personality characteristics were drawn from the data including the EPQ and SSS. Openness to experience was not assessed by any scale, and therefore it was lacking here (the NEO-PI scale was not available at that time). Life orientation was indicated by three factors: Reflectiveness (e.g., identity achievement), Life Attitudes, and Resignation (e.g., contentment without further developmental goals and, negatively, moratorium). Social functioning was indicated by five factors: Family versus Single life, Social Integration (e.g., stable working career and, negatively, number of arrests), Alcoholism, Intellectual Interests, and Party Culture.

A hierarchical clustering technique (WARD; SPSS-x package) was used for extracting personality styles from the 12 variables listed above. At first, two major clusters emerged for both men and women. One of them represented conflicted adjustment to life, and the other represented a positive adjustment. The former cluster comprised 22% of women and 25% of men. The term *conflicted* was adopted from Rank's (1945) theoretical analysis of different modes of adjustment to the developmental task of individuation through separation from parents and conventional norms: the creative, the adapted, and the conflicted (York & John, 1992). When the number of clusters was increased, the cluster for adjustment divided into two components in both sexes. One of them could be identified as adapted, whereas the other component represented a nonconventional, creative mode of adjustment, at least for women. Altogether seven clusters were separately extracted for women and men, only the three major clusters are described here (for the rest, see Pulkkinen, 1996).

Clusters for Personality Styles

Labeling the clusters extracted for women and men was difficult. In Pulkkinen's article published in 1996, similarities between the clusters she had obtained and the personality types obtained by Block (1971) were searched and shown by labels. In this article, some clusters are relabeled in order to seek for comparability with the clusters found in other studies.

Several studies have been more recently published in which the labels Resilient, Overcontrolled, and Undercontrolled personality prototypes have been identified (Robins, John, & Caspi, 1998). These terms come from the theoretical analyses of Jeanne and Jack Block (1980). Their constructs of ego-control and ego-resiliency derive from an integration of psychoanalytic ego theory and Lewin's (1951) field theory, as reviewed by Pulkkinen (1986). Ego-control refers to the control of impulse through specific ego structures, including delay of gratification, inhibition of aggression, and so on. Incorporated with Lewin's notions on the two characteristics of psychological boundaries (i.e., permeability and elasticity), undercontrol derives from excessive boundary permeability manifested in immediate expression of motivations and affects and insufficient modulation of impulses. The other end of the continuum—overcontrol—is caused by excessive boundary impermeability manifested in the inhibition of action and affect, and excessive containment of impulse.

The construct of ego-resiliency refers to the elasticity of psychological boundaries (Block & Block, 1980). At the one end of the continuum, ego-resiliency implies the ability to adapt to changing circumstances; the opposite end of the continuum—ego-brittleness—implies the inability to respond dynamically to situational requirements, a tendency to become disorganized when encountering changed circumstances or when under stress, and a difficulty in recouping after traumatic experiences. The ego-unresilient or brittle person becomes anxious when confronted by competing demands.

The Blocks' model has implications similar to those of the model of emotional and behavioral regulation (Figure 4.1). Undercontrolled and overcontrolled behaviors are close to the Type A and C behaviors, respectively, and resilient and brittle behaviors to the Type B and D behaviors, respectively. Both undercontrolled (Type A) and brittle (Type D) behaviors manifest problems with affects but for different reasons. These differences are also known in terms of externalizing and internalizing problem behaviors. The former problems are more common in males, whereas the latter are more common in females.

Gender differences in the organizing principles of the clusters for personality styles in the present study made labeling complex. The labels of the clusters are summarized in Table 4.1. The conflicted men and women differed in their personality in a way that was expressed in terms of the Undercontrolled and the Brittle (Type A and Type D, respectively). The adapted men could be identified as the Resilient (Type B) by their personality, whereas the label Traditional (York & John, 1992) fit better to the adapted women. The Traditionals did not differ by personality from the other adjusted, nonconventional female cluster. Both of them were characterized by Type B and Type C behaviors. A difference was in their family orientation or work orientation. Nonconventional women were career oriented. Helson and Srivastava (2001) have identified a female cluster called the Achiever, which obviously is close to the cluster identified here. The label Individuated, used by York and John (1992) and Pulkkinen (1996), was, however, here maintained.

The other adjusted male cluster consisted of introverted men (Type C/D), and was labeled accordingly as Introverted by Pulkkinen (1996). The label Introverted covers the characteristics of typical behavior in this cluster better than the label Overcontrolled and is, therefore, used in this article. Within the model of the emotional and behavioral regulation, high self-control may be manifested in socially active and passive behavior, but the Introverted were socially withdrawn. They were also nonconventional in a sense that they were delayed compared to the other men in the fulfillment of developmental tasks, such as getting married and having children. Also, Caspi, Bem, and Elder (1989) have found that shy individuals tend to delay entries into adult roles such as marriage.

Table 4.1   The Names of the Clusters for Personality Styles

Mode of Adjustment	Gender	Present Study	Model[1]	Pulkkinen (1996)	Other Studies
Conflicted	Males	Undercontrolled	A	Conflicted	Undercontrolled[2]
	Females	Brittle	D	Conflicted	Conflicted[3]
Adapted	Males	Resilient	B	Resilient	Resilient[2]
	Females	Traditional	B/C	Feminine	Traditional[3]
Nonconventional	Males	Introverted	C/D	Introverted	Overcontrolled[2]
	Females	Individuated	B/C	Individuated	Individuated[3]

1. Figure 4.1
2. Robins, John, and Caspi (1998)
3. York and John (1992)

Conflicted. The conflicted mode of adjustment emerged in a gender-specific way in a sense that the conflicted women ($n = 30$), called the *Brittle,* were highly introverted, whereas the conflicted men ($n = 35$), called the *Undercontrolled,* were highly nonconscientious (Pulkkinen, 1996, pp. 1293–1294). In other personality characteristics, the conflicted participants, independent of sex, were more neurotic and less agreeable than the adjusted ones, and in life orientation, they had more negative life attitudes. In social functioning, both the Brittles and the Undercontrolled were less integrated into society, and they used alcohol more heavily than their adjusted same-sex counterparts. In addition, the Undercontrolled were less family oriented but more oriented to party culture than the adjusted men, whereas the Brittles were less intellectually oriented than the adjusted women.

Adapted. For women, one of the two adjusted clusters, the *Traditionals* ($n = 48$), was characterized by a high family orientation, conscientiousness, and contentment with present achievements. For men, one of the two adjusted patterns, the *Resilients* ($n = 59$), differed from the other men in higher extraversion, positive life attitudes, and social integration in terms of stable working career. The Traditionals and the Resilients indicated the adapted mode of adjustment in a gender-specific way.

Nonconventional. Women belonging to the other adjusted cluster, the *Individuated* ($n = 59$), were characterized by high intellectual interests and reflectiveness. Men belonging to the other adjusted cluster, the *Introverted* ($n = 44$), were more introverted and conscientious than the other men. The Individuated differed from the other women in higher intellectual interests, involving longer education (70% had qualified for university studies, 26% of the other women) and higher cultural interests; higher reflectiveness, indicated by identity achievement; lower neuroticism; and lower family orientation. Only 30% of the Individuated had had children by age 27 (compared with 85% of the Traditionals and 67% of the Brittles). Correspondingly, there were more bachelors among the Introverted than among the other men. The Individuated and the Introverted had their own characteristics that marked their nonconventional adjusted profiles: cognitive orientation and introverted personality, respectively.

Social Background

In this study, the female and male personality styles were compared to each other in their social and developmental background and in their adult psychological and social functioning.

Females. The background of the Brittles differed from that of the Individuated, first, in that the parents of the Brittles were less child centered than those of the Individuated. Second, the Brittles had poorer school success at ages 8 and 14 than the Individuated, and third, the Brittles had more conduct problems than the Individuated and the Traditionals. Conduct problems covered punishment at school, truancy, smoking, drinking, and incidents with the police (Pulkkinen, 1996). Child-centered parenting describes participants' recollections of parenting practices and the home environment at age 14 (Kokko & Pulkkinen, 2000). It comprised good parental relationship, good relationship with the father, maternal support, maternal supervision, and lack of physical punishment. The socioeconomic status of the parents did not differentiate between the female clusters; it was only psychological atmosphere at home that differentiated.

Males. Differences between the male clusters did not exist in school success at age 8 or at age 14, but at age 14, the Undercontrolled exceeded the other male clusters in conduct problems. The parents of the Undercontrolled were lower in child-centeredness than the parents of the Resilients. The lowest socioeconomic status was, however, found in the parents of the Introverted. They came, more often than expected by chance, from blue-collar workers' families, whereas the Resilients had this background less often than expected by chance. The Undercontrolled had no typical socioeconomic background. Thus, both psychological atmosphere at home and socioeconomic status of the parents differentiated between the male clusters.

Continuity in Personality Characteristics

The personality style clusters extracted at age 27 were compared at ages 36 and 42 in the KSP and at ages 33 and 42 in the scales of the Big Five Personality Inventory. High differential continuity in personality characteristics was obtained through these years in the whole sample except for extraversion and neuroticism in women, which differed significantly from the stability in men (Table 4.2). Intraindividual variation across time was more common in women than in men in these temperament-based characteristics.

Vulnerability Factors at Ages 36 and 42

The KSP aims at quantifying theoretically important constructs for exploring and understanding the complicated relationships between

Table 4.2   The Stability Coefficients (Pearson Correlations) for the Karolinska Scales of Personality (KSP) and the Big Five Personality Inventory (NEO-PI)

Scales	Stability Coefficients for Men	Stability Coefficients for Women
KSP (36–42 years)	$(n = 97)$	$(n = 107)$
Extraversion	0.85	0.74
Anxiety	0.85	0.72
Conformity	0.82	0.74
Aggression	0.82	0.67
NEO-PI (33–42 years)	$(n = 89)$	$(n = 104)$
Neuroticism	0.76	0.50
Extraversion	0.81	0.49
Openness to Experience	0.79	0.82
Conscientiousness	0.64	0.60
Agreeableness	0.66	0.72

individual differences in behavior, affectivity, and functioning. The KSP includes 15 scales that are designed for the definition of certain vulnerability factors, which might help to identify individuals at risk and understand interactions between biological dispositions and situational factors. The scales were grouped for the present comparisons of the personality styles into four categories that were considered to correspond to Types A to D as follows: (1) Aggression (including Verbal Aggression, Indirect Aggression, Irritability, Suspicion, and Guilt; Type A); (2) Conformity (including Socialization and Social Desirability; Type C); and (3) Anxiety (including Somatic Anxiety, Muscular Tension, Psychic Anxiety, Psychasthenia, and Inhibition of Aggression; Type D). The fourth group of scales, assessing Extraversion–Introversion (af Klinteberg, Humble, & Schalling, 1992), includes Impulsiveness, Monotony Avoidance, and Detachment. Of them, Detachment reversed, called Sociability, was considered to represent Type B behavior. Detachment was measured by items such as, "I feel best when I keep people at a certain distance," and "I feel uncomfortable when people take me into their confidence."

The clusters for male and female personality styles extracted at age 27 were compared using Multivariate Analysis of Variance for Repeated Measures (MANOVA). This 3 (cluster) × 2 (time) analysis used the three clusters of personality styles as a between-groups variable and time as a repeated measure, enabling the investigation of (a) the level changes of the KSP variables from age 36 to 42, (b) the differences in the mean levels of these variables between clusters, and (c) the interaction of these effects. No significant changes in the average level of scores from age 36 to 42 were found in any of the four scales in men or women. There were, however, consistent mean level differences between the clusters: aggression ($p = .019$ for males, ns for females); anxiety ($p = .006$ for males, .000 for females); sociability ($p = .000$ for males, .002 for females); and conformity ($p = .000$ for males, .014 for females). The profiles of the clusters were similar for females from age 36 to 42, but two significant interactions were found for males: aggression ($p = .019$) and conformity ($p = .004$).

Conflicted. From age 36 to 42, the Undercontrolled were higher in aggression (Figure 4.2) and lower in conformity than the other men, but they did not differ from the other men in anxiety. The Brittles, on the other hand, were higher in anxiety than the other women (Figure 4.3), but lower than the Traditionals in conformity and sociability. Significant differences did not exist between the female clusters in aggression. Comparisons using

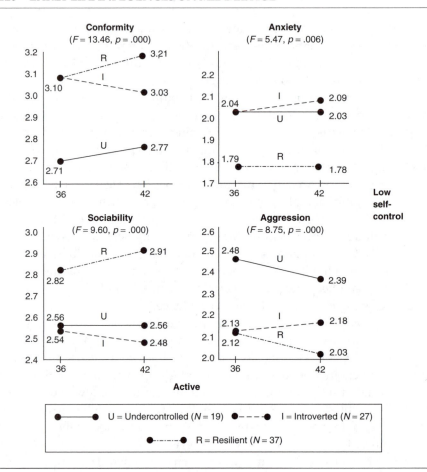

Figure 4.2   Means of Male Clusters Extracted at Age 27 in the Karolinska Scales of Personality at Ages 36 and 42

other variables for aggression (Kokko & Pulkkinen, in press), including Buss and Perry's (1992) Aggression Questionnaire, administered at ages 36 and 42, confirmed that male clusters differed in aggression at both ages in the same way as in the KSP aggression scale, but the female clusters did not differ. The results supported the observations made at age 27 on the differences between the conflicted men and women. The conflicted men, the Undercontrolled, typically displayed externalizing behavior (Type A; Figure 4.1), whereas the conflicted women, the Brittles, displayed internalizing behavior (Type D). They differed from the same-sex counterparts in a consistent way.

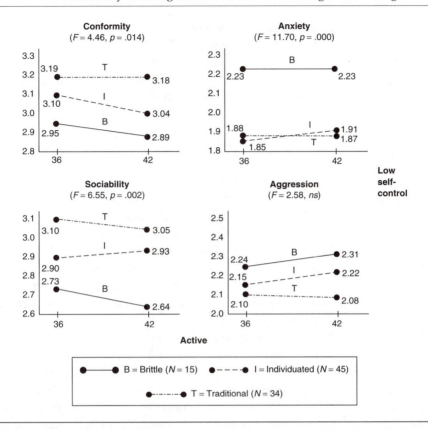

Figure 4.3   Means of Female Clusters Extracted at Age 27 in the Karolinska
Scales of Personality at Ages 36 and 42

Adapted. The Resilients were higher than the Introverted and Undercontrolled men in sociability, but lower than the Introverted in anxiety and lower than the Undercontrolled in aggression. In conformity, the Resilients were higher than the Undercontrolled. Likewise, the Traditionals were higher than the Brittles in sociability but lower than the Brittles in anxiety. In conformity, the Traditionals were higher than the Brittles. No differences existed in aggression.

Nonconventional. The Introverted men were higher in anxiety and lower in sociability than the Resilients. In conformity, they were higher and in aggression lower than the Undercontrolled. In the latter variables, there were significant interactions caused by the Introverted: Their conformity tended to decrease and aggression tended to increase, whereas the opposite trends were found in the other clusters.

The Individuated were lower in anxiety than the Brittles. They did not differ from the other women in aggression, sociability, or conformity; in these scales, their scores were consistently between those of the Brittles and the Traditionals.

Big Five Factors at Ages 33 and 42

Following the same analytical procedure as before, a decrease in the average level of scores was found in neuroticism for both genders, and an increase was found in male agreeableness and female conscientiousness (Table 4.3). The average changes were found for all female clusters; interaction was not significant in any of the scales. For males, a significant interaction was found in neuroticism. Differences between the clusters were significant in all scales for females and in three scales for males. Significant differences between the male clusters did not exist in agreeableness and openness to experience.

Differences between the Undercontrolled and the Brittles in the profiles were consistent with the differences between the clusters in externalizing and internalizing problems at age 27 and in the KSP scales (Figures 4.2 and 4.3). Compared to the same-sex counterparts, both were more neurotic, particularly the Brittles, who were more neurotic than the other women (the Undercontrolled differed from the Resilients); and both were more nonconscientious, particularly the Undercontrolled, who differed from the other men (the Brittles differed from the Traditionals). The Brittles were also highly introverted, differing from the two other female clusters.

The Resilients differed from the Undercontrolled and Introverted men in lower neuroticism, from the Introverted in higher extraversion, and from the Undercontrolled in higher conscientiousness. This pattern of emotionally stable, extraverted, and conscientious personality was common to the adapted males and females, the Resilients and the Traditionals, respectively. The Traditionals were, with the Individuated women, lower in neuroticism and higher in extraversion than the Brittles. The Traditionals were also higher in agreeableness than the other women and higher in conscientiousness than the Brittles. The Individuated women, on the other hand, were higher in openness to experience than the Brittles. This pattern fit the characteristics of the academically and culturally oriented Individuated obtained at age 27.

Table 4.3   Means of the Scores in the NEO-PI Variables at Ages 33 and 42 in Male and Female Clusters [MANOVA 3(cluster) × 2(time)]

NEO-PI Variables	Range	Conflicted Undercontrolled n = 19		Adapted Resilient n = 34		Nonconventional Introverted n = 25		Level Change p	Between Groups p	Interaction p
		33	42	33	42	33	42			
MEN										
Neuroticism	1–5	2.87	2.52	2.40	2.05	2.66	2.66	.000	.016	.011
Extraversion	1–5	3.24	3.31	3.38	3.54	2.94	2.89	ns	.001	ns
Openness	1–5	3.19	3.20	3.11	3.26	2.95	2.95	ns	ns	ns
Conscientiousness	1–5	3.18	3.32	3.65	3.80	3.62	3.60	ns	.002	ns
Agreeableness	1–5	3.32	3.37	3.44	3.58	3.45	3.58	.020	ns	ns
		Brittle n = 16		Traditional n = 33		Individuated n = 41				
		33	42	33	42	33	42			
WOMEN										
Neuroticism	1–5	3.22	2.76	2.54	2.33	2.53	2.28	.000	.000	ns
Extraversion	1–5	2.88	2.91	3.35	3.41	3.26	3.28	ns	.001	ns
Openness	1–5	3.09	3.09	3.29	3.35	3.50	3.58	ns	.006	ns
Conscientiousness	1–5	3.39	3.61	3.80	3.95	3.63	3.77	.002	.035	ns
Agreeableness	1–5	3.48	3.64	3.88	3.91	3.59	3.64	ns	.014	ns

123

The Introverted men were more introverted and neurotic than the Resilients and more conscientious than the Undercontrolled. A significant interaction in neuroticism (Table 4.3) was caused by declining neuroticism in the Resilients and Undercontrolled but not in the Introverted. The introvert, conscientious, and neurotic pattern of the Introverted was consistent with the characteristics found at age 27 and in the KSP.

Emotional and Behavioral Regulation in Perspective

The personality styles extracted at age 27 were compared in teacher ratings on socioemotional behavior at age 8 (Pulkkinen, 1996) by using Univariate Analysis of Variance (ANOVA). The variables for Type A to D behavior defined by the model of emotional and behavioral regulation (Figure 4.1) were as follows: Type A: aggression (e.g., "Hurts another child when angry by hitting, kicking, or throwing something"); Type B: constructiveness (e.g., "Acts reasonably even in annoying situations"); Type C: compliance (e.g., "Is peaceable and patient"); and Type D: anxiety (e.g., "Starts easily crying if others treat him/her nastily"). In addition, the clusters were compared in passivity (e.g., "Always silent and does not care to be busy") and high self-control (e.g., "Is a reliable classmate").

Figure 4.4 presents the means of the cluster for males in the framework of emotional and behavioral regulation. The profiles of the clusters can be compared with those at ages 36 and 42 (Figure 4.2) in aggression, anxiety, compliance/conformity, and constructiveness/sociability. Considering the interval of 34 years, the profiles and, consequently, differences between the clusters are surprisingly similar. The Undercontrolled had lower self-control than the other men, $F(2, 135) = 4.09$, $p = .019$. They were high in aggression and rather high in anxiety, although not differing significantly from the Resilients. In compliance and constructiveness, the Under-controlled were low. The Introverted, on the other hand, were high both in compliance/conformity and anxiety; they were also more passive than the Resilients, $F(2, 135) = 6.95$, $p = .001$. Besides being socially active, the Resilients were high in constructiveness and low in anxiety.

Differences between the female clusters (Figure 4.5) were smaller than between the male clusters, as in adulthood. At ages 36 and 42, the Brittles were higher than the Individuated and the Traditionals in anxiety. The Brittles also were higher than the Individuated women in social passivity, $F(2, 134) = 3.29$, $p = .040$. Significant differences between the clusters did

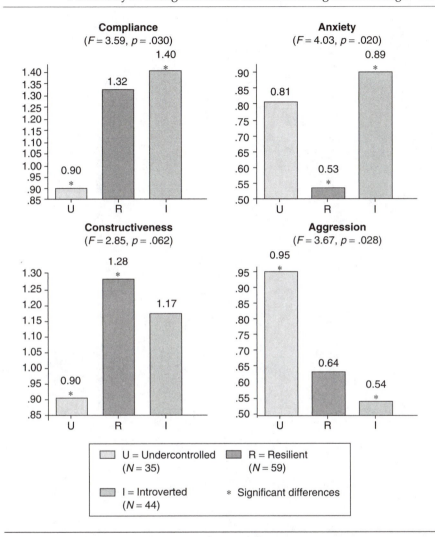

Figure 4.4   Means of Male Clusters Extracted at Age 27 in Teacher Ratings at Age 8

not exist in aggression, constructiveness, or compliance. The only trends found were that the Brittles were least constructive and the Traditionals most compliant. Childhood socioemotional characteristics were less influential organizing factors beyond the formation of female versus male personality styles.

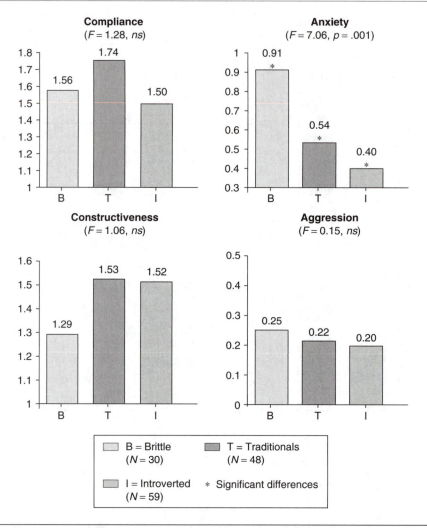

Figure 4.5   Means of Female Clusters Extracted at Age 27 in Teacher Ratings at Age 8

Psychological and Social Functioning

Differences between the clusters for personality styles were consistent in personality characteristics from childhood to middle age. At age 27 when the clusters were extracted, social functioning and aspects of psychological functioning other than personality were considered, subsumed under the title of life orientation. To see whether the clusters continued to differ in these functions or whether the personality styles moderated development in them, the clusters were compared in several indicators measured either three or two times (at ages 27, 36, and 42, or at ages 36 and 42). Some comparisons were also made in variables measured only at age 42. MANOVA was used for the comparisons when two or three measurements were available. Cross-sectional comparisons were made by one-way ANOVA and a chi-square test.

Life Orientation

Life orientation was studied with the theoretical assumption by Pulkkinen and Rönkä (1994) that there is a common underlying construct—adaptive psychological functioning—that modulates different indicators of successful development toward internal consistency. The idea was originally presented by Erikson (1950, 1968) in terms of mentally healthy functioning, as noted by Waterman (1992). The comparison of the personality clusters allowed for the analysis of whether personality clusters moderated successful development in a consistent way.

Two groups of indicators of life orientation were distinguished: those concerning self-processes and those concerning an individual's relationships with life context. In self-processes, self-esteem and identity formation were considered. There was positive development in both of them, although this was moderated by personality style. The average level of *self-esteem* increased in all male and female clusters from age 36 to 42 (Table 4.4). Across these years, the conflicted individuals, that is, the Undercontrolled and the Brittles were lower in self-esteem than others except for the Introverted men, who did not differ from the Undercontrolled in self-esteem. Among men, self-esteem was highest in the Resilients.

Each participant's identity status (diffusion, moratorium, foreclosure, and achievement) for each of five domains (religion, political opinion, occupational career, lifestyle, and intimate relationship) was assessed. Both exploration and commitment were used as criteria for identity achievement (Fadjukoff, Pulkkinen, & Kokko, 2005; Pulkkinen & Kokko, 2000). Separate scales for each of the identity statuses were created on the basis of the number of domains (from 0 to 5) in which the individual was in a particular status (Pulkkinen & Rönkä, 1994).

The level of identity achievement increased in all men and women from age 27 to 42; it was the most typical identity status at age 42, particularly

Table 4.4 Means of the Tests for Psychological Functioning at Ages 27, 36, and 42

Variables	Range	Undercontrolled			Resilient			Introverted			Level Change p	Between Groups p	Interaction p
		27	36	42	27	36	42	27	36	42			
MEN													
Self-esteem[1]	1–4		3.02	3.32		3.31	3.56		3.12	3.23	.000	.008	ns
Identity achievement[2]	0–5	0.85	1.50	2.30	1.93	1.84	2.34	0.71	1.21	1.00	.001	.000	.037
Life satisfaction[2]	1–4	2.66	2.81	2.87	3.25	3.14	3.23	2.86	2.98	3.04	.012	.000	ns
Optimism[2]	1–4	2.90	2.93	2.93	3.21	3.13	3.17	2.80	2.82	2.88	ns	.000	ns
Trust in life[2]	1–4	2.78	2.97	2.89	3.14	3.06	3.15	2.91	2.89	3.02	ns	.006	.031
Sense of coherence[3]	1–7			4.45			5.37			5.08		.000	
Psychological well-being[1]	1–4		3.01	3.03		3.27	3.26		3.06	2.95	ns	.000	ns
Depression[1]	1–4		1.54	1.73		1.40	1.38		1.42	1.45	ns	.067	ns
Psychosomatic symptoms[1]	1–4		1.69	1.64		1.51	1.47		1.61	1.55	ns	ns	ns
Self-rated health[1]	1–5		3.67	3.95		4.33	4.04		4.00	3.78	ns	.086	.027

WOMEN

Variables	Range	Brittle			Traditional			Individuated			Level Change p	Between Groups p	Interaction p
Self-esteem[1]	1–4		3.01	3.15		3.33	3.51		3.26	3.42	.000	.015	ns
Identity achievement[2]	0–5	0.75	1.44	1.81	1.09	1.29	2.26	1.70	2.19	2.89	.000	.000	ns
Life satisfaction[2]	1–4	2.90	2.91	3.04	3.05	3.08	3.15	3.02	2.97	3.08	.021	ns	ns
Optimism[2]	1–4	2.81	2.90	2.86	2.90	2.94	3.06	3.14	3.02	2.99	ns	.029	.025
Trust in life[2]	1–4	2.75	2.80	2.75	2.87	2.96	2.99	2.93	2.91	3.01	ns	.076	ns
Sense of coherence[3]	1–7	4.71				5.44			5.26			.004	
Psychological well-being[1]	1–4		3.04	3.01		3.24	3.28		3.23	3.19	ns	.015	ns
Depression[1]	1–4		1.65	1.68		1.39	1.41		1.43	1.51	ns	.013	ns
Psychosomatic symptoms[1]	1–4		1.68	1.69		1.42	1.45		1.50	1.52	ns	.002	ns
Self-rated health[1]	1–5		4.00	3.76		4.43	4.14		4.04	3.90	.032	.067	ns

1. MANOVA 3(cluster) × 2(time)
2. MANOVA 3(cluster) × 3(time)
3. ANOVA

in women; at age 36, foreclosure was the most typical status of men and women, whereas at age 27, no status was more typical than any other. Comparisons between the clusters revealed that identity achievement increased, particularly in the Undercontrolled from age 27 to 42, which reached the level of the Resilients. At the same time, moratorium decreased in the Undercontrolled. These opposite trends are consistent with the theory of identity formation.

Similar opposite changes, a decrease in moratorium and an increase in identity achievement, were found in the Individuated women. The Resilients had possibly gone through this process before age 27 because they were already high in identity achievement and low in moratorium. The highest identity diffusion was found in the Introverted at ages 27 and 42. Differences merged at age 36 when foreclosure identity was highest in all male clusters. Among women, the Brittles were higher than the Individuated in identity diffusion, whereas the Traditionals were higher than the Individuated in foreclosure identity. Due to high foreclosure identity, the Traditionals were low in moratorium throughout these years.

In the variables indicating an individual's relationships with life context, life satisfaction and expectations about the future (optimism and trust in life) were considered. There was a slight increase in *life satisfaction* from age 27 to 42 in men and women. Female clusters did not differ in life satisfaction, but among men, the Resilients were more satisfied with life than the other men.

There was no change in the average level of *optimism* among women or men in these years. There was, however, a significant Cluster × Age interaction in optimism for women resulting from a decrease of optimism in the Individuated women but an increase of optimism in the Traditionals. Optimism was lowest in the Brittles. Among men, the Resilients were higher in optimism than the other men at all ages.

The average level of *trust in life* did not change from age 27 to 42 in men or women, but differences between male clusters existed. The Resilients were higher in trustfulness than the Undercontrolled and Introverted at age 27, but this difference leveled off at age 36 and re-emerged between the Resilients and Undercontrolled at age 42.

Well-Being

Indicators of well-being included psychological well-being, depression, coherence, psychosomatic symptoms, self-rated health, and the GHQ-12.

The level of *psychological well-being* and *depression* remained the same from age 36 to 42 for men and women (Table 4.4). The adapted individuals, the Resilients and the Traditionals, were highest in well-being and lowest in depression, whereas the conflicted individuals, the Undercontrolled and the Brittles, were lowest in well-being and highest in depression, particularly at age 42. The Undercontrolled and the Brittles also were lowest in *sense of coherence* at age 42. The Introverted were closer to the Undercontrolled in well-being and depression, whereas the Individuated were closer to the Traditionals, particularly at age 36.

No changes emerged in *psychosomatic symptoms* for males or females. Nor were there differences between the male clusters, but there was a difference between female clusters: The Brittles were higher than the other women in psychosomatic symptoms at both ages. The female clusters did not, however, differ in *self-rated health;* the only trend that emerged was that the Traditionals rated their health as being better than the other women. In general, there was an average decrease in self-rated health of women from age 36 to 42. An average change or group differences did not occur in the self-rated health of men, but there was an interaction resulting from an increase in the self-rated health of the Undercontrolled, while there was a decrease in the self-rated health of other men. No changes or group differences emerged in the GHQ-12 for men or women.

Social Functioning

Social functioning was assessed in terms of work, family, and drinking behavior. Socioeconomic status at age 42 was categorized into blue-collar workers, lower white-collar workers, and higher white-collar workers. No differences existed between the male clusters, but for female clusters, differences did exist. The socioeconomic status of the Individuated was higher than that of the Brittles due to the higher proportion of the Individuated women among higher white-collar workers.

Career stability by age 27, between ages 27 and 36, and between ages 37 and 42, indicated by a scale with three categories (unstable, changeable, and stable), increased for men and women during the latest period in the conflicted individuals (the Undercontrolled and the Brittles), whose levels of career stability were generally lower than those of the Resilients and Introverted or those of the Traditionals and the Individuated, respectively. Long-term unemployment experienced between ages 27 and 36 was typical of the conflicted individuals: 22.6% of the Undercontrolled and 17.2%

of the Brittles were long-term unemployed between ages 27 and 36. It was atypical among the Resilients (1.9%). No other types or antitypes were observed: the Traditionals (2.2%), the Individuated (5.4%) and the Introverted (2.4%). At age 42, there was a similar trend among the conflicted having experienced long-term unemployment, but no statistically significant types were observed.

The improvement of the career stability of the Undercontrolled men since age 36 was reflected in their increasing mastery beliefs in the Strategy and Attribution Questionnaire (Nurmi et al., 1995). At the same time (from age 36 to 42), the task-irrelevant behavior of the Undercontrolled decreased, although it still remained higher than that of the Resilients. Success expectation increased in all men, and task-irrelevant behavior decreased. No average changes emerged in mastery beliefs. In women, the average level of success expectation increased; other significant changes or group differences did not occur.

For family, the Introverted differed from the other men. The only men who had not lived with a partner were found among the Introverted. They also had a lower number of relationships than expected by chance. The average number of children was lower in the Introverted than in the other men.

The Resilients and the Undercontrolled, and correspondingly, the Traditionals and the Brittles, did not differ in number of children. The conflicted individuals, the Undercontrolled and the Brittles, were married less often than the adapted individuals, the Resilients and the Traditionals, respectively. Several relationships were more common among the Undercontrolled than among the other men. The Individuated women did not differ from the other women in any of the family variables.

Drinking behavior is one of the markers of social functioning in Finnish culture because heavy drinking is common. It affects people's health, work, and family life. The frequency of drinking increased from age 27 to 42 in men, as well as the amount of alcohol consumed per year. The consumption was higher in the Undercontrolled than in the Introverted, and the former were drunk more often than the Introverted. The Undercontrolled received higher scores than other men (particularly the Resilients) on alcoholism screening tests (CAGE and the Minnesota Alcoholism Screening Test) at ages 36 and 42. The frequency of drinking and the consumption of alcohol also increased among women from age 27 to 42. Differences between the female clusters did not exist in the consumption of alcohol or in the scores of the alcoholism screening tests.

Summary of the Findings

This article introduced the heuristic model of emotional and behavioral regulation, devised in 1968 to depict the function of cognitive control in the regulation of emotional expressions and consequent interindividual differences in positive and problem behaviors. In recent years, emotion regulation has become a common paradigm in psychological research, but long-term longitudinal studies are still pending. In the JYLS, the variables chosen for the study in 1968 were aimed to map the behavioral variation described by the model. In adulthood, the scope of the JYLS has been expanded to many spheres of life, but based on data collected on personality, the study of continuity in high and low self-control of emotional behavior across 34 years and concomitant aspects of social and psychological functioning has been possible. The sample represents the age cohort group born in 1959, which means that more variation in behavior can be detected than with samples limited to a selected group, such as college students. The major findings are as follows:

1. The kinds of behavior that indicate low self-control of negative emotions, Type A for aggressive behavior and Type D for anxious behavior, are, independent of whether variable-oriented or person-oriented (functional or typological) approaches are applied, risk factors for later vulnerability to aggressive and anxious behaviors, low psychological well-being, and problems in social functioning, such as long-term unemployment, use of alcohol, criminality, and poor intimate relationships. Passive and anxious behavior (Type D) is a more significant risk factor in women than in men, whereas aggressive behavior (Type A) is more significant in men.

2. The kinds of behavior that indicate high self-control of negative emotions, Type B for constructive behavior and Type C for compliant behavior, are resource factors for later career orientation and other aspects of adaptive social functioning in adulthood, as well as for sociability, conformity, and psychological well-being, indicated by, for instance, self-esteem, identity achievement, and sense of coherence. For females, socially active constructive behavior (Type B) is a more significant resource factor for positive development than compliance (Type C). Constructive behavior and compliant behavior do not differ as a resource factor in men.

3. Significant continuity from childhood to adulthood exists in the configuration of characteristics describing emotional and behavioral regulation.

4. The focus of this article was in adult development studied in a person-oriented way. Personality styles extracted at age 27 using all available data on personality characteristics, social behavior, and life orientation were comparable to typologies in other studies. There are some major differences to be noted. First, the commonly used label for a conflicted style, the Undercontrolled, fits only for males because of the involvement of aggressive behavior, whereas the label the Brittle better describes female anxious-loaded conflicted behavior. Second, characteristics that indicate emotional and behavioral regulation were highly influential organizing factors beyond the formation of adaptive styles in men. The Resilient men were socially active and well-controlled, differing from the Introverted men, who were characterized by both compliance/conformity and anxiety. The results confirmed that the label Introverted fits them better than the label Overcontrolled, which, in the model of emotional and behavioral regulation, would only describe Type C behavior. Third, differences in female adaptive behavior were more notably formed on the basis of academic success and social roles than emotional and behavioral regulation. Adaptive but nonconventional (Individuated) women were open to experience and oriented to studies and career, whereas the Traditionals were more family oriented and agreeable.

5. Differences between the personality styles remained unchanged from age 36 to 42, as indicated by the means of the clusters in four categories of scales from the KSP corresponding to Types A to D in the model of emotional and behavioral regulation, and from age 33 to 42, as indicated by the means of the clusters in the Big Five factors of personality.

6. The profiles and, consequently, differences between the clusters were very similar at age 8 compared to those in adulthood. For males, significant differences in all types of behavior existed both in childhood and in adulthood. Differences between the male clusters at age 8 were more pronounced than those between the female clusters and even more so in adulthood. The most consistent differences between the female clusters existed in anxiety.

7. Differences between the personality style clusters were significant and consistent across years in several indicators of psychological and social functioning from early adulthood to early middle age. The conflicted individuals—the Undercontrolled men and the Brittle women—were

lower in all measured variables for adaptive behavior and higher in depression. As shown elsewhere (Pulkkinen, Nurmi, & Kokko, 2002), the clusters at age 36 also differed in unifying life themes as perceived by the interviewers. Typically, these themes focused on conflicts and constraints that limited the attainment of age-related developmental goals. Individuals on successful tracks had a capacity to cope with them, but the conflicted individuals were struggling with problems in profession, social relationships, and lifestyles.

8. Changes in the average level of vulnerability factors (KSP) from age 36 to 42 did not exist. In the Big Five factors, the most consistent finding was the decrease of neuroticism from age 33 to 42. In accordance with it, the average level of self-esteem, identity achievement, and life satisfaction increased. In other variables for psychological functioning, average level changes did not emerge.

9. Personality styles formulated in a holistic way also functioned as significant moderators of adult development. The results showed that neuroticism and aggression did not decrease in the Introverted as they did in the other men. Correspondingly, their conformity decreased, whereas it increased in the other men. This finding is in accordance with the results by Morizot and Le Blanc (2003), who found that overcontrolled men differed in their 30s from other men in conjugal and work problems that tended to decrease in other men. On the other hand, our results showed that positive development emerged in the Undercontrolled men compared to the other men: Their identity achievement increased highly, career stability increased, task-irrelevant behavior decreased, and self-rated health improved, although their drinking was still heavy. Our results also showed that optimism tended to decrease in the career-oriented Individuated women from early adulthood to early middle age, whereas it increased in the family-oriented Traditional women. This finding may reflect women's difficulties in career achievements.

10. Adult individuals do not form a homogeneous group as often implicitly assumed when adult development is described normatively. For understanding and supporting individual development, it would be relevant to identify an individual's personality style. It could be easily approximated within the broad categories described in this article.

References

Adler, A. (1969). *The science of living.* New York: Anchor Books. (Original work published 1929)

af Klinteberg, B., Humble, K., & Schalling, D. (1992). Personality and psychopathy of males with a history of early criminal behaviour. *European Journal of Personality, 6,* 245–266.

af Klinteberg, B., Schalling, D., & Magnusson, D. (1990). Childhood behaviour and adult personality in male and female subjects. *European Journal of Personality, 4,* 57–71.

Antonovsky, A. (1987). *Unraveling the mystery of health. How people manage stress and stay well.* San Francisco: Jossey-Bass.

Aro, H. (1988). *Stress development and psychosomatic symptoms in adolescence. Study of 14 to 16 year old school children* (Acta Universitatis Tamperensis, Series A, Whole No. 242). Tampere, Finland: University of Tampere.

Asendorpf, J. B., & van Aken, M. A. G. (1999). Resilient, overcontrolled, and under-controlled personality prototypes in childhood: Replicability, predictive power, and the trait-type issue. *Journal of Personality and Social Psychology, 77,* 815–832.

Bergman, L. R., Magnusson, D., & El-Khouri, B. M. (2003). *Studying individual development in an interindividual context: A person-oriented approach.* Mahwah, NJ: Erlbaum.

Block, J. (1971). *Lives through time.* Berkeley, CA: Bancroft Books.

Block, J. H., & Block, J. (1980). The role of ego-control and ego-resiliency in the organization of behavior. In W. A. Collins (Ed.), *Minnesota Symposia on Child Psychology* (Vol. 13, pp. 39–101). Hillsdale, NJ: Erlbaum.

Buss, A. H., & Perry, M. (1992). The Aggression Questionnaire. *Journal of Personality and Social Psychology, 63,* 452–459.

Caspi, A. (1998). Personality development across the life course. In N. Eisenberg (Ed.), *Social, emotional, and personality development* (Handbook of Child Psychology, Vol. 3, pp. 311–388). New York: Wiley.

Caspi, A., Bem, D. J., & Elder, G. (1989). Continuities and consequences of interactional styles across the life course. *Journal of Personality, 57,* 375–406.

Caspi, A., & Roberts, B. W. (1999). Personality continuity and change across the life course. In L. A. Pervin & O. P. John (Eds.), *Handbook of personality: Theory and research* (2nd ed., pp. 300–326). New York: Guilford Press.

Caspi, A., Wright, B. R. E., Moffitt, T. E., & Silva, P. A. (1998). Early failure in the labor market: Childhood and adolescent predictors of unemployment in the transition to adulthood. *American Sociological Review, 63,* 424–451.

Costa, P. T., Jr., & McCrae, R. R. (1985). *The NEO Personality Inventory manual.* Odessa, FL: Psychological Assessment Resources.

Depue, R. (1987). *General Behavior Inventory.* Ithaca, NY: Cornell University, Department of Psychology.

Digman, J. M. (1997). Higher-order factors of the Big Five. *Journal of Personality and Social Psychology, 73*, 1246–1256.

Elder, G. H., Jr. (1998). Life-course and human development. In R. M. Lerner (Ed.), *Theoretical models of human development* (Handbook of Child Psychology, Vol. 1, pp. 939–991). New York: Wiley.

Erikson, E. H. (1950). *Childhood and society.* New York: Norton.

Erikson, E. H. (1968). *Identity: Youth and crisis.* New York: Norton.

Ewing, J. A. (1984). Detecting alcoholism, the CAGE questionnaire. *Journal of the American Medical Association, 252*, 1905–1907.

Eysenck, H. J. (1997). Personality and experimental psychology: The unification of psychology and the possibility of a paradigm. *Journal of Personality and Social Psychology, 73*, 1224–1237.

Eysenck, H. J., & Eysenck, S. B. G. (1975). *Manual of the Eysenck Personality Questionnaire.* London: Hodder & Stoughton.

Fadjukoff, P., Pulkkinen, L., & Kokko, K. (2005). Identity processes in adulthood: Diverging domains. *Identity: An International Journal of Theory and Research, 5*, 1–20.

Fergusson, D. M., Horwood, L. J., & Lynskey, M. T. (1997). The effects of unemployment on psychiatric illness during young adulthood. *Psychological Medicine, 27*, 371–381.

Friedman, M., & Rosenman, R. H. (1974). *Type A behavior and your heart.* New York: Knopf.

Goldberg, D. P. (1972). *The detection of psychiatric illness by questionnaire.* London: Oxford University Press.

Hanisch, K. A. (1999). Job loss and unemployment research from 1994–1998: A review and recommendations for research and intervention. *Journal of Vocational Behavior, 55*, 188–220.

Hart, D., Atkins, R., & Fegley, S. (2003). Personality and development in childhood: A person-centered approach. *Monographs of the Society for Research in Child Development, 68*, vii–109.

Havinghurst, R. J. (1948). *Developmental tasks and education.* New York: McKay.

Helson, R., & Srivastava, S. (2001). Three paths of adult development: Conservers, Seekers, and Achievers. *Journal of Personality and Social Psychology, 80*, 995–1010.

Hull, C. L. (1943). *Principles of behavior.* New York: Appleton-Century-Crofts.

Kagan, J. (1971). *Change and continuity in infancy.* New York: Wiley.

Kinnunen, U., & Pulkkinen, L. (2003). Childhood socioemotional characteristics as antecedents of marital stability and quality. *European Psychologist, 8*, 223–237.

Knuuttila, S., & Sihvola, J. (1998). How the philosophical analysis of emotions was introduced. In J. Sihvola & T. Engberg-Pedersen (Eds.), *The emotions in Hellenistic philosophy* (The New Synthese Historical Library, Vol. 46, pp. 1–19). Dordrecht, Netherlands: Kluwer Academic.

Kokko, K., Bergman, L. R., & Pulkkinen, L. (2003). Child personality characteristics and selection into long-term unemployment in Finnish and Swedish longitudinal samples. *International Journal of Behavioral Development, 27,* 134–144.

Kokko, K., & Pulkkinen, L. (1998). Unemployment and psychological distress: Mediator effects. *Journal of Adult Development, 5*(4), 205–217.

Kokko, K., & Pulkkinen, L. (2000). Aggression in childhood and long-term unemployment in adulthood: A cycle of maladaptation and some protective factors. *Developmental Psychology, 36,* 463–472.

Kokko, K., & Pulkkinen, L. (in press). Stability of aggressive behavior from childhood to middle age in women and men. *Aggressive Behavior.*

Kokko, K., Pulkkinen, L., & Puustinen, M. (2000). Selection into long-term unemployment and its psychological consequences. *International Journal of Behavioral Development, 24,* 310–320.

Kristenson, H., & Trell, E. (1982). Indicators of alcohol consumption: Comparisons between a questionnaire (Mm-MAST), interviews and gammaglutamyl transferase (GGT) in a health survey of middle-aged males. *British Journal of Addiction, 77,* 297–304.

Lachman, M. E., & Bertrand, R. M. (2001). Personality and the self in midlife. In M. E. Lachman (Ed.), *Handbook of midlife development* (pp. 279–309). New York: Wiley.

Laursen, B., Pulkkinen, L., & Adams, R. (2002). The antecedents and correlates of agreeableness in adulthood. *Developmental Psychology, 38,* 591–603.

Levinson, D. (1978). *The seasons of a man's life.* New York: Knopf.

Levinson, D. (1986). A conception of adult development. *American Psychologist, 41,* 3–13.

Lewin, K. (1951). *Field theory in social science: Selected theoretical papers* (D. Cartwright, Ed.). New York: Harper.

Magnusson, D., & Stattin, H. (1998). Person-context interaction theories. In R. M. Lerner (Ed.), *Theoretical models of human development* (Handbook of Child Psychology, Vol. 1, pp. 685–759). New York: Wiley.

Marcia, J. E. (1966). Development and validation of ego identity status. *Journal of Personality and Social Psychology, 3,* 551–558.

Miller, N. E. (1959). Liberalization of basic S-R concepts: Extension to conflict behavior, motivation, and social learning. In S. Koch (Ed.), *Psychology: A study of a science* (Vol. 2, pp. 196–292). New York: McGraw-Hill.

Morizot, J., & Le Blanc, M. (2003). Searching for a developmental typology of personality and its relations to antisocial behaviour: A longitudinal study of an adjudicated men sample. *Criminal Behaviour and Mental Health, 13,* 241–277.

Nurmi, J.-E., Salmela-Aro, K., & Haavisto, T. (1995). The Strategy and Attribution Questionnaire: Psychometric properties. *European Journal of Psychological Assessment, 11,* 108–121.

Pitkänen, L. (1969). *A descriptive model of aggression and nonaggression with applications to children's behaviour* (Jyväskylä Studies in Education, Psychology and Social Research, Whole No. 19). Jyväskylä, Finland: University of Jyväskylä.

Pulkkinen, L. (1982). Self-control and continuity from childhood to adolescence. In B. P. Baltes & O. G. Brim, Jr. (Eds.), *Life-span development and behavior* (Vol. 4, pp. 63–105). New York: Academic Press.

Pulkkinen, L. (1986). The role of impulse control in the development of antisocial and prosocial behavior. In D. Olweus, J. Block, & M. Radke-Yarrow (Eds.), *Development of antisocial and prosocial behavior: Theories, research, and issues* (pp. 149–175). New York: Academic Press.

Pulkkinen, L. (1992). Life-styles in personality development. *European Journal of Personality, 6*(2), 139–155.

Pulkkinen, L. (1995). Behavioral precursors to accidents and resulting physical impairment. *Child Development, 66,* 1660–1679.

Pulkkinen, L. (1996). Proactive and reactive aggression in early adolescence as precursors to anti- and prosocial behavior in young adults. *Aggressive Behavior, 22,* 241–257.

Pulkkinen, L. (2000). Developmental psychology II: Adulthood and aging. In K. Pawlik & M. R. Rosenzweig (Eds.), *The International Handbook of Psychology* (pp. 261–282). London: Sage.

Pulkkinen, L. (2004). A longitudinal study on social development as an impetus for school reform towards an integrated school day. *European Psychologist, 9,* 125–141.

Pulkkinen, L., Fyrstén, S., Kinnunen, U., Kinnunen, M-L., Pitkänen, T., & Kokko, K. (2003). *40+ Erään ikäluokan selviytymistarina* [40+ A successful transition to middle adulthood in a cohort of Finns] (Rep. No. 349). Jyväskylä, Finland: University of Jyväskylä, Department of Psychology.

Pulkkinen, L., & Hämäläinen, M. (1995). Low self-control as a precursor to crime and accidents in a Finnish longitudinal study. *Criminal Behaviour and Mental Health, 5,* 424–438.

Pulkkinen, L., & Kokko, K. (2000). Identity development in adulthood: A longitudinal study. *Journal of Research in Personality, 34,* 445–470.

Pulkkinen, L., Nurmi, J.-E., & Kokko, K. (2002). Individual differences in personal goals in mid-thirties. In L. Pulkkinen & A. Caspi (Eds.), *Paths to successful development: Personality in the life course* (pp. 331–352). Cambridge, UK: Cambridge University Press.

Pulkkinen, L., Nygren, H., & Kokko, K. (2002). Successful development: Childhood antecedents of adaptive psychosocial functioning in adulthood. *Journal of Adult Development, 9,* 251–265.

Pulkkinen, L., Ohranen, M., & Tolvanen, A. (1999). Personality antecedents of career orientation and stability among women compared to men. *Journal of Vocational Behavior, 54,* 37–58.

Pulkkinen, L., & Pitkänen, T. (1994). A prospective study of the precursors to problem drinking in young adulthood. *Journal of Studies on Alcohol, 55,* 578–587.

Pulkkinen, L., & Rönkä, A. (1994). Personal control over development, identity formation, and future orientation as components of life orientation: A developmental approach. *Developmental Psychology, 30,* 260–271.

Pulver, A., Allik, J., Pulkkinen, L., & Hämäläinen, M. (1995). A Big Five Personality Inventory in two non-Indo-European languages. *European Journal of Personality, 9,* 109–124.

Rank, O. (1945). *Will therapy and truth and reality.* New York: Knopf.

Robins, R. W., John, O. P., & Caspi, A. (1998). The typological approach to studying personality. In R. B. Cairns, L. R. Bergman, & J. Kagan (Eds.), *Methods and models for studying the individual* (pp. 135–160). Thousand Oaks, CA: Sage.

Robins, R. W., & Tracy, J. L. (2003). Setting an agenda for a person-centered approach to personality development. *Monographs of the Society for Research in Child Development, 68,* 110–122.

Rönkä, A., Kinnunen, U., & Pulkkinen, L. (2000). The accumulation of problems of social functioning as a long-term process: Women and men compared. *International Journal of Behavioral Development, 24,* 442–450.

Rönkä, A., Oravala, S., & Pulkkinen, L. (2002). I met this wife of mine and things got onto a better track. *Journal of Adolescence, 25,* 47–63.

Rönkä, A., & Pulkkinen, L. (1995). Accumulation of problems in social functioning in young adulthood: A developmental approach. *Journal of Personality and Social Psychology, 69*(2), 381–391.

Rosenberg, M. (1965). *Society and the adolescent self-image.* Princeton, NJ: Princeton University Press.

Rothbart, M., & Bates, J. (1998). Temperament. In N. Eisenberg (Ed.), *Social, emotional, and personality development* (Handbook of Child Psychology, Vol. 3, pp. 105–176). New York: Wiley.

Rothbart, M. K., & Putnam, S. P. (2002). Temperament and socialization. In L. Pulkkinen & A. Caspi (Eds.), *Paths to successful development: Personality in the life course* (pp. 19–45). Cambridge, UK: Cambridge University Press.

Rutter, M. (1984). Continuities and discontinuities in socioemotional development: Empirical and conceptual perspectives. In R. Harmon & R. Emde (Eds.), *Continuities and discontinuities in development.* New York: Plenum.

Ryff, C. (1989). Happiness is everything, or is it? Explorations on the meaning of psychological well-being. *Journal of Personality and Social Psychology, 57,* 1069–1081.

Selzer, M. L. (1971). The Michigan Alcoholism Screening Test: The quest for a new diagnostic instrument. *American Journal of Psychiatry, 127,* 1653–1658.

Sihvola, J. (1996). Emotional animals: Do Aristotelian emotions require beliefs? *Apeiron, 29,* 105–144.

Statistics Finland. (2002). *Statistical Yearbook of Finland 2002.* Keuruu, Finland: Otava.

Vaillant, G. E., & Milofsky, E. (1980). The natural history of male psychological health: IX. Empirical evidence for Erikson's model of the life cycle. *American Journal of Psychiatry, 137,* 1348–1359.

Waterman, A. S. (1992). Identity as an aspect of optimal psychological functioning. In G. R. Adams, T. P. Gullotta, & R. Montemayor (Eds.), *Adolescent identity formation* (pp. 50–72). Newbury Park, CA: Sage.

York, K. L., & John, O. P. (1992). The four faces of Eve: A typological analysis of women's personality at midlife. *Journal of Personality and Social Psychology, 63,* 494–508.

Zuckerman, M. (1979). *Sensation seeking: Beyond the optimal level of arousal.* Hillsdale, NJ: Erlbaum.

Five

Impact of Past Transitions on Well-Being in Middle Age

Pasqualina Perrig-Chiello
and Sonja Perren

R ecent advances in research on middle age have shown that the ongoing demographic, economic, technical, cultural, and social changes have produced unprecedented diversity or variability in individuals of this age group. What in fact characterizes contemporary midlife is a growing diversity in roles, relationships, and resources, as people who are the same age can be at vastly different family or career stages (Moen & Wethington, 1999). This phenomenon has been referred to by some authors as the age-irrelevant society (Kohli & Künemund, 2004; Neugarten & Hagestad, 1976) or as the deinstitutionalization of the life course (Held, 1986). The current scientific debate focuses on whether the life course remains standardized (or "age-graded") or whether this standardization has been eroded in favor of a pluralization of lifestyles (Zapf, 1995). From a psychological perspective, this issue goes beyond the simple question whether life courses are still standardized or not. What is really of interest is the question whether and how this observed destandardization or increased variability has an impact on lifelong development and future well-being. The debate on an age-irrelevant society is indeed a very broad issue and a real desideratum in the agenda of midlife research. In this chapter, we will have the opportunity to consider some aspects of this debate.

When exactly is midlife? We can observe a general implicit consensus in literature assuming that middle age begins somewhere around 40 years and ends at about age 60 (Levinson, Darrow, Klein, Levinson, & McKee, 1978). However, there are different explicit approaches to answer the question about the time span of middle age—answers which are not concurrent but rather complement one another, focusing on central aspects of that life stage. One possibility is the statistical approach of defining midlife as the mean life expectancy from birth divided by 2 (in Switzerland, this would be 43 years for women and 39 years for men). Another approach postulates that the distinction of different life stages, such as middle age, mirrors the social regulation of the life course. It is a fact that working life has a structural function within the life course in our society; middle age is the time period following the development of a career and preceding retirement. Finally, it has been argued that the construct "middle age" stands for a subjective representation about one's position within the life course, for a "state of mind" (Fiske, 1979, p. 23). This subjective meaning is undoubtedly influenced by the typical biographical transitions that take place for a majority of this age group. In this sense, we can speak of middle age as an intersubjective interpretation of a certain phase in the life course with specific developmental tasks and themes. Considering these different definitions, we found it appropriate for our research to de-limit midlife as the time between the ages of 40 and 55.

Although it has been repeatedly suggested in lifespan psychology to study pathways or transitions rather than isolated stages—these being empirically valid metaphors of the life course—the majority of studies on midlife development have concentrated on this single life stage without considering the life history of individuals in terms of experiences and transitions in youth and young adulthood, all of which might shape the quality of present and future existence. Recent advances within a life course framework have begun to focus on life pathways, considering developmental transitions, trajectories and turning points over the life course (Wethington, Cooper, & Holmes, 1997; Wheaton & Gotlib, 1997; Willis & Reid, 1999; see also Pulkkinen, Feldt, & Kokko, Chapter 4, this volume). Some authors (Elder & Crosnoe, 2002; Grossmann & Grossmann, 1998) have emphasized the importance of past experiences and consequently the fact that individuals are the product of their life history as well as of situational demands, opportunities, and barriers. It has been assumed that the way in which individuals cope with the large number of normative and nonnormative transitions in adulthood may strongly influence their way of adapting to the challenges of later life, but little research has been done on this topic so far. Others have criticized the lack of reliable data on this concern (Rutter, 1996). The lack of data is especially striking for research on middle age. Therefore, the questions of how middle-aged persons have experienced past transitions and how these specific experiences may affect current well-being and subsequent aging are critical to an understanding of midlife development. Considering the changing societal context (shifting demographics and rapid societal change), along with the fact that people during midlife have more responsibilities (familial, professional, and public) than at any other time in life, it is surprising that well-being in midlife and its developmental determinants have seldom been an explicit target of scientific inquiry (Keyes & Ryff, 1999).

Biographical Transitions From a Life Course Perspective

Recent advances in lifespan developmental psychology suggest that individual lives can be characterized as a series of interrelated transitions. Biographical transitions define points in the life course when roles are transformed, redefined, and left behind for new ones. Life is full of transitions: starting school, puberty, finishing school, starting work, leaving home, getting married, having children, menopause, retirement, death of parents, and so forth. Transitions are therefore significant benchmarks in the human life cycle, which involve individual changes and role adaptations over the life span and give shape and direction to various aspects of a person's life (Mercer, Nichols, & Doyle, 1989; Sugarman, 2001).

Transitions can be classified—depending on their causal origin—as history-graded (wars, political and economical crises), normative age-graded (age-normed transitions such as puberty, climacteric change), and nonnormative (idiosyncratic, or "silent," because they are unexpected and not determined by age norms or age expectations; transitions such as accidents, losses, illness). Furthermore, it is assumed that transitions are embedded in trajectories, which give them meaning (Baltes, Reese, & Lipsitt, 1980; Elder, 1998). In this chapter, we will concentrate on both individual age-normed (-graded) and nonnormative transitions. The life course perspective assumes that the content and timing of age-normed transitions are dependent on biological heritage as well as on the historical, demographical, and social structural factors that shape the typical life course of individuals (Elder & Rockwell, 1979). Biological maturation sets the boundaries for the occurrence of normative social transitions, such as readiness for leaving the parental home or having children. Other transitions are socially regulated. For example, developmental trajectories are subject to gender differences, meaning that women's transitions may differ from those of men mainly because of the different societal expectations or circumstances. Besides these age-normed transitions, there are significant sudden changes that may launch a person on a new developmental path at almost any stage of life (Kuhlen, 1959). These unique, nonnormative transitions are usually unexpected and therefore associated with considerable stress (Chiriboga, 1997). In fact, the emotional valence of transitions—that is, how good or bad a transition has been experienced emotionally and remembered—may play an equally important role in subsequent well-being, in addition to the impact of the timing or degree of anticipation of the event. Considering the fact that little work has been done on individual, group, and gender differences concerning the differential impact of earlier transitions on midlife adaptation, this chapter will highlight the predictive power of (a) timing and emotional valence of age-normed transitions and (b) earlier stressors such as nonnormative transitions on well-being in middle age and on expectations of old age.

Well-Being and Its Relation to Biographical and Psychosocial Resources

The relationship between well-being and its correlates and predictors has received much attention in recent research on successful developmental adaptation and aging. A review of the literature reveals a considerable amount of divergence in definitions of what "well-being" is (Kahneman, Diener, & Schwarz, 1999; Keyes, Shmotkin, & Ryff, 2002; Ryan & Deci, 2000). This diversity of definitions supports a multidimensional nature of the construct. In the field of positive psychology, there exist various conceptions about well-being, most of them focusing mainly on *psychological* well-being (Ryff, 1989); this type of well-being is in contrast to physical and social well-being. The majority of theories of well-being are based on bottom-up models. Well-being is understood from the bottom up, by reference to lower-order structural units or antecedents (determinants, predictors), which are defined on different levels from objective predictors (such as neurological, biological, and physiological variables) to subjective ones (such as physical, psychological, and social resources). Bottom-up approaches assume that the only way to understand and effect a change in well-being is to modify the predictor characteristics (Kahneman et al., 1999; Kozma, Stones, & McNeil, 1991).

Our approach to the conceptualization of well-being is also based on a bottom-up model and focuses on positive functioning founded in developmental, clinical, and mental health literature (Kahneman et al., 1999; Ryff, 1989). We conceptualize well-being as a multidimensional construct involving psychological well-being (life satisfaction, life purpose, mastery) and future expectations (for details, especially on psychometric quality, see Perrig-Chiello, 1997). Good functioning on these dimensions depends on the lower-order structural units, which can be grouped into two categories: (a) the currently disposable psychosocial resources and (b) the biographical resources. The biographical resources consist of the actual sequence of transitions and life events (incidence, timing, duration) and of the remembered emotional valence of these events. The psychosocial resources are a combination of individual features (such as personality and coping strategies) and of social networks (such as partnerships, children, family ties, and friends). Figure 5.1 illustrates our assumptions concerning the dynamics of biographical transitions, psychosocial resources, and well-being, all of which will be outlined later in this chapter.

The Dynamics of Biographical Transitions, Resources, and Well-Being: A Theoretical Framework

The question regarding the extent to which actual early life biographical transitions shape future development and how they predict well-being in middle age and future expectations of old age has attracted increasing attention from researchers in developmental psychology (Pulkkinen & Caspi, 2002). Research on this topic started from very different conceptual bases. The main approaches were growth models, lifespan models, and

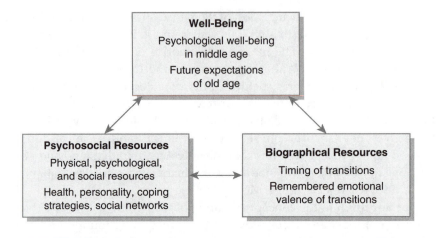

Figure 5.1   Well-Being and Its Psychosocial and Biographical Preconditions

life course models. These approaches differ in their scope and the extent to which different behavioral mechanisms and goals have an impact on successful development. Key areas of focus are, for example, the successful resolution of psychosocial crises (Erikson, 1959), accomplishment of developmental tasks (Havighurst, 1972), the "social clock" in particular cultures (Helson, Mitchell, & Moane, 1984), social trajectories (Elder, 1998), emotion regulation (Pulkkinen, Nygren, & Kokko, 2002), and attachment or resiliency (Grossmann & Grossmann, 1998; Werner & Smith, 2003). Common to all these approaches is their focus on the question on how individuals handle age-graded tasks and transitions over the life span.

Based on our model (Figure 5.1) and on the status quo of current research, we want to highlight in this chapter (a) the long-term impact that age-normed transitions can have on well-being, especially in midlife, and (b) the question how nonnormative transitions might affect subsequent development, particularly adjustment in middle age.

Early Age-Normed Transitions and Their Long-Term Impact on Well-Being in Middle Age

One hundred years ago, the life course was highly unpredictable as death was a ubiquitous fate that could occur at any stage of life. With the increasing advancement of social and medical care for the majority of the population and the longer life expectancy associated with it, the life course became more and more predictable. Given these societal changes, since the middle of the 20th century, psychological theories of normative development have proposed that individuals are confronted with an age-related order of developmental tasks throughout life (Havighurst, 1953; Erikson, 1968). These theories focus on the age-structured, individual life plan and on the typical sequences or pathways in which a multitude of roles are adopted, fulfilled, and terminated (e.g., entering/finishing school, puberty/becoming an adult, leaving home, marrying, having children, retiring). According to this perspective, the successful transition into, and the adoption of, age-specific roles are among the main developmental tasks to be fulfilled by individuals (Elder & Caspi, 1990). Age-normed transitions reflect the socially shared expectations about age-appropriate behavior, which in its turn is highly dependent on chronological age. This is especially true for transitions in childhood and adolescence (e.g., maturation and the correlated social expectations concerning gender roles, embodiment in the adult world of work and relationships).

Given the rapid societal and demographical changes, it has been argued that transitions are being experienced on a less normative and more individuated basis (e.g., a 40-year-old woman can become a mother or else a grandmother for the first time; a 50-year-old man may be professionally burned out, whereas a woman of the same age can restart her professional career full of motivation). That is, the timing of occupational training, marriage, parenthood, and retirement tends to be increasingly idiosyncratic, so that biographies now are less and less similar (Chiriboga, 1989; Kohli, 1986). This debate has initiated research around the following questions: Is the life course still normatively structured? Are the factors of age and timing of transitions still relevant for successful development in later life? Considering the existing literature on this matter, we can observe that changes in the normativity of life course patterns and transitional series vary across different cultural settings, social status, gender, and different phases of the life course (Wrosch & Freund, 2001).

It has been shown that life course patterns in Germany are more stable than in the United States or in Great Britain (Mayer, 1998). Results from our own research demonstrate that in Switzerland—similarly to Germany—life course pathways are still experienced as relatively stable and very similar concerning age and timing of transitions in a representative sample of middle-aged persons (Perrig-Chiello & Höpflinger, 2004). Our results suggest, for example, that due to the relatively lower mobility, stronger family ties, and higher social pressure (in comparison to the United States), the majority of middle-aged women in Switzerland are confronted with the obligation to help their frail and dependent parents (Perrig-Chiello & Sturzenegger, 2001). These results concur with those of other studies that have found evidence that even today, individuals' development seems to be related to an age-graded structuring of the life course (i.e., different life tasks are sequenced in an age-related order), even if in some studies a broadening of the age range has been observed, in which certain transitions occur or are expected to occur (Heckhausen, 1997; Neugarten, 1968; Nurmi, 1992; Settersten & Hagestad, 1996).

The Importance of the Transition to Adulthood for Successful Adaptation in Later Life

Societal regulation of the timing is not equal for all age groups. Events in childhood and adolescence are much more age-normed and regulated than are events in the later years. Obviously, social norms for the socialization phase are still quite rigid, for example, concerning school and vocational training and establishing families. This fact implies, at the same time, that this phase is a critical one in the sense that missing the right timing of an age-normed transition (which would represent a violation of social norms) would probably lead to social sanctions and far-reaching negative consequences for future development. This is especially true for middle-aged adults, because at this biographical point it becomes evident that the options for realizing goals or tasks are more and more limited (limited time left, limited professional options, biological [fertility] deadline for women, etc.).

In fact, there is empirical evidence that timing, sequencing, and experience of early life events lead to various outcomes later in the life course and can have enduring consequences by affecting subsequent transitions, even after many years and decades have passed. Based on secondary analysis of three large-scale population surveys of adults, Kessler, Gillis-Light, Magee, Kendler, and Eaves (1997) found a significant relationship between retrospectively reported measures of specific childhood adversity during age-normed transitions and several dimensions of adult psychopathology. Many studies have shown a range of effects later in life following the experience of specific transitions, especially in adolescence (e.g., psychological functioning during puberty and adolescence was significantly correlated with that in middle and old age; Clausen, 1991;

Hogan, 1981; Vaillant, 1990). In the same vein, Caspi (1993) has shown that some life course events can have a significant impact on the organization of the future self; the transition from childhood to adulthood was the most vulnerable and had the most impact on future development. Based on data from the Berkeley Guidance Study, the Berkeley Growth Study, and the Adolescent (Oakland) Growth Study, Clausen (1993) has argued that adolescent planful competence (in the sense of fulfillment of developmental tasks concerning academic and occupational achievement) has a substantial bearing on successful role performance in later adulthood. Consistent with the findings of Clausen (1993), Laub and Sampson (1998) found empirical evidence that adolescent competence emerges as an important influence on later developmental outcomes (in young adulthood and in middle age) despite controlling for measures such as intelligence and family background. Results from the Flanders prospective longitudinal study by Verhofstadt-Denève, Schittekatte, and Van Leeuwen (2003) indicate a significant relationship between psychosocial experiences during adolescence (e.g., early school leaving) and degree of well-being in young adulthood for both sexes, but especially for women. The cumulative negative developmental consequences of early school leaving, such as low self-esteem and greater risk of unemployment, also were shown by other studies (Dooley & Prause, 1997; Menaghan, 1997).

However, the question of timing is crucial not only for the rather socially determined transitions, such as school leaving and occupation, which have a far-reaching effect on later development, but also for the more biologically determined ones, like puberty and the developmental tasks directly related to it (such as developing a good body image and gender identity, which are biologically as well as socially determined). It has been argued that being off-time concerning puberty has negative developmental consequences (Brim & Ryff, 1980; Caspi & Moffitt, 1991). Koff and Rierdan (1993) found in their study that early adolescent girls with advanced pubertal development have an elevated risk of developing a negative body image and eating disorders. However, it has to be specified that gender differences may play a decisive role concerning the question of whether or not being off-time with puberty has a negative developmental effect. Results of different studies suggest negative outcomes for women but not for men (Clausen, 1975; Ewert, 1984).

There are different theoretical and empirical approaches to demonstrating the significant impact of the transition to adulthood on future development, including midlife. According to Erikson, the way in which the major task of adolescence—the achievement of a secure sense of identity—is resolved is determinant for future experiences such as the generativity task in midlife (Erikson, 1968). Findings from a longitudinal study conducted by Josselson (1987) show that the configuration of identity in adolescence forms the templates for adulthood, and as Vandewater and Stewart (1997) point out, identity development (identity generally thought of as an accomplishment of adolescence) has important consequences for midlife well-being. In the same vein, Levinson and associates (1978) have formulated four major tasks that have to be fulfilled during this crucial transition and which determine future development: formulating a life's dream, forming mentor relationships, establishing an occupation, and establishing love and family relationships. These are indeed tasks that should constitute the solid base for future outcomes, especially for generative behavior. There is empirical evidence that successful accomplishment of developmental tasks at an earlier stage of development sets the scene for later psychological health (Stewart, Ostrove, & Helson, 2001). Finally, Ryff and Heidrich's (1997) study shows that normative events and transitions early in life are significant predictors of multiple aspects of present and future well-being for different age groups (young, middle, and old age). Taken together, there is impressive empirical evidence that the transition to adulthood, specifically puberty, is a crucial one for predicting development in later adulthood.

Negative Nonnormative Risks: Impact of Resilience and Biographical Turning Points for Midlife Development

A few longitudinal studies in Europe and the United States were conducted to investigate the impact of adverse experiences in childhood or adolescence on later development (Clausen, 1993; Elder, 1999; Hagnell, Essen-Möller, Lanke, Öjesjö, & Rorsman, 1990; Vaillant, 1990; Werner & Smith, 2003). Many of those study participants have now reached midlife. Biological and psychosocial risk factors, such as perinatal stress, parental psychopathology, or poverty, as well as stressful life events, such as parents' divorce or abuse were of research interest. From a life course perspective, such events can be regarded as negative nonnormative transitions. One of the most striking findings of different studies is the surprisingly high percentage of persons, even of high-risk samples, who show positive psychosocial adaptation in midlife, despite having had a difficult childhood (Werner & Smith, 2003).

What we can learn from these studies is that various life course trajectories can lead to being well and healthy in midlife. Some of the high-risk individuals never showed signs of maladjustment (i.e., they seemed to be "vulnerable but invincible"; Werner, 1996), whereas others could recover from maladjustment in earlier developmental stages. For the first group of individuals, the *process of resilience* is important; for the second group, we speak of *turning points*. Resilience is a dynamic process that allows maintaining positive adjustment despite negative experiences (Luthar, Cicchetti, & Becker, 2000). Recovering from a negative life trajectory (e.g., from delinquency) can be considered as a turning point (Rutter, 1996).

Resilience and Protective Factors

Most of the larger longitudinal studies on risk and resilience, which include participants in middle age, were conducted in the United States; data on large European samples are quite scarce. One exception is the Lundby Study, a prospective, longitudinal population study (original $N = 2,550$) on mental health, which started in 1947 in Sweden (Hagnell et al., 1990). Cederblad (1996) interviewed participants of the Lundby study when they were in middle age (42–56 years old). Persons ($n = 148$) who had three or more childhood psychiatric risk factors were interviewed. The interviews were designed to detect salutogenetic factors in the lives of the participants. Three out of four were functioning well in midlife despite having been exposed to various psychiatric risk factors in childhood (e.g., death of parents, divorce, abuse). Protective factors were intellectual capacity and self-esteem in childhood, a desire to change one's fate in adolescence, as well as growing up in a small family with a trusting relationship with one of the parents (Cederblad, 1996; Cederblad, Dahlin, Hagnell, & Hansson, 1994).

In the United States, Ryff and collaborators investigated the life histories of some women of the Wisconsin Longitudinal Study and identified different pathways to resilience in midlife. Good early starting resources, high-quality social relationships, job achievements, and a positive self-evaluation served as protective factors (Ryff, Singer, & Seltzer, 2002). In sum, various protective factors were identified, covering mainly two dimensions: personal resources (e.g., easy temperament, high self-esteem, internal locus of control) and positive social relationships (e.g., positive parenting or forming supportive social relationships outside the family).

Biographical Turning Points

In their Kauai Study, Werner and Smith (2003) examined the developmental trajectories of the entire population of children born on the island of Kauai in 1955 from birth on. About one third of the children were subject to at least one risk factor for their future development such as perinatal stress, poverty, substance abuse, or mental illness in the family. Two-thirds of these "high-risk" children had serious learning or behavior problems by the time they were ten, and mental health problems, juvenile delinquency records, or pregnancy by age 18. One-third of high-risk children, however, never seemed to develop serious problems. The children of the Kauai study have now also reached midlife (Werner & Smith, 2003). Most participants showed a successful adaptation and high psychological well-being in middle adulthood. This was true for the resilient participants (the ones who never showed maladjustment or mental health problems) as well as for a part of the troubled adolescents. Most participants with serious coping problems in midlife (about 16% of the cohort) also were troubled adolescents with learning and mental health problems or delinquency. However, when taking a prospective look, only a small proportion of troubled adolescents or children with adverse childhood experiences had poor outcomes in midlife. For a considerable number of the teenage mothers, delinquent boys, and individuals with learning or mental health problems, the opening up of opportunities in young and middle adulthood led to positive changes in their life course. Continuing education, vocational skills acquired in military service, geographical moves, marriage to a stable partner, conversion to being an active participant of a church, recovery from a life-threatening illness or accident, as well as psychotherapy were identified as turning points (Werner & Smith, 2003). Military service was identified as being a positive turning point in the lives of the economically disadvantaged men of the Berkeley and Oakland cohorts (Elder, 1986). This latter finding points to important sociohistorical and cultural differences, which have to be considered when investigating turning points in people's lives. For example, military service in Switzerland is mandatory and is thus an age-normed transition for young men, whereas in other countries, for example, the United States, military service has more profound implications for a person's profession and living conditions and may thus, in fact, represent a turning point. Human development is characterized by continuities and discontinuities (Rutter, 1989). Results of longitudinal studies encompassing childhood to midlife show, in an impressive manner, that biographical turning points may lead to an improvement in psychosocial adaptation and well-being in middle age.

An Illustrative Example: A Longitudinal Study on Biographical Transitions, Life Perspectives, and Well-Being in Midlife

To illustrate what has been said so far, and to supply some additional empirical evidence from a Swiss perspective, we will present results from a large interdisciplinary project titled "Transitions and Life Perspectives in Middle Age" (Perrig-Chiello, Höpflinger, Kaiser, & Sturzenegger, 1999).

Rationale and Description of the Study

The rationale of this project is a transactional model of personality, which claims that individuals try to cope with age-normed (e.g., climacteric change, departure of the children) and nonnormative (e.g., divorce, health problems) transitions by activating their available external and personal resources (e.g., Perren & Perrig-Chiello, 2003; Perrig-Chiello & Sturzenegger, 2001). This view postulates that individuals—based on their biographical experience—develop strategies that allow them to adapt their life perspectives to bring continuity to their lives and to ensure their well-being. In this chapter, we especially want to highlight the results in connection with the question of the impact of past transitions on both current well-being and anticipation of old age (Perrig-Chiello, Höpflinger, et al., 1999; Perrig-Chiello & Höpflinger, 2004).

First, we will focus on the question of the timing and emotional valence of age-normed and nonnormative transitions—in childhood, adolescence, and young adulthood—experienced by a sample of Swiss persons in midlife. Second, we are interested in the predictive power of the retrospective emotional appraisal of these past transitions for current psychological well-being in midlife and for expectations of well-being in old age. Special attention is given to age, gender, current living condition, and personality differences.

Participants

Two hundred and sixty-eight middle-aged persons (197 women, 71 men) participated in the interview study (mean age = 47.2 years). The sample is a subsample of a larger survey study ($N = 1,015$) and can be considered as being representative of a healthy, middle-aged, urban population in Switzerland (Perrig-Chiello, Höpflinger, et al., 1999). Participants belonged to two age groups: The younger group was at the transition to midlife (40–45 years old), "late baby boomers" born between 1953 and 1958. The older group was in the middle of midlife (50–55 years old), "early baby boomers" born between 1943 and 1948. Fifty-two percent of the participants belonged to the younger age group (mean age = 42.3 years), 48% to the older age group (mean age = 52.1 years). The early social context of the older age group was rather conservative and restrictive. They were born during and directly after World War II, which was a constant threat for Switzerland because of its neutral status; they had their schooling in the 1950s and puberty before 1968. The younger age group went to school in the early 1960s and experienced puberty around 1968, which is a societal turning point standing for more personal freedom, more openness, and less commitment to traditional norms.

Our sample included men and women varying in marital status, parenthood, and employment status. The sample included "double-track women" (married with children, with employment; 21.6%), "conventional housewives" (married with children, without employment; 19.3%), "single mothers" (single with children; 18.5%), "single women" (single without children; 11.3%), "working fathers" (married with children, with employment; 25.7%), and "single men" (single without children; 4.8%).

Procedure and Instruments

Participants completed two questionnaires (psychological well-being and personality) and were given an in-depth interview on biographical transitions (timing and emotional valence of age-normed and nonnormative transitions; Perrig-Chiello & Höpflinger, 2004). The crucial variables were assessed using the procedure we discuss next.

A list of age-normed and frequent non–age-normed transitions was presented, and participants indicated the age at which the specific transition occurred (*timing*). In addition, the *emotional valence* of each event as experienced at that time was assessed. The list referred to transitions across the whole life span (from school entry, puberty, first love through retirement and grandparenthood). At this point in time, participants had already experienced a series of transitions in the past, were currently undergoing others, and anticipated possible future ones. In addition to identifying the age-normed transitions, participants were asked to indicate other (nonnormative) transitions or life events in their biographies. They also indicated timing and emotional valence of these nonnormative transitions. Emotional valence of the anticipated transition to old age (*anticipation "being old"*) was also assessed.

Psychological well-being in middle age was assessed, including the dimensions of life satisfaction, life purpose, and mastery (for more details on this instrument, see Perrig-Chiello, 1996, 1997). *Physical well-being* was assessed by a single-item question on subjective health self-evaluation. *Personality* was assessed by means of the NEO-Five Factor Inventory (Costa & McCrae, 1985), the five factors being neuroticism, extraversion, openness to experience, conscientiousness, and agreeableness.

Age-Normed Transitions— Timing, Emotional Valence, and Their Impact on Well-Being in Middle Age

Timing of Age-Normed Transitions

Timing of age-normed transitions was examined for group differences in age, gender, and living conditions in midlife (single men, married men with children, single women, single-parent women, conventional homemaker and mother, double-track women; for more details, see Perrig-Chiello & Perren, in press). The results yielded significant gender and age group differences. As can be seen in Table 5.1, the women participants experienced puberty at an earlier age than did men. They also reported leaving home, getting married, and having their first child earlier than did men (see Table 5.1).

Furthermore, significant age group differences emerged regarding timing of puberty and leaving home. For all these transitions, the older age group reported a later onset (see Table 5.1). Finally, we found significant differences concerning the timing of transitions of the different living conditions of middle-aged persons. Women who were single parents entered puberty at a significantly earlier age than the others, and single women left home at a significantly earlier age than the others.

Table 5.1 Timing of Experienced Age-Normed Transitions by Gender, Age Groups, and Living Conditions (Means and Standard Deviations)

Transition	Gender		Age Group		Living Condition in Midlife					
	Men (N = 71)[a]	Women (N = 197)	40-45 (N = 141)	50-55 (N = 127)	Double-track women (N = 69)	Conventional housewives (N = 51)	Single women (N = 30)	Single-parent women (N = 47)	Single men (N = 13)	Married men with children (N = 58)
School entry	6.7	6.7	6.8	6.6	6.7	6.8	6.8	6.7	6.6	6.7
	(0.5)	(0.6)	(0.6)	(0.5)	(0.5)	(0.5)	(0.8)	(0.5)	(0.5)	(0.5)
Puberty	14.4	13.4	13.4	14.0	13.5	13.4	13.5	13.1	14.9	14.3
	(1.7)	(1.4)	(1.5)	(1.6)	(1.5)	(1.4)	(1.7)	(1.2)	(3.0)	(1.3)
First employment	20.7	19.8	20.0	20.0	20.4	19.1	20.1	19.6	21.0	20.6
	(4.6)	(3.2)	(3.5)	(3.8)	(3.1)	(3.0)	(3.4)	(3.4)	(5.6)	(4.4)
First love	18.0	18.4	17.9	18.7	17.9	18.1	19.7	18.5	18.8	17.9
	(3.8)	(3.3)	(3.3)	(3.5)	(3.0)	(3.4)	(3.9)	(2.9)	(4.0)	(3.8)
Leaving home	22.0	20.6	20.6	21.4	20.5	20.7	20.0	20.8	23.3	21.7
	(3.1)	(3.4)	(3.7)	(2.9)	(3.1)	(2.7)	(3.8)	(4.1)	(3.1)	(3.1)
Getting married	26.5	25.0	25.7	25.1	25.0	25.3	25.8	24.5	26.7	26.5
	(4.1)	(4.6)	(5.0)	(3.8)	(3.9)	(5.1)	(4.0)	(5.1)	(5.7)	(3.8)
Birth of first child	30.1	27.8	28.8	28.0	28.6	27.9	—	26.6	24.7	30.5
	(4.5)	(4.9)	(4.8)	(5.0)	(4.3)	(5.6)	—	(4.9)	(2.2)	(4.4)

a. Transitions were not experienced by all participants. Thus, sample sizes vary (total $N > 225$).

Despite the postulate in the literature that the timing of transitions is becoming more and more idiosyncratic, the biographies of our sample showed considerable similarity in the timing of these transitions, with only small variation in age for childhood, adolescence, and young adulthood. However, it is also true that there are some important age group and gender differences to be taken into account and that—especially in middle adulthood—a greater variation in the nature and timing of experienced transitions is to be observed.

The detected age and gender differences in timing of transitions may underline their biological regulation but still with considerable societal input. Women report experiencing the onset of puberty significantly earlier than men. This is even true for the women of the older age group, who report having experienced the onset of puberty later than the younger group. Even though the two age groups are only 10 years apart, this fact reflects the secular acceleration of puberty. The other reported significant gender difference in the timing of transitions reflects the ongoing strong social regulation of transitions: Women still leave home, marry, and have children at an earlier point in time than do men. In Western culture, the Swiss culture included, women are still expected to be younger than their partners and the fathers of their children; furthermore, they are expected to be autonomous and able to run their own household at an earlier age than men (de Vries & Watt, 1996). Finally, our results show that both single-parent women and single women had significant earlier onsets of age-normed transitions (puberty and departure from home). It has to be specified here that these two groups of women are the ones with the most restricted resources (either social or financial), the most problems (health problems, financial problems), and the lowest physical and psychological well-being (Kaiser & Perrig-Chiello, 2000). These results indicate that these two groups can be seen as problem groups, an assumption that will be confirmed by our next analysis concerning the emotional valence of age-normed and nonnormative transitions.

Emotional Valence of Age-Normed Transitions

In addition to asking about the timing of transitions, we asked participants to indicate, in retrospect, how they had emotionally experienced the transitions at that time. The results yielded several significant main effects for gender but not for age. Women experienced school entry more positively but evaluated their transition to marriage and becoming parents more negatively than did men (Figure 5.2).

Figure 5.2   Emotional Valence of Age-Normed Transitions by Gender

Although the literature reports considerable gender differences concerning the number of remembered relational and romantic life events (women reporting significantly more events than men), better recollection does not seem to be associated with more positive memories. In our sample, women evaluated their transition to marriage and parenthood more negatively than did men. It seems that for women, these transitions represent radical changes with far-reaching effects in life trajectories. From the perspective of Swiss middle-aged women, becoming a wife and mother still seems to imply a much more substantial role change than it does for men. In contrast, men have not had to change their career plans or their role in the labor force, which is known to be an important source of purposive activity, independence, social relations, and self-respect (Moen & Wethington, 1999). Finally, the comparison of the overall emotional estimation of the past age-normed transitions with the different living condition groups is revealing. Our results show significant differences, with single-parent women and single men having the lowest emotional overall estimation of their past transitions and working fathers, working mothers, and housewives having the highest one.

Prior Age-Normed Transitions and
Personality as Predictors of Well-Being in Middle Age

Hierarchical regression analyses were performed to evaluate the predictive power of emotional valence of experienced transitions, together with personality variables, for psychological and physical well-being and anticipation of "being old." Age group and gender, emotional valence of transitions from childhood to young adulthood (school entry, puberty, first love, job entry, marriage, birth), as well as personality variables, served as independent variables. We entered age group and gender as block 1, emotional valence of transitions as block 2, and personality variables as block 3. Anticipation of being old (emotional valence), psychological well-being (the sum of the three subtests: "mastery," "sense of life," and "satisfaction with life"), and physical well-being served as dependent variables. Results reveal that anticipation of the transition to old age ("becoming old") was best predicted by the emotional valence of puberty and also by neuroticism (see Table 5.2). The more negatively puberty was experienced, and the higher the neuroticism score, the more negatively the transition to old age was anticipated.

Emotional valence of puberty also was a significant predictor of psychological well-being in middle age, but only before entering personality variables into the model. Psychological well-being in middle age was predicted in the final model by neuroticism and conscientiousness. Low scores for neuroticism and high scores for conscientiousness were associated with high psychological well-being. As can be seen in Table 5.2, a major increase in overall model fit was observed when the personality variables were included in the prediction of psychological well-being in midlife. Finally, neuroticism predicted physical well-being, but physical well-being did not seem be related to the experience of past transitions.

Our results confirm other empirical findings, namely, that the transition to adulthood is a crucial biographical transition for predicting future developmental perspectives. Even after controlling for age and gender, the remembered emotional valence of this specific transition (puberty) still has a significant impact on anticipation of old age in middle-aged persons. It has been suggested that puberty can be seen as an anchor point from which we begin the story of our adult lives, and that the memories from this period help us define who we are later in life (Fitzgerald, 1988; Fitzgerald & Shifley-Grove, 1999; Rybash, 1999). According to Erikson (1959), the way in which the major task of adolescence (the achievement of a secure sense of identity) is resolved determines the way future life

Table 5.2 Age-Normed Transitions and Personality Predicting Well-Being in Midlife: Results of the Hierarchical Regression Analysis

Model	Independent Variables	Psychological Well-Being in Midlife	Physical Well-Being in Midlife	Anticipation "Being Old"[a]
Model I	Gender (female = 1)	−.12**	−.11	−.06
	Age group (older = 1)	.09	.02	.08
Model II	Gender	−.15	−.07	−.01
	Age group	.08	.01	.07
	School entry (EV)[b]	−.08	.00	−.00
	Puberty (EV)	.18*	.02	.19*
	First love (EV)	.02	−.04	.13
	Leaving home (EV)	.01	−.05	.06
	Job entry (EV)	.15	.04	.15
	Getting married (EV)	.12	.09	.11
	Birth first child (EV)	−.02	.07	−.02
Model III	Gender	.01	.03	.05
	Age group	.03	−.02	.05
	School entry (EV)	−.06	.03	−.02
	Puberty (EV)	.08	−.05	.18*
	First love (EV)	.05	−.02	.13
	Leaving home (EV)	−.03	−.07	.05
	Job entry (EV)	.02	−.04	.13
	Getting married (EV)	.09	.05	.11
	Birth first child (EV)	−.05	.05	−.02
	Neuroticism	−.53**	−.35**	−.19*
	Extraversion	.01	.05	.01
	Openness	−.05	−.07	.03
	Conscientiousness	.18*	.05	−.01
	Agreeableness	−.02	−.03	−.10
Model Summary	Model I	$R^2 = .05$; $F_{change} = 4.6**$	$R^2 = .01$; $F_{change} = 1.1$	$R^2 = .01$; $F_{change} = 0.9$
	Model II	$R^2 = .13$; $F_{change} = 2.1*$	$R^2 = .03$; $F_{change} = 0.3$	$R^2 = .13$; $F_{change} = 3.0*$
	Model III	$R^2 = .42$; $F_{change} = 15.7**$	$R^2 = .15$; $F_{change} = 4.8**$	$R^2 = .16$; $F_{change} = 1.2$

a. Values represent betas ($N = 175$); b. EV = emotional valence.

$^*p < .05$; $^{**}p < .01$.

events will be experienced. Findings from a longitudinal study conducted by Josselson (1987) did indeed show that the configuration of identity in adolescence forms the template for adulthood.

Our results show further that the predictive power of the emotional valence of puberty is no longer significant when personality variables are considered as predictors for current psychological well-being in midlife. These results indicate that the reconstruction of one's own past (i.e., the reconstruction of past transitions) is strongly related to personality factors. In fact, there is empirical evidence that a person's coping style and adaptive devices in early adolescence are important in determining their future life course (Elder & Crosnoe, 2002; Moen, 1997; Vaillant, 1977).

The other important finding concerns both of the groups differing in living conditions: the single-parent women and the single women. Both have a significant earlier onset of two important age-normed transitions in their earlier years: puberty and departure from home. Furthermore, they reported more nonnormative transitions and showed lower overall emotional valence of past transitions (see Table 5.3). Singles also have the lowest level of psychological and physical well-being. As already mentioned in the theoretical section of this chapter, being off-time in age-normed transitions can have negative consequences on well-being. Our results show that this deteriorating effect persists many years later. We can speculate that the direct negative effects of being off-time at the time an early-life transition occurs could impact subsequent nonnormative transitions as consequences (broken relationships, involuntary pregnancies, etc.).

Nonnormative Transitions: Timing, Emotional Valence, and Agency

Nonnormative Transitions Over the Life Course

In addition to the previously presented age-normed transitions, participants were asked to indicate (nonnormative) transitions or life events in their lives. A total of 443 life events were mentioned. Seventy-three percent of the participants reported one or more nonnormative transition; 29% of these transitions concerned the marital relationship; 25% illness, accidents, and death; 16% job and education; 13% family issues; 11% living arrangements; and 5% other issues (see Table 5.3). The reported nonnormative transitions range from very negative events (e.g., suicide or accidents of close persons) to very positive events (e.g., adoption of a child). There was considerable interindividual variability in the number and content of experienced nonnormative transitions. Women reported significantly more nonnormative transitions than did men. Men nominated more positive nonnormative transitions than women. Nonnormative transitions were unevenly distributed across the life span; that is, 8% occurred in childhood (0–14 years), 12% in adolescence (15–22 years), 40% in young adulthood (23–35 years), and 41% in adulthood (35–55 years).

The nonnormative transitions were categorized based on their content and on their causality, that is, whether the transition was caused by external forces (e.g., illness or death of a spouse) or whether it was self-initiated (self-agency; e.g., new job or new vocational training). More than half (61%) of the transitions involved self-agency. Transitions with self-agency were evaluated mainly as positive, whereas transitions that were induced by external forces were mostly negatively connotated (with self-agency: $M = 6.14$, $SD = 3.63$; without self-agency: $M = 2.40$, $SD = 2.31$). Men reported more nonnormative transitions with than without self-agency (75.6% vs. 24.4%), whereas women reported about the same percentage of each kind of transition (58.1% vs. 41.9%; Perren & Perrig-Chiello, 2002).

Self-agency of transitions was significantly associated with developmental stages. In childhood, only 21% of transitions involved self-agency, in adolescence 47%, in young adulthood 72%, and in adulthood 62%. Moreover, nonnormative transitions in childhood were more negatively experienced than transitions in later life (childhood: $M = 2.39$, $SD = 2.55$; adolescence: $M = 4.57$, $SD = 3.97$; young adulthood: $M = 5.07$, $SD = 3.64$; adulthood: $M = 4.67$, $SD = 3.63$).

Nonnormative Transitions and Living Conditions in Midlife

The analysis of variance regarding the number of transitions shows significant effects of living conditions in middle age. Single women and single mothers named more nonnormative transitions than did working mothers, working fathers, and single men. The overrepresentation of nonnormative transitions among single mothers and single women was partly due—as expected—to more frequent mentions of marital relationship transitions. But single women also named job and education transitions more frequently than did married women. Single mothers nominated family issues transitions more frequently. Single women not only experienced more frequently separations and forming of new relationships, they were

Table 5.3 Nonnormative Transitions: Frequency of Nominations, Timing, and Emotional Valence

Main Category	Categories, Differentiated	Frequency of Nominations			Timing	Emotional Valence
		Women (count)	Men (count)	Total (in %)	M (SD)	M (SD)
Illness, accidents, and death	Illness (own)	23	7	7%	30.9 (14.2)	1.6 (1.0)
	Illness (others)	14	2	4%	34.3 (9.5)	2.2 (1.5)
	Accident (own)	5	1	1%	28.5 (15.9)	2.8 (4.0)
	Accident (others)	2	1	1%	23.3 (7.8)	1.7 (1.2)
	Therapy	5	2	2%	38.4 (9.5)	8.0 (3.2)
	Suicide attempt (own)	3		1%	21.0 (10.1)	2.3 (2.3)
	Suicide/-attempt (others)	7		2%	26.0 (11.2)	1.9 (1.6)
	Death among friends	8		2%	32.8 (8.6)	3.1 (2.6)
	Death in family	28	4	7%	32.3 (12.6)	2.1 (1.9)
	Total	**95**	**17**	**25%**	**31.4 (12.3)**	**2.4 (2.3)**
Marital relationship	New relationship	22	9	7%	31.7 (6.6)	8.3 (1.9)
	Break-up/separation/divorce	80	19	22%	36.3 (8.1)	3.8 (3.1)
	Total	**102**	**28**	**29%**	**35.3 (8.0)**	**4.9 (3.4)**
Family issues	Adoption	2	2	1%	33.5 (2.6)	10.0 (0.0)
	Miscarriage, abortion	23		5%	29.4 (8.6)	2.3 (1.9)
	Family/education	11	4	3%	37.1 (8.6)	3.7 (3.4)
	Parents/sisters, brothers	8		2%	29.8 (16.4)	3.3 (3.4)
	Divorce (others)	7	1	2%	26.0 (19.7)	1.4 (0.7)
	Total	**51**	**7**	**13%**	**31.3 (11.8)**	**3.2 (3.1)**

(Continued)

165

Table 5.3 (Continued)

Main Category	Categories, Differentiated	Frequency of Nominations			Timing	Emotional Valence
		Women (count)	Men (count)	Total (in %)	M (SD)	M (SD)
Job and education	Continuing education	22	10	7%	28.0 (8.4)	8.0 (3.0)
	Job situation	32	7	9%	40.0 (9.3)	7.0 (3.4)
	Total	**54**	**17**	**16%**	**35.0 (10.7)**	**7.5 (3.3)**
Living arrangements	Traveling	17	7	5%	25.0 (6.6)	8.9 (2.2)
	Moving, living conditions	11	5	4%	29.0 (12.9)	5.7 (4.1)
	Institutionalization	6	1	2%	10.9 (5.6)	2.7 (3.0)
	Total	**34**	**13**	**11%**	**24.2 (10.9)**	**6.9 (3.8)**
Other	Conflicts	4		1%	37.8 (12.9)	5.0 (3.5)
	Sexual abuse	3		1%	13.0 (6.6)	1.0 (0.0)
	Interests, personality	8	5	3%	31.0 (12.4)	7.2 (3.9)
	Other	4	1	1%	28.0 (19.3)	6.0 (3.2)
	Total	**19**	**6**	**6%**	**29.2 (14.7)**	**5.8 (3.8)**

also more frequently challenged by having a new job or starting a new professional formation. Living conditions in midlife were significantly associated with the self-agency of nonnormative transitions. Single men and working fathers reported the most transitions with self-agency, and the lowest percentage was found among housewives, that is, women who had chosen a traditional family career.

Nonnormative Transitions and Personality as Predictors of Psychological Well-Being in Midlife

Life Domains and Well-Being. Singles did not only experience nonnormative transitions more frequently in their life course, but they also had significantly lower psychological well-being than married participants. Psychological well-being in midlife was significantly associated with nonnormative transitions in various life domains. The more positive marital relationship transitions and job and education transitions were experienced, the higher psychological well-being in midlife.

Next, we investigated whether the experience of nonnormative transitions in various life domains predicted psychological well-being in midlife. The hierarchical regression analyses show significant effects of past nonnormative transitions as well as current living conditions. The emotional valence of marital relationship transitions significantly predicted psychological well-being in midlife even when controlling for current marital status, personality, gender, and cohort effects (see Table 5.4). Single persons who described the forming and breaking of intimate relationships as negative experiences had the lowest well-being in midlife.

Developmental Stages and Well-Being. We expected that nonnormative transitions in different developmental stages are associated with psychological well-being in midlife. The correlation analysis shows that the emotional valence of experienced nonnormative transitions in adolescence and young adulthood are significantly positively associated with psychological well-being in midlife. Again, we computed a hierarchical regression analysis to control for sociodemographics and personality variables. The predictive value of emotional valence of nonnormative transitions in young adulthood remained significant, even when controlling for cohort and gender effects, personality, current marital status. and the emotional valence of the other nonnormative transitions. Transitions in young adulthood involved mainly transitions with self-agency; thus, persons who have a sense of self-determination of their development and who could realize some of their goals had a more positive well-being in midlife.

Table 5.4   Nonnormative Transitions and Personality Predicting Well-Being in Midlife: Results of the Hierarchical Regression Analysis

Model	Independent Variables	Psychological Well-Being in Midlife[a]
Model III	Gender (female = 1)	.044
	Age group (older = 1)	.132*
	Marital status in midlife (married = 1)	.193**
	Illness, accidents, and death (EV)[b]	.050
	Marital relationship (EV)	.123*
	Family issues (EV)	.083
	Job and education (EV)	.053
	Living arrangements (EV)	.004
	Neuroticism	−.406**
	Extraversion	.046
	Conscientiousness	.191**
	Openness	−.020
	Agreeableness	−.043
Model Summary	Model I	$R^2 = 12; F_{change} = 10.2$**
	Model II	$R^2 = .19; F_{change} = 3.5$**
	Model III	$R^2 = .40; F_{change} = 14.5$**

a. Values represent betas; b. EV = emotional valence; persons who did not report nonnormative transitions were assigned the sample mean of emotional valence.

*$p < .05$; **$p < .01$; $N = 221$.

Nonnormative Transitions as Risk or Protective Factors for Adjustment in Middle Age

The retrospective reporting of nonnormative life course transitions of persons in middle age yielded a very high interindividuality and heterogeneity. Our results replicate findings of studies with prospective designs. Our results emphasize (a) the importance of past and current biographical transitions regarding partnerships and social relations for well-being in midlife, (b) the significance of self-regulation in human development, (c) gender differences in reconstructing one's past, and (d) the role of nonnormative transitions in young adulthood as an important predictor for development in middle age.

Social Relationships. Most nonnormative transitions reported by our participants involved social relationships, ranging from illness and death of relatives or friends to separations and partnership conflicts, but also included starting new intimate relationships or adopting a child. Thus, our life course is in fact characterized by "linked lives" (Elder, 1998). Experiences concerning intimate relationships seem to be particularly important, as they are associated with psychological well-being in midlife. Having no partner or spouse in midlife predicted lower psychological well-being as did having experienced nonnormative transitions (e.g., a separation) in a negative way.

Between Human Agency and Destiny. Our participants reported heterogeneous nonnormative transitions, some of them representing self-regulated actions and others being fateful events. From a theoretical viewpoint, humans can be considered agents of their development (Heckhausen, 2002). Our study showed that self-initiated life events are very important when evaluating one's biography. Studies on resilience repeatedly demonstrate that an internal locus of control is a protective factor (e.g., Cederblad, 1996). Various research traditions show that self-efficacy, or sense of coherence, a sense of control, or self-regulation is associated with well-being and health (Antonovsky, 1987; Diener, Suh, Lucas, & Smith, 1999; Perrig-Chiello, Perrig, & Stähelin, 1999). Moreover, turning points, which involve a certain amount of choice, were then and later on more positively evaluated (Rönkä, Oravala, & Pulkkinen, 2003). Our study also shows that events that are self-initiated are more positively experienced.

Gender Differences. As nominating and evaluating past nonnormative transitions involves a certain amount of reconstruction, it also mirrors personality aspects. The reported transitions partly reflect real developmental changes but also their subjective (re)interpretations, which are related to individual differences such as gender. The finding that men reported more positive nonnormative transitions and more frequently self-determined transitions than did women might reflect a gender bias, which means that men are more likely to reinterpret their biographies in terms of self-determination and have thus more positive memories of their past development than women.

Developmental Paths. The reported nonnormative transitions in childhood were mainly caused by external forces and are negatively experienced. In that developmental period, people seem to have fewer opportunities to assert themselves and therefore may have less mastery. Self-initiated transitions have their peak in young adulthood. Our results suggest that young adulthood is a period that provides many opportunities for self-regulation and human agency. It seems thus to be an important developmental stage and may even represent a turning point that affects psychological well-being in midlife. In young adulthood, we may overcome adverse experiences in childhood if we have more possibilities to actively create and alter our life course trajectories. In sum, critical life events do not only have an impact on well-being and health in the aftermath of the event (Schwarzer & Schulz, 2003), but also seem to be relevant when individuals have a retrospective look on their own developmental pathways.

Paths to Successful Development in Midlife: A Synopsis

Our study shows in an impressive manner the importance of past biographical transitions for well-being in middle age and anticipation of old age. Based on the status quo of literature as well as on our results, we have gained some important insights, which allow drawing conclusions concerning the determinants of successful paths to midlife well-being.

(a) *The social resources:* First of all we have to consider that for today's middle-aged cohorts in Switzerland, the social context was and still is relevant for the regulation of their developmental trajectories. Age-normed transitions and role changes and social expectations associated with them were still a reality and a challenge, especially in the young years (e.g., puberty) of this cohort. That means that the fulfillment of these age-normed tasks was quite crucial and had an enduring impact on later development. In a small—and mostly rural—country as Switzerland is, social norms and expectations still have a considerable impact on individual development because of the lower mobility, tighter family ties, and stronger familial and societal expectations and obligations.

(b) *Biographical resources:* We can further assume that the missing of age-normed transitions was associated with an increased probability to experience consecutive nonnormative transitions. This cumulative effect begins already in earlier years and has negative consequences far into middle age.

Here the importance of primary and secondary prevention in early life becomes evident. The interruption of such a build-up of negative sequence by providing support early in life would be an important element for future successful development.

(c) *Psychological resources:* Developmental pathways are dependent not only on social context and biographical background but also to a great extent on individual resources, such as personality, agency, and self-regulation. In fact, there is considerable empirical evidence that a person's coping style and adaptive devices in early adolescence are important in determining his or her future life course. Our results indicate that personality factors are indeed strongly related to psychological well-being and the reconstruction of one's own past. This point brings us to the crucial question, whether it is the objectively experienced transition per se that has a long-term effect or whether it is rather the subjective post-hoc interpretation that matters. The question of the validity of retrospective data has been discussed controversially (Rutter, 1996). In our view, there are two good arguments for the adequacy of working with retrospective data:

1. There is empirical evidence that retrospective reports on biographical events converge in a significant way with the data from prospective longitudinal studies (Costa & McCrae, 1989; McCrae & Costa, 1990).

2. From a memory-theoretical perspective, the question whether the objective experience or the subjective post-hoc interpretation of past transitions counts is not crucial at all for the study of later well-being (Perrig-Chiello & Perrig, 2004). In fact, all autobiographical memories are subjective personal reconstructions of the past, and it is the emotional quality of the memory that accounts for actual well-being and not the objective event per se (Schacter, 1996; Schwarz & Strack, 1999; Keyes & Ryff, 1999).

All these insights emphasize both the considerable impact of early experiences on developmental adaptation and psychological well-being in middle age and the crucial importance of the self variable (i.e., the personal reconstruction of the life course, i.e., one's life review). In accordance with this, the conclusions to be drawn are twofold: First, prevention and health promotion in early years have to be taken seriously; second, individuals in middle age still have a considerable number of possibilities to "compose their own life" (Bateson, 1990).

References

Antonovsky, A. (1987). *Unraveling the mystery of health: How people manage stress and stay well.* San Francisco: Jossey-Bass.

Baltes, P. B., Reese, H. W., & Lipsitt, L. P. (1980). Life-span developmental psychology. *Annual Review of Psychology, 31,* 65–110.

Bateson, M. C. (1990). *Composing a life.* New York: Plenum.

Brim, O. G., & Ryff, C. D. (1980). On the properties of life events. In P. B. Baltes & O. G. Brim, Jr. (Eds.), *Life-span development and behavior* (Vol. 3, pp. 367–388). New York: Academic Press.

Caspi, A. (1993). Why maladaptive behaviors persist: Sources of continuity and change across the life course. In D. C. Funder, R. D. Parke, C. Tomlinson-Keasey, & K. Widaman (Eds.), *Studying lives through time: Personality and development* (pp. 343–376). Washington, DC: American Psychological Association.

Caspi, A., & Moffitt, T. E. (1991). Individual differences are accentuated during periods of social change: The sample case of girls at puberty. *Journal of Personality and Social Psychology, 61,* 157–168.

Cederblad, M. (1996). The children of the Lundby Study as adults: A salutogenic perspective. *European Child and Adolescent Psychiatry, 5,* 38–43.

Cederblad, M., Dahlin, L., Hagnell, O., & Hansson, K. (1994). Salutogenic childhood factors reported by middle-aged individuals. Follow-up of the children from the Lundby Study grown up in families experiencing three or more childhood psychiatric risk factors. *European Archives of Psychiatry and Clinical Neurosciences, 244,* 1–11.

Chiriboga, D. A. (1989). Mental health at the midpoint: Crisis, challenge, or relief? In S. Hunter & M. Sundel (Eds.), *Mid-life myths: Issues, findings, and practice implications* (pp. 116–144). Newbury Park, CA: Sage.

Chiriboga, D. A. (1997). Crisis, challenge, and stability in middle years. In M. E. Lachman & J. B. James (Eds.), *Multiple paths of mid-life development.* (pp. 293–322). Chicago: University of Chicago Press.

Clausen, J. A. (1975). The social meaning of differential physical and sexual maturation. In S. E. Dragastin & G. Elder (Eds.), *Adolescence in the life cycle: Psychological change and the social context* (pp. 25–47). New York: Halsted.

Clausen, J. A. (1991). Adolescent competence and the shaping of the life course. *American Journal of Sociology, 96,* 805–842.

Clausen, J. A. (1993). *American lives: Looking back at the children of the Great Depression.* New York: Free Press.

Costa, P. T., & McCrae, R. R. (1985). *Manual for the NEO Personality Inventory.* Odessa, FL: Psychological Assessment Resources.

Costa, P. T., & McCrae, R. R. (1989). Personality continuity and the changes of adult life. In M. Storand & G. R. Vandenbos (Eds.), *The adult years: Continuity and change* (pp. 45–77). Washington, DC: American Psychological Association.

de Vries, B., & Watt, D. (1996). A lifetime of events: Age and gender variations in the life story. *International Journal of Aging and Human Development, 42*, 81–102.

Diener, E., Suh, E. M., Lucas, R. E., & Smith, H. L. (1999). Subjective well-being: Three decades of progress. *Psychological Bulletin, 125*, 276–302.

Dooley, D., & Prause, J. A. (1997). School-leavers' self-esteem and unemployment: Turning point or a station on a trajectory? In I. H. Gotlib & B. Wheaton (Eds.), *Stress and adversity over the life course. Trajectories and turning points* (pp. 91–114). Cambridge, UK: Cambridge University Press.

Elder, G. H. (1986). Military times and turning points in men's lives. *Developmental Psychology, 22*, 233–245.

Elder, G. H. (1998). The life course as developmental theory. *Child Development, 69*, 1–12.

Elder, G. H. (1999). *Children of the Great Depression*. Boulder, CO: Westview Press.

Elder, G. H., & Caspi, A. (1990). Studying lives in a changing society: Sociological and personological explorations. In A. Rabin, R. Zucker, R. Emmons, & S. Frank (Eds.), *Studying persons and lives* (pp. 201–247). New York: Springer.

Elder, G. H., & Crosnoe, R. (2002). The influence of early behavior patterns on later life. In L. Pulkkinen & A. Caspi (Eds.), *Paths to successful development* (pp. 157–177). Cambridge, UK: Cambridge University Press.

Elder, G. H., & Rockwell, R. C. (1979). The life course and human development: An ecological perspective. *International Journal of Behavioural Development, 2*, 1–21.

Erikson, E. H. (1959). *Identity and the life cycle*. New York: International University Press.

Erikson, E. H. (1968). *Identity: Youth and crisis*. New York: Norton.

Ewert, O. M. (1984). Psychische Begleiterscheinungen des puberalen Wachstums-schubs bei männlichen Jugendlichen—eine retrospektive Untersuchung [Psychological consequences of pubteral growth in male adolescents—A retrospective study]. *Zeitschrift für Entwicklungspsychologie und Pädagogische Psychologie, 16*, 1–11.

Fiske, M. (1979). *Middle age: The prime of life?* New York: Harper & Row.

Fitzgerald, J. M. (1988). Vivid memories and the reminiscence phenomenon: The role of a self narrative. *Human Development, 31*, 261–273.

Fitzgerald, J. M., & Shifley-Grove, S. S. (1999). Memory and affect: Autobiographical memory distribution and availability in normal and recently detoxified alcoholics. *Journal of Adult Development, 6*, 11–19.

Grossmann, K. E., & Grossmann, K. (1998). Développement de l'attachement et adaptation psychologique du berceau au tombeau [Attachment development and psychological adaptation from birth to death]. *Enfance, 3*, 44–68.

Hagnell, O., Essen-Möller, E., Lanke, J., Öjesjö, L., & Rorsman, B. (1990). *The incidence of mental illness over a quarter of a century. The Lundby Longitudinal Study of mental illnesses in a total population based on 42,000 observation years*. Stockholm: Almqvist & Wiksell International.

Havighurst, R. J. (1953). *Human development and education*. London: Longman.

Havighurst, R. J. (1972). *Developmental tasks and education* (3rd ed.). New York: McKay.

Heckhausen, J. (1997). Developmental regulation across adulthood: Primary and secondary control of age-related challenges. *Developmental Psychology, 33,* 176–187.

Heckhausen, J. (2002). Developmental regulation of life course transitions: A control theory approach. In L. Pulkkinen & A. Caspi (Eds.), *Paths to successful development* (pp. 257–280). Cambridge, UK: Cambridge University Press.

Held, T. (1986). Institutionalization and deinstitutionalization of the life course. *Human Development, 29,* 157–162.

Helson, R., Mitchell, V., & Moane, G. (1984). Personality and patterns of adherence and nonadherence to the social clock. *Journal of Personality and Social Psychology, 46,* 1079–1096.

Hogan, D. P. (1981). *Transitions and social change: The early lives of American men.* New York: Academic Press.

Josselson, R. (1987). *Finding herself: Pathways to identity development in women.* San Francisco: Jossey-Bass.

Kahneman, D., Diener, E., & Schwarz, N. (Eds.). (1999). *Well-being: The foundations of hedonic psychology.* New York: Russell Sage.

Kaiser, A., & Perrig-Chiello, P. (2000). Weibliche Lebenswelten und Wohlbefinden im mittleren Lebensalter [Women's environments and well-being in middle age]. In E. Thommen & H. Kilcher (Eds.), *Comparer ou prédire. Exemples de recherches comparatives en psychologie aujourd'hui* (pp. 153–163). Fribourg, Switzerland: Editions Universitaires.

Kessler, R. C., Gillis-Light, J., Magee, W. J., Kendler, K. S., & Eaves, L. J. (1997). Childhood adversity and adult psychopathology. In I. H. Gotlib & B. Wheaton (Eds.), *Stress and adversity over the life course* (pp. 29–49). Cambridge, UK: Cambridge University Press.

Keyes, C. L. M., & Ryff, C. D. (1999). Psychological well-being in mid-life. In S. L. Willis & J. D. Reid (Eds.), *Life in the middle: Psychological and social development in middle age* (pp. 161–182). San Diego, CA: Academic Press.

Keyes, C. L. M., Shmotkin, D., & Ryff, C. D. (2002). Optimizing well-being: The empirical encounter of two traditions. *Journal of Personality and Social Psychology, 82,* 1007–1022.

Koff, E., & Rierdan, J. (1993). Advanced pubertal development and eating disturbance in early adolescent girls. *Journal of Adolescent Health, 14,* 433–439.

Kohli, M. (1986). Social organization and subjective construction of the life course. In A. B. Sorensen, F. E. Weinert, & L. R. Sherrod (Eds.), *Human development and the life course: Multidisciplinary perspectives* (pp. 272–292). Hillsdale, NJ: Erlbaum.

Kohli, M., & Künemund, H. (2004). Die Grenzen des Alters–Strukturen und Bedeutungen [The limits of aging—Structures and meanings]. In P. Perrig-Chiello & F. Höpflinger (Eds.), *Jenseits des Zenits. Frauen und Männer in der zweiten Lebenshälfte* (pp. 37–61). Bern, Switzerland: Haupt.

Kozma, A., Stones, M. J., & McNeil, J. K. (1991). *Psychological well-being in later life.* Toronto, Ontario, Canada: Butterworths.

Kuhlen, R. G. (1959). Aging and life-adjustment. In J. E. Birren (Ed.), *Handbook of aging and the individual* (pp. 852–897). Chicago: University of Chicago Press.

Laub, J. H., & Sampson, R. J. (1998). The long-term reach of adolescent competence: Socioeconomic achievement in the lives of disadvantaged men. In A. Colby, J. James, & D. Hart (Eds.), *Competence and character through life* (pp. 89–113). Chicago: University of Chicago Press.

Levinson, D. J., Darrow, D. N., Klein, E. B., Levinson, M. H., & McKee, B. (1978). *The seasons of a man's life.* New York: Knopf.

Luthar, S., Cicchetti, D., & Becker, B. (2000). The construct of resilience: A critical evaluation and guidelines for future work. *Child Development, 71,* 543–562.

Mayer, K. U. (1998). Lebensverlauf [Life process]. In B. Schäfers & W. Zapf (Eds.), *Handwörterbuch zur Gesellschaft Deutschlands* (pp. 438–451). Opladen, Germany: Leske & Budrich.

McCrae, R. R., & Costa, P. T. (1990). *Personality in adulthood.* New York: Guilford Press.

Menaghan, E. G. (1997). Intergenerational consequences of social stressors: Effects of occupational and family conditions on young mothers and their children. In I. H. Gotlib & B. Wheaton (Eds.), *Stress and adversity over the life course. Trajectories and turning points* (pp. 114–133). Cambridge, UK: Cambridge University Press.

Mercer, R. T., Nichols, E. G., & Doyle, G. C. (1989*). Transitions in a woman's life. Major life events in developmental context.* New York: Springer.

Moen, P. (1997). Women's roles and resilience: Trajectories of advantage or turning points? In I. H. Gotlib & B. Wheaton (Eds.), *Stress and adversity over the life course* (pp. 133–159). Cambridge, UK: Cambridge University Press.

Moen, P., & Wethington, E. (1999). Mid-life development in a life course context. In S. L. Willis & J. D. Reid (Eds.), *Life in the middle. Psychological and social development in middle age* (pp. 3–25). San Diego, CA: Academic Press.

Neugarten, B. L. (1968). The awareness of middle age. In B. L. Neugarten (Ed.), *Middle age and aging* (pp. 22–28). Chicago: University of Chicago Press.

Neugarten, B. L., & Hagestad, G. O. (1976). Age and the life course. In R. Binstock & E. Shanas (Eds.), *Handbook of aging and social sciences* (pp. 35–55). New York: Van Nostrand Reinhold.

Nurmi, J.-E. (1992). Age differences in adult life goals, concerns, and their temporal extension: A life course approach to future-oriented motivation. *International Journal of Behavioral Development, 15,* 487–508.

Perren, S., & Perrig-Chiello, P. (2002, August). *Silent life-course transitions from a mid-life perspective—between human agency and destiny.* Poster presentation at the Biennial Meeting of The International Society for the Study of Behavioural Development (ISSBD), Ottawa, Ontario, Canada.

Perren, S., & Perrig-Chiello, P. (2003). Das Erleben von Krankheit und Tod im mittleren Erwachsenenalter [The experience of illness and death in middle-aged adults]. In P. Perrig-Chiello & F. Höpflinger (Eds.), *Gesundheitsbiographien. Variationen und Hintergründe* (pp. 135–151). Bern, Switzerland: Huber.

Perrig-Chiello, P. (1996). Wie können wir Wohlbefinden erfassen? [How can we measure well-being?]. In H. W. Heiss, F. Huber, B. Peter, & H. B. Stähelin (Eds.), *Wohlbefinden im Alter—geriatrische und gerontologische Strategien* (pp. 7–17). Reinach, Switzerland: Roche Pharma.

Perrig-Chiello, P. (1997). *Ressourcen des Wohlbefindens im Alter* [Resources for well-being in old age]. Weinheim, Germany: Juventa.

Perrig-Chiello, P., & Höpflinger, F. (2004). *Zwischen den Generationen—Frauen und Männer im mittleren Lebensalter* [Between generations—Women and men in middle age]. Zürich, Switzerland: Seismo-Verlag.

Perrig-Chiello, P., Höpflinger, F., Kaiser, A., & Sturzenegger, M. (1999). Psychosoziale Aspekte der Lebensbedingungen von Frauen und Männern im mittleren Lebensalter [Psychosocial aspects of the living conditions of women and men in middle age]. *Zeitschrift für Familienforschung, 11*, 5–27.

Perrig-Chiello, P., & Perren, S. (in press). Biographical transitions from a mid-life perspective. *Journal of Adult Development.*

Perrig-Chiello, P., & Perrig, W. (2004). The impact of personality, context and memorized life transitions on well-being. In R. Levy (Ed.), *Advances in interdisciplinary life course research.* Manuscript in preparation.

Perrig-Chiello, P., Perrig, W. J., & Stähelin, H. B. (1999). Health control beliefs in old age—Relationship with subjective and objective health and health behavior. *Journal of Psychology, Health & Medicine, 4*, 84–94.

Perrig-Chiello, P., & Sturzenegger, M. (2001). Social relations and filial maturity in middle-aged adults: Contextual conditions and psychological determinants. *Zeitschrift für Gerontologie und Geriatrie, 34*, 21–27.

Pulkkinen, L., & Caspi, A. (2002). *Paths to successful development personality in the life course.* Cambridge, UK: Cambridge University Press.

Pulkkinen, L., Nygren, H., & Kokko, K. (2002). Successful development: Childhood antecedents of adaptive psychosocial functioning in adulthood. *Journal of Adult Development, 9*, 251–265.

Rönkä, A., Oravala, S., & Pulkkinen, L. (2003). Turning points in adults' lives: The effect of gender and the amount of choice. *Journal of Adult Development, 10*, 203–215.

Rutter, M. (1989). Pathways from childhood to adult life. *Journal of Child Psychology and Psychiatry, 30*, 23–51.

Rutter, M. (1996). Transitions and turning points in developmental psychopathology: As applied to the age span between childhood and mid-adulthood. *International Journal of Behavioral Development, 19*, 603–626.

Ryan, R. M., & Deci, E. L. (2000). On happiness and human potentials: A review of research on hedonic and eudaimonic well-being. *Annual Review of Psychology, 52*, 141–166.

Rybash, J. M. (1999). Aging and autobiographical memory: The long and bumpy road. *Journal of Adult Development, 6,* 1–10.

Ryff, C. D. (1989). Happiness is everything, or is it? Explorations on the meaning of psychological well-being. *Journal of Personality and Social Psychology, 57,* 1069–1081.

Ryff, C. D., & Heidrich, S. M. (1997). Experience and well-being: Explorations on domains of life and how they matter. *International Journal of Behavioral Development, 20,* 193–206.

Ryff, C. D., Singer, B. H., & Seltzer, M. M. (2002). Pathways through challenge: Implications for well-being and health. In L. Pulkkinen & A. Caspi (Eds.), *Paths to successful development* (pp. 302–328). Cambridge, UK: Cambridge University Press.

Schacter, D. L. (1996). *Searching for memory. The brain, the mind, and the past.* New York: Basic Books.

Schwarz, N., & Strack, F. (1999). Reports of subjective well-being: Judgmental processes and their methodological implications. In D. Kahneman, E. Diener, & N. Schwarz (Eds.), *Well-being. The foundations of hedonistic psychology* (pp. 61–85). New York: Russell Sage.

Schwarzer, R., & Schulz, U. (2003). Stressful life events. In A. M. Nezu, C. M. Nezu, & P. A. Geller (Eds.), *Health psychology* (Handbook of Psychology, Vol. 9, pp. 27–49). New York: Wiley.

Settersten, R. A., & Hagestad, G. O. (1996). What's the latest? Cultural age deadlines for educational and work transitions. *The Gerontologist, 36,* 602–613.

Stewart, A. J., Ostrove, J. M., & Helson, R. (2001). Middle aging in women: Patterns of personality change from the 30s to the 50s. *Journal of Adult Development, 8,* 23–37.

Sugarman, L. (2001). *Life-span development. Frameworks, accounts and strategies* (2nd ed.). East Sussex, UK: Psychology Press.

Vaillant, G. E. (1977). *Adaptation to life.* Boston: Little, Brown.

Vaillant, G. E. (1990). Avoiding negative life outcomes: Evidence from a forty-five year study. In P. B. Baltes & M. M. Baltes (Eds.), *Successful aging: Perspectives from the behavioral sciences* (pp. 323–358). New York: Cambridge University Press.

Vandewater, E. A., & Stewart, A. J. (1997). Women's career commitment patterns and personality development. In M. E. Lachman & J. B. James (Eds.), *Multiple paths of mid-life development* (pp. 375–411). Chicago: University of Chicago Press.

Verhofstadt-Denève, L., Schittekatte, M., & Van Leeuwen, K. (2003). Gender differences in developmental pathways on self-evaluation from adolescence into adulthood: The Flanders Longitudinal Study. *International Journal of Adolescent Medicine and Health, 15,* 139–152.

Werner, E. E. (1996). Vulnerable but invincible: High risk children from birth to adulthood. *European Child and Adolescent Psychiatry, 5*(Suppl. 1), 47–51.

Werner, E. E., & Smith, R. S. (2003). *Journeys from childhood to mid-life: Risk, resilience, and recovery.* Ithaca, NY: Cornell University Press.

Wethington, E., Cooper, H., & Holmes, C. S. (1997). Turning points in mid-life. In I. H. Gotlib & B. Wheaton (Eds.), *Stress and adversity of the life course* (pp. 215–231). Cambridge, UK: Cambridge University Press.

Wheaton, B., & Gotlib, I. H. (1997). Trajectories and turning points over the life course: Concepts and themes. In I. H. Gotlib & B. Wheaton (Eds.), *Stress and adversity over the life course* (pp. 1–29). Cambridge, UK: Cambridge University Press.

Willis, S. L., & Reid, J. D. (1999). *Life in the middle. Psychological and social development in middle age.* San Diego, CA: Academic Press.

Wrosch, C., & Freund, A. M. (2001). Self-regulation of normative and non-normative developmental challenges. *Human Development, 44,* 264–283.

Zapf, W. (1995). Entwicklung und Sozialstruktur moderner Gesellschaften [The development and social structure of modern societies]. In H. Korte & B. Schäfers (Eds.), *Einführung in die Hauptbegriffe der Soziologie* (pp. 181–191). Opladen, Germany: Leske & Budrich.

Six

Cognitive Development in Midlife

Mike Martin and Daniel Zimprich

T he group of middle-aged adults between the ages of roughly 40 and 65 years gains growing interest from the public and scientists alike because it currently represents one of the largest age groups in Europe and the United States. A better understanding of midlife cognitive development and related factors might become increasingly important as these cohorts reach old age, and cognitive aging affects an increasingly large proportion of the overall population. In this chapter, we review selected literature on cognitive development in middle adulthood. Our focus is on cognitive development because cognition is one of the key competencies needed in young and old age to meet the challenges of education, job demands, and everyday life (M. M. Baltes & Lang, 1997; Martin & Mroczek, in press).

Parts of the preparation of this chapter were supported by grant SNF 101411–103525/1 to M. Martin, D. Zimprich, and M. Kliegel.

Studies of cognitive development in midlife can be characterized by two main approaches. On one hand, the decline of cognitive resources is a main concern for persons from middle age onward (Lawton et al., 1999). Thus, studies on midlife cognition have focused on the question of whether groups at risk for decline in early old age could be identified. The timely identification of at-risk individuals would permit preventive measures targeted at early stages of decline (see Schaie, 2000). One could speculate that middle age would be an ideal time for preventive measures because the performance around a lifetime peak level increases the likelihood of training gains. In addition, even though declines in performance are from a high starting level, these first signs of decline might be salient enough to motivate persons to participate in cognitive trainings. On the other hand, midlife might be characterized by cognitively demanding activities and relatively high levels of cognitive performance. Thus, there is an interest in examining if and how demanding activities and a wide spectrum of interests in middle age may protect middle-aged adults from cognitive decline or at least provide compensatory potential for the later years of life.

Although studies observe high mean levels of cognitive performance across middle age, it can be argued theoretically that middle age differs from both young and old age in several ways. First, different developmental tasks and everyday demands (Havighurst, 1948/1982; Sternberg, Grigorenko, & Oh, 2001) in midlife versus young and old age make person-environment interactions hardly comparable between midlife and other ages. For instance, it is hard to see in which way the challenge of schooling in young age or of retirement in old age is comparable to challenges at midlife, which consist of work and family environments requiring the particular skills of organizing, planning, problem solving, and multitasking (Schooler, 1999). For example, family obligations peak in middle-aged adults who are in good health, have numerous elderly kin, and have children just moving out and establishing their own families (Hogan, 1987; Rossi & Rossi, 1990). In the same vein, raising children is a typical demand around the ages of 25 to 40, but rarely so at age 60 (Hogan, 1987). In the work domain, average job demands and workloads increase from age 25 to age 40 and then decrease toward age 60 to 70 (Townsend, 2001).

Second, in young age, cognitive development is strongly influenced by formal training and characterized by shared and homogeneous environments such as school classes or peer groups (Espy, Molfese, & DiLalla, 2001).

In old age, cognitive development becomes increasingly dependent on physiological factors such as sensory and sensorimotor functions (P. B. Baltes & Lindenberger, 1997; Li & Lindenberger, 2002; Lindenberger & Baltes, 1994; see also Hofer, Berg, & Era, 2003). In middle adulthood, after having reached a high level, cognitive performance will be shaped strongly by individual environments (see Sternberg et al., 2001). Different job environments have been shown to influence development of cognitive skills (Kirlik & Bisantz, 1999). This can be explained by assuming that in particular job environments, individuals will engage in similar cognitive activities, for example, reading particular instructions, thinking about how to achieve particular goals, planning particular behaviors, or regulating success or failure in achieving subgoals. All individuals may achieve their goals, all will have used at least some of the same underlying abilities, and all will have practiced particular skills. Thus, compared to young and old age, in midlife one would expect more differentiated, that is, less correlated, patterns of particular cognitive functions. This expected differential influence of developmental contexts, such as from professional, family, or social life, would suggest large individual differences within age groups and across middle adulthood that are potentially enlarged by individual differences in activities aiming at improving or maintaining current levels of cognitive functioning, such as participating in memory trainings (West & Tomer, 1989).

Third, developmental potential in young age is needed to support natural maturation and academic achievement (Rees & Palmer, 1970) and to prepare for job demands (Havighurst, 1948/1982). In old age, cognitive training may serve to prevent consequences of age-associated decline, although effects are typically small (Ball et al., 2002; Willis & Schaie, 1986). In middle age, cognitive potential is typically used to develop job-specific skills, thus contributing to the development of highly job-specific and individualized change trajectories (Moen & Wethington, 1999). In addition, the effects of and transfer from cognitive trainings are likely to be higher in midlife than in young or old age (Kliegl, Philipp, Luckner, & Krampe, 2001), and different biological or hormonal changes may influence cognition in middle compared with young and old age (Seeman, Singer, Ryff, Dienberg-Love, & Levy-Storms, 2002).

Fourth, cognitive development in middle age can be characterized by rather high mean levels of cognitive performance (Willis & Schaie, 1999). In young age, the level of cognitive performance across many different tasks increases; thus, development is generally characterized by increases in performance from low to high levels. In old age, cognitive performance eventually demonstrates declines; thus, development is characterized by decreases in performance from a high starting level. Overall, the high or even peak level of performance at middle age (Willis & Schaie, 1999), combined with a different direction of mean change, may represent a qualitative difference from other age groups. In fact, changes from peak performance are less likely to influence everyday life, and thus might not be comparable to increases from a lower level, such as in young age groups, or decreases from a high level until potentially affecting the level of independence in everyday life such as in very old age.

Cognitive Development Across Middle Age

The Seattle Longitudinal Study (Schaie, 1996) has provided detailed insights into the developmental trajectories of several intellectual functions across middle age (see Willis & Schaie, 1999). The data suggest that for inductive reasoning, vocabulary, verbal memory, and spatial orientation, the average performance peaks occur in the ages from the early 40s to 60s, with fluid intelligence abilities showing earlier declines than crystallized abilities. For perceptual speed and numerical ability, performance peaks before midlife and declines through midlife and into old age. Willis and Schaie conclude that "for four of the six abilities studied, middle-aged individuals are functioning at a higher level than they did at age 25" (p. 238). Examining the mean trajectories of the four abilities peaking in midlife would suggest that middle adulthood could be characterized as stable with relatively small mean changes. This explains why a number of longitudinal studies include middle-aged adults as a comparison group, but only few include the examination of changes in cognitive performance across midlife (Bosma, van Boxtel, Ponds, Houx, & Jolles, 2003; Finkel, Pedersen, & Harris, 2000; Lamar, Resnick, & Zonderman, 2003; Maitland, Intrieri, Schaie, & Willis, 2000). However, the data based on mean changes of all six cognitive and intellectual functions demonstrate that within the same time period, patterns of increases, declines, and stability can be observed with substantial intraindividual variability. This suggests that middle age should not be taken as a period of the life span that is mainly, or only, characterized by stability. Instead, in middle age, different types of cognitive change occur within and across abilities (Dixon, De Frias, & Maitland, 2001). Thus, the different types of changes in particular cognitive functions across middle age require explanations.

Examining Different Types of Change

The question of whether cognitive performance changes during middle adulthood is not just a yes-or-no question. In fact, change in cognitive performance may manifest itself along several dimensions, each of which covers different aspects of change. One might distinguish between structural change, absolute change, differential change, change in divergence, and general versus specific change (Hertzog & Dixon, 1996). In what follows, we discuss these different aspects of change and related empirical findings in turn. Note that although the emphasis is on longitudinal change, one might argue that some of these aspects of change might also be examined by comparing different age groups, conditional on the assumption that cohort effects do not play a major role in cognitive development in middle adulthood.

Structural change (or stability) refers to the persistence of covariation patterns among variables across time or in different age groups. Although in principle it is possible to compare the equality of covariance matrices directly (Perlman, 1980), the usual procedure is to utilize factor analysis techniques in order to exclude covariance differences due to measurement error (Bollen, 1989). Within factor analysis models, structural stability is labeled measurement invariance, which implies that the variables in question are unbiased with respect to specific selection variables, for example, time of measurement or age at measurement.

Measurement invariance is an issue of degree (Bollen, 1989; Meredith, 1993) regarding the level of invariance obtained and is based on whether increasingly stringent constraints result in model misfit. *Configural invariance* refers to the same pattern of factors and factor loadings in different subgroups (e.g., age groups). Configural invariance holds, for example, if in a sample of persons aged 40 and a sample of persons aged 60, a battery of six cognitive measures would be described adequately by two correlated factors with the same measures loading on the first factor (say, Tests 1–3) and the same measures loading on the second factor (say, Tests 4–6) in both age groups. *Metric or pattern invariance* requires the (unstandardized) factor loadings to be equal in different subgroups. On a conceptual level, metric or pattern invariance ensures that there is no interaction between group membership and factor scores. Such an interaction would be a form of bias because for a given factor score on a latent variable, the regression of observed scores on it would depend on group membership. In addition to metric invariance, *strong invariance* requires the latent intercepts of the observed indicators to be equal across groups. Conceptually, the requirement of equal latent intercepts tests whether one group scores consistently higher (or lower) on the measures than other groups for each value of the factor (weighted by the factor loadings). Eventually, *strict invariance* adds the requirement of equal residual variances across groups. To understand the requirement of equal residual variances on a conceptual level, suppose that a test is utilized for an admission decision and a certain ability level as measured by the factor is needed. If the decision were based on the observed scores, the number of incorrect admissions and incorrect rejections would be higher in groups with larger residual variances.

As Meredith (1993; see also Meredith & Horn, 2001) has demonstrated, for structural stability to hold, strong invariance should be established; in other words, across time or across different age groups (or both), the configuration of factors, the factor loadings, and the latent intercepts of the manifest indicators should be equal. As some developmental psychologists argue (P. B. Baltes, Reese, & Nesselroade, 1977), the importance of structural stability stems from the fact that it represents a prerequisite for interpreting change (or stability). Specifically, only the existence of strong invariance renders the comparison of cognitive measures meaningful, either across time or across different age groups (or both). Thus, strong invariance or structural stability has to be established before other forms of change (or stability) can be investigated.

Empirical research on structural stability of cognitive abilities in middle adulthood is sparse at present. Taub, McGrew, and Witta (2004), for example, found metric invariance to hold for the Wechsler Adult Intelligence Scale - 3rd edition (WAIS-III) across 13 age groups in 2,450 individuals aged 16 to 89, implying that, across the whole adult life span and, thus, also across middle adulthood, factor loadings of the WAIS-III subtests remained stable. Schaie, Maitland, Willis, and Intrieri (1998) investigated longitudinal measurement invariance of six primary mental abilities (Inductive Reasoning, Spatial Orientation, Perceptual Speed, Numeric Facility, Verbal Ability, and Verbal Recall) across a 7-year period in a sample of 984 individuals, disaggregated into six age groups (32, 46, 53, 60, 67, and 76 years at first testing). They found that, longitudinally, strong invariance was present in the middle-aged groups only. Schaie (1996) established metric invariance for the same primary mental abilities in a sample of 1,621 individuals subdivided into nine age groups (mean ages of 29, 39, 46, 53, 60, 67, 74, 81, and 90).

Horn and McArdle (1992) reported that in the standardization sample ($N = 1{,}880$) of the Wechsler Adult Intelligence Scale-Revised (WAIS-R), strong invariance was found for a complex two-factor model of the subtests in four age groups (16–22, 30–40, 50–60, and 67–72 years of age). To summarize, previous findings indicate that the structure of cognitive abilities is rather stable in middle adulthood in the sense that metric invariance or strong invariance seems to hold. Note, however, that different degrees of factorial invariance have to be reexamined and, possibly, reestablished in every new sample and for the measures used in a study to assess cognitive abilities. Thus, measurement invariance is an essential part of research that should be investigated in studies that aim to examine the other aspects of cognitive change in middle adulthood.

A special field of empirical research with respect to structural change or stability is the question of differentiation or dedifferentiation of cognitive abilities with advancing age (Ghisletta & Lindenberger, 2003; Zelinsky & Lewis, 2003). Note that differentiation or dedifferentiation of cognitive abilities in middle adulthood does not exclude structural stability, because (de-) differentiation commonly involves the covariances between measurement-invariant factors. Hence, structural stability and (de-)differentiation do not contradict each other, but, again, a prerequisite for (de-)differentiation is structural stability. Some cross-sectional studies have provided empirical support for cognitive dedifferentiation in the elderly (Babcock, Laguna, & Roesch, 1997; P. B. Baltes et al., 1980; Hertzog & Bleckley, 2001). By contrast, in other cross-sectional studies, contrary findings (i.e., a differentiation of cognitive abilities with age) have been reported (Cunningham, Clayton, & Overton, 1975; Schmidt & Botwinick, 1989; Tomer & Cunningham, 1993), or results supported neither differentiation nor dedifferentiation (Bickley, Keith, & Wolfle, 1995; Cunningham & Birren, 1980; Juan-Espinosa, García, Colom, & Abad, 2000; Juan-Espinosa et al., 2002; Park et al., 2002). Thus, the question of dedifferentiation would profit from a longitudinal examination. To our knowledge, the only longitudinal study examining dedifferentiation, albeit in old age, was conducted by Anstey, Hofer, and Luszcz (2003). In a sample of 1,823 individuals aged 70 years and older, they did not find consistent patterns of dedifferentiation. Hence, at present, the evidence for dedifferentiation in middle adulthood is sparse.

Absolute change (or stability) refers to constancy in the quantity or amount of a cognitive ability over time or across age. Although one might be interested in cognitive change in individual persons, absolute change is usually examined using average (i.e., sample values of groups of) persons. Traditionally, sample means of cognitive abilities have been compared across time or in different age groups in order to test for absolute continuity (Schaie, 1996). Using latent growth models, Finkel, Reynolds, McArdle, Gatz, and Pedersen (2003) found that across a 6-year period, the longitudinal rate of decline in a sample of 590 adults aged 44 to 88 years accelerated from middle to later adulthood for four of five cognitive abilities, the common element of which was perceptual speed. A single-slope estimate provided sufficient description of the data for another five cognitive measures, meaning that the rate of decline in these abilities did not differ by age group. Thus, accelerating decline at the transition from middle to late adulthood seems to be evident for some, but not all, cognitive abilities. Similarly, Finkel, Pedersen, Plomin, and McClearn (1998) reported that middle-aged adults (55 years) performed significantly better than old adults (83 years) in all of a battery of 14 cognitive variables. The largest age differences in mean performance were found for measures of perceptual speed. Soederberg Miller and Lachman (2000) investigated whether midlife is a time of peak performance in the area of cognitive functioning. Comparing the average performance of 84 young adults (25–39 years), 108 middle-aged adults (40–59 years), and 67 older adults (60–75 years) in speed, reasoning, short-term memory, and vocabulary, they found that middle-aged adults showed little or no cognitive declines on speed, reasoning, and short-term memory measures relative to the young and outperformed the young on vocabulary. Relative to the elderly, middle-aged adults scored higher on all tasks except vocabulary, for which there were no differences.

An alternative procedure would consist of establishing structural stability and then testing for differences in factor means across time or different age groups. Doing so would minimize the influence of measurement error and, at the same time, warrant that the measures used are unbiased with respect to time and age. Horn and McArdle (1992), for example, after establishing strong invariance, found that compared to young (16–22 years) and old (67–72 years) adults, the average verbal cognitive component in the WAIS-R was highest in both middle-aged adult groups (30–40, 50–60 years), whereas the average performance cognitive component was highest in the younger age group and the younger of the two middle-aged cohorts. Specifically, the effect size for the verbal cognitive component was about Cohen's $d = .40$, indicating a small to medium performance difference favoring middle-aged adults (Cohen, 1987). A similar effect size was found for the performance cognitive component, showing that the 50- to 60-year-old participants scored, on average, about $d = .38$ below the younger adults and the 30- to 40-year-olds. Schaie et al. (1998), after having established strict invariance, reported that across a 7-year longitudinal time period, those aged 60 to 67 declined on the primary mental ability factors Inductive Reasoning, Spatial Orientation, Verbal Comprehension, Numeric Facility, and Perceptual Speed, but not Verbal Recall; those aged 53 to 60 remained stable on five of the six cognitive abilities with statistically significant decline evidenced only for Numeric Facility; and those aged 46 to 53 were stable on four of the six abilities and showed improved performance for the Verbal Comprehension and Verbal Recall factors (see also Schaie, 1996, pp. 126–129). Overall, with respect to the more crystallized or pragmatic cognitive abilities, middle-aged adults show a peak performance, whereas for the more fluid or mechanic cognitive abilities at the end of the period of midlife, a decline in performance is present.

A limitation of comparing means across time, different age groups, or both is that mean stability in middle adulthood might mask individual differences in cognitive development. That is, mean stability might appear in the presence of individually differing changes; for example, one half of the sample might increase in cognitive abilities and the other half decreases to the same amount (Hertzog & Dixon, 1996). To check for individual differences in change, stability of individual differences over time is required. That is, examining absolute change in middle age requires longitudinal data to determine the influence of environmental factors on cognitive development, the effects of chronic stressors on cognitive performance, the interaction between changes in different cognitive domains, and cohort differences between early and late middle age in the amount of cognitive performance change.

Differential change (or stability) refers to the consistency of individual differences in cognitive abilities across time. Empirically, the consistency of individual differences is often indexed by a correlation coefficient between two adjacent measurement occasions. For this reason, differential change can only be assessed longitudinally (and not cross-sectionally, i.e., across age groups). Conceptually, differential change implies that some individuals change to a larger (or smaller) amount than others, such that the rank order of individuals is different at different time points. Traditionally, correlations across time have been computed for observed measures of cognitive abilities (e.g., sum scores). Although according to classical test theory, random errors should cancel out across repeated assessments such that the correlation of scores should be uncontaminated by (random) measurement error, there might be other systematic influences that may qualify the comparison of observed scores across time. Again, a possible strategy to diminish such unwanted influences might be to establish strong invariance and to calculate the correlation across time between factors. However, to protect against unique systematic influences such as some forms of retesting effects (e.g., reduced test anxiety, learning, etc.), no statistical approach is optimal. Rather, this would require considering possible retesting effects in the design of a study, for example, by including independent samples at later measurement occasions (Schaie, 1996).

A problem with differential change is that it is difficult to judge when stability is low enough to consider it practically important. Thus, a stability of .90 might be considered high enough by some researchers to regard change of relative positions as negligible, whereas other researchers may emphasize the fact that stability is not perfect, from which one could conclude that there is differential change.

A strength of examining differential change is that relative change, that is, the degree to which individuals' cognitive performance changes in similar directions over time, is considered. However, from a low stability implying pronounced differential change, we do not know whether the sample of persons—let alone an individual person—increases or decreases in their cognitive ability level. Moreover, using correlations, we also do not know whether variances (i.e., the amount of interindividual differences) change across time.

Change (or stability) of divergence refers to the fact that using correlations, we do not know whether variances change over time. That is, across time there might be perfect differential stability and no absolute change, but variances might increase or decrease (Preece, 1982). This would still be indicative of individual differences in change, although both the mean level and rank order of individuals might be perfectly preserved across time (Hertzog & Dixon, 1996).

Examination of the age-related changes in variances in cognitive performance across middle age is needed to determine the degree to which there might be differential developments between populations at risk for further and stronger declines and populations repeatedly profiting from gains in performance because they are starting from high levels of performance. A better understanding of the processes leading to this dissociation of development could point to events or ages in the life course when persons respond particularly strongly to even small improvements or declines in performance, thus setting the stage for a developmental trajectory of life-long gains or lifelong losses in performance.

General versus specific change (or stability). Change in different cognitive abilities might or might not be correlated across persons. The question is whether or not there is an overall commonality in change of different cognitive abilities. If changes in cognitive abilities are highly related, this would suggest one factor, or at least very few factors, responsible for the individual changes observed; this factor would explain a similarly large degree of cognitive change in most individuals. This could occur in stable environmental conditions leading to very similar cognitive activations or when similar physiological processes are strongly influencing performance despite environmental variations between persons and over time (Pedersen & Lichtenstein, 1997; Pedersen, Spotts, & Kato, Chapter 3, this volume).

Intraindividual variability (or stability). Until recently, most longitudinal studies of cognitive aging have focused on mean changes and declines in cognitive performance as people age (Schaie & Hofer, 2001). Although the focus on mean change has not emphasized between-person differences in intraindividual variability in cognitive functioning, intraindividual variability has long been considered an interesting outcome in itself (Nesselroade, 1991). There is now sufficient empirical evidence to establish that intraindividual variability is a substantial source of systematic performance variability between people, especially in adults (Hultsch, Hertzog, Small, McDonald-Miszczak, & Dixon, 1992; Martin & Hofer, 2004; Nesselroade, 2001). In fact, recent studies suggest that intraindividual variability may predict later cognitive difficulties in older age (MacDonald, Hultsch, & Dixon, 2003; Rabbitt, Osman, Moore, & Stollery, 2001; Rowe & Kahn, 1997; Schaie, 2000). Even within the middle adult age range, there seem to be substantial interindividual differences in intraindividual change in particular cognitive functions (Ghisletta, Nesselroade, Featherman, & Rowe, 2002; Zimprich & Martin, 2002). Willis and Schaie (1999), in their review of longitudinal data on cognition, point out that there are significant individual differences above and beyond differences depending on design (i.e., cross-sectional vs. longitudinal) and length of longitudinal interval. This renders it meaningful to examine individual differences in change in cognitive functioning across midlife.

Once sufficient data on midlife cognition are available, it can be established to which degree individual differences in developmental changes might be due to (a) individual differences in usage and training (Bosma et al., 2003; Hultsch, Hertzog, Small, & Dixon, 1999), (b) individual differences in the interaction between environmental demands and age-related levels of performance (Sparrow & Davies, 1988), or (c) individual differences in resilience (Staudinger, Marsiske, & Baltes, 1995) and compensatory processes individuals apply to maintain a high level of everyday functioning (Freund & Baltes, 2002). It would also be possible to examine the role of individual differences in the effects of differentiation in early middle age and dedifferentiation processes in the transition from middle to old age (Reinert, Baltes, & Schmidt, 1965). Finally, it could be examined to which degree interindividual differences in intraindividual change across middle adulthood are related to changes in other cognitive (and noncognitive) domains.

It should be noted that as the six aspects of change discussed so far refer to groups of persons (the way persons are investigated empirically), it is impossible to conclude that the same change takes place for all individuals. Strictly speaking, with the exception of general versus specific change, the change observed in groups of middle-aged individuals might not capture the change of any individual person. Assuming, however, that the group change is representative of individual changes, the merit of examining groups is the generalizability of findings due to more representative selections of samples and more reliable measurements of cognitive functioning.

Changes in Cognitive Performance in Early and Late Middle Age

To examine changes in cognitive performance across middle adulthood, a number of different approaches and data may be used. For illustrative purposes, we will be using longitudinal data from the Interdisciplinary Study on Adult Development (ILSE; Martin, Grünendahl, & Martin, 2001). ILSE is an ongoing interdisciplinary longitudinal study of the psychological, physical, and social antecedents and consequences of aging among two groups of participants: a cohort born in the years 1930 to 1932 and a cohort born 1950 to 1952. Earlier analyses with the older cohort demonstrated substantial amounts of interindividual differences in several aspects of cognitive change over time (Martin & Zimprich, 2003; Zimprich, Martin, & Kliegel, 2003). However, similar questions have not yet been addressed with the early middle-aged cohort of the study. Currently available for this cohort are data from two measurement occasions, the first (T1) in 1995 and the second (T2) in 1999, that is, a longitudinal time period of approximately 4 years. We selected those $N = 479$ participants from the 1950–1952 cohort—of originally 501 participants at T1—who had complete data records for the variables of interest at both measurement occasions. Mean age of the sample at T1 (1995) was 43.8 years ($SD = 0.91$ years). Of the 479 participants, 226 (47%) were female.

Measures

Processing Speed

Processing speed was assessed using the Digit Symbol Substitution subtest of the German Version of the WAIS-R (Tewes, 1991) and the d2-Test (Brickenkamp & Zillmer, 1998). The Digit Symbol Substitution (DS) subtest requires using a code table of numbers paired with symbols in order to fill in as many correct symbols under the numbers of the answer sheet as possible. Scored are the numbers of correctly copied symbols within 90 seconds (possible range: 0–67 points). The d2-Test is composed of items that consist of the letters "d" or "p" with one, two, three, or four dashes arranged either individually or in pairs above and below the letter. There are 14 lines of 47 characters each for a total of 658 items. The participant is given 20 seconds to scan each line and mark all "d's" with two dashes. According to the authors, the d2-Test measures processing speed, rule compliance, and quality of performance (Brickenkamp & Zillmer, 1998). For the analyses (described next), two manifest indicators of processing speed were constructed from the d2-Test by summing the results of the first seven lines (d2_1, possible range: 0–329 points) and the results of the second seven lines (d2_2, possible range: 0–329 points). All three indicators of processing speed were divided by 10 in order to make them numerically more comparable to the memory indicators (see Marsh, Hau, Balla, & Grayson, 1998).

Memory

At both measurement occasions, memory was assessed using three different measures—an immediate picture recall task (PR), an immediate word recall task (WR), and a delayed word recognition task (DW)—from a major German gerontological test battery (Nuremberg Inventory of Old Age; Oswald & Fleischmann, 1995). For the immediate picture recall task (PR), seven pictures of objects were presented to the participants for 3 seconds each. Immediately after presentation of all pictures, participants were asked to recall as many objects as possible. Scored was the number of correctly recalled objects (possible range: 0–7 points). For the immediate word recall task (WR), a list of 12 common, two-syllable German words was read aloud to the participants. Instantly after presentation, participants were asked to recall as many words as possible. Scored was the number of correctly recalled words (possible range: 0–12 points). For the delayed word recognition task (DW), after a 30-minute interval, 24 words (12 identical to previously presented words and 12 distractor words) were read aloud to the participants. Participants had to decide which words they had been presented already in the immediate word recall task. Scored was the number of correctly recognized words (possible range: 0–12 points).

Modeling Different Types of Change in Early Middle Adulthood

The objective of our analysis was to examine absolute change, differential change, change of divergence, general change, and specific change in the age group of persons in early middle adulthood, that is, in their 40s. Despite relatively high individual levels of performance that could potentially lead to ceiling effects in memory assessments, the examination of different types of changes in early middle age may highlight the importance of examining change in an age group that has mostly been seen as stable in their performance. The final model displays the relations between measures at the two measurement occasions. Before discussing the implications, we will briefly go through the findings.

Structural Stability

In a first model, configural invariance across the 4-year period was tested by specifying the same confirmatory factor model, that is, a processing speed and a memory factor at both measurement occasions, but without any across-time constraints. To scale the latent variables, the means and variances were fixed to zero and one, respectively, for processing speed and memory at T1 and T2. Additionally, we freely estimated the across-time covariances between the residuals of the d2-Test indicator (d2_2) at T1 and T2, the digit symbol substitution test (DS) at T1 and T2, the picture recall test (PR) at T1 and T2, and the delayed word recall test (DW) at T1 and T2 (see Figure 6.1). Model 0 achieved an excellent fit

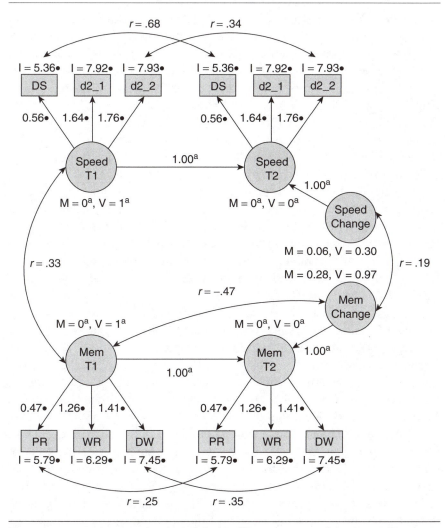

Figure 6.1   A Longitudinal Model of Different Aspects of Cognitive Change in Early Midlife Based on Data From 41- to 43-Year-Olds Followed Up for 4 Years

NOTES: $N = 479$, $\chi^2 = 146.14$, $df = 61$, $p < .05$, CFI = 0.996, RMSEA = 0.054. I = intercept, M = mean, V = variance, • denotes a parameter constrained to be equal over time, [a] denotes a fixed parameter. Except from correlations, all parameter estimates are nonstandardized. DS = Digit Symbol Substitution, d2_1 = First half of the d2-Test, d2_2 = second half of the d2-Test, Mem = Memory, PR = Picture Recall, WR = Word Recall, DW = Delayed Word Recognition.

($\chi 2 = 88.94$, $df = 44$, $p < .05$, CFI $= 0.998$, RMSEA $= 0.046$), implying that configural invariance holds across the two measurement occasions. Next, in Model 1, pattern or metric invariance was imposed by constraining factor loadings to be equal across time, while at the same time the variances of processing speed and memory at T2 were estimated freely. Although Model 1 also evinced an excellent fit ($\chi 2 = 103.89$, $df = 48$, $p < .05$, CFI $= 0.997$, RMSEA $= 0.049$), it represented a statistically significant decrease in fit compared to Model 0 ($\Delta \chi 2 = 14.95$, $\Delta df = 4$, $p < .05$). Note, however, that the change in the CFI was only 0.001, which indicated a fit difference of virtually no practical relevance. Thus, from Model 1, one might conclude that pattern or metric invariance holds for both the processing speed and the memory factors across the 4-year period. Subsequently, in Model 2, strong invariance was tested by constraining the latent intercepts of the manifest indicators to be equal across time, whereas the means of processing speed and memory at T2 were estimated freely. Model 3 showed an excellent fit as well ($\chi 2 = 116.29$, $df = 52$, $p < .05$, CFI $= 0.997$, RMSEA $= 0.051$), but with a statistically significant loss in model fit compared to the previous model ($\Delta \chi 2 = 12.40$, $\Delta df = 4$, $p < .05$). However, because there was no change in the CFI, one might consider this loss in fit as of no practical importance, implying that the hypothesis of strong invariance could not be rejected. Eventually, in Model 3, strict invariance was introduced by setting across-time equality constraints on the residual variances of all manifest indicators. Despite these restrictions, Model 3 exhibited an excellent fit ($\chi 2 = 143.20$, $df = 58$, $p < .05$, CFI $= 0.996$, RMSEA $= 0.055$), even though compared to Model 2, fit had decreased significantly ($\Delta \chi 2 = 26.91$, $\Delta df = 4$, $p < .05$). A comparison of the CFIs of both models indicated that the loss in fit due to imposing equal residual variances across time was negligible from a substantive point of view (ΔCFI $= -0.001$). Therefore, we kept Model 3 as adequately describing the data of both the processing speed and memory indicators at T1 and T2. Parameter estimates of Model 3 are depicted in Figure 6.1.

To summarize, a comparison of nested models imposing more and more equality constraints showed that strict variance holds with respect to processing speed and memory across the 4-year longitudinal time period. From this, one might conclude that at both T1 and T2, the measurement of processing speed and memory was identical in the sense that at both occasions, the same entity was assessed. At the same time, the fact that strict invariance was established rendered the analyses of other aspects of change meaningful.

Absolute Change

After having established strict invariance, the means of the processing speed and the memory factor were tested for statistically significant differences across time. Because the means of both variances were constrained to equal zero at T1, factor means significantly different from zero at T2 reflected a significant change in average performance across time.

The mean of the processing speed factor at T2 was 0.057 ($SE = 0.028$) and significantly different from zero ($p < .05$). Hence, on average, participants increased in processing speed performance across the 4-year period. However, the effect size of this increase was small ($d = 0.05$), implying that, although the average change in processing speed was statistically significant, there were only minor, but reliable, enhancements in processing speed across 4 years.

The statistically significant mean of the memory factor at T2 was estimated as 0.281 ($SE = 0.058$, $p < .05$). This implied that, on average, memory performance increased between T1 and T2. Effect size was $d = 0.27$, which, according to common standards, would be considered a small effect. Compared to the average increase in processing speed, however, the average increase in memory performance was more pronounced, indicating that, longitudinally, participants improved their memory performance more than they improved their speed performance.

To sum up, for both processing speed and memory performance, an average longitudinal increase was found. Although in both cognitive abilities the effect size of this mean increase was small, for memory the average improvement across the 4-year longitudinal period was more pronounced.

Differential Change

Differential change was assessed by correlating the processing speed and memory factors at T1 and T2. For processing speed, the covariance between T1 and T2 factor scores was 0.96 ($SE = 0.03$, $p < .05$), corresponding to a correlation of $r = 0.87$, indicating a relatively high level of differential stability or, in turn, a comparatively small amount of differential change. By contrast, the longitudinal covariance for memory performance was 0.53 ($SE = 0.06$, $p < .05$), corresponding to a correlation of $r = 0.52$. Hence, differential change across the 4-year period was more pronounced in memory performance than in processing speed, implying that relative positions of participants changed more in memory functioning than in speed of processing.

Change of Divergence

As mentioned earlier, the variances of both the processing speed and the memory factor at T1 were fixed to equal one in order to scale the latent variables. At T2, the variance of the processing speed factor was 1.21 ($SE = 0.06$) and significantly different from zero ($p < .05$). To test for change in the variance of the speed factor across time, the variance of processing speed at T2 was fixed to equal one and the fit of the resulting model was compared to the fit of Model 3. The difference in model fit amounted to $\Delta\chi2 = 13.4$, which, with $df = 1$, was statistically significant ($p < .05$). Thus, the variance increase of processing speed across the 4-year period was reliable, indicating that individual differences increased over time. The variance of memory at T2 was 1.012 ($SE = 0.11$) and significantly different from zero. Following the same procedure as for processing speed, the difference in model fit was $\Delta\chi2 = 0.05$, which, with $df = 1$, was not statistically significant. Hence, by contrast to processing speed, the variance of memory did not change reliably across time, showing that the amount of individual differences in memory performance remained stable.

General Versus Specific Change

So far, the investigation of different aspects of change in processing speed and memory in middle-aged adults has led to a rather complex picture. In both cognitive abilities, after establishing structural stability, an average increase of performance was observed across the 4-year period, albeit the increase was more pronounced for memory. With respect to differential change, longitudinal change in relative positions was present in both processing speed and memory; however, it was more pronounced in memory performance. Eventually and only in processing speed was there a change in diversity, indicating that individual differences increased over time.

One way to combine all this information into one model, but from a different perspective, is to utilize latent change models (McArdle & Nesselroade, 1994). In these models, the explicit focus is on change, not stability. Figure 6.1 depicts the finally accepted latent change model for processing speed and memory. By constraining the regression of speed at

T2 on speed at T1 to equal one, perfect stability was imposed on the covariance, mean, and variance for processing speed across time. All departures from perfect stability are then captured in a latent residual variable named "speed change." The same constraint is applied to memory performance, resulting in latent variable named "mem(ory) change." Change is modeled on the latent level, which has the advantage that the contamination by measurement error—a typical problem of differences between manifest variables—is reduced. Note that the means of speed change and memory change latent variables correspond to the mean changes reported earlier. The variances of the speed change and memory change latent variables are different, however, which is due to the fact that perfect stability is imposed. Both variances are statistically different from zero ($p < .05$), implying that there are reliable individual differences in the amount of change across time in processing speed and memory. In other words, diverging from the perspective of testing for a change in variance across time, now the focus is on whether individuals differ in their amount of change across time.

The utilization of latent change models allows for examining the fifth aspect of change, namely, whether cognitive changes are general or specific. For general changes to be present, one would expect that a change in speed would be accompanied by a proportional change in memory. Empirically, this would correspond to a strong correlation between speed and memory changes. For specific changes, in turn, the relation between longitudinal changes in speed and memory should only weakly be correlated, implying that the change in both cognitive abilities is only loosely coupled. For the model depicted in Figure 6.1, the correlation between changes was $r = .19$, showing that, although statistically significant, individual differences in processing speed changes were weakly associated with individual differences in memory changes in early middle adulthood. More specifically, speed and memory changes shared about 4% of common variance, from which one might conclude that the changes in these cognitive abilities are rather independent.

Discussion

We started out by claiming that the examination of cognitive development in middle age profits from going beyond a focus on mean changes or mean stability and that it is essential to examine the validity of theoretical approaches to lifespan development. It is, for instance, of theoretical importance whether speed and memory changes are related or unrelated across middle adulthood. If unrelated, this suggests a process of differentiation across middle age; that is, performance changes in different domains of cognitive functioning are differentially dependent on particular environmental or individual conditions, such as provided by the work and family environment. A strong relation would suggest a high degree of interdependence of cognitive functions and would also support the view of a common factor explaining most changes in most domains of cognitive functions (Baltes & Lindenberger, 1997). The combination of examining relations between intraindividual changes across several cognitive domains in early versus late middle adulthood also allows us to examine whether, as would be suggested by the lifespan literature and mean-based findings of peak performances in middle age, early middle adulthood is characterized by increasing differentiation and late middle adulthood by increasing dedifferentiation.

Examining different aspects of individual differences in change across middle adulthood can also help to relate changes in cognitive functioning to current theoretical explanations of lifelong cognitive development. Some theoretical concepts have related individual differences in cognitive functioning changes to the onset of physiological decline, for example, by centering the examination of longitudinal change around the occurrence of a particular event that has the potential of influencing many facets of cognitive functioning, such as hormonal changes in midlife or indications of dementia (Sliwinski, Hofer, Hall, Bushke, & Lipton, 2003). Others have suggested relating individual differences in performance changes to differences in usage and training of particular cognitive skills (Schooler, 1999) and have highlighted the potential influence of age by contextual demands effects, for example, when one assumes that the amount of individual training becomes more important for successful job performance. Finally, individual differences in different aspects of cognitive change may be related to individual differences in resilience and compensatory processes to maintain high and stable levels of cognitive performance. In this case, examining individual differences in change, other than mean level changes, allows us to examine individual trajectories of compensatory behaviors, relate trajectories across cognitive functioning domains, and focus on explaining the level of stability in a particular outcome that is achieved by the interaction of these trajectories (Martin & Hofer, 2004; Zimprich, Hofer, & Aartsen, 2004; Zimprich, Martin, & Kliegel, 2003).

The analysis we presented examines different aspects of change in early middle adulthood, and we have related these changes to observed developmental trends in young old age. We have demonstrated that structural stability in factors explaining cognitive performance exists; that absolute change exists with respect to processing speed and memory over several years of observation; that differential change was much higher for memory performance than for speed; that change in variance of speed, but not in memory, occurred; and that, when examining individual differences in speed and memory changes, changes in speed and memory performance were specific, and not general.

First of all, these results substantiate earlier findings of mean levels of cognitive performance across middle age (Willis & Schaie, 1999). In addition, they provide new information on the types of changes occurring in early versus late middle adulthood. The findings suggest that there are substantial differences in the types, direction, and size of different types of change between early and late middle age. For example, the relation between individual differences in 4-year longitudinal speed and memory changes is minimal in early middle age (4% shared variance) and in the range of 25% in late middle age (Zimprich & Martin, 2002). We also observed more differential change in memory than speed in early middle age. This might suggest that individually different and varying environmental demands and conditions in early middle age are related to memory performance, but not speed. In other words, memory performance is more malleable by environmental factors, whereas speed performance depends on a different, environment-independent influence, such as physical functioning. If that were true, then the question of differentiation and dedifferentiation in adulthood could be asked differently. Differentiation of particular cognitive functions in this case would depend on the influence of different factors, that is, an environmental and a physiological one. It would be important to know if, for cognitive functions that can be influenced by environmental factors, we would find differentiation (due to the differential influence of the environment) or dedifferentiation (due to the influence of shared environments). In fact, we might expect both, depending on the kind of environmental influence and the cognitive domain examined. Once we have more data on the environmental demand characteristics across middle age, including larger age ranges within middle age, and add longer periods of observation, it will be possible to elaborate a clearer picture of the influence of environmental demands on the level of differentiation and dedifferentiation across middle age.

A limitation in the theorizing and empirical examination of cognitive development across adulthood has been the use of more or less extended longitudinal studies with single measurement occasions. As Willis and Schaie (1999) have pointed out, there are differences in the reported longitudinal findings due to differences in the length of the longitudinal measurement interval (Zimprich et al., 2004). From a theoretical standpoint, the use of measurement-intensive designs with repeated measures within each measurement occasion might be another aspect of change that, in the future, could provide more insights into the processes responsible for the empirical relation between functioning in different cognitive domains or even between cognitive and noncognitive domains such as emotional or affective development (Martin & Hofer, 2004; Martin & Zimprich, 2003; Neiss & Almeida, 2004). This would support a process-oriented account of longitudinal change in cognitive functioning. In fact, compensatory processes might explain which declines in particular cognitive functions may lead to increases in other domains of cognitive or noncognitive functioning. Within the same person, the burst design allows researchers to examine to what degree individual differences in cognitive functioning can be accounted for by environmental influences such as stress, and may determine the relations between variability of earlier stress, of current stress, and of later stress and cognition or health variables (to see if short-term stress reactivity might be predictive of long-term changes in stress reactivity and long-term effects on cognition or health).

Overall, examining different aspects of change in middle age poses new theoretical challenges and new empirical questions that complement the existing findings on mean level changes in adulthood. In fact, the focus on individual differences in different aspects of change in cognitive functioning across middle adulthood highlights that despite relatively high mean levels of performance, a large amount of developmental change occurs in midlife. Focusing on these aspects of change clearly suggests a need for more data and more specific change theories on development across middle adulthood.

References

Anstey, K. J., Hofer, S. M., & Luszcz, M. A. (2003). Cross-sectional and longitudinal patterns of dedifferentiation in late-life cognitive and sensory function: The effects of age, ability, attrition, and occasion of measurement. *Journal of Experimental Psychology: General, 132,* 470–487.

Babcock, R. L., Laguna, K. D., & Roesch, S. C. (1997). A comparison of the factor structure of processing speed for younger and older adults: Testing the assumption of measurement equivalence across age groups. *Psychology and Aging, 12,* 268–276.

Ball, K., Berch, D. B., Helmers, K. F., Jobe, J. B., Leveck, M. D., Marsiske, M., et al. (2002). Effects of cognitive training interventions with older adults. *Journal of the American Medical Association, 288,* 2271–2281.

Baltes, M. M., & Lang, F. R. (1997). Everyday functioning and successful aging: The impact of resources. *Psychology and Aging, 12,* 433–443.

Baltes, P. B., Cornelius, S. W., Nesselroade, J. R., & Willis, S. L. (1980). Integration versus differentiation of fluid/crystallized intelligence in old age. *Developmental Psychology, 16,* 625–635.

Baltes, P. B., & Lindenberger, U. (1997). Emergence of a powerful connection between sensory and cognitive functions across the adult life span: A new window to the study of cognitive aging? *Psychology and Aging, 12,* 395–409.

Baltes, P. B., Reese, H. W., & Nesselroade, J. R. (1977). *Life-span developmental psychology: Introduction to research methods.* Monterey, CA: Brooks/Cole.

Bickley, P. G., Keith, T. Z., & Wolfle, L. M. (1995). The three-stratum theory of cognitive abilities: Test of the structure of intelligence across the life span. *Intelligence, 20,* 309–328.

Bollen, K. A. (1989). *Structural equations with latent variables.* New York: Wiley.

Bosma, H., van Boxtel, M. P. J., Ponds, R. W., Houx, P. J., & Jolles, J. (2003). Education and age-related cognitive decline: The contribution of mental workload. *Educational Gerontology, 29,* 165–173.

Brickenkamp, R., & Zillmer, E. (1998). *The d2 test of attention* (1st U.S. ed.). Seattle, WA: Hogrefe & Huber.

Cohen, J. (1987). *Statistical power analysis for the behavioral sciences* (Rev. ed.). Hillsdale, NJ: Erlbaum.

Cunningham, W. R., & Birren, J. E. (1980). Age changes in the factor structure of intellectual abilities in adulthood and old age. *Educational and Psychological Measurement, 40,* 271–290.

Cunningham, W. R., Clayton, V., & Overton, W. (1975). Fluid and crystallized intelligence in young adulthood and old age. *Journal of Gerontology, 30,* 53–55.

Dixon, R. A., De Frias, C. M., & Maitland, S. B. (2001). Memory in midlife. In M. E. Lachman (Ed.), *Handbook of midlife development* (pp. 248–278). New York: Wiley.

Espy, K. A., Molfese, V. J., & DiLalla, L. F. (2001). Effects of environmental measures on intelligence in young children: Growth curve modeling of longitudinal data. *Merrill Palmer Quarterly, 47,* 42–73.

Finkel, D., Pedersen, N. L., & Harris, J. R. (2000). Genetic mediation of the association among motor and perceptual speed and adult cognitive abilities. *Aging, Neuropsychology, and Cognition, 7,* 141–155.

Finkel, D., Pedersen, N. L., Plomin, R., & McClearn, G. E. (1998). Longitudinal and cross-sectional twin data on cognitive abilities in adulthood: The Swedish Adoption/Twin Study of Aging. *Developmental Psychology, 34,* 1400–1413.

Finkel, D., Reynolds, C. A., McArdle, J. J., Gatz, M., & Pedersen, N. L. (2003). Latent growth curve analyses of accelerating decline in cognitive abilities in late adulthood. *Developmental Psychology, 39*, 535–550.

Freund, A. M., & Baltes, P. B. (2002). The adaptiveness of selection, optimization, and compensation as strategies of life management: Evidence from a preference study on proverbs. *Journals of Gerontology: Psychological and Social Sciences, 57B*, P426–P434.

Ghisletta, P., & Lindenberger, U. (2003). Age-based structural dynamics between perceptual speed and knowledge in the Berlin Aging Study: Direct evidence for ability dedifferentiation in old age. *Psychology and Aging, 18*, 696–713.

Ghisletta, P., Nesselroade, J. R., Featherman, D. L., & Rowe, J. W. (2002). The structure, validity and predictive power of weekly intraindividual variability in health and activity measures. *Swiss Journal of Psychology, 61*, 73–83.

Havighurst, R. J. (1982). *Developmental tasks and education*. New York: McKay. (Original work published 1948)

Hertzog, C., & Bleckley, K. (2001). Age differences in the structure of intelligence: Influences of information processing speed. *Intelligence, 29*, 191–217.

Hertzog, C., & Dixon, R. A. (1996). Methodological issues in research on cognition and aging. In F. Blanchard-Fields & T. M. Hess (Eds.), *Perspectives on cognitive change in adulthood and aging* (pp. 66–121). Boston: McGraw-Hill.

Hofer, S. M., Berg, S., & Era, P. (2003). Evaluating the interdependence of aging-related changes in visual and auditory acuity, balance, and cognitive functioning. *Psychology and Aging, 18*, 285–305.

Hogan, D. P. (1987). Demographic trends in human fertility, and parenting across the life span. In J. B. Lancaster, J. Altmann, A. S. Rossi, & L. R. Sherrod (Eds.), *Parenting across the life span* (pp. 315–350). New York: De Gruyter.

Horn, J. L., & McArdle, J. J. (1992). A practical and theoretical guide to measurement invariance in aging research. *Experimental Aging Research, 18*, 117–144.

Hultsch, D. F., Hertzog, C., Small, B. J., & Dixon, R. A. (1999). Use it or lose it: Engaged lifestyle as a buffer of cognitive decline in aging? *Psychology and Aging, 14*, 245–263.

Hultsch, D., Hertzog, C., Small, B. J., McDonald-Miszczak, L., & Dixon, R. A. (1992). Short-term longitudinal change in cognitive performance in later life. *Psychology and Aging, 7*, 571–584.

Juan-Espinosa, M., García, L. F., Colom, R., & Abad, F. J. (2000). Testing the age differentiation hypothesis through Wechsler's scales. *Personality and Individual Differences, 29*, 1069–1075.

Juan-Espinosa, M., García, L. F., Escorial, S., Rebollo, I., Colom, R., & Abad, F. J. (2002). Age dedifferentiation hypothesis: Evidence from the WAIS-III. *Intelligence, 30*, 395–408.

Kirlik, A., & Bisantz, A. M. (1999). Cognition in human-machine systems: Experiential and environmental aspects of adaptation. In A. P. Hancock (Ed.),

Human performance and ergonomics: Handbook of perception and cognition series (2nd ed., pp. 47–68). San Diego, CA: Academic Press.

Kliegl, R., Philipp, D., Luckner, M., & Krampe, R. T. (2001). Face memory skill acquisition. In N. Charness & D. C. Park (Eds.), *Communication, technology and aging: Opportunities and challenges for the future* (pp. 169–186). New York: Springer.

Lamar, M., Resnick, S. M., & Zonderman, A. B. (2003). Longitudinal changes in verbal memory in older adults: Distinguishing the effects of age from repeat testing. *Neurology, 60,* 82–86.

Lawton, M. P., Moss, M., Hoffman, C., Grant, R., Ten Have, T., & Kleban, M. H. (1999). Health, valuation of life, and the wish to live. *The Gerontologist, 39*(4), 406–416.

Li, K., & Lindenberger, U. (2002). Relations between aging sensory/sensorimotor and cognitive functions. *Neuroscience and Biobehavioral Reviews, 26,* 777–783.

Lindenberger, U., & Baltes, P. B. (1994). Sensory functioning and intelligence in old age: A strong connection. *Psychology and Aging, 9,* 339–355.

MacDonald, S. W. S., Hultsch, D. F., & Dixon, R. A. (2003). Performance variability is related to change in cognition: Evidence from the Victoria Longitudinal Study. *Psychology and Aging, 18,* 510–523.

Maitland, S. B., Intrieri, R. C., Schaie, K. W., & Willis, S. L. (2000). Gender differences and changes in cognitive abilities across the adult life span. *Aging, Neuropsychology, and Cognition, 7,* 32–53.

Marsh, H. W., Hau, K. T., Balla, J. R., & Grayson, D. (1998). Is more ever too much? The number of indicators per factor in confirmatory factor analysis. *Multivariate Behavioral Research, 33,* 181–220.

Martin, M., Grünendahl, M., & Martin, P. (2001). Age differences in stress, social resources and well-being in middle and older age. *Journal of Gerontology: Psychological Sciences, 56,* P214–P222.

Martin, M., & Hofer, S. M. (2004). Intraindividual variability, change, and aging: Conceptual and analytical issues. *Gerontology, 50,* 7–11.

Martin, M., & Mroczek, D. K. (in press). Are personality traits across the lifespan sensitive to environmental demands? *Journal of Adult Development.*

Martin, M., & Zimprich, D. (2003). Are changes in cognitive functioning in older adults related to subjective complaints? *Experimental Aging Research, 29,* 335–352.

McArdle, J. J., & Nesselroade, J. R. (1994). Using multivariate data to structure developmental change. In H. W. Reese & S. H. Cohen (Eds.), *Life-span developmental psychology: Methodological contributions* (pp. 223–267). Hillsdale, NJ: Erlbaum.

Meredith, W. (1993). Measurement invariance, factor analysis, and factorial invariance. *Psychometrika, 58,* 525–543.

Meredith, W., & Horn, J. (2001). The role of factorial invariance in modeling growth and change. In L. M. Collins & A. G. Sayer (Eds.), *New methods for the analysis of change* (pp. 203–240). Washington, DC: American Psychological Association.

Moen, P., & Wethington, E. (1999). Midlife development in a life course context. In S. L. Willis & J. D. Reid (Eds.), *Life in the middle* (pp. 3–23). San Diego, CA: Academic Press.

Neiss, M., & Almeida, D. M. (2004). Age differences in the heritability of mean and intraindividual variation of psychological distress. *Gerontology, 50,* 22–27.

Nesselroade, J. R. (1991). The warp and the woof of the developmental fabric. In R. M. Downs & L. S. Liben (Eds.), *Visions of aesthetics, the environment and development: The legacy of Joachim F. Wohlwill* (pp. 213–240). Hillsdale, NJ: Erlbaum.

Nesselroade, J. R. (2001). Intraindividual variability in development within and between individuals. *European Psychologist, 6,* 187–193.

Oswald, W. D., & Fleischmann, U. M. (1995). *Nürnberger Altersinventar (NAI)* [Nuremberg Age Inventory]. Göttingen, Germany: Hogrefe.

Park, D. C., Lautenschlager, G., Hedden, T., Davidson, N. S., Smith, A. D., & Smith, P. K. (2002). Models of visuospatial and verbal memory across the adult life span. *Psychology and Aging, 17,* 299–320.

Pedersen, N. L., & Lichtenstein, P. (1997). Biometric analyses of human abilities. In C. Cooper & V. Varma (Eds.), *Processes in individual differences* (pp. 125–147). London: Routledge.

Perlman, M. D. (1980). Unbiasedness of the likelihood ratio tests for equality of several covariance matrices and equality of several multivariate normal populations. *Annals of Statistics, 8,* 247–263.

Preece, P. F. (1982). The fan-spread hypothesis and the adjustment for initial differences between groups in uncontrolled studies. *Educational and Psychological Measurement, 42,* 759–762.

Rabbitt, P., Osman, P., Moore, B., & Stollery, B. (2001). There are stable individual differences in performance variability, both from moment to moment and from day to day. *Quarterly Journal of Experimental Psychology: Human, 54A,* 981–1003.

Rees, A. H., & Palmer, F. H. (1970). Factors related to change in mental test performance. *Developmental Psychology, 3,* 57.

Reinert, G., Baltes, P. B., & Schmidt, L. R. (1965). Faktorenanalytische Untersuchungen zur Differenzierungshypothese der Intelligenz [Factor analytic studies on the differentiation hypothesis of intelligence]. *Psychologische Forschung, 28,* 246–300.

Rossi, A. S., & Rossi, P. H. (1990). *Of human bonding.* New York: Aldine de Gruyter.

Rowe, J. W., & Kahn, R. L. (1997). Successful aging. *Gerontologist, 37,* 433–440.

Schaie, K. W. (1996). *Intellectual development in adulthood—The Seattle Longitudinal Study.* Cambridge, UK: Cambridge University Press.

Schaie, K. W. (2000). The impact of longitudinal studies on understanding development from young adulthood to old age. *International Journal of Behavioral Development, 24,* 257–266.

Schaie, K. W., & Hofer, S. M. (2001). Longitudinal studies in aging research. In K. W. Schaie & J. E. Birren (Eds.), *Handbook of the psychology of aging* (pp. 53–77). San Diego, CA: Academic Press.

Schaie, K. W., Maitland, S. B., Willis, S. L., & Intrieri, R. C. (1998). Longitudinal invariance of adult psychometric ability factor structures across 7 years. *Psychology and Aging, 13*, 8–20.

Schmidt, D. F., & Botwinick, J. (1989). A factorial analysis of the age dedifferentiation hypothesis. In K. W. Schaie & V. L. Bengtson (Eds.), *The course of later life: Research and reflections* (pp. 87–92). New York: Springer.

Schooler, C. (1999). The workplace environment: Measurement, psychological effects, and basic issues. In S. L. Friedman & T. D. Wachs (Eds.), *Measuring environment across the life span* (pp. 229–246). Washington, DC: American Psychological Association.

Seeman, T. E., Singer, B. H., Ryff, C. D., Dienberg-Love, G., & Levy-Storms, L. (2002). Social relationships, gender, and allostatic load across two age cohorts. *Psychosomatic Medicine, 64*, 395–406.

Sliwinski, M. J., Hofer, S. M., Hall, C., Bushke, H., & Lipton, R. B. (2003). Modeling memory decline in older adults: The importance of preclinical dementia, attrition and chronological age. *Psychology and Aging, 18*, 658–671.

Soederberg Miller, L. M., & Lachman, M. E. (2000). Cognitive performance and the role of control beliefs in midlife. *Aging, Neuropsychology, and Cognition, 7*, 69–85.

Sparrow, P. R., & Davies, D. R. (1988). Effects of age, tenure, training, and job complexity on technical performance. *Psychology and Aging, 3*, 307–314.

Staudinger, U. M., Marsiske, M., & Baltes, P. B. (1995). Resilience and reserve capacity in later adulthood: Potentials and limits of development across the life span. In D. Cicchetti & D. J. Cohen (Eds.), *Risk, disorder, and adaptation* (Developmental Psychopathology, Vol. 2, pp. 801–847). Oxford, UK: Wiley.

Sternberg, R. J., Grigorenko, E. L., & Oh, S. (2001). The development of intelligence at midlife. In M. E. Lachman (Ed.), *Handbook of midlife development* (pp. 217–247). New York: Wiley.

Taub, G. E., McGrew, K. S., & Witta, E. L. (2004). A confirmatory analysis of the factor structure and cross-age invariance of the Wechsler Adult Intelligence Scale-Third Edition. *Psychological Assessment, 16*, 85–89.

Tewes, U. (1991). *Hamburg-Wechsler-Intelligenztest für Erwachsene, Revision 1991* (2. Aufl [Hamburg-Wechsler Intelligence Test for Adults, 1991 revision (2nd ed.)]. Bern, Switzerland: Huber.

Tomer, A., & Cunningham, W. R. (1993). The structure of cognitive speed measures in old and young adults. *Multivariate Behavioral Research, 28*, 1–24.

Townsend, B. (2001). Dual-earner couples and long work hours: A structural and life course perspective. *Berkeley Journal of Sociology, 45*, 161–179.

West, R. L., & Tomer, A. (1989). Everyday memory problems of healthy older adults: Characteristics of a successful intervention. In P. J. Whitehouse &

G. C. Gilmore (Eds.), *Memory, aging, and dementia: Theory, assessment, and treatment* (pp. 74–98). New York: Springer.

Willis, S. L., & Schaie, K. W. (1986). Training the elderly on the ability factors of spatial orientation and inductive reasoning. *Psychology and Aging, 1,* 239–247.

Willis, S. L., & Schaie, K. W. (1999). Intellectual functioning in midlife. In S. L. Willis & J. D. Reid (Eds.), *Life in the middle* (pp. 234–247). San Diego, CA: Academic Press.

Zelinsky, E. M., & Lewis, K. L. (2003). Adult age differences in multiple cognitive functions: Differentiation, dedifferentiation, or process-specific change? *Psychology and Aging, 18,* 727–745.

Zimprich, D., Hofer, S. M., & Aartsen, M. J. (2004). Short-term versus long-term longitudinal changes in processing speed. *Gerontology, 50,* 17–21.

Zimprich, D., & Martin, M. (2002). Can longitudinal changes in processing speed explain longitudinal age changes in fluid intelligence? *Psychology and Aging, 17,* 690–695.

Zimprich, D., Martin, M., & Kliegel, M. (2003). Subjective cognitive complaints, memory performance, and depressive affect in old age: A change-oriented approach. *International Journal of Aging and Human Development, 57,* 339–366.

PART III

Impact of Middle Age on Functioning in Late Life

Seven

The Development of Physical and Mental Health From Late Midlife to Early Old Age

Dorly J. H. Deeg

M idlife is a period of life that is sandwiched between young adulthood and older age. It is a seemingly inconspicuous period, in which stability is the expected norm, and no major changes are expected to occur—as opposed to the periods preceding and following midlife. Perhaps for this reason, midlife in itself has received little attention in the scientific literature. Most literature that covers midlife considers it either as an outcome of earlier life exposures and experiences (Kuh & Ben-Shlomo, 2004) or as a determinant of changes and developments in older age (Holahan, Holahan, & Wonacott, 1999; Strandberg, Strandberg, Salonmaa, Pitkala, & Miettinen, 2003). The image that emerges from the scarce academic publications that focus on midlife is one of a period of optimal functioning in various aspects of mental health and competence (Clark-Plaskie & Lachman, 1999; Keyes & Ryff, 1999; Neugarten, 1976), whereas the first aging-related health problems may start presenting themselves (Merrill & Verbrugge, 1999). The popular literature, on the other hand, frequently associates the term *midlife* with the term *crisis* (Sheehy, 1976).

In short, a dualistic view of midlife exists: as one of both crisis and stability (Lachman, 2004). During midlife, many life events and changes occur in similar frequencies as in other phases of life and are associated with similar characteristics. Among these are acute illness, divorce, and job loss. This being said, it must also be noted that there is a huge body of literature on "the change," that is, on changes related to menopause in women. Among the 208 relevant titles that came up in a literature search based on the keywords "midlife" and "health," 54 dealt with menopause. This shows that researchers, like other human beings, are drawn by obvious changes and distinctive events. The question, of course, is whether the less obvious changes or even the presumed uneventfulness of middle age are not equally relevant objects for study when placed in a life-course perspective. In the view of Baltes (1987), there is a shifting balance of gains and losses throughout the life span. Is it not possible that in midlife, a large heterogeneity of gains and losses is hidden behind uneventful averages?

The age range of 55–65, termed *late midlife*, is currently considered the last phase of middle adulthood. Either end of this age range, of course, is up for discussion. If the beginning of late midlife is marked by changes such as children leaving the home, this age may vary with the average age of childbearing. In the Netherlands, for instance, the age at which mothers get their first child has increased from 24 to 29 years during the past decades (Statistics Netherlands, 1999). Likewise, if the average age at retirement is considered to mark the end of late midlife, this age is likely to vary across time and country. Whereas in the United States, no legal retirement age exists, but the age at which younger workers are entitled to old age security has moved up to age 67, in the Netherlands, the legal retirement age is 65, but over 90% of employees retire earlier using pre-pension schemes (Henkens & Van Solinge, 2003). Regardless of its exact limits, the late-midlife age group is currently showing an unprecedented increase in size because it includes the earliest baby boomers, for whom the first birth cohort is 1946. Because life expectancy for this age group amounts to some 20 additional years beyond retirement age, it is important to consider the influence of the changes during late middle adulthood on the quality of life during these later years. However, little is known about the development of physical and mental health from this transitional period into early old age and how the various social changes experienced in late middle adulthood affect development in old age. Moreover, the development of physical and mental health during this period is likely to be affected by experiences earlier in the life course.

As opposed to earlier phases of midlife, late midlife is a period in which several obvious changes are likely to occur. Such changes may include the death of a parent, the last child leaving the parental home, becoming a grandparent, the preparation for retirement, and in most cases actual retirement. Many people in this age range experience their first confrontation with health problems. The wide variety of possible (social) changes implies that this age group shows substantial heterogeneity. On balance, one might state that losses start to dominate gains (Baltes, 1987).

Heterogeneity or variability is a useful concept in the study of midlife. Changes in physical and mental health are conceptualized as different trajectories for those doing well and those doing worse (Lachman, 2004). These trajectories, in turn, are studied in relation to gains and losses in various domains. A second useful concept is the interrelatedness of changes; rather than singling out one factor, the interplay of personal, social, and health factors is studied (Lachman, 2004). Furthermore, sociodemographic factors exert an influence that can be assessed relatively easily, although the explanation of these influences may be more difficult to achieve. For example, middle-aged persons with lower socioeconomic status have been shown to experience negative changes earlier in life than adults with higher status (Marmot et al., 1998). And there are obvious gender differences: Women experience some changes earlier than men (e.g., retirement) and other changes later than men (e.g., fatal chronic illness).

This chapter describes the transition from late middle age to early old age, in terms of physical and mental health, from the vantage point of late midlife as a starting point for older age. Due consideration is given to heterogeneity, both in the development of physical and mental health and in the social factors that are related to these developments. These social factors are grouped according to their temporal relation with the transitions studied: *Baseline* factors include characteristics of late midlife, at the starting point of the period of transition; *early life* factors include characteristics of childhood, adolescence, or young adulthood that may exert influence on transitions from late midlife; and *concurrent changes* include typical changes in social factors during late midlife and early old age. What is known from the literature on this transition will be reviewed. As there is practically no longitudinal research following a single group of individuals from late midlife to early old age in terms of their physical and mental health, new data are presented derived from the Longitudinal Aging Study Amsterdam (LASA; Deeg, Beekman, Kriegsman, & Westendorp-de Serière, 1998).

Historic and Social Context

The cohort that has been followed from late midlife to early old age in the LASA was born in 1927–1937. This paragraph describes the historical context in which this cohort grew up and provides the development during their lives of social indicators such as fertility, labor market participation, and education.

This cohort spent the first years of their lives during the years of the economic crisis of the 1930s. As least as disruptive were the years of World War II, when the Netherlands was occupied by fascist Germany (1940–1945), which were experienced by all members of this cohort earlier or later during their childhood. For example, during the famine of the Dutch Hunger Winter (1944–1945), they were aged 7 to 17. This cohort made the transition to young adulthood during the period of "Restoration" of the nation after World War II. Although the Marshall Plan helped alleviate the most urgent lack of basic needs, for several years, food and luxury articles were still rationed. The postwar baby boom peaked in the late 1940s, with a high fertility rate of almost 4 children born to each woman of childbearing age, and lasted until 1970, the decade after which the fertility rate dropped from 2.8 to 1.6 (Statistics Netherlands, 1999). The baby boom caused a lack of housing, which was not alleviated for decades.

Another consequence of the long duration of the Dutch baby boom was the long duration of the low labor market participation of women. During the first half of the 20th century, 25% of women of working age (15–65 years) had a paid job. In this period, it was customary that young women stopped working after marriage. In contrast to other European countries, the percentage of women participating in the labor market stayed at 25% throughout the 1970s. Only in the 1980s did this percentage start rising, reaching 45% in the year 2000. This rise was visible in women at all ages, but was most notable in women aged 40 years and older (Statistics

Netherlands, 2004). Thus, from 1992 to 2002, the period during which the LASA cohort was followed from late midlife to early old age, female labor market participation at ages 55 to 59 rose from 18% to 35%, and at ages 60 to 64, from 4% to 7%. At the same time, the labor market participation of men declined because in young adulthood, men spent an increasing number of years in education, and in late midlife, they made increasing use of pre-pension schemes that were financially favorable, or, in the decreasing economic tide of the 1980s, were dismissed with what was euphemistically called "age dismissal." This trend was halted in the mid-1990s, when the Netherlands went through a period of economic prosperity. Labor market participation among men aged 55 to 59 rose from 58% in 1995 to 73% in 2002 and among men aged 60 to 64, from 17% to 27%.

The recent rise in labor market participation may be partly due to the rise in level of education in subsequent cohorts. Whereas in the cohorts born in the 1920s, men had on average 8 and women 7 years of schooling, the number of years rose steadily until both men and women born in the 1960s had an average of 13 years of schooling (Statistics Netherlands, 1999).

The Longitudinal Aging Study Amsterdam

The LASA is an ongoing, interdisciplinary study on changes in physical, emotional, cognitive, and social functioning; interrelations between these domains of functioning; and potential determinants and consequences of changes in functioning. Its main goal is to supply insights that enhance the autonomy, quality of life, and social integration of older persons (Deeg, Knipscheer, & Van Tilburg, 1993; Deeg & Westendorp-de Serière, 1994).

The LASA cohort started with a stratified random sample of 3,107 participants aged 55 to 85 in 1992–1993. The sample was taken from municipal registries in 11 cities and towns, based in three socioculturally distinct geographical areas. The northeast of the Netherlands is traditionally Protestant, the south is traditionally Roman Catholic, and the west is the most secularized area. In each area, a larger sized city and several smaller towns were included. Thus, the sample can be considered to reflect the national distribution of population density. The sample consists of age and sex strata that are weighted according to expected mortality, so that 5 years after baseline each 5-year age group would include equal numbers of men and women. For the initial sample, the upper age limit of 85 years was chosen because beyond this age a high nonresponse was expected, whereas it was considered easier to keep participants in the study once they had participated, and so with time, the sample would include sufficient numbers of the oldest-old. The lower age limit of 55 years was chosen because it was considered important to have data on the changes in functioning that precede ages 65 and over that are generally considered as "older age." Moreover, a sizeable proportion of the Dutch population aged 55 to 64 years shares characteristics with those 65 and over because of early retirement.

All LASA participants are followed up every 3 years, and at this moment the data span a period of nine years (from 1992–1993 to 2001–2002). Each data collection cycle includes identical interviews and measurements of physical, cognitive, emotional, and social functioning as well as possible determinants and consequences of changes in functioning. These data provide the opportunity to examine various changes in living conditions and to relate these changes to the development of physical and mental health.

Study Sample

At the origin of the LASA in 1992–1993, there were 966 participants aged 55 to 64 years: 499 (51.7%) men and 467 (48.7%) women. These participants were born in 1928–1937 and transited from late midlife to early old age during the study period of 9 years. At the end of this period, their ages were 64 to 73 years. Across the 9 years, complete data are available for 849 persons (88% of baseline participants); of these, 100 (10%) had died. The subjects who dropped out for reasons other than mortality ($n = 117, 12\%$) were more often based in the west and northeast than in the south but did not differ significantly from the continuing participants on other sociodemographic characteristics.

Measures

Measures of physical and mental health include two indicators of each domain. Physical health is assessed by self-reported functional limitations (Kriegsman, Deeg, Van Eijk, Penninx, & Boeke, 1997) and self-rated health (Deeg & Kriegsman, 2003). Mental health is covered by a depressive symptoms scale (Beekman et al., 1997; Radloff, 1977) and a loneliness scale (De Jong Gierveld & Kamphuis, 1985). As the main purpose of this chapter is to show the variability in the development from late midlife to early old age for each indicator of physical and mental health, trajectories are constructed based on cluster analyses of the scores at the four observation cycles (Deeg, in press; Singer & Ryff, 2001). A common procedure in longitudinal research is to study only those subjects who survived the study period. However, such findings are likely to be biased because the survivors are a healthy selection of the initial cohort. Therefore, those who died during the 9 years of follow-up in the LASA study were considered to have followed a separate trajectory.

Potential determinants of trajectories of intraindividual change are baseline characteristics, early-life experiences, and concurrent changes. Selected baseline characteristics include sociodemographics (age, gender, education), health problems (functional limitations, self-rated health), family relations (living with a partner), and social position (having paid work, income). Early-life experience includes socioeconomic status of the participants' parents, which is combined with the educational level attained by the participants into a measure of social mobility (Broese van Groenou, 2003). Concurrent changes are selected based on their salience in late midlife (Lachman, 2004) and include retirement from paid work, loss of income, and changes in partner status.

Changes in Physical and Mental Health

This section provides an overview of the literature on physical and mental health in late midlife, with a special focus on the Netherlands. In reviewing the evidence, differences between men and women are described, as the data are usually reported according to gender. This section furthermore describes new data on trajectories in physical and mental health during the transition from late midlife to early old age, based on the LASA.

Life Expectancy

Ultimate indicators of health and well-being are mortality and life expectancy. At age 55 in the year 2000, life expectancy in the Netherlands is an additional 24 years for men and 28 years for women, and at age 65, life expectancies for men and women are still an additional 15 and 20 years, respectively (Statistics Netherlands, 2004). Moreover, since 1950, life expectancy at age 55 has increased by 2 years in men, and by 4 years in women. The cohorts that entered late midlife during the 1990s had lost only 15% (men) and 10% (women) to mortality (Tabeau, Van Poppel, & Willekens, 1994). These numbers show some variation across developed nations, among which the Netherlands occupies a place in the upper half (Van der Wilk, Achterberg, & Kramers, 2001). Clearly, on average, death has been a relatively rare event for those entering late midlife.

Physical Health

Physical health includes specific conditions and symptoms as well as general indicators such as functional limitations, activities of daily living (ADL) and instrumental activities of daily living (IADL) disability, and self-rated health.

Despite the considerable number of remaining years of life, during late midlife the likelihood of health problems, some of which are related to aging, starts to increase. Table 7.1 lists the top five most prevalent chronic conditions by age and gender in the Netherlands (Van den Berg Jeths, Poos, & Ruwaard, 1993). In midlife, chronic conditions are not necessarily life threatening. In the group aged 45 to 64 years, arthritis ranks first among both men (6%) and women (9%). Respiratory diseases, including asthma, rank second, again in both men (5%) and women (3%). Other high-ranking conditions in this age group are depression (men, 4% and women, 3%) and angina pectoris (men, 4% and women, 2%). Notably, the top five most prevalent chronic conditions for men and women differ only in one condition: For men, they include myocardial infarction (4%), and for women, they include diabetes (3%).

The transition from late midlife to early old age is marked by a substantial increase in the prevalence of chronic conditions. However, these are still not necessarily life threatening. In the group aged 65 to 74 years, the list of the top five most prevalent conditions is still headed by arthritis, in both men (16%) and women (26%). Respiratory diseases still feature in the top five (13% in men, 4% in women) but no longer occupy second place. Angina pectoris has moved up in both men (13%) and women (8%). Diabetes is still in the top five among women (7%) but not among men. Also, depression features in the top five in women (4%) but no longer in men. In contrast, myocardial infarction in men has tripled (15%) and now occupies second place. Moreover, stroke enters the top five in men, with a prevalence of 6%.

For the group aged 45 to 64 years in the United States, similar top five chronic conditions for men and women have been reported, including heart disease in men and diabetes and psychiatric disorders in women

Table 7.1   Top Five Most Prevalent Chronic Conditions[1] in Midlife and Early
                   Old Age by Gender in the Netherlands (Van den Berg Jeths et al.,
                   1993) and the United States (Verbrugge & Patrick, 1995)

The Netherlands

Men 45–64 years	%	Women 45–64 years	%
1 Osteoarthritis	5.9	1 Osteoarthritis	9.0
2 Asthma and COPD[2]	5.1	2 Asthma and COPD	3.1
3 Depression	4.3	3 Diabetes	2.6
4 Myocardial Infarction	4.3	4 Depression	2.5
5 Angina Pectoris	3.8	5 Angina Pectoris	1.7

Men 65–74 years	%	Women 65–74 years	%
1 Osteoarthritis	16.0	1 Osteoarthritis	26.0
2 Myocardial Infarction	14.7	2 Angina Pectoris	8.1
3 Asthma and COPD	13.4	3 Diabetes	6.9
4 Angina Pectoris	12.8	4 Depression	4.2
5 Stroke	6.2	5 Asthma and COPD	4.2

United States

Men 45–64 years	%	Women 45–64 years	%
1 Essential Hypertension	22.5	1 Essential Hypertension	27.7
2 Ischemic Heart Disease	12.5	2 Malignant Neoplasms	12.8
3 Diabetes	9.1	3 Diabetes	12.5
4 Malignant Neoplasms	8.3	4 Urinary System Diseases	9.0
5 Prostate and Other Male Genital Problems	7.4	5 Anxiety States and Other Neuroses	9.0

1. Based on reasons (principal diagnoses) for visits to office-based physicians
2. Chronic obstructive pulmonary disease

(Merrill & Verbrugge, 1999; Verbrugge & Patrick, 1995). Depending on the system of registration, however, conditions may be reported differently. Thus, malignant neoplasms are absent from the Netherlands top five because the registration system used classifies neoplasms according to site instead of lumping all neoplasms together, like the U.S. registration system. A notable difference is also the high rank of hypertension for both U.S. men and women. Possibly, in the United States, unlike in the Netherlands, it is routine practice to have one's blood pressure taken, so that high blood pressure is more often established.

Clearly, for men, entering early old age implies being exposed to increasing risks of fatal diseases, whereas for women, the burden of diseases certainly increases, but these are associated with a limited risk of death. Thus, in late midlife, the well-known gender paradox of health starts to emerge: Women live longer than men but spend more of their remaining years in poorer health. The top five lists demonstrate that whereas men more often have fatal diseases, women more often have disabling, nonfatal diseases (Verbrugge & Patrick, 1995).

As suggested by the prevalence of potentially disabling conditions, the prevalence of functional limitations in late midlife is not negligible. In the LASA study, limitations in (i.e., difficulty performing) three activities were determined: climbing 15 steps, cutting toenails, and using own or public transportation. Eighteen percent of those aged 55 to 64 years reported difficulty doing at least one activity, and this percentage rose to 37% in the group aged 65 to 74 years (Kriegsman et al., 1997). The level of functional limitations and disability is higher in older women than in older men, a consistent finding across developed countries (Laditka, 2002). In the Netherlands, the gender difference appeared true for both age groups (i.e., 55–64 years and 65–74 years; Deeg & Pot, 1997). However, in late midlife, the gender difference could be explained by other sociodemographic factors that are associated with poor health. In particular, adjustment for the lower level of education of women and their higher frequency of living alone rendered the gender difference insignificant. These two factors were also strongly predictive of functional status in samples of late-middle-aged Americans (Pope, Sowers, Welch, & Albrecht, 2001; Waite & Hughes, 1999). In early old age, the gender difference in disability in the Dutch sample persisted despite adjustment for other sociodemographic factors. The discussion of the top five chronic conditions in men and women suggests that this gender difference may be due to a gender difference in the severity or fatality of the conditions. However, further analysis showed that the gender difference in disability was only partly attributable to the higher prevalence of nonfatal diseases in women. Additionally, it may be attributable to the higher mortality in men, once they have a potentially fatal disease (Deeg, Portrait, & Lindeboom, 2002).

In addition to functional limitations and disability, health experienced by the subject, termed self-rated health, is a widely used measure of general health. Self-rated health shows cultural variations (Jylhä, Guralnik, Ferrucci, Jokela, & Heikkinen, 1998). In the Netherlands, the prevalence of fair or poor self-rated health in late midlife is 32%, and in early old age, 36% (Broese van Groenou & Deeg, 2000). As opposed to disability, self-rated health does not show a steep age gradient of decline. Part of the explanation for this lack of age-related decline may be that self-ratings of health are associated with personality factors such as openness to experience, extraversion, conscientiousness, and neuroticism (Goodwin & Engstrom, 2002). It has been shown that these personality factors are largely stable during the life span (McCrae & Costa, 2003). As is the case with functional limitations, women report poorer health than men. In the LASA sample, no gender difference was apparent in the group aged 55 to 64 years. In contrast, in the early old age group of 65 to 74 years, a gender difference emerged (reports of fair or poor health in men: 31%, and in women: 40%). This gender difference persisted after adjustment for other sociodemographic characteristics, the most influential of which was level of education (Deeg & Pot, 1997). Again, for middle-aged samples in other developed countries, similar associations of self-rated health and socioeconomic status have been reported (Marmot et al., 1998; Miech & Hauser, 2001; Wilson, 2001). An Australian study found that despite the gender difference in level of self-rated health, men and women experience similar symptoms (Calvaresi & Bryan, 2003).

Trajectories of Physical Health

The LASA study provides data on changes in physical health from late midlife to early old age. The variability in patterns of change was studied by determining trajectories for two general health indicators: functional limitations and self-rated health.

Functional Limitations

Rather than focus on disability, the end stage of the disablement process, the LASA study focuses on functional limitations, which conceptually precede disability (Verbrugge & Jette, 1994). The measure of functional limitations was based on self-reports assessing the degree of difficulty with the following three activities: climbing stairs, cutting one's own toenails, and using own or public transportation (Deeg, in press; Kriegsman et al., 1997). The selected activities are expected to be sensitive to changes over time because having difficulty doing them indicates mild levels of functional limitation, which are more likely to occur in late middle age than the more severe limitations indicated by difficulty doing ADL activities. The response categories ranged from 0 = no difficulty to 3 = not able to perform. The items were summed to a functional limitations score ranging from 0 to 9. At baseline, the mean and standard deviation were 0.4 + 1.2.

Cluster analysis produced two meaningful clusters in addition to those who died (Figure 7.1). The majority of subjects (78%) are grouped in the "stable low limitations" cluster. Throughout the study period, they show scores well below 1. Another 8% experienced increases in limitations during the 9-year study period. This is a very small minority. Note, however, that their functional limitations score increased by at least three standard deviations. An additional cluster included 13% of all subjects who died during the 9 years of follow-up. They had an average initial score of 1.0, which is slightly higher than the average for the total sample. The observation that

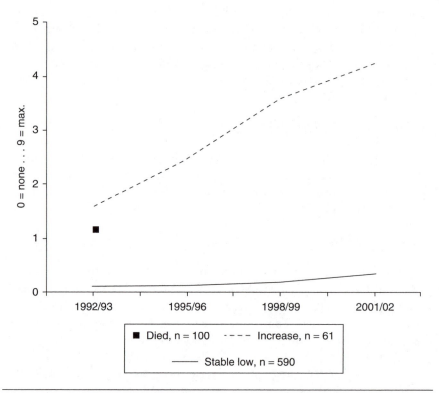

Figure 7.1   Nine-Year Trajectories of Functional Limitations, Longitudinal Aging Study Amsterdam

the cluster "died" is larger than the cluster "increasing limitations" suggests that mortality in late midlife is not always preceded by a period of functional decline.

Self-Rated Health

Self-rated health was assessed with the widely used question, "How in general is your health?" with response categories ranging from 1 = excellent to 5 = poor (Deeg & Kriegsman, 2003). At baseline, when the respondents were aged 55 to 64 years, the mean and standard deviation were 2.3 and 0.9, respectively.

Three trajectories were established using cluster analysis (Figure 7.2). The additional trajectory "died" had an initial average score of 2.7. The largest cluster (61%) includes the subjects who rated their health as "stable

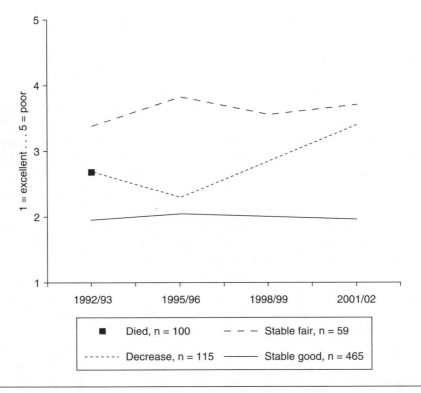

Figure 7.2   Nine-Year Trajectories of Self-Rated Health, Longitudinal Aging Study Amsterdam

good" throughout the 9-year study period, with an average score of 2, corresponding to "good" self-rated health. A second cluster identified subjects whose self-rating of health decreased (15%). Their average score rose over the 9 years to 3.4, indicating "fair" health. A third cluster had "stable fair" ratings of their health throughout the 9 years (8%), with average scores slightly fluctuating between 3 and 4.

Comparison of the two sets of trajectories shows that the subjective component of health as expressed in self-ratings shows more variability than the more objective component of health as determined by functional limitations. In particular, the cluster "decreasing self-rated health" was larger (15%) than the cluster "increasing limitations" (8%). A third cluster with stable, fair ratings of health emerged, whereas in terms of functional limitations, no such group was identified. It seems likely that compared with more specific assessments of functional limitations, self-assessments of general health may capture health problems earlier (Idler & Benyamini, 1997).

Mental Health

Mental health is the most widely studied aspect of health in midlife. The 208 relevant titles resulting from a literature search using keywords "midlife" and "health" produced 64 publications on mental health. Mental health is, in fact, an umbrella concept, including a range of more specific concepts, such as psychological well-being, psychological distress, positive and negative affect, psychiatric disorders, adjustment to life, and positive relations with others. Some authors include personal dispositions such as self-esteem, environmental mastery, and personal growth in the concept of mental health (Helson & Srivastava, 2001; Maier & Lachman, 2000; Marks & Lambert, 1998; Ryff & Heidrich, 1997). The most widely studied indicator of mental health is depression, or depressed mood. Social aspects of mental health, such as perceived relations with others, are only rarely studied (Maier & Lachman, 2000; Raikkonen, Matthews, & Kuller, 2001). Nevertheless, because social changes are likely to occur in late midlife, it seems important to examine the social aspect of mental health as an outcome, in addition to depressed mood. The definition of loneliness appropriately covers this aspect: "Loneliness is a situation experienced by the individual as one where there is an unpleasant or inadmissible lack of (quality of) certain relationships" (De Jong Gierveld, 1998, p. 73).

Trajectories of Mental Health

The LASA study provides data on changes in mental health from late midlife to early old age in terms of depressive symptoms and loneliness.

Depression

Depressive symptoms are assessed using the 20-item Center for Epidemiologic Studies Depression scale (CES-D; Beekman et al., 1997; Radloff, 1977). For each item, the response categories are $0 =$ (almost) never to $3 =$ (almost) always. The maximum scale score is 60, and the cut-off for clinically relevant depressive symptoms is 16. This scale has been shown to have good psychometric properties in the older population. At baseline, the average score and standard deviation in the late-midlife age group were 6.9 and 7.2, respectively.

Cluster analysis produced four trajectories of depressive symptoms in addition to the trajectory "died" (Figure 7.3). The latter trajectory had a baseline mean score of 8.0. As observed for self-rated health, there were two stable trajectories: one "stable low depression" (22%) and one "stable high depression" (17%). Notably, the "stable low" trajectory includes considerably fewer subjects, and the "stable high" trajectory includes considerably more subjects than was the case for self-rated health. Moreover, the "stable high" trajectory had average scores that were near the cutoff (16) for clinically relevant depressive symptoms throughout the study period of 9 years (scores 11.8 to 14.6). In fact, during the study period, 35% to 46% of this group scored above this cutoff. The largest cluster indicated a trajectory of increasing symptoms (34%). Another sizable cluster showed a trajectory of decreasing symptoms (13%). Note, however, that the average scores in the latter two trajectories varied between 3.0 and 8.7. Only a small minority of persons grouped in these clusters actually had clinically relevant depressive symptoms (7% at the last observation of the "increasing" trajectory and 12% at the first observation of the "decreasing" trajectory). Most variability, therefore, takes place at levels of depressive symptoms below clinical relevance. However, these levels are not necessarily harmless, as it has been shown that they predict increases in functional limitations (Penninx, Deeg, Van Eijk, Beekman, & Guralnik, 2000).

Loneliness

The second indicator of mental health captures loneliness. This concept was measured using the 11-item De Jong Gierveld loneliness scale

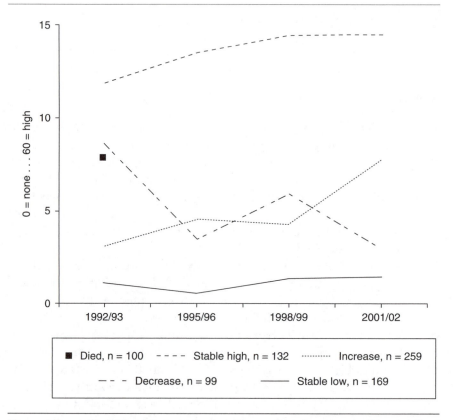

Figure 7.3   Nine-Year Trajectories of Depressive Symptoms, Longitudinal Aging Study Amsterdam

(De Jong Gierveld & Kamphuis, 1985). Each item has three response categories, of which the middle response and the response indicating loneliness are combined into one score. The maximum scale score is 11. A cutoff was determined in order to be able to apply the scale for population-based interventions. This cutoff for relevant loneliness is 3 (Van Tilburg & De Jong Gierveld, 1999). In the late-midlife sample, the average and standard deviation were 1.6 and 2.3, respectively.

Similar to the cluster analyses for depressive symptoms, cluster analysis of loneliness produced four trajectories in addition to the trajectory "died" (Figure 7.4). The trajectory "died" had an average initial score of 2.2, again, higher than average. The largest trajectory was "stable low loneliness" (43%), with near-zero scores throughout the study period. The

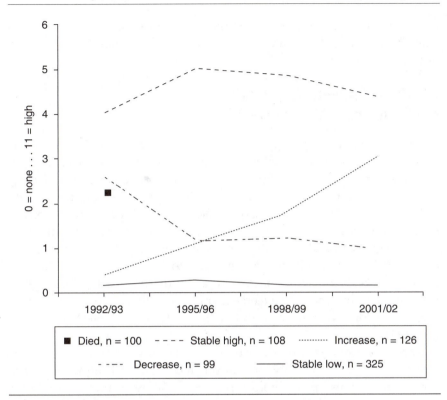

Figure 7.4   Nine-Year Trajectories of Loneliness, Longitudinal Aging Study
Amsterdam

"stable high" trajectory constituted 14% of the sample, with average
scores well above the cutoff for relevant loneliness. The increasing trajectory constituted 17% of the sample. On average, the increase was to score
3 at the final observation cycle. At that time, 68% scored 3 or higher on the
loneliness scale. A slightly smaller cluster showed a trajectory (13%) of
decreasing loneliness.

Considering both indicators of mental health, clearly more variability
was shown in the trajectories of depressive symptoms than in those of
loneliness, as a smaller proportion of the sample was represented in the
"stable low" trajectory in depressive symptoms than in the comparable
cluster for loneliness. However, there was also a marked correspon-
dence between the two sets of trajectories. In contrast to the indicators
of physical health, depressive symptoms and loneliness each showed a

trajectory of decline in mental health. These observations show that at least in mental health, changes during late midlife to early old age can be multidirectional.

Interplay Between Trajectories of Physical and Mental Health

Having established the heterogeneity of intraindividual changes in late midlife and early old age, we now move on to examine the extent of their interrelatedness. This is best performed in the survivors: As the trajectory "died" is common to all four indicators, including this trajectory would inflate the correlations. Because the trajectories cannot be considered as ordinal variables, approximations of a correlation are derived from multinomial regression models, using the pseudo-R (Nagelkerke, 1991). Moderate correlations exist between both indicators of physical heath, as well as between both indicators of mental health (each $R = 0.42$). The highest correlation is observed between self-rated health and depression ($R = 0.46$). Functional limitations and loneliness show the lowest correlation ($R = 0.17$).

These correlations should be understood as overall measures of the interplay between trajectories in various indicators of health. The multinomial models also provide information on the association of a specific trajectory in one health indicator with a specific trajectory in another health indicator. These associations were generally in the expected direction, with two exceptions concerning the trajectory "decreasing depressive symptoms." This trajectory correlated with "*in*creasing functional limitations" and with "*de*creasing self-rated health." An explanation of this seeming anomaly may be that a remitted depressive period preceded actual changes in health. This interpretation is supported by evidence that depression is associated with subsequent mortality and functional decline (Penninx, Geerlings, Deeg, Beekman, & Van Tilburg, 1999; Penninx et al., 2000).

In all, the moderate size of these correlations suggests that the trajectories in the various aspects of health show limited overlap. Foremost, they demonstrate the diversity and limited interrelatedness among various health indicators in this phase of life. It must be emphasized that the correlations were computed among surviving subjects. A speculative interpretation of the moderate size of the correlations may be that adults who survive this phase of life still have sufficient resources at their disposal to keep losses in one aspect of health limited to this one aspect. This is in contrast with older age, during which a loss in one aspect of health may give rise to losses in other aspects of health (Birren & Cunningham, 1985).

Baseline Sociodemographic Determinants of Health Change

Among the potential sociodemographic determinants of trajectories of physical and mental health, gender, age, and education are fixed characteristics of an individual in this age group. Other sociodemographic characteristics such as income, work, and partner status are likely to change.

In this section, the predictive ability of sociodemographic characteristics, as measured at the beginning of the LASA study period for trajectories defined in the subsequent 9 years, is examined. Concurrent changes in income, work, and partner status are reported in a later section.

Quantification of Sociodemographic Characteristics

The LASA sample included 52% male and 48% female subjects. Due to the stratified sampling procedure, the group aged 60 to 64 years was slightly better represented than the group aged 55 to 59 years (54% vs. 46%, respectively). In this sample, 32% had elementary schooling or less, 35% had 2 to 4 years of additional schooling (mostly vocational), 19% had completed secondary schooling, and 14% had college or higher education. Regarding income, the respondents were asked to state the net amount of the total household income. When the respondents were living with their partner, this amount was multiplied by 0.7 to achieve comparability with one-person households (Broese van Groenou & Deeg, 2000). Then, income was recoded into two categories, the lowest one indicating the Dutch definition of "minimum income" (i.e., Dfl 1,250 in 1992). At baseline, 12% of the LASA late-midlife sample had a minimum income or less. Having paid work was reported by 30% of the sample at baseline; 64% reported having had paid work in the past, and 6% reported never having had paid work. Among those who had had paid work in the past, 23% had completely retired at baseline. Their mean age at retirement was 55 years ($SD = 10$ years). Finally, 83% of the baseline sample reported living with their partner, and 17% had no partner in their household.

Table 7.2   Correlates of Trajectory "Died"

Early Life Characteristics	Baseline Characteristics		Concurrent Changes	
Upward educational ↓ mobility	Older age	↑	Early retirement	↑
	Female sex	↓	Change in partner status ↑	
	Education		Change in income	↓
	Partner in household ↓			
	Income			
	Paid work			

NOTES: Upward arrow = significantly greater mortality risk; downward arrow = significantly smaller mortality risk; no arrow = no significant association with mortality ($p > 0.05$).

Associations With Mortality

As the trajectory "died" is common to all four health indicators, the determinants of this trajectory are examined separately (Table 7.2, column 2). In a logistic regression model including all potential sociodemographic determinants, the following variables were independently associated with mortality: male sex, older age, and not living with a partner. Education, income, and paid work did not account for significant variance in mortality in late midlife. The three significant associations (sex, age, not living with a partner) persisted when the baseline values of all health indicators were included in the model. Among the latter, only the indicators of physical health (i.e., functional limitations, self-reported health) were associated with mortality.

Associations With Trajectories Among Survivors

To examine the predictive ability of sociodemographic characteristics for the distinct trajectories for each health indicator, four multivariable multinomial regression models were used (one model for each health indicator). In each model, the reference trajectory was defined as "stable low," and the risk of each trajectory other than "stable low" was compared with the reference trajectory.

The independent predictive ability of the baseline sociodemographic characteristics appeared limited (Table 7.3, upper part). The arrows in the figure indicate the directionality of the relationship. The number of arrows indicates the number of trajectories for which the variable was a

Table 7.3   Correlates[1] of Trajectories Among Survivors

	FL	SRH	Dep	Lon
Baseline				
Older age	ns	ns	↓	ns
Female sex	ns	ns	↑↑↑	ns
Low education	ns	ns	ns	ns
Partner in household	ns	ns	ns	↓↑
Low income	ns	ns	ns	ns
Paid work	ns	↑	↓	ns
Early Life				
Upward educational mobility	ns	ns	↓	ns
Concurrent				
Early retirement	ns	ns	↑	ns
Change in income	ns	ns	ns	↑
Change in partner status	↑	ns	↑↑	↑↑↓

NOTES: FL = functional limitations; SRH = self-rated health; Dep = depression; Lon = loneliness; *ns* = nonsignificant (*p* > 0.05).

1. The number of arrows indicate the number of trajectories for which a significant association is observed (*p* < 0.05). See the note to Table 7.2 for the meaning of the arrows. For each health measure, the reference category is "stable low" (for SRH, "stable good").

significant predictor. Increase in functional limitations was not predicted by any sociodemographic characteristic. Stable fair self-rated health was predicted by no longer doing paid work, with a sizable odds ratio of 4.8. Decreasing self-rated health was not predicted by any sociodemographic characteristic. The trajectories of depressive symptoms were more satisfactorily predicted. Female gender showed an increased risk for all three trajectories compared to "stable low," with odds ratios for the trajectories of "stable high," "increasing symptoms," and "decreasing symptoms" being 3.4, 2.1, and 2.8, respectively. Moreover, the risk of the trajectory "stable high depressive symptoms" was greater among the younger subjects (aged 55–59 at baseline), with an odds ratio of 2.4. Furthermore, this trajectory was more often observed among subjects who had never had a paid job (*OR* = 4.3) and among subjects who had no current paid work (*OR* = 2.7). Trajectories of loneliness were predicted by one prominent sociodemographic characteristic: not living with a partner. The odds of "singles" for the trajectory "stable high loneliness" was 3.0. Moreover, subjects who had no partner at baseline were more likely to follow the trajectory "decreasing loneliness." The latter finding suggests a certain adaptation to the partnerless state across the 9-year study.

Early Life Determinants of Health Change

Recently, the implications of early life experiences and events for midlife and older age have gained attention among both social scientists (George, 1996; Giele & Elder, 1998) and epidemiologists (Kuh & Ben-Shlomo, 2004). One of the best-studied factors is socioeconomic status of the family of origin. Most of these studies, however, have examined a single end point, such as mortality, or the incidence of a chronic condition, or psychological well-being at a certain age (Marmot et al., 1998). No studies so far have examined the association of early life characteristics with trajectories from midlife to old age.

In the LASA study, information on the education level of the father of the subject was available (Broese van Groenou, 2003). The combination of father's educational status and subject's level of education determines "upward mobility." In the late midlife sample, 39% showed upward mobility, implying that whereas their fathers had elementary schooling or less, they themselves attained education levels higher than elementary schooling. A minority of the sample (27%) came from a family headed by a father with elementary schooling or less and did not attain a higher level of education themselves during their lives (stable low status). The remaining 34% of the sample had a father with higher than elementary schooling and attained similar levels of schooling themselves (stable high status).

Association With Mortality and Trajectories of Physical and Mental Health

In the Dutch late-midlife sample, stable low socioeconomic status was associated with a 1.8 increased mortality as compared to stable high socioeconomic status (Table 7.2, column 1). Upward mobility carried the same risk of mortality as stable high status. However, mobility in socioeconomic status did not show substantial associations with trajectories among survivors (Table 7.3). The only trajectory for which the stable low status showed an increased risk was "increasing depression" ($OR = 1.8$).

The lack of significant associations is surprising, because an earlier study in the full LASA sample aged 55 to 85 years (Broese van Groenou, 2003) at baseline found independent associations of mobility in socioeconomic status with physical and mental health.

There are two tentative explanations for this discrepancy. First, the influence of mobility in socioeconomic status is stronger in older age than in late midlife. Second, mobility in socioeconomic status affects level of health but not changes in health. To examine the second hypothesis, the analyses were repeated examining the level of functioning on the four health indicators at baseline. These analyses revealed that also in the late midlife group, stable low mobility status was associated with an increased risk of functional limitations. However, the baseline values of self-rated health, depressive symptoms and loneliness, were not affected. Thus, the influence of long-term low socioeconomic status seems weaker in late midlife than in older age. This influence of long-term low socioeconomic status appears to be most directly related to objective health indicators such as mortality and the level of functional limitations, but less so to indicators of mental health.

Concurrent Correlates of Health Change

During late midlife, several changes in engagement with the social world are expected. Retirement is the change that is most generally experienced, although its timing depends on sociocultural factors and differs across nations. In the Netherlands, many people start thinking about retirement in their early 50s, and most people have retired from the labor force well before the legal retirement age of 65 years. The average age of voluntary retirement is 60 years (Henkens & Van Solinge, 2003). Retirement usually has consequences for one's income position, one's family relations, and one's social role. When retirement is not voluntary, income may decrease. In all cases, whether retirement is voluntary or not, what is gained is leisure time. The way this time is filled may have consequences for health in the years ahead and even for old-age mortality (Glass, Mendes de Leon, Marottoli, & Berman, 1999; Lennartsson & Silverstein, 2001).

The scientific literature on the effects of retirement on health and well-being is ambiguous. Although early studies reported increased risk of psychological distress and mortality following retirement (Cumming & Henry, 1961; Haynes, McMichael, & Tyroler, 1978), more recent studies have reported increased well-being (Nuttman-Shwartz, 2004; Reitzes, Mitran, & Fernandez, 1996). The current view is that not all retirees are the same and that their health and well-being depend on their work history, the way the transition to retirement took place, their current income position, and time elapsed since retirement (Gall, Evans, & Howard, 1997; Marshall, Clarke, & Ballantyne, 2001).

Other changes during late midlife are not normative to this phase but may occur at any age (Lachman, 2004). Nevertheless, some changes start to occur more frequently. An example is death of the partner. Neugarten (1976) addressed the issue of timing of widowhood. She found that when widowhood is experienced "off-time" (before most people lose their spouses), the consequences for health and well-being are worse than when widowhood is experienced "on-time." More recently, this view has been debated, as life events involving loss have been shown to have similar associations with depressive symptoms across age groups (Nolen-Hoeksema & Ahrens, 2002). However, as with retirement, it is difficult to generalize across all persons bereaved because other factors such as marital history and concurrent changes such as loss of income may influence outcomes (Earle, Smith, Harris, & Longino, 1998; Tucker et al., 1996; Van Grootheest, Beekman, Broese van Groenou, & Deeg, 1999).

Quantification of Concurrent Changes

From the LASA study, three concurrent changes were selected: retirement, change in partner status, and change in income. Of these three changes, retirement was experienced by all subjects earlier or later, except by the small minority (9%) who had never had a paid job. This minority consisted mostly of women (96% of this group). Among those who had participated in the labor market, 23% had retired at baseline. Among those who experienced retirement during the study period, the majority (76%) retired within three years from baseline, whereas 16% retired after the first three years of the study period. Only 4 persons had not retired by the end of the study period. The average age at retirement was 61 for men ($SD = 4$ years) and 59 for women ($SD = 9$ years). Change in partner status, in contrast, was experienced by a minority of 14%, whereas 72% had a stable partner and 14% had no partner throughout the study period. Among those who experienced a change in partner status, 11% lost their partner and 3% found a new partner or experienced multiple changes in partner status. Change in income was more equally distributed. Among the late-midlife sample, 20% experienced a decrease in income from above to below the minimum level, whereas 7% experienced an increase in income from below to above the minimum. The majority (61%) had an income above the minimum throughout the study, and 12% had an income below the minimum throughout the study period.

To examine the possibility that one change may lead to another, the intercorrelations between the three changes were calculated. Similar to the procedure for the intercorrelations between the trajectories of the four health indicators (see section titled "Changes in Physical and Mental Health"), the pseudo-R from multinomial regression models was determined. This pseudo-R, however, was quite low. Between timing of retirement and change of partner status, as well as between timing of retirement and change in income, the correlation was minimally significant ($R = 0.17$) given the sample size, but the correlation between change in partner status and change in income was not significant. More detailed examination of the interplay between the changes revealed that most of the overall correlation of timing of retirement with change in partner status, as well as with change in income, can be traced to the subgroup that had never had a job. This group, the majority of which are women, had higher chances of having no partner or losing their partner and had a lower chance of having a stable high income.

Associations of Concurrent Changes With Mortality

All associations of concurrent changes with trajectories of physical and mental health were examined in multivariable regression models adjusting for baseline determinants. First, associations of concurrent changes with the trajectory "died" were examined, as this trajectory is common to all four physical and mental health trajectories (Table 7.2, column 3). No significant association was observed between changes in work status and mortality, although the early retirees showed a nonsignificant increased risk compared with those who retired later on ($OR = 2.3$, $p > 0.05$). Change in partner status, in contrast, was significantly associated with mortality. In particular, those who lost their partner during the first three years of the study period had a substantially increased risk of mortality ($OR = 9.4$) compared with those who had a stable partner throughout the study period. Change in income was also significantly associated with mortality, but contrary to the expected direction, a decrease in income to a level below the minimum was associated with a lower risk of mortality compared with having an income above the minimum throughout the study period ($OR = 0.35$). This finding suggests that the detrimental effect of lowered income level may need to be studied over a longer time period than was used in this study.

Associations of Concurrent Changes With Trajectories Among Survivors

Moving on to the trajectories of physical and mental health among the survivors (Table 7.3), it appears that change in work status was not significantly associated with any health trajectory. There was a nonsignificant increased risk for those who retired early to be in the stable depressive symptoms cluster ($OR = 2.1$, $p > 0.05$). Change in income only showed a significant association with loneliness. A decrease in income was inversely associated with a decreasing trajectory of loneliness. In other words, those whose income stayed stable above the minimum had a 2.1 higher chance to follow a trajectory of decreasing loneliness than those whose income decreased.

In contrast to change in work status and income, change in partner status had a more pervasive effect on trajectories of physical and mental health. Not living with a partner throughout the study period was associated with increasing functional limitations ($OR = 2.3$). Thus, a stable partnerless status was the only concurrent factor that affected trajectories of physical health among survivors. Regarding mental health, loss of the partner during the study period was significantly associated with stable high depressive symptoms ($OR = 4.7$) and with increasing depressive symptoms ($OR = 2.5$). Equally strong effects of loss of the partner were observed for trajectories of loneliness. Compared to those who had a stable partner, those who lost their partner were 3.1 times more likely to follow a trajectory of stable loneliness across the study interval and 3.3 times more likely to follow a trajectory of increasing loneliness. Moreover, those who had no partner throughout the study period were 4.9 times more likely to follow a trajectory of stable loneliness as compared to those who did have a partner throughout the study interval. On the other hand, those who had no partner were also 2.7 times more likely to experience a decrease in their loneliness, suggesting an improvement in social well-being in a subgroup of the partnerless. Finally, those who found a new partner showed a marginal increased chance of decreasing loneliness

($OR = 3.1, p > 0.05$). As this is a small group, the analysis may lack sufficient power for a statistical test to reach significance.

Conclusion

This chapter's aims were to describe changes in physical and mental health from late midlife to early old age. In particular, the focus was on revealing heterogeneity in intraindividual change and interrelatedness among trajectories in the various domains of health. In comparing the trajectories of functional limitations, self-rated health, depressive symptoms, and loneliness, it can be concluded that there is considerable heterogeneity. While sharp declines in health were not yet pervasive, mortality had occurred for a substantial 13% of the study sample, and both increases and decreases in mental health were observed. It must be noted that most mental health trajectories showed movement in the "healthy" part of the scales, although a minority had persistently high levels of depressive symptoms and loneliness. Concerning interrelatedness, the findings showed only low to moderate associations between the various trajectories. This was true for the trajectories of physical and mental health, and likewise, the concurrent changes in work, income, and partner status showed very limited associations.

Examination of the impact of sociodemographic characteristics on the different trajectories of physical and mental health showed that socioeconomic status in terms of a low income or a low level of education did not have the unfavorable effect that was expected, based on the literature. Only when early-life socioeconomic status was considered could it be demonstrated that those who came from a low status background and achieved no upward mobility had more physical health problems than the more fortunate in the sample. Furthermore, concurrent decrease in income was associated with unfavorable trajectories of loneliness. With respect to work status, not having paid work was associated with stable high trajectories of poorer self-rated health and of depressive symptoms. Moreover, early retirement was associated with a somewhat increased risk of mortality and stable depressive symptoms, both of which may be attributable to preexisting health problems not captured by controlling for functional status and self-rated health (Ferraro, 2001).

Not living with a partner was the characteristic most strongly associated with loneliness. Concurrent changes in partner status, in particular, partner loss and staying partnerless, were associated with unfavorable trajectories in functional limitations, loneliness, and depressive symptoms. Nevertheless, some positive findings were that a subgroup of the partnerless experienced a decrease in loneliness, as did those who found a new partner. Furthermore, female gender, independent of partner status, was associated with unfavorable trajectories of depressive symptoms. Male gender was independently associated with mortality. An intriguing finding, finally, concerned age: Whereas older age was associated with increased mortality, younger age was independently associated with stable high depressive symptoms among the survivors.

Insight into the transition from late midlife to early old age is important, as this transition marks the entrance into older age. In this sense, the way this transition is experienced is expected to have a pervasive influence on the experience of old age. As the current average life expectancy of an additional 15 to 20 years for persons aged 65 is still increasing, the number of remaining years amounts to about a quarter of the total lifetime. Therefore, it is paramount to enter old age in optimal physical and mental health. This chapter has shown for which population groups this is already realized and for which other population groups interventions might be beneficial.

It should be emphasized that this cohort's transition from late midlife to early old age was likely influenced by the historic time during which it took place, as well as by the historic events that occurred during their development from childhood to young adulthood. These historic circumstances were severe for virtually the whole cohort. In contrast, the optimism of the postwar years marked their entry into adulthood. Against this background, this cohort stands out; its uniqueness is further enhanced by the social and political circumstances surrounding their middle years. Because of the government's encouragement of early retirement during those years, the average age of retirement of this cohort will be the lowest ever. To the extent that early retirement has unfavorable effects, as shown in the data discussed in this chapter, these effects might be unique to this specific cohort.

Future cohorts will be different in a number of respects. On the positive side, they will have experienced fewer hardships during their younger years, grown up in smaller families, and obtained better schooling. On the negative side, they will have experienced more hardships during their middle years (in the 1980s) when securing and maintaining a stable labor market position became more difficult. Furthermore, in the 1990s, the

Dutch government put restrictions on the social security benefits in cases of prolonged illness, to the effect that the pressure to continue labor market participation increased. Now, in the early 21st century, the government is discouraging early retirement by restricting pre-pension schemes. These restrictions, although considered unfair by many citizens, may not necessarily have a negative effect on the health of those entering early old age. Other, most likely negative, developments affecting currently middle-aged cohorts are the increasing secularization and divorce rates. The data presented show that changes in partner status had the most pervasive effect on trajectories of physical and mental health. The future will show how these positive and negative aspects balance out in their effects on physical and mental health in early old age.

References

Baltes, P. B. (1987). Theoretical propositions of life-span developmental psychology: On the dynamics between growth and decline. *Developmental Psychology, 23*, 611–626.

Beekman, A. T., Deeg, D. J., Van Limbeek, J., Braam, A. W., De Vries, M. Z., & Van Tilburg, W. (1997). Criterion validity of the Center for Epidemiologic Studies Depression scale (CES-D): Results from a community-based sample of older subjects in the Netherlands. *Psychological Medicine, 27*, 231–235.

Birren, J. E., & Cunningham, W. R. (1985). Research on the psychology of aging: Principles, concepts, and theory. In J. E. Birren, & K. W. Schaie (Eds.), *Handbook of the psychology of aging* (2nd ed., pp. 3–34). New York: Van Nostrand Reinhold.

Broese van Groenou, M. I. (2003). Ongelijke kansen op een goed oude dag. Sociaal-economische gezondheidsverschillen bij ouderen vanuit een levensloopperspectief [Unequal chances of a good old age. Socio-economic health differences in older adults from a life course perspective]. *Tijdschrift voor Gerontologie en Geriatrie, 34*, 196–207.

Broese van Groenou, M. I., & Deeg, D. J. H. (2000). Sociaal-economische dimensies van veranderingen in gezondheid bij ouderen [Socio-economic dimensions of changes in the health of older adults]. *Tijdschrift voor Gezondheidswetenschappen, 78*, 294–302.

Calvaresi, E., & Bryan, J. (2003). Symptom experience in Australian men and women in midlife. *Maturitas, 44*, 225–236.

Clark-Plaskie, M., & Lachman, M. E. (1999). The sense of control in midlife. In S. L. Willis & J. D. Reid (Eds.), *Life in the middle. Psychological and social development in middle age* (pp. 181–208). San Diego, CA: Academic Press.

Cumming, E., & Henry, W. E. (1961). *Growing old*. New York: Basic Books.

Deeg, D. J. H. (in press). Longitudinal characterization of course types of functional limitations. *Disability and Rehabilitation*.

Deeg, D. J. H., Beekman, A. T. F., Kriegsman, D. M. W., & Westendorp-de Serière, M. (Eds.). (1998). *Autonomy and well-being in the aging population II: Report from the Longitudinal Aging Study Amsterdam 1992-1996*. Amsterdam: VU University Press.

Deeg, D. J. H., Knipscheer, C. P. M., & Van Tilburg, W. (1993). *Autonomy and well-being in the aging population. Concepts and design of the Longitudinal Aging Study Amsterdam* (NIG-Trendstudies, No. 7). Bunnik: Netherlands Institute of Gerontology.

Deeg, D. J. H., & Kriegsman, D. M. W. (2003). Concepts of self-rated health: Specifying the gender difference in mortality risk. *The Gerontologist, 43*, 376–386.

Deeg, D. J. H., Portrait, F., & Lindeboom, M. (2002). Health profiles and profile-specific health expectancies of older women and men: The Netherlands. *Journal of Women and Aging, 14*, 27–46.

Deeg, D. J. H., & Pot, A. M. (1997). Gezondheid van ouderen [Health in older persons]. In T. Lagro-Janssen & G. Noorden-bos (Eds.), *Sekseverschillen in ziekte en gezondheid* (pp. 133–145). Nijmegen, Netherlands: Uitgeverij SUN.

Deeg, D. J. H., & Westendorp–de Serière, M. (Eds.). (1994). *Autonomy and well-being in the aging population I: Results from the Longitudinal Aging Study Amsterdam 1992-1993*. Amsterdam: VU University Press.

De Jong Gierveld, J. (1998). A review of loneliness: Concept and definitions, determinants and consequences. *Reviews in Clinical Gerontology, 8*, 73–80.

De Jong Gierveld, J., & Kamphuis, F. H. (1985). The development of a Rasch-type loneliness scale. *Applied Psychological Measurement, 9*, 289–299.

Earle, J. R., Smith, M. H., Harris, C. T., & Longino, C. F. (1998). Women, marital status, and symptoms of depression in a midlife national sample. *Journal of Women and Aging, 10*, 41–57.

Ferraro, K. F. (2001). Aging and role transitions. In R. H. Binstock & L. K. George (Eds.), *Handbook of aging and the social sciences* (5th ed., pp. 313–330). San Diego, CA: Academic Press.

Gall, T. L., Evans, D. R., & Howard, J. (1997). The retirement adjustment process: Changes in the well-being of male retirees across time. *Journals of Gerontology: Psychological Sciences, 52B*, 110–117.

George, L. K. (1996). Missing links: The case for a social psychology of the life course. *The Gerontologist, 36*, 248–255.

Giele, J. Z., & Elder, G. H., Jr. (1998). Life course research: Development of a field. In J. Z. Giele & G. H. Elder, Jr. (Eds.), *Methods of life course research. Qualitative and quantitative approaches* (pp. 5–27). Thousand Oaks, CA: Sage.

Glass, T., Mendes de Leon, C., Marottoli, R. A., & Berkman, L. F. (1999). Population based study of social and productive activities as predictors of survival among elderly Americans. *British Medical Journal, 319*, 478–483.

Goodwin, R., & Engstrom, G. (2002). Personality and the perception of health in the general population. *Psychological Medicine, 32,* 325–332.

Haynes, S. G., McMichael, A. J., & Tyroler, H. A. (1978). Survival after early and normal retirement. *Journal of Gerontology, 33,* 269–278.

Helson, R., & Srivastava, S. (2001). Three paths of adult development: Conservers, seekers, and achievers. *Journal of Personality and Social Psychology, 80,* 995–1010.

Henkens, K., & Van Solinge, H. (2003). *Het eindspel: werknemers, hun partners en leidinggevenden over uittreden uit het arbeidsproces* [The end game: Employees, their partners and executives about retirement from employment]. Assen, Netherlands: Van Gorcum.

Holahan, C. K., Holahan, C. J., & Wonacott, N. L. (1999). Self-appraisal, life satisfaction, and retrospective life choices across one and three decades. *Psychology and Aging, 14,* 238–244.

Idler, E. L., & Benyamini, Y. (1997). Self-rated health and mortality: A review of twenty-seven community studies. *Journal of Health and Social Behavior, 38,* 21–37.

Jylhä, M., Guralnik, J. M., Ferrucci, L., Jokela, J., & Heikkinen, E. (1998). Is self-rated health comparable across cultures and genders? *Journals of Gerontology: Social Sciences, 53B,* 144–152.

Keyes, C. L. M., & Ryff, C. D. (1999). Psychological well-being in midlife. In S. L. Willis & J. D. Reid (Eds.), *Life in the middle. Psychological and social development in middle age* (pp. 161–180). San Diego, CA: Academic Press.

Kriegsman, D. M., Deeg, D. J., Van Eijk, J. T., Penninx, B. W., & Boeke, A. J. (1997). Do disease specific characteristics add to the explanation of mobility limitations in patients with different chronic diseases? A study in the Netherlands. *Journal of Epidemiology and Community Health, 51,* 676–685.

Kuh, D., & Ben-Shlomo, Y. (Eds.). (2004). *A life course approach to chronic disease epidemiology* (2nd ed.). Oxford, UK: Oxford University Press.

Lachman, M. E. (2004). Development in midlife. *Annual Review of Psychology, 55,* 305–331.

Laditka, S. B. (Ed.). (2002). *Health expectancies of older women: International perspectives.* New York: Haworth Press.

Lennartsson, C., & Silverstein, M. (2001). Does engagement with life enhance survival of elderly people in Sweden? The role of social and leisure activities. *Journals of Gerontology: Social Sciences, 56B,* 335–342.

Maier, E. H., & Lachman, M. E. (2000). Consequences of early parental loss and separation for health and well-being in midlife. *International Journal of Behavioral Development, 24,* 183–189.

Marks, N. F., & Lambert, J. D. (1998). Marital status continuity and change among young and midlife adults: Longitudinal effects on psychological well-being. *Journal of Family Issues, 19,* 652–686.

Marmot, M. G., Fuhrer, R., Ettner, S. L., Marks, N. F., Bumpass, L. L., & Ryff, C. D. (1998). Contribution of psychosocial factors to socioeconomic differences in health. *Milbank Memorial Fund Quarterly, 76,* 403–448.

Marshall, V. W., Clarke, P. J., & Ballantyne, P. J. (2001). Instability in the retirement transition. Effects on health and well-being in a Canadian study. *Research on Aging, 23,* 379–409.

McCrae, R., & Costa, P. T. (Eds.). (2003). *Personality in adulthood: A five factor theory perspective* (2nd ed.). New York: Guilford Press.

Merrill, S. S., & Verbrugge, L. M. (1999). Health and disease in midlife. In S. L. Willis & J. D. Reid (Eds.), *Life in the middle. Psychological and social development in middle age* (pp. 77–103). San Diego, CA: Academic Press.

Miech, R. A., & Hauser, R. M. (2001). Socio-economic status and health at midlife: A comparison of educational attainment with occupation based indicators. *Annals of Epidemiology, 11,* 75–84.

Nagelkerke, N. J. D. (1991). A note on a general definition of the coefficient of determination. *Biometrika, 78,* 691–692.

Neugarten, B. (1976). Adaptation and the life cycle. *Counseling Psychologist, 6,* 16–20.

Nolen-Hoeksema, S., & Ahrens, C. (2002). Age differences and similarities in the correlates of depressive symptoms. *Psychology and Aging, 17,* 116–124.

Nuttman-Shwartz, O. (2004). Like a high wave: Adjustment to retirement. *The Gerontologist, 44,* 229–236.

Penninx, B. W. J. H., Deeg, D. J. H., Van Eijk, J. T. M., Beekman, A. T. F., & Guralnik, J. M. (2000). Changes in depression and physical decline in older adults: A longitudinal perspective. *Journal of Affective Disorders, 61,* 1–12.

Penninx, B. W. J. H., Geerlings, S. W., Deeg, D. J. H., Beekman, A. T. F., & Van Tilburg, W. (1999). Minor and major depression and the risk of death in older persons. *Archives of General Psychiatry, 56,* 889–896.

Pope, S. K., Sowers, M. R., Welch, G. W., & Albrecht, G. (2001). Functional limitations in women at midlife: The role of health conditions, behavioral and environmental factors. *Women's Health Issues, 11,* 494–502.

Radloff, L. S. (1977). The CES-D scale: A self-report depression scale for research in the general population. *Applied Psychological Measurement, 1,* 385–401.

Raikkonen, K., Matthews, K. A., & Kuller, L. H. (2001). Trajectory of psychological risk and incident hypertension in middle-aged women. *Hypertension, 38,* 798–802.

Reitzes, D. C., Mitran, E. J., & Fernandez, M. (1996). Does retirement hurt well-being? Factors influencing self-esteem and depression among retirees and workers. *The Gerontologist, 36,* 649–656.

Ryff, C. D., & Heidrich, S. M. (1997). Experience and well-being: Exploration on domains of life and how they matter. *International Journal of Behavioral Development, 20,* 193–206.

Sheehy, G. (Ed.). (1976). *Passages.* New York: Dutton.

Singer, B., & Ryff, C. D. (2001). Person-centered methods for understanding aging: The integration of numbers and narratives. In R. H. Binstock & L. K. George

(Eds.), *Handbook of aging and the social sciences* (5th ed., pp. 44–65). San Diego, CA: Academic Press.

Statistics Netherlands. (1999). *Vital events. Past, present and future of the Dutch population.* Voorburg/Heerlen: Statistics Netherlands.

Statistics Netherlands. (2004). *Working population by sex.* Retrieved July 2004 from http://statline.cbs.nl

Strandberg, T. E., Strandberg, A., Salonmaa, V. V., Pitkala, K., & Miettinen, T. A. (2003). *International Journal of Obesity, 27,* 950–954.

Tabeau, E., Van Poppel, F., & Willekens, F. (1994). *Mortality in the Netherlands 1850–1991. The data base.* The Hague: Netherlands Interdisciplinary Demographic Institute.

Tucker, J. S., Wingard, D. L., Friedman, H. S., & Schwartz, J. E. (1996). Marital history at midlife as a predictor of longevity: Alternative explanations to the protective effect of marriage. *Health Psychology, 15,* 94–101.

Van den Berg Jeths, A., Poos, M. J. J. C., & Ruwaard, D. (1993). Aanwezigheid van ziekten en aandoeningen [Prevalence of diseases and disorders]. In D. Ruwaard & P. G. N. Kramers (Eds.), *Volksgezondheid Toekomst Verkenning. De gezondheidstoestand van de Nederlandse bevolking in de periode 1950–2010* [Public Health Forecast. The health status of the Dutch population in the period 1950–2010]. National Institute of Public Health and the Environment (pp. 135–145). The Hague, Netherlands: Sdu Publishers.

Van der Wilk, E. A., Achterberg, P. W., & Kramers, P. G. N. (2001). *Long live the Netherlands! An analysis of trends in Dutch life expectancy in a European context.* Bilthoven, Netherlands: National Institute of Public Health and the Environment.

Van Grootheest, D. S., Beekman, A. T. F., Broese van Groenou, M. I., & Deeg, D. J. H. (1999). Sex differences in depression after widowhood. Do men suffer more? *Social Psychiatry and Psychiatric Epidemiology, 34,* 391–398.

Van Tilburg, T. G., & De Jong Gierveld, J. (1999). Cesuurbepaling van de eenzaamheidsschaal [Cut points on the De Jong Gierveld loneliness scale]. *Tijdschrift voor Gerontologie en Geriatrie, 30,* 158–163.

Verbrugge, L. M., & Jette, A. (1994). The disablement process. *Social Science and Medicine, 38,* 1–14.

Verbrugge, L. M., & Patrick, D. L. (1995). Seven chronic conditions: Their impact on US adults' activity levels and use of medical services. *American Journal of Public Health, 85,* 173–182.

Waite, L. J., & Hughes, M. E. (1999). At risk on the cusp of old age: Living arrangements and functional status among Black, White and Hispanic adults. *Journals of Gerontology: Social Sciences, 54,* 136–144.

Wilson, S. E. (2001). Socio-economic status and the prevalence of health problems among married couples in late midlife. *American Journal of Public Health, 91,* 131–135.

Eight

Cognitive Trajectories in Midlife and Cognitive Functioning in Old Age

Sherry L. Willis and K. Warner Schaie

A major distinction among lifespan psychological theories is their differing position on stability versus change in middle age. Theories focusing on aspects of ego development or the self have suggested that major intrapsychic changes occur in midlife (Erikson, 1980; Levinson, 1978; Whitbourne, 1986). These theories focus on qualitative change and vary in the extent to which change is considered normative or universal. The midlife crisis first described by Jaques (1965) and expanded on by Levinson (1978) represents the most dramatic example of intrapsychic change said to occur in middle age.

Trait theories, in contrast, such as those concerned with personality (Costa & McCrae, 1980; McCrae & Costa, 1984) or intelligence (Schaie, 1996, 2005), have depicted midlife as a period of considerable stability with relatively little intraindividual change occurring, at least when studied at the aggregate level (see also Martin & Zimprich, Chapter 6, this volume). Costa and McCrae (1993) and Costa et al. (1999) have written extensively on interindividual stability in personality traits; individuals maintain the same rank ordering on a personality trait in comparison to others in the group across adulthood. Similarly, ability performance has been reported in longitudinal studies of mental abilities as representing a flat plateau with little change in slope in midlife; these findings have been interpreted to indicate that there is considerable intraindividual stability in the middle years (Dixon, de Frias, & Maitland, 2001; Schaie, 1984, 1996; Willis & Schaie, 1999). The study of stability in personality or ability traits has focused primarily on possible change in the *level* of functioning, with less examination or concern regarding *slope*. Recently, however, there has been increasing interest in studying individual differences in both level and slope. An aggregate or mean level approach to the study of cognition is likely to mask the subgroups of individuals that exhibit either positive or negative slope trajectories in midlife. In this chapter, we utilize data from the Seattle Longitudinal Study (SLS) to explore individual differences in trajectories of cognitive change during midlife and discuss possible factors associated with variability in change trajectories.

We begin by briefly reviewing some of the major propositions of life-span development theory as they may apply to study of cognition in midlife (Baltes, 1987; Baltes & Baltes, 1990; Baltes, Staudinger, & Lindenberger, 1999). We then discuss some of the limitations in the design of prior research on cognitive functioning in midlife and consider how these limitations may have contributed to a stability view of adult cognition in middle age. We present two types of data on ability performance in midlife from the SLS: (a) normative performance data indicating considerable stability in cognitive functioning in midlife and (b) cognitive change trajectories. The latter suggest that for subgroups of individuals, change in both level and slope does occur in the middle years. We then consider whether cognitive change in midlife may be predictive of cognitive functioning in old age, and we provide illustrative data from the SLS showing that for some individuals, midlife change trajectories are related to long-term outcomes, such as cognitive impairment in old age. We next briefly review current research on select factors (e.g., chronic disease, biomarkers, and the work environment) that have been reported to be associated with differential cognitive change trajectories in middle age. Structural changes in the brain that occur in midlife or early old age in healthy adults are considered. We conclude that there is growing evidence of considerable individual differences in cognitive functioning in midlife, and variability in cognitive trajectories in midlife may predict clinically meaningful outcomes in old age.

Midlife Development From Lifespan Theory

Lifespan theory focuses on the salience of balancing contrary forces in midlife (Baltes et al., 1999; Staudinger & Bluck, 2001). Indeed, the relative stability that appears to characterize midlife may be a reflection of this "balance" of contrary forces in development. A major proposition of lifespan theory is that development at all life stages involves both gains (growth) and losses (decrement). A unique feature of midlife may be that it is the developmental period characterized by a "tie" in the relation of gains and losses; some domains of functioning are still increasing, many domains are being maintained, and others are beginning to decline. This tie in gains and losses in midlife is said to be associated with a balance in midlife in the impact of biology and culture. While age-related decline in biological functioning may begin to occur in midlife, the complexity and sophistication of cultural structures to support development may peak in middle age. Early midlife may be the peak time to reap the cultural assets of education, career, relationships, and family. Indeed, culture and environment are believed to play an increasingly important role in adult development, as compared with early development. Related to the gain-loss ratio and to the biology-culture dynamics is the proposition dealing with allocation of resources across the life span. In early life, resources are allocated to growth, whereas in old age, resources are allocated to regulation of loss. Staudinger and Bluck (2001) have suggested that in midlife, resources may be primarily allocated to maintenance and recovery; however, some resources are still allocated to growth or regulation of loss. Thus, again midlife is a unique developmental phase in which allocation of resources may be balanced between growth, maintenance, and regulation of loss.

Limitations of Prior Research on Midlife

It is ironic that currently there may be a greater variety of theories of midlife development than there are longitudinal data sets against which to evaluate such theories. The paucity of literature on midlife cognition, for example, was illustrated by a literature search for studies of memory in middle age, conducted by Dixon and colleagues (Dixon et al., 2001) for the first handbook on midlife development (Lachman, 2001). The authors reported that an average of five articles containing midlife participants were published annually during the past 20 years. However, virtually none of these studies was focused primarily on midlife; the articles were identified only because they included a middle age group. Moreover, the vast majority of studies were cross-sectional in design (Bäckman & Nilsson, 1996). Dixon et al. (2001) concluded that there is little evidence of programmatic research on memory in midlife with different authors employing alternative sets of tasks as well as utilizing diverse definitions of middle age.

The paucity of longitudinal data specifically targeting middle age is due, in part, to limitations in the design of many past aging studies (Dixon et al., 2001). The traditional extreme age group comparative design (young adults compared with old adults) of many cognitive aging studies in the past few decades has resulted in serious design limitations for building a lifespan perspective of adult cognitive development. Comparison of only two age groups implies the assumption of a linear trajectory of change, with performance in midlife assumed to fall midway between young and old age. Given only two data points, nonlinear forms of developmental trajectories could not be tested. Moreover, the assumption that the extreme groups differed primarily as a function of age was problematic because the old and young also differed on other variables related to cognition, such as health, job status, sensory deficits, and educational attainment.

More recent studies have involved research designs that included a group in middle age. However, often the age range for the midlife group has been considerably larger than the age ranges for the young or older groups, as later adulthood is now segmented into young-old, old-old, and very old age. Moreover, cohort comparisons of midlife adults, when at the same chronological age, may be particularly important. A number of life-span developmentalists (Baltes, 1987; Schaie, 1984; Staudinger & Bluck, 2001) have proposed that midlife is the period most heavily impacted by sociocultural events, rather than biological events, given that puberty is past and the biological decline of old age is only at an early stage.

Cognitive Functioning in Midlife: Findings From the Seattle Longitudinal Study

In our prior research on midlife cognition within the SLS, we have focused on normative change in ability performance in middle age (Schaie, 2005; Willis, 1987; Willis & Schaie, 1999). That is, we have presented *average* estimates of cognitive change for all SLS participants studied over a given age range. We have reported cohort differences in level of ability performance in midlife (e.g., baby boomers vs. parents of baby boomers; Willis & Schaie, 1999). However, even in cohort-related analyses, the focus was comparison of cohort differences, *averaged* across all members of a cohort at a given age period (Willis, 1989).

Figure 8.1 presents the typical finding of stability in cognitive performance in midlife (age range 39–60 years) when data are aggregated across all SLS participants studied longitudinally over this age range. Performance is shown for six abilities: verbal meaning, spatial orientation, inductive reasoning, number, word fluency, and delayed recall (Schaie, 1996, 2005). For these six mental abilities, the magnitude of change across the 21-year period is less than 0.2 standard deviation (*SD*) units. No statistically reliable age-related change is shown for any ability. Cognitive functioning at the aggregate level thus supports the position of lifespan developmental theory that

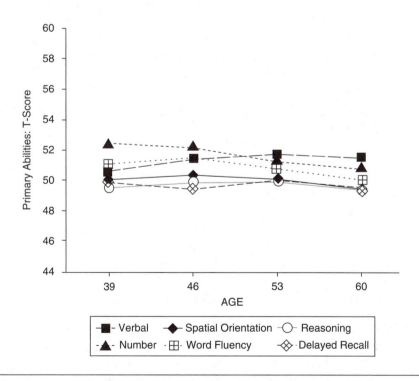

Figure 8.1   Primary Mental Abilities: Longitudinal Change in Midlife

because both gains and losses occur in midlife, the relative balance of gains and losses in middle age may create the illusion of stability.

Different Trajectories of Cognitive Change in Midlife

Lifespan developmental theory, however, also maintains that there are individual differences in the experience of middle age (Schaie, 1989a, 1989b). Individuals vary in the relative amount of gains and losses experienced in midlife. Variability in patterns of gains and losses becomes evident when subgroups of individuals varying in cognitive change trajectories are studied, rather than focusing on the mean or aggregate level (Schaie & Willis, 1993).

In this section, we present new findings related to different patterns or trajectories of cognitive change across midlife for abilities studied in the SLS. We focus on three cognitive abilities studied in the SLS: number, delayed recall, and word fluency (Thurstone & Thurstone, 1949). As shown in Figure 8.1, all three abilities exhibit patterns of stability in midlife when examined at the aggregate or mean level. These abilities represent distinct domains of cognition. Number ability represents the crystallized intelligence domain, which in cross-sectional studies appears to be maintained into old age because of negative cohort differences, but which in longitudinal studies shows decline beginning in early old age (Schaie, 2005). Episodic memory, as represented by delayed memory recall, is one of the most widely studied abilities in cognitive aging (Hultsch, Hertzog, Dixon, & Small, 1998); showing age-related decline in the 60s, it is the ability most commonly associated with early stages of cognitive impairment and dementia (Albert & Killiany, 2001; Petersen, 2003). Word fluency is a measure of executive functioning representing higher-order cognitive skills required for executing complex tasks of daily living (Lezak, 1995; Willis, Allen-Burge, et al., 1998). In the SLS, we have found midlife performance on both delayed recall and word fluency to be predictive of neuropsychologists' ratings of cognitive impairment in old age, as discussed in a later section of this chapter.

Development of Cognitive Change Trajectories

Midlife change in these abilities was studied over a 14-year interval, involving two 7-year intervals and three data points (age 46, 53, and 60 years). Ability change was examined at the individual level ($N = 433$). Defining cognitive change trajectories required consideration of both level of performance at baseline (age 46; intercept) and rate of change over the 14-year period (slope). For each of the three abilities, participants were classified as having reliably declined (decliners), improved (gainers), or remained stable (stable) over the 14-year interval. The statistical criterion for the definition of individual decline or gain was one standard error of measurement or greater over the 14-year period. Subjects were classified by defining a one standard error of measurement confidence interval about their baseline score (age 46; Dudek, 1979; Schaie & Willis, 1986; Willis & Schaie, 1986). If their score at age 60 fell below or above this interval, they were classified as having declined or gained, respectively. Standard errors of measurement (T-score units) for the three abilities were number = 6; delayed recall = 6; word fluency = 6. The proportions of participants classified as stable for number, delayed recall, word fluency were 79%, 53%, 69%, respectively. The proportions classified as having declined were 15%, 31%, and 20%, respectively; those having gained were 6%, 16%, and 11%, respectively. Thus, although Figure 8.1 presents a normative pattern of stability across midlife, the above procedure indicates that 15% to 31% of individuals have declined on at least one of the three abilities, whereas 6% to 16% have gained on at least one of the abilities. However, the nature of cognitive change trajectories for a given individual varies by ability. Only 2% of the sample had gained on at least two of the three abilities, and only 13% had declined on at least two of the three abilities. Delayed recall was the ability exhibiting the greatest proportion of individuals showing either decline (31%) or gain (16%).

In the second step of the analysis of change trajectories, the distribution of scores at baseline (age 46) for each of the three abilities was examined and divided into tertiles. Each participant was classified in terms of intercept at age 46 (i.e., tertile) and slope across the 14-year interval (decline, stable, gain). Repeated measures analyses of variance indicated a significant interaction between slope status and age for each of the three abilities. However, the triple interaction between slope status, tertile (intercept), and age was not significant for any ability, indicating that the interaction of age and slope did not vary by intercept. Hence, Figures 8.2, 8.3, and 8.4 present the interaction of slope status and age averaged across tertiles at baseline.

Number Ability: Cognitive Change Trajectories

Figure 8.2 presents age-related change in number ability for individuals classified as having remained stable, declined, or increased over the

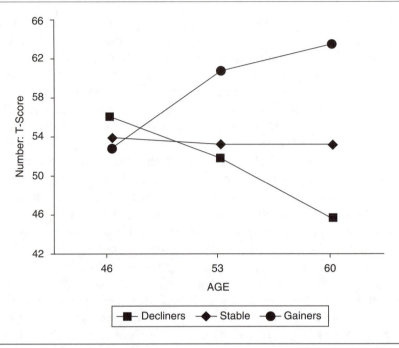

Figure 8.2   Age-Related Change in Number Ability for Individuals Classified as Remaining Stable, Declined, or Increased

14-year interval. At age 46, performance levels of the three groups were roughly comparable: The difference between the decline group and the other two groups was approximately 0.2 SD units. However, by age 53, the gainers diverged significantly from the stables and decliners, and by age 60, the gainers were performing more than 1 SD unit above the stable group. In contrast, although stables and decliners did not differ in performance level at age 46, by age 60, the decline group performed almost 0.8 SD units below the stable group.

Delayed Recall: Cognitive Change Trajectories

Figure 8.3 presents age-related change for the delayed recall ability for the three groups. At age 46, the group of decliners did not differ in performance level from the stable group but did differ from the performance of gainers (0.2 SD units). By age 53, all three groups differed significantly in level of performance. By age 60, the decline group was performing more

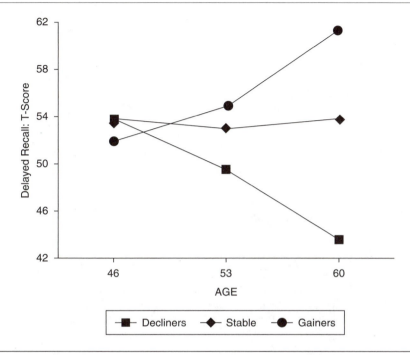

Figure 8.3   Age-Related Change for the Delayed Recall Ability for Individuals Classified as Remaining Stable, Declined, or Increased

than 1 *SD* unit below stables, whereas the gainer group was performing approximately 0.8 *SD* units above the stable group.

Word Fluency: Cognitive Change Trajectories

Figure 8.4 presents age-related change for the word fluency ability for the three groups. The stable, decline, and gain groups did not differ significantly at age 46. However, at age 53 and age 60, the decline group was performing at a level significantly below both the stable and gain groups. The gain group at age 53 and age 60 was performing at a significantly higher level than the stable group. The decline group had dropped over the 14-year period by 1 *SD* unit, whereas the gain group had increased by almost 1 *SD* unit.

In summary, these data indicate that although there is considerable stability in cognitive functioning when studied at the aggregate level,

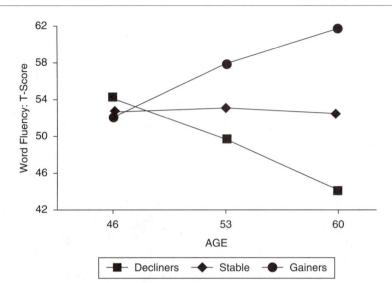

Figure 8.4   Age-Related Change for the Word Fluency Ability for Individuals Classified as Remaining Stable, Declined, or Increased

there are wide individual differences in patterns of cognitive change for subgroups of individuals in midlife. Individuals included in these analyses were functioning at quite comparable performance levels at age 46. By age 60, however, performance of the subgroups had diverged dramatically, with group differences on the order of 1 *SD* unit.

Association of Midlife Cognitive Change and Cognitive Impairment in Old Age

Given the wide individual differences in cognitive change trajectories in midlife, the question arises whether there is an association between cognition in middle age and subsequent functioning in old age (Schaie, 1984). Of particular concern is the question whether there is an association between negative cognitive trajectories in midlife and cognitive impairment in later adulthood.

Findings from a limited number of prospective studies indicate a lengthy preclinical phase of cognitive impairment that may extend up to several decades preceding the diagnosis of onset of Alzheimer's disease

(AD). In a study on normal aging in twins, LaRue and Jarvik (1987) noted deficits on multiple cognitive measures for those diagnosed as having dementia 20 years later. Snowdon and colleagues (1996) found that impoverished linguistic ability, when the participants were in their 20s, was associated with the clinical expression of AD almost 60 years later (Snowdon et al., 1997). In the Framingham study cohort, presence or absence of probable AD during a 22-year surveillance period was related to initial test performance (M. F. Elias et al., 2000; M. F. Elias & Robbins, 1991; Linn et al., 1995). In a prospective study over 15 years, healthy adults who eventually developed dementia performed less well on psychometric testing at initial assessment (Rubin et al., 1998).

Most current prospective studies of the preclinical phase, however, may have begun too late. While the length of the preclinical phase shown in prospective studies is impressive, participants at initial assessment were typically already in old age (Petersen, 2003). Most current short-term longitudinal prospective studies of cognitive risk for dementia originate in young-old age, or even in old-old age, but not in middle age. Entry age for the Framingham study was 65 years (M. F. Elias, Robbins, Elias, & Streeten, 1998; M. F. Elias & Elias, 1997) and 64 years for the Rubin et al. (1998) study. In the very well-characterized Kungsholmen study (Fratiglioni et al., 1991) entry age was 75 years. As initial assessment of individuals in their early 60s has been found to be predictive, the question arises whether cognitive status or change even earlier in midlife may provide important information about the preclinical phase. Current prospective studies on adults in their mid-60s and older must meet the challenge of differentiating older adults experiencing normative age-related change from adults experiencing preclinical decline, given the onset of normative age-related decline for fluid-type abilities is in the 60s (Hultsch et al., 1998; Schaie, 2005). However, cognitive decline in midlife is clearly nonnormative, and hence, prospective studies beginning in midlife may have particular merit.

While significant age-related decline is not normative until after age 60 on most ability measures, there are wide individual differences in rate of change as shown in Figures 8.2, 8.3, and 8.4. Having demonstrated different trajectories of cognitive change in midlife for the SLS cohorts (birth years 1907–1941), we then compared the magnitude of change in midlife for two subgroups from these cohorts: participants rated in old age as *normal* versus *cognitively impaired* by two neuropsychologists based on performance on a neuropsychological test battery.

Figure 8.5 presents the magnitude of decline in midlife for those rated as normal as compared with those who were cognitively impaired in old age. Significant group differences in midlife were found for four SLS measures (immediate and delayed recall, fluency, speed)—all of these measures map on the cognitive domains of interest as precursors of impairment (Figure 8.5, top graph). For the group subsequently rated as impaired in old age, magnitude of decline over the 46 to 60 age interval was on the order of 0.30 to 0.40 SD units for the SLS memory and fluency measures and on the order of 0.20 SD units for SLS speed.

The magnitude of midlife decline for the impaired-in-old-age group was on the order of the magnitude of decline shown from age 60 to 74 in normative aging samples (Schaie, 2005). Specifically, average decline from age 60 to 74 was 0.36 SD units on delayed recall, whereas the to-be-impaired group showed this level of impairment (0.38 SD units) from age 46 to 60. Equally important is that normal and impaired in old age did not differ in midlife performance on ability measures of verbal, spatial orientation, or number (Figure 8.5, bottom graph)—thus, group differences in decline in midlife did not occur for all abilities. Rate of decline in midlife differed only on memory, fluency, and speed—cognitive domains of interest as precursors of impairment.

Age of onset of decline and rate of decline varies by ability, and there are wide individual differences in rate and onset of decline. Rabbit (1993) posed the question, "Does it all go together, when it goes?" SLS findings and findings from other longitudinal studies (e.g., Hultsch et al., 1998) do not support the perspective of global decline.

Potential Factors Associated With Differential Cognitive Trajectories in Midlife

Within the study of cognitive aging, relatively limited attention has been given to factors associated with level and rate of change in abilities in midlife. However, in related fields such as neuropsychology, neurology, health psychology, and behavioral genetics, there is growing evidence for the impact of disease, biomarkers, and life experiences on cognition in middle age. In a recent review of factors associated with cognitive change in 34 longitudinal studies, Anstey and Christensen (2000) concluded that education, hypertension, objective health status, cardiovascular disease, and the APO-E gene are the factors most consistently related to cognitive

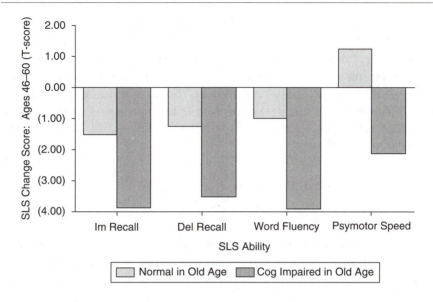

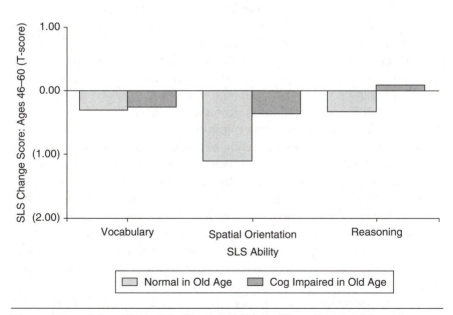

Figure 8.5   Magnitude of Decline in Midlife for Those Rated as Normal
Compared With Those Cognitively Impaired in Old Age

change across adulthood. Although risk factors for cognitive decline have received far greater attention, there is growing recognition of the role of protective factors in cognitive maintenance and plasticity. Protective factors are important as possible mechanisms to be targeted in preventive interventions. In addition, protective factors are of interest due to the dramatic increase in the level of protective factors such as education and occupational status that have occurred for recent-born, compared to early-born, cohorts.

Risk Factors for Midlife Cognitive Decline

Hypertension

Hypertension is one of the earliest manifestations of cardiovascular disease and has been one of the most extensively investigated diseases with respect to cognitive functioning (M. F. Elias, Elias, & Elias, 1990; Waldstein & Elias, 2001). There is now evidence indicating that hypertension is associated with poorer cognitive performance among adults not only in old age but at all adult ages. While the impact of hypertension on cognition in old age is well established, recent findings by P. K. Elias and colleagues have further established the role of hypertension on cognitive functioning in young and middle adulthood (M. F. Elias, Elias, Robbins, Wolf, & D'Agostino, 2001; P. K. Elias, Elias, Robbins, & Budge, 2004). Indeed, several studies suggest that cognitive performance differences are greater between young hypertensives (younger than 50 years) and normotensives than between late midlife hypertensives (50–70 years) and normotensives (M. F. Elias, Schultz, et al., 1990; Waldstein et al., 1996). Hypertension in early midlife is of particular concern, given that duration or lifetime exposure to elevated blood pressure may be a particularly important predictor of cognitive outcomes in old age (Knopman et al., 2000; Swan, Carmelli, & LaRue, 1996). Several epidemiological studies have found that higher blood pressure levels during middle age predict poorer cognitive outcomes in old age (Launer, Masaki, Petrovitch, Foley, & Havlik, 1995; Swan et al., 1996). In a 20-year longitudinal study, the magnitude of cognitive decline was 12.1% greater for persons who were hypertensive than for those who were never hypertensive. Thus, chronic hypertension is associated not only with level of performance but also with accelerated longitudinal decline in cognition (M. F. Elias, Robbins, & Elias, 1996; M. F. Elias et al., 1998; Knopman et al., 2000).

Hypertension has been associated with lower performance levels on tests of attention, learning and memory, executive functions, and visuospatial, psychomotor, and perceptual abilities (M. F. Elias & Robbins, 1991; M. F. Elias et al., 1987; P. K. Elias et al., 1995; Waldstein & Elias, 2001). Crystallized verbal abilities appear to be less affected.

Hypertension and Multiple Risk Factors

A limitation of many studies examining the impact of hypertension on cognition has been lack of consideration of multiple risk factors (e.g., gender, education, smoking, obesity, diabetes), as comorbidities are common among hypertensives. The number of risk factors has been significantly related to lower cognitive functioning. For each increase in the number of risk factors, the risk of performing in the lower quartile of distribution of cognitive scores for Learning and Memory increased by 39%. Moreover, studies assessing the long-term duration of risk factors showed a much stronger relationship with cognition (M. F. Elias et al., 1998).

Diabetes

In 20 case control studies of the association between cognitive function and Type 2 diabetes in older adults, almost all found cognitive impairment, with learning and memory abilities showing the most pronounced deficits, but also evidence for effects on attention, psychomotor speed, and problem solving (Strachan, Deary, Ewing, & Frier, 1997). Virtually all these studies have been cross-sectional with small sample sizes; thus, the long-term relationship between cognition and diabetes has not been examined. In addition, these studies have not taken into account common disorders that accompany diabetes and normal aging, such as cerebrovascular disease, hypertension, and impaired vision. Large-scale epidemiological studies support the findings of case control studies, but most epidemiological studies have been cross-sectional with the exception of the Framingham Health Study, which showed strong evidence of a causal relationship between diabetes and cognitive dysfunction (P. K. Elias et al., 1997); duration of diabetes was associated with poorer performance on verbal memory and abstract reasoning tests.

Biomarkers

Cholesterol and Cognition

The existing literature suggests that complex relationships exist between serum lipids and cognitive function (Muldoon, Flory, & Ryan, 2001). In healthy samples, certain abilities may be inversely associated with serum cholesterol level, whereas other aptitudes appear to be positively correlated with cholesterol concentration. Low serum cholesterol has been found to be associated with better memory and crystallized intelligence performance (Muldoon, Ryan, Matthews, & Manuck, 1997). On the other hand, studies also show that high serum cholesterol may be associated with optimal mental speed and mental flexibility. For example, high serum cholesterol was associated with less decline in digit-symbol substitution test performance over 5 years in middle-aged twins (Swan, LaRue, Carmelli, Reed, & Fabsitz, 1992).

What might explain these seemingly conflicting findings regarding the association of cholesterol and cognition? Muldoon et al. (1997) found that compared with people with high cholesterol, those with relatively low cholesterol (hypocholesterolemia) have more education, have a lower body mass index, have lower blood pressure, and are less likely to smoke. One possibility is that people with a wide range of crystallized knowledge are most aware of the health risks of certain behaviors and, thus, are more likely to adopt lifestyles that maintain lower cholesterol levels (Muldoon et al., 2001). According to this hypothesis, causality is in the direction of crystallized intelligence affecting health-related behaviors, resulting in reduced serum cholesterol concentrations. These questions can only be addressed in longitudinal studies in which the reciprocal associations between longitudinal trajectories of cognition and health outcomes can be examined.

APO-E

The ε4 allele of the APO-E gene is associated with an increased risk for AD and may modify the age of onset of AD (Saunders et al., 1993). An individual with no copies of the ε4 allele has a lifetime risk of developing AD of 9%, whereas the presence of one ε4 allele increases lifetime risk for AD to 29% (Swartz, Black, & St. George-Hyslop, 1999). However, there is accumulating evidence that the greater significance of APO-E ε4 may be in its association with age-related decline in cognitive performance rather than for the risk of developing AD (Carmelli et al., 1998; Hyman et al., 1996; Riley et al., 2000). In a study of adults with an average age of 45 (age range 24–60 years), individuals with an ε4 allele had lower scores on learning and memory tasks than did individuals with no ε4 allele (Flory, Manuck, Ferrell, Ryan, & Muldoon, 1999); no effect of the ε4 allele was found on measures of psychomotor speed or attention.

APO-E ε4 may be associated with earlier brain volumetric change, possibly evident in midlife. Nondemented ε4 carriers aged 45 to 70 years have been found to have smaller hippocampal volumes (Plassman et al., 1997), a faster rate of atrophy in the hippocampus (Moffat, Szekely, Zonderman, Kabani, & Resnick, 2000), and decreased blood flow in the temporal and parietal lobes (Reiman et al., 1996; Small et al., 1995). The presence of a single ε4 allele was also found to be associated with increased rate of hippocampal volume loss ($p < .03$) in healthy women in their 60s (Cohen, Small, Lalonde, Friz, & Sunderland, 2001). However, hippocampal volume loss was not correlated with changes in any of the cognitive measures.

APO-E ε4 genotype may play a modifier role with respect to other risk factors and cognition (Haan, Shemanski, Jagust, Manolio, & Kuller, 1999). The APO-E ε4 genotype is a risk factor for atherosclerosis (Hofman et al., 1997), coronary heart disease (Davignon et al., 1988; Mahley, 1988; P. Wilson et al., 1994), and hypertension (Metter & Wilson, 1993; Warden & Thompson, 1994). After adjusting for lipids and other risk factors, the APO-E ε4 genotype is the strongest genetic determinant for coronary heart disease in both men and women (P. Wilson et al., 1994). It promotes increased levels of circulating cholesterol (Escargueil-Blanc, Salvayre, & Negre-Salvayre, 1994). Larson et al. (1990; see also Jarvik et al., 1995) have reported that APO-E ε4 may moderate the relationship between cholesterol and dementia; effects of ε4 on cholesterol metabolism were not independent of its effects on dementia. Only longitudinal studies have the long-term multiability data sets capable of examining these alternative explanations for the role of APO-E ε4 across the adult life span.

Protective Factors

Education

Education has proven to be the most consistent nonbiological correlate of both cognitive level and rate of change (Anstey & Christensen, 2000). Moreover, educational level is associated with cognitive change not only in old age but also throughout adulthood (Farmer, Kittner, Rae, Barko, & Regier, 1995; Lyketsos, Chen, & Anthony, 1999). Education most often predicts change in crystallized abilities, memory, and mental status and is less consistently predictive of change in fluid abilities and speed. In the MacArthur Studies of Successful Aging, education was the best predictor of change in cognition (Albert et al., 1995). The effects of education on cognitive change remain when controlling for factors such as age, gender, race, and health. However, among hypertensives, relatively lower levels of education were associated with poorer neuropsychological function, whereas more highly educated hypertensives and normotensives (more than 16 years education) showed comparable performance (M. F. Elias et al., 1987).

Educational level increased significantly across birth cohorts in the first half of the 20th century. Hauser and Featherman (1976) report a total increase of about 4 years of education from the cohort born in 1897 to the cohort born in 1951. Intergenerational differences in level of schooling peaked among men born just after World War I; a deceleration has occurred across more recent cohorts.

Several explanations for the effect of education on cognitive change have been proposed. One explanation maintains that education may serve as a proxy for factors such as health behavior, socioeconomic status, occupational hazards, or nutrition, which affect cognitive change and covary with education. Alternatively, education may produce direct effects on brain structure through an increase in number of synapses or vascularization (Greenough, Larson, & Withers, 1985).

It has also been hypothesized that education does not alter vulnerability to disease but rather delays the appearance of clinical symptoms by postponing the point at which a sufficient number of abnormalities have accumulated. Moreover, education's impact on brain structure may continue throughout life by instilling lifelong habits of mental stimulation that produce neurochemical or structural alternations in the brain that are themselves protective. Thus, although formal education is acquired early in life, the effects of education on brain function would be mediated by habits that are maintained throughout life. A third hypothesis is that education may protect and preserve learning acquired through schooling but not the rate of biological decline. Greater expertise in crystallized knowledge would compensate for, or disguise, the rate of biological aging in the well educated. Because crystallized intelligence increases through most of adulthood and declines only in late life, the positive effects of education would be expected to increase progressively into midlife and old age (Christensen et al., 1997).

Environmental Complexity and the Nature of Work

Schooler and colleagues have examined the effects of environmental demand, particularly in the work context, on adult cognition (Schooler,

1987, 1990, 1998). Recent findings are particularly relevant to midlife cognition (DeFrias & Schaie, 2001). The reciprocal relationship between substantively complex activities (work, leisure) and cognition has been examined longitudinally over three decades. Job conditions involving self-directed, substantively complex work increase intellectual flexibility and self-direction. Recent findings indicate that the reciprocal relationship between substantively complex work and cognition is even stronger for men in late midlife than was found previously in younger men (Schooler, Mulatu, & Oates, 1999, 2004). In addition, Schooler's work suggests that there are age-cohort differences in work complexity; older age–cohort workers were found to do less substantively complex work.

Schooler and colleagues (Schooler, 1998; Schooler et al., 2004) suggest that if technical and economic development in a society leads to more complex environments, including intellectually demanding work conditions, such increased environmental complexity should result in higher levels of intellectual functioning. Environmental complexity is defined by stimulus and demand characteristics; the more diverse the stimuli, the greater the number of decisions required, the greater the number of factors to be taken into account in making decisions, the more complex the environment. Cognitively demanding complex environments lead not only to higher intellectual functioning, but greater valuation of self-direction and autonomy (Schooler, 1990). A self-directed, substantively complex environment impacts cognitive functioning, not only in young adulthood, but also in midlife and old age (Attwell, 1987; Schooler et al., 2004). Cognitive variability may be due, in part, to variability in individuals' involvement in complex, self-directed activities.

In the SLS, we have examined the association of work variables to retirement status and cognitive functioning over a 7-year interval, with age and education as covariates. SLS participants who continued to work scored higher on immediate recall than those who retired during the 7-year interval (DeFrias & Schaie, 2001). Those participants reporting higher job complexity scored higher on immediate recall than those with low complexity. In addition, those reporting low complexity in their jobs declined on Fluency over the 7-year interval.

Cognitive Engagement

Recent research on cognitive engagement provides further support for the importance of environmental stimulation on cognition in middle and later adulthood (Kramer & Willis, 2003; R. S. Wilson et al., 1999). Katzman (1993) has proposed that persons with higher educational levels are more resistant to the effects of dementia as a result of having greater cognitive reserve and increased complexity of neuronal synapses. Like education, participation in work or leisure activities may lower the risk of dementia by improving cognitive reserve (Scarmeas, Levy, Tang, Manly, & Stern, 2001; Wang, Karp, Winblad, & Fratiglioni, 2002).

Two recent studies examined prospectively the association of cognitive activities and risk of dementia. In the Religious Orders Study (R. S. Wilson et al., 2002), cognitive activity was assessed at baseline and members followed for approximately 5 years. A 1-point increase in cognitive activity score was associated with a 33% reduction in risk of AD. However, members were very highly educated and were aged 60 to 70 years on average at baseline. In the Bronx Aging Study (Verghese et al., 2003), similar findings were reported. Again, members were aged 75 to 85. Thus, longitudinal studies examining the impact of cognitive activity across the life span on subsequent cognitive decline are needed.

Although these results suggest that such activities have a protective role, there is an alternative explanation. In dementia, there is a long period of cognitive decline preceding diagnosis (M. F. Elias et al., 2000; Small, Fratiglioni, Viitanen, Winblad, & Bäckman, 2000). Reduced participation in activities during this preclinical phase of dementia may be the consequence, and not the cause, of cognitive decline. Resolution of this issue requires a long period of observation before diagnosis to disentangle the effects of preclinical dementia.

In an early study (Gribbin, Schaie, & Parham, 1980), four groups of SLS participants with distinctly different lifestyles were compared on magnitude of cognitive decline over 7- and 14-year intervals. Magnitude of cognitive decline varied by lifestyle group for verbal, spatial, reason, and fluency abilities. The lifestyle group most fully engaged in social and leisure activities and with high socioeconomic status showed greater maintenance of cognitive ability over 7- and 14-year intervals. The greatest cognitive decline occurred for those with the lowest activity engagement.

Exercise

In the Anstey and Christensen (2000) review of factors associated with cognitive change, findings were mixed on the effect of physical activity. However, in a recent meta-analysis of fitness intervention studies, Colcombe and Kramer (2002) found that fitness effects were selective and that aerobic fitness training had a substantially larger positive impact on tasks with large executive control components. In the MacArthur Studies of Successful Aging (Albert et al., 1995), self-report of strenuous daily physical activity was one of four significant predictors of cognitive change. Carmelli et al. (1998) found that individuals (aged 65–86) who improved on a cognitive composite reported the highest physical activity; individuals who declined cognitively reported significantly lower exercise levels than those not declining. However, Hultsch et al. (1999) found that physical activity did not affect memory over 6 years. In the Midlife in the United States study, Markus and colleagues (2004) found educational differences in health practices, with college-educated individuals reporting a higher rate of exercise and a lower rate of smoking. There have been several studies supporting the effects of physical activity on brain function and cognition. Active older adults have been shown to maintain more consistent cerebral perfusion (Rogers, Meyer, & Mortel, 1990), to have shorter event-related potential latencies, and to demonstrate higher cognitive scores (Dustman et al., 1990).

The Brain and Cognitive Performance in Midlife and Old Age

Although brain atrophy in patients with mild cognitive impairment and AD has been found, research on brain change in healthy adults experiencing normal aging is limited (Albert & Killiany, 2001). The majority of studies examining the association of age and brain volume have been cross-sectional. In aging healthy adults, brain regions are affected differentially. The prefrontal cortex (PFC) appears to be the most vulnerable, whereas the effect of aging on the hippocampus (HC) is moderate and on the entorhinal cortex (EC) is relatively spared (Du et al., 2003; Raz, 2000; Raz, Rodrigue, Head, Kennedy, & Acker, 2004). In contrast, in the course of AD, pathological changes in the EC and HC precede those in the PFC (Braak & Braak, 1991; Laakso, 2002; Thompson et al., 2003). Although shrinkage of both the HC (Xu et al., 2000) and EC (Dickerson et al., 2001) is associated with concurrent AD and predicts clinical deterioration (Jack et al., 2000), volume reduction in the EC is viewed as the earliest indicator of incipient conversion from preclinical cognitive impairment to dementia (Dickerson et al., 2001; Killiany et al., 2000).

A few longitudinal studies of volumetric change have been reported. Raz and colleagues (Raz, Rodrigue, Head, Kennedy, & Acker, 2004) recently reported on change over a 5-year period in EC and HC volume assessed twice in healthy adults, mean age 57 years (range 26–82 years), educational level 16 years. It was hypothesized that the EC volume declines at a slower rate than the HC volume. HC volume exhibited significant age-related differences at baseline and at follow-up and shrunk at a faster pace (0.86% per annum) than the EC volume (0.33% per annum); no EC shrinkage was observed in adults under age 50. However, participants over age 50 showed increased annual shrinkage of the HC (1.18%) as well as EC shrinkage (0.53% per annum). Thus, there were markedly different age trends for the HC and EC. However, both regions showed increased shrinkage for older participants (50+ years). In a follow-up study, Rodrigue and Raz (2004) examined the association of memory performance with volumetric decline over 5 years in the HC, EC, and PFC regions. Longitudinal decline in the entorhinal region was associated with poorer performance on a composite declarative memory measure, including the Wechsler Memory Scale Logical Memory and California Verbal Learning Test. Decline in the HC and PFC regions, however, was not significantly associated with poorer memory performance. The correlation between EC decline and the memory composite was on the order of $r = .40$.

Cross-sectional studies have reported a significant relationship between volumetric measures of the frontal cortex and tasks of executive function. Raz, Gunning-Dixon, Head, Dupuis, and Acker (1998) reported that volume of the prefrontal cortex was inversely correlated with performance on the Wisconsin Card Sorting Test. In addition, at an early stage of learning to solve the Tower of Hanoi puzzle, speed and efficiency were associated with age, PFC volume, and working memory in healthy adults (Raz, Dixon, Head, Dupuis, & Acker, 1998). When hypertensive participants were excluded, the effect of prefrontal shrinkage on executive aspects of performance was no longer significant, but the effect of working memory remained. Moreover, in a study examining the neural substrates of age-related differences in mental imagery, it was suggested that age-related shrinkage of the PFC and age-related declines in working memory are associated with age deficits in visual-spatial imagery tasks (Raz, Briggs, Marks, & Acker, 1999).

Hypertension has been associated with smaller PFC and underlying white matter volumes and increased frontal white-matter hypertensities (WMH; Raz, Rodrigue, & Acker, 2003). Likewise, smaller PFC and WMH have been associated with age-related deficits in executive functioning (Gunning-Dixon & Raz, 2000; Raz et al., 1998). The effect of untreated hypertension has also been found to affect a number of cognitive tasks, in particular, executive functions, speed of processing, and memory (Brady, Spiro, McGlinchey-Berroth, Milberg, & Gaziano, 2001; P. K. Elias et al., 1995; Waldstein, Manuck, Ryan, & Muldoon, 1991). Thus, PFC shrinkage and WMH may mediate the effects of hypertension on cognitive performance, including executive functioning and speed of processing. In support of this hypothesis, Raz and colleagues have found that hypertensives committed significantly more perseverative errors (an index of prefrontal dysfunction) while showing no differences on tests of working memory, fluid intelligence, and vocabulary.

Summary and Future Directions

We began this chapter by briefly reviewing some of the major propositions of lifespan development theory as they may apply to the study of cognition in midlife. That is, while trait theorists have argued for considerable intraindividual stability in midlife, ego psychologists have proposed that substantial qualitative changes such as the "midlife crisis" (Jaques, 1965) may prevail for many individuals during this life stage. We noted that this discrepancy may be attributable, in part, to the prevailing focus in studies of ability and personality development on changes in aggregate means (level) rather than on differences between individual change trajectories (slope).

Data from the SLS were then presented that show aggregate stability over the midlife period for selected abilities. However, when individual trajectories are disaggregated into subtypes of stables, decliners, and gainers (using a 1 standard error of measurement criterion), it is found that although the majority of individuals remain stable over the age range from 46 to 60 years, there are significant subsets of individuals that show significant gain or decline across midlife. The proportion of gainers and decliners differ by ability; the proportion of decliners is greatest for measures of immediate and delayed memory.

We next considered whether cognitive change in midlife predicted long-term outcomes, such as cognitive impairment in old age. Illustrative data from the SLS showed that for some individuals, midlife change trajectories could be related to cognitive impairment in old age. In particular, measures of immediate and delayed recall, fluency, and speed were identified as early predictors.

Cognitive psychologists have given only limited attention to risk factors associated with cognitive change in midlife. We therefore reviewed the literature in neuropsychology, health psychology, and behavioral genetics to identify risk factors that have been related to cognition and that deserve greater attention in studies of cognitive aging. These risk factors associated with lower performance on many cognitive functions include the early occurrence of hypertension, diabetes, serum cholesterol, and allele 4 of the APO-E gene.

But, while a number of physiological influences pose risks for the maintenance of optimal cognitive function, there are also a number of protective factors that have been identified in well-functioning, midlife individuals that predict better cognitive performance in old age. These protective factors include high levels of education, environmental complexity, the nature of work, cognitive engagement, and exercise. Here, we suggested a number of mechanisms that might explain the favorable effects attributed to these protective factors.

Finally, we reviewed evidence on the relation of changes in brain and cognitive performance in midlife and old age. As yet, there is a paucity of longitudinal evidence on structural changes in brain volume. However, it does appear that in normal individuals, the PFC is most vulnerable to aging, the HC is moderately affected, and the EC is relatively spared. By contrast, in the cognitively impaired, the EC is the first part of the brain likely to be affected.

We conclude then that many of the phenomena of cognitive aging, at least in those individuals who will eventually become cognitively impaired or those who represent the sparse group of the unusually well-functioning "super-aged," can be traced back to physiological and behavior changes that begin in midlife (or even earlier). Hence, attempts at long-term prediction of either cognitive impairment or successful aging must be based on studies that begin at much earlier ages than do most studies currently in progress.

There is a complex interaction between genetic predispositions, onset of chronic disease, and protective factors based on lifestyles often associated with the availability of economic resources that is likely to account for substantial proportions of variance associated with the individual differences in midlife cognitive functions we have described. Future cognitive aging studies will therefore require much better assessment of both risk factors and protective factors.

Finally, a better understanding of structural and functional changes in the brain will facilitate an understanding of how the risk and protective factors identified—which we now know to be associated with cognitive aging—play out at the neurophysiological level. Not the least of such analyses, however, will require further inquiry into possible reciprocal relationships between changes in the brain and changes in behavior.

References

Albert, M. S., Jones, K., Savage, C. R., Berkman, L., Seeman, T., Blazer, D., et al. (1995). Predictors of cognitive change in older persons: MacArthur Studies of Successful Aging. *Psychology and Aging, 10,* 578–589.

Albert, M. S., & Killiany, R. J. (2001). Age-related cognitive change and brain-behavior relationships. In J. E. Birren & K. W. Schaie (Eds.), *Handbook of the psychology of aging* (5th ed., pp. 161–185). San Diego, CA: Academic Press.

Anstey, K., & Christensen, H. (2000). Education, activity, health, blood pressure and Apolipoprotein E as predictors of cognitive change in old age: A review. *Gerontology, 46,* 163–177.

Attwell, P. (1987). The deskilling controversy. *Work and Occupation, 14,* 323–346.

Bäckman, L., & Nilsson, L.-G. (1996). Semantic memory functioning across the adult life span. *European Psychologist, 1,* 27–33.

Baltes, P. B. (1987). Theoretical propositions of life-span developmental psychology: On the dynamics between growth and decline. *Developmental Psychology, 23,* 611–626.

Baltes, P. B., & Baltes, M. M. (1990). *Successful aging: Perspectives from the behavioral sciences.* New York: Cambridge University Press.

Baltes, P. B., Staudinger, U. M., & Lindenberger, U. (1999). Lifespan psychology: Theory and application to intellectual functioning. *Annual Review of Psychology, 50,* 471–502.

Braak, H., & Braak, E. (1991). Neuropathological staging of Alzheimer-related changes. *Acta Neuropathology, 82,* 239–259.

Brady, C., Spiro, A., McGlinchey-Berroth, R., Milberg, W., & Gaziano, J. (2001). Stroke risk predicts verbal fluency decline in healthy older men. Evidence from the normative aging study. *Journals of Gerontology: Series B: Psychological Sciences and Social Sciences, 56,* 340–346.

Carmelli, D., Swan, G. E., Reed, T., Miller, B., Wolf, P. A., Jarvik, G. P., et al. (1998). Midlife cardiovascular risk factors, ApoE, and cognitive decline in elderly male twins. *American Academy of Neurology, 50,* 1580–1585.

Christensen, H., Korten, A. E., Jorn, A. F., Henderson, A. S., Jacomb, P. A., Rodgers, B., et al. (1997). Education and decline in cognitive performance; compensatory but not protective. *International Journal of Geriatric Psychiatry, 12,* 323–330.

Cohen, R. M., Small, C., Lalonde, F., Friz, J., & Sunderland, T. (2001). Effect of apolipoprotein E genotype on hippocampal volume loss in aging healthy women. *Neurology, 57,* 2223–2228.

Colcombe, S., & Kramer, A. F. (2002). Fitness effects on the cognitive function of older adults: A meta-analytic study. *Psychological Science, 14,* 125–130.

Costa, P. T., Jr., & McCrae, R. R. (1980). Still stable after all these years: Personality as a key to some issues in adulthood and old age. In P. B. Baltes and O. G. Brim, Jr. (Eds.), *Life span development and behavior* (Vol. 3, pp. 65–102). New York: Academic Press.

Costa, P. T., Jr., & McCrae, R. R. (1993). Stability and change in personality from adolescence through adulthood. In C. A. Halverson, G. A. Kohnstamm, & R. P., Martin (Eds.), *The developing structure of temperament and personality from infancy to adulthood.* Hillsdale, NJ: Erlbaum.

Costa, P. T., Jr., McCrae, R. R., Martin, T. A., Oryol, V. E., Senin, I. G., Rukavishnikov, A. A., et al. (1999). Personality development from adolescence through adulthood: Further cross-cultural comparisons of age differences. In V. J. Molfese & D. Molfese (Eds.), *Temperament and personality development across the life span* (pp. 235–252). Mahwah, NJ: Erlbaum.

Davignon, J., Bouthillier, D., Nestruck, A. C., & Sing, C. F. (1988). Apolipoprotein E polymorphism and atherosclerosis: Insight from the study of octogenarians. *Trans America Clinic Association, 99,* 100–110.

DeFrias, C., & Schaie, K. W. (2001). Perceptions of work environment and cognitive performance. *Experimental Aging Research, 27,* 67–81.

Dickerson, B. C., Goncharova, I., Sullivan, M. P., Forchetti, C., Wilson, R. S., Bennett, D. A., et al. (2001). MRI-derived entorhinal and hippocampal atrophy in incipient and very mild Alzheimer's disease. *Neurobiology of Aging, 22,* 747–754.

Dixon, R. A., de Frias, C. M., & Maitland, S. B. (2001). Memory in midlife. In M. E. Lachman (Ed.), *Handbook of midlife development* (pp. 248–278). New York: Wiley.

Du, A. T., Schuff, N., Zhu, X. P., Jagust,W. J., Miller, B. L., Reed, B. R., et al. (2003). Atrophy rates of entorhinal cortex in AD and normal aging. *Neurology, 60,* 481–486.

Dudek, F. J. (1979). The continuing misinterpretation of the standard error of measurement. *Psychological Bulletin, 86,* 335–337.

Dustman, R. E., Emmerson, R. Y., Ruhling, R. O., Shearer, D. E., Steinhaus, L. A., Johnson, S. C., et al. (1990). Age and fitness effects on EEG, ERPs, visual sensitivity, and cognition. *Neurobiology of Aging, 11,* 193–200.

Elias, M. F., Beiser, A., Wolf, P. A., Au, R., White, R. F., & D'Agostino, R. B. (2000). The preclinical phase of Alzheimer disease: A 22-year prospective study of the Framingham Cohort. *Archives of Neurology, 57,* 808–813.

Elias, M. F., Elias, J. W., & Elias, P. K. (1990). Biological and health influences on behavior. In J. E. Birren & K. W. Schaie (Eds.), *Handbook of the psychology of aging* (3rd ed., pp. 80–102). San Diego, CA: Academic Press.

Elias, M. F., & Elias, P. K. (1997). Active life expectancy: Conceptual model for research on competency? In S. Willis, K. W. Schaie, & M. Hayward (Eds.), *Societal mechanisms for maintaining competence in old age* (pp. 35–49). New York: Springer.

Elias, M. F., Elias, P. K., Robbins, M. A., Wolf, P. A., & D'Agostino, R. B. (2001). Cardiovascular risk factors and cognitive functioning: An epidemiological perspective. In S. Waldstein & M. F. Elias (Eds.), *Neuropsychology of cardiovascular disease* (pp. 83–104). Mahwah, NJ: Erlbaum.

Elias, M. F., & Robbins, M. A. (1991). Longitudinal studies of disease and cognitive function: Where have all the subjects gone? In L. M. Collins & J. L. Horn (Eds.), *Best methods for the analysis of change* (pp. 264–275). Washington, DC: American Psychological Association.

Elias, M. F., Robbins, M. A., & Elias, P. K. (1996). A 15-year longitudinal study of Halstead-Reitan neuropsychological test performance. *Journal of Gerontology: Psychological Sciences, 51B*, P331–P334.

Elias, M. F., Robbins, M. A., Elias, P. K., & Streeten, D. H. P. (1998). A longitudinal study of blood pressure in relation to performance on the Wechsler Adult Intelligence Scale. *Health Psychology, 17*, 486–493.

Elias, M. F., Robbins, M. A., Schultz, N. R., Streeten, D. H., & Elias, P. K. (1987). Clinical significance of cognitive performance by hypertensive patients. *Hypertension, 9*, 192–197.

Elias, M. F., Schultz, N. R., Robbins, M. A., & Elias, P. K. (1990). A longitudinal study of neuropsychological performance by hypertensives and normotensives: A third measurement point. *Journal of Gerontology: Psychological Sciences, 44*, 25–28.

Elias, P. K., D'Agostino, R. B., Lias, M. F., & Wolf, P. A. (1995). Blood pressure, hypertension, and age as risk factors for poor cognitive performance. *Experimental Aging Research, 21*, 393–417.

Elias, P. K., Elias, M. F., D'Agostino, R. B., Cupples, L. A., Wilson, P. W., Silbershatz, H., et al. (1997). NIDDM and blood pressure as risk factors for poor cognitive performance. *Diabetes Care, 20*, 1388–1395.

Elias, P. K., Elias, M. F., Robbins, M. A., & Budge, M. M. (2004). Blood pressure related cognitive decline: Does age make a difference? *Hypertension, 44*, 1–6.

Erikson, E. H. (1980). *Identity and the life cycle.* New York: Norton.

Escargueil-Blanc, I., Salvayre, R., & Negre-Salvayre, A. (1994). Neurosis and apotosis induced by oxidized low density lipoprotein occur through two calcium-dependent pathways in lymphoblastoid cells. *FASEB Journal, 8*, 1075–1080.

Farmer, M. E., Kittner, S. J., Rae, D. S., Barko, J. J., & Regier, D. A. (1995). Education and change in cognitive function: The Epidemiologic Catchment Area Study. *Annals of Epidemiology, 5*, 1–7.

Flory, J. D., Manuck, S. B., Ferrell, R. E., Ryan, C. M., & Muldoon, M. F. (1999). APOE e4 allele is associated with lower memory scores in middle aged adults. *Psychosomatic Medicine, 61*, 257.

Fratiglioni, L., Grut, M., Forsell, Y., Viitanen, M., Grafstrom, M., Holmen, K., et al. (1991). Prevalence of Alzheimer's disease in an elderly urban population: Relationship with sex and education. *Neurology, 41*, 1886–1891.

Greenough, W. T., Larson, J. R., & Withers, G. S. (1985). Effects of unilateral and bilateral training in a reaching task on dendritic branching of neurons in the rat motor-sensitivity forelimb cortex. *Behavioral Neural Biology, 44*, 301–314.

Gribbin, K., Schaie, K. W., & Parham, I. A. (1980). Complexity of life style and maintenance of intellectual abilities. *Journal of Social Issues, 36*, 47–61.

Gunning-Dixon, F., & Raz, N. (2000). The cognitive correlates of white matter abnormalities in normal aging: A quantitative review. *Neuropsychology, 14*, 224–232.

Haan, M. N., Shemanski, L., Jagust, W. J., Manolio, T. A., & Kuller, L. (1999). The role of APOE e4 in modulating effects of other risk factors for cognitive decline in elderly persons. *Journal of the American Medical Association, 282*, 40–46.

Hauser, R. M., & Featherman, D. L. (1976). Equality of schooling: Trends and prospects. *Sociology of Education, 49*, 99–120.

Hofman, A., Ott, A., Breteler, M., Bots, M. L., Slooter, A., van Harskamp, F., et al. (1997). Atherosclerosis, apolipoprotein E, and prevalence of dementia and Alzheimer's disease in the Rotterdam Study. *The Lancet, 349*, 151–154.

Hultsch, D. F., Hertzog, C., Dixon, R. A., & Small, B. J. (1998). *Memory change in the aged.* Cambridge, UK: Cambridge University Press.

Hultsch, D. F., Hertzog, C., Small, B., & Dixon, R. A. (1999). Use it or lose it: Engaged lifestyle as a buffer of cognitive decline in aging? *Psychology and Aging, 14*, 245–263.

Hyman, B. T., Gomez-Isal, T., Briggs, M., Chung, H., Nichols, S., Kohut, F., et al. (1996). Apolipoprotein E and cognitive change in an elderly population. *Annals of Neurology, 40*, 55–66.

Jack, C. R., Jr., Petersen, R. C., Xu, Y., O'Brien, P. C., Smith, G. E., Ivnik, R. J., et al. (2000). Rates of hippocampal atrophy correlate with change in clinical status in aging and AD. *Neurology, 55*, 484–489.

Jaques, E. (1965). Death and the midlife crisis. *International Journal of Psychoanalysis, 46*, 502–514.

Jarvik, G. P., Wijsman, E. M., Kukull, W. A., Schellenberg, G. D., Yu, C., & Larson, E. B. (1995). Interactions of apolipoprotein E genotype, total cholesterol level, age, and sex in prediction of Alzheimer's disease: A case control study. *Neurology, 45*, 1092–1096.

Katzman, R. (1993). Education and the prevalence of dementia and Alzheimer's disease. *Neurology, 43*, 13–20.

Killiany, R. J., Gomez-Isla, T., Moss, M., Kikinis, R., Sandor, T., Jolesz, F., et al. (2000). Use of structural magnetic resonance imaging to predict who will get Alzheimer's disease. *Annals of Neurology, 47*, 430–439.

Knopman, D. S., Boland, L. L., Folsom, A. R., Mosley, T. H., McGovern, P. G., Howard, G., et al. (2000). Cardiovascular risk factors and longitudinal cognitive changes in middle age adults. *Neurology, 54* (Suppl. 3), 42–48.

Kramer, A. F., & Willis, S. L. (2003). Cognitive plasticity and aging. In B. H. Ross (Ed.), *The psychology of learning and motivation: Advances in research and theory* (Vol. 43, pp. 267–302). San Diego, CA: Academic Press.

Laakso, M. P. (2002). Structural imaging in cognitive impairment and the dementias: An update. *Current Opinion in Neurology, 15*, 415–421.

Lachman, M. E. (Ed.). (2001). *Handbook of midlife development.* New York: Wiley.

Larson, E. B., Kukull, W. A., Teri, L., McCormick, W., Pfanschmidt, M., Van Belle, G., et al. (1990). University of Washington's Alzheimer's Disease Patient Registry (ADPR): 1987-1988. *Aging, 2*, 404–408.

LaRue, A., & Jarvik, L. F. (1987). Cognitive function and prediction of dementia in old age. *International Journal of Aging and Human Development, 25*, 79–89.

Launer, L. J., Masaki, K., Petrovitch, H., Foley, D., & Havlik, R. J. (1995). The association between midlife blood pressure levels and late life cognitive function. *Journal of the American Medical Association, 274*, 1846–1851.

Levinson, D. J. (1978). *The seasons of a man's life.* New York: Knopf.

Lezak, M. D. (1995). *Neuropsychological assessment* (3rd ed.). New York: Oxford University Press.

Linn, R. T., Wolf, P. A., Bachman, D. L., Knoefel, J. E., Cobb, J. L., Belanger, A. J., et al. (1995). The "preclinical phase" of probable Alzheimer's disease: A 13-year prospective study of the Framingham cohort. *Archives of Neurology, 52*, 485–490.

Lyketsos, C. G., Chen, L. S., & Anthony, J. C. (1999). Cognitive decline in adulthood: An 11.5-year follow-up of the Baltimore Epidemiologic Catchment Area Study. *American Journal of Psychiatry, 156*, 58–65.

Mahley, R. W. (1988). Apolipoprotein E: Cholesterol transport protein with expanding role in cell biology. *Science, 240*, 622–630.

Markus, H. R., Ryff, C. D., Curham, K. B., & Palmersheim, K. A. (2004). In their own words: Well-being in midlife among high school-educated and college educated adults. In O. G. Brim, C. D. Ryff, & R. C. Kessler (Eds.), *How healthy are we? A national study of well-being in midlife* (pp. 273–319). Chicago: University of Chicago Press.

McCrae, R. R., & Costa, P. T. (1984). *Emerging lives, enduring dispositions: Personality in adulthood.* Boston: Little, Brown.

Metter, E. J., & Wilson, R. S. (1993). *Vascular dementias.* New York: Oxford University Press.

Moffat, S. D., Szekely, C. A., Zonderman, A. B., Kabani, N. J., & Resnick, S. M. (2000). Longitudinal change in hippocampal volume as a function of apolipoprotein E genotype. *Neurology, 55*, 134–136.

Muldoon, M. F., Flory, J. D., & Ryan, C. M. (2001). Serum cholesterol, the brain, and cognitive functioning. In S. Waldstein & M. F. Elias (Eds.), *Neuropsychology of cardiovascular disease* (pp. 37–59). Mahwah, NJ: Erlbaum.

Muldoon, M. F., Ryan, C. M., Matthews, K. A., & Manuck, S. B. (1997). Serum cholesterol and intellectual performance. *Psychosomatic Medicine, 59*, 382–387.

Petersen, R. C. (Ed.). (2003). *Mild cognitive impairment: Aging to Alzheimer's disease.* Oxford, UK: Oxford University Press.

Plassman, B. L., Welsh-Bohmer, K. A., Bigler, E. D., Johnson, S. C., Anderson, C. V., Helms, M. J., et al. (1997). Apolipoprotein E epsilon 4 allele and hippocampal volume in twins with normal cognition. *Neurology, 48,* 985–989.

Rabbit, P. M. A. (1993). Does it all go together when it goes? The Nineteenth Bartlett Memorial Lecture. *Quarterly Journal of Experimental Psychology: Human Experimental Psychology, 46,* 385–434.

Raz, N. (2000). Aging of the brain and its impact on cognitive performance: Integration of structural and functional findings. In F. I. Craik & T. A. Salthouse (Eds.), *Handbook of aging and cognition* (pp. 1–90). Mahwah, NJ: Erlbaum.

Raz, N., Briggs, S., Marks, W., & Acker, J. (1999). Age-related deficits in generation and manipulation of mental images: II. The role of the dorsolateral prefrontal cortex. *Psychology and Aging, 14,* 436–444.

Raz, N., Dixon, F. M., Head, D. P., Dupuis, J. H., & Acker, J. D. (1998). Neuroanatomical correlates of cognitive aging: Evidence from structural MRI. *Neuropsychology, 12,* 95–106.

Raz, N., Gunning-Dixon, F., Head, D., Dupuis, J., & Acker, J. (1998). Neuro-anatomical correlates of cognitive aging: Evidence from structural magnetic resonance imaging. *Journal of Neuropsychology, 121,* 95–114.

Raz, N., Rodrigue, K., & Acker, J. (2003). Hypertension and the brain: Vulnerability of the prefrontal regions and executive functioning. *Behavioral Neuroscience, 117,* 1169–1180.

Raz, N., Rodrigue, K. M., Head, D., Kennedy, K. M., & Acker, J. D. (2004). Differential aging of the medial temporal lobe: A study of a five-year change. *Neurology, 62,* 433–439.

Reiman, E. M., Caselli, R. J., Yun, L. S., Chen, K., Bandy, D., Minoshima, S., et al. (1996). Preclinical evidence of Alzheimer's disease in persons homozygous for the e4 allele for apolipoprotein E. *New England Journal of Medicine, 334,* 752–758.

Riley, K. P., Snowdon, D. A., Saunders, A. M., Roses, A. D., Mortimer, J. A., & Nanayakkara, N. (2000). Cognitive function and apolipoprotein E in very old adults: Findings from the Nun Study. *Journal of Gerontology: Social Sciences, 55B,* S69–S75.

Rodrigue, K. M., & Raz, N. (2004). Shrinkage of the entorhinal cortex over five years predicts memory performance in healthy adults. *The Journal of Neuroscience, 24,* 956–963.

Rogers, R. L., Meyer, J. S., & Mortel, K. F. (1990). After reaching retirement age physical activity sustains cerebral perfusion and cognition. *Journal of the American Geriatrics Society, 38,* 123–128.

Rubin, E. H., Storandt, M., Miller, J. P., Kinscherf, D. A., Grant, E. A., Morris, J. C., et al. (1998). A prospective study of cognitive function and onset of dementia in cognitively healthy elders. *Archives of Neurology, 55,* 395–401.

Saunders, A. M., Hulette, O., Welsh-Bohmer, K. A., Schmechel, D. E., Crain, B., Burke, J. R., et al. (1993). Specificity, sensitivity and predictive value of apolipoprotein-E genotyping for sporadic Alzheimer's disease. *Lancet, 348,* 90–93.

Scarmeas, N., Levy, G., Tang, M. X., Manly, J., & Stern, Y. (2001). Influence of leisure activity on the incidence of Alzheimer's disease. *Neurology, 57,* 2236–2242.

Schaie, K. W. (1984). Midlife influences upon intellectual functioning in old age. *International Journal of Behavioral Development, 7,* 463–478.

Schaie, K. W. (1989a). The hazards of cognitive aging. *Gerontologist, 29,* 484–493.

Schaie, K. W. (1989b). Individual differences in rate of cognitive change. In V. L. Bengtson & K. W. Schaie (Eds.), *The course of later life: Research and reflections* (pp. 65–85). New York: Springer.

Schaie, K. W. (1996). *Intellectual development in adulthood: The Seattle Longitudinal Study.* New York: Cambridge University Press.

Schaie, K. W. (2005). *Developmental influences on adult intelligence: The Seattle Longitudinal Study.* New York: Oxford University Press.

Schaie, K. W., & Willis, S. L. (1986). Can intellectual decline in the elderly be reversed? *Developmental Psychology, 22,* 223–232.

Schaie, K. W., & Willis, S. L. (1993). Age difference patterns of psychometric intelligence in adulthood: Generalizability within and across ability domains. *Psychology and Aging, 8,* 44–55.

Schooler, C. (1987). Cognitive effects of complex environments during the life span: A review and theory. In C. Schooler & K. W. Schaie (Eds.), *Cognitive functioning and social structure over the life course* (pp. 24–49). Norwood, NJ: Ablex.

Schooler, C. (1990). Psychosocial factors and effective cognitive functioning in adulthood. In J. E. Birren & K. W. Schaie (Eds.), *Handbook of the psychology of aging* (3rd ed., pp. 347–358). San Diego, CA: Academic Press.

Schooler, C. (1998). Environmental complexity and the Flynn effect. In U. Neisser (Ed.), *The rising curve: Long-term gains in IQ and related measures* (pp. 67–79). Washington, DC: American Psychological Association.

Schooler, C., Mulatu, M. S., & Oates, G. (1999). The continuing effects of substantively complex work on the intellectual functioning of older workers. *Psychology and Aging, 14,* 483–506.

Schooler, C., Mulatu, M. S., & Oates, G. (2004). Occupational self-direction, intellectual functioning, and self-directed orientation in older workers: Findings and implications for individuals and societies. *American Journal of Sociology, 110,* 161–197.

Small, B. J., Fratiglioni, L., Viitanen, M., Winblad, B., & Bäckman, L. (2000). The course of cognitive impairment in preclinical Alzheimer disease: Three- and 6-year follow-up of a population-based sample. *Archives of Neurology, 57,* 839–844.

Small, G. W., Mazziotta, J. C., Collins, M. T., Baxter, L. R., Phelps, M. E., Mandelkern, M. A., et al. (1995). Apolipoprotein E type 4 allele and cerebral glucose metabolism in relatives at risk for familial Alzheimer disease. *Journal of the American Medical Association, 273*, 942–947.

Snowdon, D. A., Greiner, L. H., Mortimer, J. A., Riley, K. P., Greiner, P. A., & Markesbery, W. R. (1997). Brain infarction and the clinical expression of Alzheimer disease. The Nun Study. *Journal of the American Medical Association, 277*, 813–817.

Snowdon, D. A., Kemper, S. J., Mortimer, J. A., Greiner, L. H., Wekstein, D. R., & Markesbery, W. R. (1996). Linguistic ability in early life and cognitive function and Alzheimer's disease in late life: Findings from the Nun Study. *Journal of the American Medical Association, 275*, 528–532.

Staudinger, U. M., & Bluck, S. (2001). A view of midlife development from life-span theory. In M. E. Lachman (Ed.), *Handbook of midlife development* (pp. 3–39). New York: Wiley.

Strachan, M. W., Deary, I. J., Ewing, F. M. E., & Frier, B. M. (1997). Is type II diabetes associated with an increased risk of cognitive dysfunction? *Diabetes Care, 20*, 438–445.

Swan, G. E., Carmelli, D., & LaRue, A. (1996). Relationship between blood pressure during middle age and cognitive impairment in old age: The Western Collaborative Group Study. *Aging, Neuropsychology and Cognition, 3*, 241–250.

Swan, G. E., LaRue, A., Carmelli, D., Reed, T. E., & Fabsitz, R. R. (1992). Decline in cognitive performance in aging twins. Heritability and biobehavioral predictors from the National Heart, Lung, and Blood Institute Twin Study. *Archives of Neurology, 49*, 476–483.

Swartz, R., Black, S., & St. George-Hyslop, P. (1999). Apolipoprotein E and Alzheimer's disease: A genetic, molecular and neuroimaging review. *Canadian Journal of Neurological Science, 26*, 77–88.

Thompson, P. H., Hayashi, K., de Zubicaray, G., Janke, A., Rose, S., Semple, J., et al. (2003). Dynamics of gray matter loss in Alzheimer's disease. *Journal of Neuroscience, 23*, 994–1005.

Thurstone, L. L., & Thurstone, T. G. (1949). *Examiner Manual for the SRA Primary Mental Abilities Test* (Form 10–14). Chicago: Science Research Associates.

Verghese, J., Lipton, R. B., Katz, M., Hall, C. B., Derby, C. A., Kuslansky, G., et al. (2003). Leisure activities and the risk of dementia in the elderly. *New England Journal of Medicine, 348*, 2508–2516.

Waldstein, S., & Elias, M. F. (Eds.). (2001). *Neuropsychology of cardiovascular disease.* Mahwah, NJ: Erlbaum.

Waldstein, S. R., Jennings, J. R., Ryan, C. M., Muldoon, M. F., Shapiro, A. P., Polefrone, J. M., et al. (1996). Hypertension and neuropsychological performance in men: Interactive effects of age. *Health Psychology, 15*, 102–109.

Waldstein, S. R., Manuck, S. B., Ryan, C. M., & Muldoon, M. F. (1991). Neuropsychological correlates of hypertension: Review and methodological considerations. *Psychological Bulletin, 110*, 451–468.

Wang, H. X., Karp, A., Winblad, B., & Fratiglioni, L. (2002). Late life engagement in social and leisure activities is associated with a decreased risk of dementia: A longitudinal study from the Kungsholmen project. *American Journal of Epidemiology, 155,* 1081–1087.

Warden, B. A., & Thompson, E. (1994). Apolipoprotein E and the development of atherosclerosis. *Laboratory Medicine, 25,* 449–455.

Whitbourne, S. K. (1986). *The me I know: A study of adult identity.* New York: Springer-Verlag.

Willis, S. L. (1987). Adult intelligence. In S. Hunter & M. Sundel (Eds.), *Midlife myths: Issues, findings, and practice applications* (pp. 97–111). Newbury Park, CA: Sage.

Willis, S. L. (1989). Cohort differences in cognitive aging: A sample case. In K. W. Schaie & C. Schooler (Eds.), *Social structure and aging: Psychological processes* (pp. 94–112). Hillsdale, NJ: Erlbaum.

Willis, S. L., Allen-Burge, R., Dolan, M. D., Bertrand, R. M., Yesavage, J., & Taylor, J. (1998). Everyday problem solving among individuals with Alzheimer's disease. *Gerontologist, 38,* 569–577.

Willis, S. L., & Schaie, K. W. (1986). Training the elderly on the ability factors of spatial orientation and inductive reasoning. *Psychology and Aging, 1,* 239–247.

Willis, S. L., & Schaie, K. W. (1999). Intellectual functioning in midlife. In S. Willis & J. Reid (Eds.), *Life in the middle* (pp. 233–247). San Diego, CA: Academic Press.

Wilson, P., Myers, R. H., Larson, M. G., Ordovas, J. M., Wolf, P. A., & Schaefer, E. J. (1994). Apolipoprotein E alleles, dyslipidemia, and coronary heart disease: The Framingham Offspring Study. *Journal of the American Medical Association, 272,* 1666–1671.

Wilson, R. S., Bennett, D. A., Beckett, L. A., Morris, M. C., Gilley, D. W., et al. (1999). Cognitive activity in older persons from a geographically defined population. *Journal of Gerontology B: Psychological Sciences, 54,* P155–P160.

Wilson, R. S., Mendes de Leon, C. F., Barnes, L. L., Scheider, J. A., Bienias, J. L., et al. (2002). Participation in cognitively stimulating activities and risk of incident. *Alzheimer Disease, 287,* 742–748.

Xu, Y., Jack, C. R., O'Brien, P. C., Kokmen, E., Smith, G. E., Ivnik, R. J., et al. (2000). Usefulness of MRI measures of entorhinal cortex versus hippocampus in AD. *Neurology, 54,* 1760–1767.

Nine

Self-Development at Midlife

Lifespan Perspectives on Adjustment and Growth

Jessica Dörner, Charlotte Mickler,
and Ursula M. Staudinger

R esearch on lifespan development so far clearly has concentrated on the study of childhood, adolescence, young adulthood, and old age; relatively few studies have concentrated on the period in between, that is, midlife. How do the two decades from age 40 to age 60—what we call *midlife*—differ from earlier or later years? How may the events and experiences taking place during this period influence personality development in midlife? To answer these questions, let us take a brief look at the life of middle-aged adults in Western industrialized nations today.

First of all, a majority of persons at this age are employed (e.g., 92% of the mixed gender sample by Diehl, Hastings, & Stanton, 2001) and often caught in the throes of career transitions like reentry into the labor force, holding the ground against younger colleagues, or facing declining career opportunities and retirement (e.g., Roberts & Friend, 1998). Role changes take place in private life as well: Typically, it is the time when children are becoming adults and moving out, leaving the parents in the "empty nest" alone with each other again (e.g., Crowley, Hayslip, & Hobdy, 2003; Morfei, Hooker, Carpenter, Mix, & Blakeley, 2004; Stewart & Ostrove, 1998). Caretaking sometimes reappears on the agenda as parents grow to be increasingly frailer and physically dependent. One's own physical functioning becomes an issue (usually not before age 50), when some more marked signs of biological decline—such as decrease in muscle strength and sensory functioning and increasing likelihood of cardiovascular diseases—make themselves felt, and women go through menopause (e.g., Hooker & Kaus, 1994; Klohnen, Vandewater, & Young, 1996; Lachman, 2004; Staudinger & Bluck, 2001). All in all, these descriptions render a rather bleak view of midlife, in line with the common use of *midlife* as a prefix for *crisis*. Yet, while all these events can be substantial physical and psychological stressors, it is at the same time important to consider that midlife also is a time of reaping the harvest from our efforts in education, career, parenthood, partnership, and social relations.

We are, for instance, at the height of social power and have access to a rich supply of social support. Even though the social networks are shrinking throughout adulthood, social satisfaction is steadily on the rise (e.g., Lansford, Sherman, & Antonucci, 1998). Thus, it comes as no surprise that self-esteem—at least according to cross-sectional data—is never higher than around the age of 60 (Robins, Trzesniewski, Tracy, Gosling, & Potter, 2002), the sense of personal control and power is at its peak (for an overview, see Clark-Plaskie & Lachman, 1999), and subjective well-being tends to be at least considerably higher than in young adulthood (Keyes, Shmotkin, & Ryff, 2002). Taken together, in contrast to younger adults, middle-aged individuals are much more secure about themselves and the paths they are following (e.g., Cross & Markus, 1991; Franz, 1994; Heckhausen, 1999), without feeling overly grandiose or afraid. Unlike many younger adults, most of them have made their peace with societal expectations and have found decent arrangements to meet both personal goals and environmental demands. Yet, in comparison with older adults, middle-aged adults tend to be more egocentric and also more vital and vigorous in pursuing their concerns (McAdams, 2001; Stewart & Vandewater, 1998).

Combining risks and resources in such a pronounced manner makes midlife a potentially intriguing life phase for the study of self and personality.

Thus, the goal of this chapter is to describe theories and empirical results related to the development and growth of self and personality during midlife. Although we are far from exhausting all available models and results, we at least want to draw some first conclusions regarding the opportunities, risks, and challenges that individual self-development typically encounters during the middle years. We start out by introducing the distinction between development in the sense of adjustment and development in the sense of growth.

The Distinction Between Adjustment and Growth

We do not intend to go into detail of this highly complex discussion here, but we would like to offer the following clarification. Whenever taking a lifespan perspective on development, development is not equated with growth but rather defined as a ratio of gains and losses. Thus, the following question arises: What are gains and what are losses with regard to personality development (see Baltes, Lindenberger, & Staudinger, 1998)? In the present chapter, we focus on the gain side of self-development, implying, however, that also losses arise while pursuing these gain trajectories (this is what lifespan development is all about). We suggest that at least two different underlying dimensions in defining gains in personality development can be distinguished: One is gains in terms of degrees of *adjustment* to the challenges and tasks of everyday life, and the other is gains in terms of *growth* as defined in theories of personality "maturation" (e.g., Allport, 1961; Bühler, 1959; Cloninger, 2003; Erikson, 1959; Freud, 1917/1993; Jung, 1934/2001; Loevinger, 1976; Maslow, 1968; Rogers, 1961). Personality growth, for instance, implies critical self-reflection, self-transcendence, and moving beyond the given. Adjustment focuses on mastering the demands of everyday life and its various roles (work, family), that is, social and practical competences, reliability, and emotional stability. These two developmental goals, adjustment and growth, are not completely independent, but they do seem to follow different trajectories and demonstrate drastically different base rates (for more extensive discussion of this argument, see Staudinger & Kunzmann, 2005). Adjustment in personality functioning is observed normatively as we age. It is one of the few areas that show age-related increase. This is not the case for growth. Few individuals follow growth trajectories as they move through midlife (see, e.g., Staudinger, 1999). After having introduced this basic distinction, we now proceed to describe the external and internal developmental contexts that come with midlife.

Does Midlife Foster Adjustment and Growth? A View From Classic Midlife Theories

There seems to be something scary about midlife as we approach it. This is not only reflected by the popular literature and music of our times, but also by psychologists such as Jung, who wrote that "as a childish person shrinks back from the unknown in the world and in human existence, so the grown man shrinks back from the second half of life. It is as if unknown and dangerous tasks were expected of him" (Jung, 1934/2001, p. 108; see also Staudinger & Bluck, 2001; Stewart & Ostrove, 1998).

Midlife Asks for a Change in Priorities: Jung, Levinson, Bühler, and Peck

But what are these "unknown and dangerous" tasks the middle-aged are supposed to fulfill? Many tasks of midlife certainly cannot be mastered by the skills and talents that proved successful in the past: A mother can hardly rely solely on her motherly qualities once her children leave the house; a partnership built on physical attractiveness might not offer what it used to; a business woman might experience how her former monopolized domains of achievement are gradually being conquered by younger generations. Jung perceived the age of midlife the most decisive turning point in life. According to him, the task of the second half of life is a stage of turning inward, of "illuminating" the self, instead of shedding one's light or energy on worldly achievements. As the first half of life seems to be characterized by "our entrenchment in the outer world, the propagation of our kind and the care of our children . . . moneymaking, social existence, family and posterity" (Jung, 1934/2001, p. 112), the second half should be dedicated to culture. Similar to how older people in ancient cultures were viewed, Jung envisioned the elders as bearers and guardians of cultural myth and truth. As such, according to Jung, middle age is a time where personality growth is doomed to thrive or die, depending on whether one decides to follow the familiar path and continue to strive for the goals of youth, eventually leading into a dead end, or whether one succeeds to withdraw from previous habits and ambitions and to turn into a new direction. This idea is probably captured best in what has become a classic quotation concerning midlife: "We cannot live the afternoon of life according to the program of life's morning—for what was great in the morning will be little at evening, and what in the morning was true will at evening have become a lie" (Jung, 1934/2001, p. 111).

This aspect is also central to the theory of Levinson (1986), who thought of midlife as a stage where persons had achieved earlier goals and now were striving for a more general purpose in life. As a consequence, midlife for Levinson presented a time for turning inward, in search for one's true values, goals, and desires, "a new step in individuation" (Levinson, 1986, p. 5). As Levinson's empirical results suggest, in men, this step is often manifested by a shift in priorities from career- and achievement-related endeavors to private and family-oriented ones. Two more recent studies seem to confirm these assumptions (Brandtstädter, Renner, & Baltes-Götz, 1989; Franz, 1994). In both samples, there was a slight, but significant, increase in the importance of "private" issues, such as self-development and family-related themes at the expense of achievement and career goals. This is also supported by research on value change, which demonstrates that terminal values increase in importance as compared to instrumental values in the course of adulthood (Ryff, 1979, 1982, 1984; Ryff & Baltes, 1976). Bühler's psychology of human strivings presents another related idea. Bühler (1968) emphasized that at middle age, considerations of past, present, and future do not stand separately as before, but finally merge in forming motivational forces. Whereas the child's strivings mostly concern the present and consequently are aimed at immediate comfort, the goals of midlife stretch further into the future and tap on knowledge acquired in the past.

Peck (1956, 1968) suggested an additional explanation for value change in midlife. He argued that in order to age successfully, persons have to learn to accept bodily changes. As a consequence, Peck assumed that starting in midlife, we change our value hierarchies such that we favor psychological and cognitive resources above physical strength or appearance. Note, however, that all of these authors regarded value change during midlife as an ideal rather than a reality. Jung (1934/2001) even believed that the normal process of aging involves tendencies of values becoming more rigid around middle age, even to the degree of fanaticism.

In sum, the work of the authors just discussed suggests that midlife entails the adoption of a new perspective. This perspective is narrower and, at the same time, more intense than earlier perspectives: narrower in the sense of directing increasing attention toward oneself, and more intense in the sense of a deeper, more thorough reflection of problems. As such, these views may be classified as proclaiming growth rather than adjustment as a midlife theme. They do not, however, explicitly address base rates of these growth phenomena. This leads to the question of whether they concern the average midlifer or only a small subgroup of individuals moving through midlife.

Time for Agency or Time for Communion?
Midlife From the Eriksonian Perspective

The most influential theory of age-graded life tasks clearly is the theory of Erik Erikson. Erikson's phase of midlife starts somewhat earlier than that of Jung. Midlife sets in once the life task of accomplishing an intimate relationship has been mastered (cf. Stewart & Vandewater, 1998). Hence, the very themes that Jung saw as the substantial duties of a younger person, that is, "moneymaking, social existence, family and posterity" (Jung, 1934/2001, p. 112), represent an important part of what Erikson's middle-aged adult is occupied with. These differences in perspective may also be related to the different cultural and historical contexts within which the respective theories were developed. For instance, average life expectancy during Jung's time was considerably lower than in Erikson's time, possibly explaining the greater similarity between middle and old age in Jung's writings. Whatever the case, the differences between Erikson's and Jung's perspectives on midlife can also be reconciled by distinguishing early from late midlife (cf. Staudinger & Bluck, 2001).

Empirical results also support this distinction between early and late midlife. For instance, there is evidence of a great number of external changes taking place around the age of 50 (e.g., Helson & Wink, 1992; Klohnen et al., 1996). Examples of these changes include alterations in household composition—accordingly, the number of women living with children decreases considerably (from 75% at age 43 to 25% at age 52)—and physical changes, for example, menopause and a relatively sudden increase in number of physical complaints (Hooker & Kaus, 1994; Lachman, 2004). These external changes, in turn, may engender and reinforce internal changes. For example, Rosenberg, Rosenberg, and Farrell (1999), although uncovering a substantial shift in patterns of personal narratives at midlife, locate this change "more in late (fifth decade) rather than early (fourth decade) middle age" (Rosenberg et al., 1999, p. 67).

But let's return to Erikson. In Erikson's (1950/1995) theory of the eight ages of man, midlife is seen from a lifespan perspective; that is, life tasks are generally age graded, but they also accumulate across life. His stages of industry, intimacy, and generativity are respectively expressed in the challenges of career, marriage, and parenting. All three remain important across adulthood, whereas the challenge of generativity versus stagnation is specific to midlife. Accordingly, once individuals have accomplished intimacy with another person, their interest should move further, and their focus of investment should shift toward "that which is being generated . . . in the meeting of bodies and minds" (Erikson, 1950/1995, p. 240). Hence, in a symbolic sense, the person's focus should be put onto what he or she has to pass on to younger generations, may it be knowledge, care, love, or material possessions (for an overview, see McAdams, 2001). If persons fail to accomplish such transcendence of self-interest, they are doomed to stagnate in the attempt of establishing pseudo-intimacy, often accompanied by personal impoverishment. Thus, with regard to passing on the cultural heritage, the Jungian idea and the Eriksonian idea of midlife seem to converge again. In Erikson's view, however, the middle-aged person participates much more actively in social life.

Drawing on the work of Erikson (e.g., 1959, 1950/1995) and Kotre (e.g., 1984), McAdams and his colleagues (e.g., McAdams, 2001; McAdams & de St. Aubin, 1998; McAdams, Diamond, de St. Aubin, & Mansfield, 1997) developed an integrative model of generativity, also addressing the ambiguity, or "the motivational paradox" (McAdams, 2001, p. 405), inherent in the concept: On the one hand, generative persons are driven by a need of self-expansion, keen to leave an imprint on the world after them, or even more, to create a counterpart according to their own image that will survive their own efforts. On the other hand, generativity comprises the "need to be needed," that is, the need to take care, to nurture, and to give. Thus, generativity entails both agency and communion; one reflecting the achievement-oriented tasks associated with midlife, the other the social tasks.

Neugarten and Havighurst:
Emphasis on Agency and Social Approval

Agency (rather than retreat from the outer world) appeared to be of striking importance in the interviews conducted by Neugarten and colleagues in the 1960s. In what she called "executive processes of personality," Neugarten (1968) summarized what appeared in the self-reports of some select middle-aged females and males: Both genders described, as an especially rewarding experience of midlife, knowing their capacities and potential life difficulties well; this resulted, in turn, in a pervasive sense of mastery and competence. This idea is illustrated best by the comment of a female participant: "I know what will work in most situations, and what will not. I am well beyond the trial-and-error stage of youth. I now have a set of guidelines . . . And I am practiced . . ." (p. 87). In the more recent past, Neugarten's observations have been replicated, especially with regard to female samples. Analyzing the interview statements of three female samples of different cohorts, Stewart and Ostrove (1998) concluded that, regardless of age, the participants voiced "an exuberance . . . hard to miss, along with a sense of personal authority and agency" (p. 1191). For example, one woman said,

> In my 20s . . . we simultaneously thought we had all the power in the world and that we had no power at all. Neither was true. . . . I now have a much more limited, more accurate, and in some important ways more energizing and empowering sense of my own powers and limitations. (p. 1190)

Havighurst's theory (1972) offers yet another integrative view on life tasks during midlife development. Clearly, Havighurst's idea of ideal development is a story of gaining social approval. He claimed,

> The tasks the individual must learn—the developmental tasks of life—are those things that constitute healthy and satisfactory growth [termed *adaptation* in this chapter] within our society. They are the things a person must learn if he is to be judged and to judge himself to be a reasonably happy and successful person. (p. 2)

Therefore, according to Havighurst, the life tasks of midlife adults are centered on social responsibilities. According to his approach, however, middle-aged adults' main focus is not exclusively limited to psychosocial tasks (e.g., career and relationships), but also includes biological tasks such as learning to accept physiological changes at midlife as well as assuming social responsibilities in a broader sense.

Having reviewed theories of developmental tasks of midlife, we may conclude that there are two diverging trends. Following Erikson, Neugarten, and Havighurst, middle age is a phase of still increasing societal impact, of commitment and engagement for goals that lie beyond mere self-interest. According to this notion, middle-aged individuals are settled, and thrive, after they have invested in developing their social position for a long time. Feeling on top of things, they experience a heightened sense of self-confidence and competence. If this portrayal of middle age is correct, we should find middle-aged adults to be socializers, instead of being socialized, and "drivers," instead of being "driven" (Neugarten, 1968). Their personality should show proof of interactive and communicative skills, adjustment, high self-esteem, life satisfaction, and feelings of competence; in short, they should exhibit psychosocial adjustment (see Helson & Wink, 1987). At the same time, we would not necessarily expect growth in the sense of personal wisdom. After all, according to this view, middle-aged adults are preoccupied with problems outside and not inside of themselves. Even the sense of mastery and agency reported by Neugarten's participants, while certainly being of high importance for everyday problem solving, is of lesser significance in terms of growth, where self-reflection, conceiving ambiguities, and questioning one's mastery is of prime importance (e.g., Staudinger, Dörner, & Mickler, in press).

But there is another view of midlife, emerging especially from the writings of Jung, Levinson, Peck, and Bühler. These psychologists tend to regard midlife as a time of retreat and contemplation, followed by questions and doubts concerning previously obeyed norms, and in turn, doubts about oneself. In this light, midlife might well be perceived as a kind of crisis with potential for growth. Mastery of this crisis may leave persons calmer, stronger, and more aware of themselves. Based on this view, middle-aged adults should also be characterized by high levels of contemplation, self-reflection, doubt, and uncertainty alongside a certain confidence and self-trust. Social norms are questioned and examined rather than adopted. In other words, midlife then would be a phase of personal growth rather than psychosocial adjustment. Most likely, these two views on midlife are not mutually exclusive; rather, they apply to varying degrees. We would like to suggest that *normative* development in midlife and into old age leads to psychosocial adjustment. Only a select group of individuals characterized by a given constellation of person characteristics and a firm motivation to find out about themselves may make progress on the road toward personal wisdom (cf. Staudinger et al., in press). When reviewing the empirical evidence, we will see that indeed both types of developmental paths occur. Before we get to this evidence, however, we will discuss characteristics of the social context in midlife and how this context influences self-development during midlife.

Social Norms at Midlife: Banister or Burden on the Way to Adjustment and Growth?

Ontogeny proceeds not only in the context of age-related ontogenetic time, but also in the context of historical cohort time (Baltes et al., 1998). Thus, individual development is shaped not only by biological (e.g., physical maturation) and idiosyncratic influences (e.g., getting hurt in an accident) but also by history-graded influences (e.g., war, Zeitgeist) affecting all members of a certain birth cohort in a similar way (Baltes, Reese, & Lipsitt, 1980; Baltes, Reese, & Nesselroade, 1977/1988). The tremendous impact of historical changes on individual development has been documented by numerous studies (e.g., Baltes, 1968; Caspi, 1987; Elder, 1998; Riegel, 1972; Schaie, 1965). Gender norms are a particularly prominent example of how history-graded influences impact human development (cf. Huyck, 1999; Moen & Wethington, 1999). Applying this argument to the influence of historical times on adjustment and growth, it can, for instance, be speculated that personal growth may be more likely under highly challenging historical circumstances (e.g., war, authoritarian regime) than during smooth times.

When we talk about the role of social norms in the following section, we will adopt two different points of view. First, we will briefly review some literature on the importance of norm adherence versus norm defiance with regard to adjustment and growth, thereby drawing especially on Neugarten's concept of the "social clock." With regard to this topic, it is important to note that norms, as well as the degree of "tightness" versus "looseness" of these norms (Triandis, 2004)—that is, the degree to which social norms are considered as obligatory—are subject to change (Baltes et al., 1980). Thus, any evidence cited here has to be viewed within its historical and cultural context and cannot be generalized beyond these limits. As a second issue, following hypotheses proposed by Jung and Gutmann, we will address the development of gender-related personality attributes.

Age-Related Norms in Midlife

Neugarten's theory suggests that neither the quality nor the frequency of events decides about the course of midlife. According to this view, what is more important for psychosocial adjustment in midlife is appropriate timing. According to Neugarten, there exists "a prescriptive timetable for the ordering of major life-events," "imbedded throughout the cultural fabric of adult life" (Neugarten, Moore, & Lowe, 1965, p. 711; for experimental testings of this hypothesis, see Krueger, Heckhausen, & Hundertmark, 1995; Settersten & Mayer, 1997). The social clocks (Neugarten et al., 1965, p. 711) are of particular importance when it comes to midlife. There are two reasons for this: First, younger adults are usually granted lenience in trying themselves out, and as a consequence, a variety of life paths seem appropriate for them (e.g., Bühler, 1935). Similarly, but for other reasons, no strict rules exist for old age; old age is simply too young from a historical point of view for clear role models to exist (Riley, Kahn, Foner, & Mack, 1994). As a consequence, societal expectations tend to be much more codified and structured in middle age than in young and old adulthood (Diehl et al., 2001). Additionally, as middle-aged adults are the ones who assume the most responsibilities both within a family and a societal context, they can least afford to digress from what they are supposed to do.

Certainly, we have to consider that this is a historical snapshot and that circumstances most likely will change. Time will show how much of this characterization will survive historical change in social circumstances. There is some reason to believe that midlife across historical time is the period in the life span that is most closely linked to carrying out and maintaining social structures; thus, mean levels may change across historical time, but patterns are preserved. In this vein, both Neugarten and Havighurst argued for the relevance and validity of social norms in midlife. Havighurst, for instance, posits that through social experience as manifested in adults' life tasks, individuals do become not only more skilled but also more complied with social conventions in the course of the life span. In sum, Neugarten and Havighurst both suggested that an adherence to social norms is of special importance during midlife and that nonadherence might entail serious consequences for a person's well-being and present a challenge to be mastered on the road to psychosocial adjustment.

Do consequences of adherence or nonadherence matter only for well-being, life-satisfaction, and social functioning (psychosocial adjustment), or do they pertain to other indicators of positive development, such as personal growth? One could argue that it is indeed the "on-time" decisions that render development smooth and thus create the ideal prerequisites for a high level of well-being, an indicator often used to measure adjustment. However, often it is not the smooth, but the rough times, the frictions and conflicts that promote new insights into ourselves (e.g.,

Staudinger, 2001). Therefore, the often conflict-laden "off-time" decisions might entail a higher potential for stimulating personal growth.

In a longitudinal study comparing women who followed the traditional female clock with both those who followed a delayed female pattern and those who followed a male pattern through midlife, tremendous developmental differences were identified (Helson, Mitchell, & Moane, 1984). It is important to mention that participants of this study were born in the period of 1936 to 1938, thus growing up in an era where the adherence to traditional gender paths was strongly reinforced. Already at the first time of measurement (young adulthood), the groups differed in attitudes and goals. Women following the female pattern appeared to be significantly stronger marked by social adjustment and respect for social conventions and showed a greater sense of societal responsibility as well as optimism and confidence in the future (Helson et al., 1984; see also Helson & Picano, 1990). However, if they happened to have bad luck with their marriages, they showed strong negative effects on their subjective well-being.

In terms of personal growth, social clock adherence did not seem to offer any advantages (Helson & Wink, 1987); in fact it even turned out to be detrimental when associated with a lack of challenges (e.g., keeping up the conventional homemaking role; Helson & Roberts, 1994). Thus, accommodative challenges turned out to be a crucial factor in promoting personal growth for those women who had succeeded in professional careers independent from whether they had partners, children, or both or were single women (Helson & Roberts, 1994; see also Stewart & Ostrove, 1998).

In sum, the studies show that adherence to the social clock alone—that is, without taking into account congruence with individual aspirations—neither fosters successful adjustment nor promotes personality growth. In fact, to keep in tune with the social clock, despite feelings of dissatisfaction with the current situation, turned out to be destructive in terms of both aspects. However, if societal expectations can be brought in line with personal needs and goals, competence and adjustment result. Finally, personal growth had no relationship with social clock adherence, but it did have a relationship with the occurrence and mastery of life-course challenges. Taken together, conforming to societal expectations can support well-being if it corresponds to personal needs and goals; however, for personal growth, it seems to be of higher importance to seek and master challenges embodied sometimes by the very transcendence of social norms.

Gender-Related Norms in Midlife

Jung introduced a notion that deals with norms from a somewhat different perspective. He observed that at midlife, similar to the profound changes in attitudes and character, "man's values and even his body tend to undergo a reversal into the opposite" (1934/2001, p. 110), a "gender cross-over" (Gutmann, 1987; see also Labouvie-Vief, 1994). According to Jung's argument, men in midlife have used up their supply of masculine resources and have only the smaller amount of feminine "substance" left over, whereas women in midlife discover their masculine side. This reversal, in turn, has implications for needs and motivations. According to Jung, men at the stage of decreasing masculinity often abandon their competitive endeavors. Women, on the other hand, often show "an uncommon masculinity and an incisiveness which push the feelings and the heart aside" (1934/2001, p. 110). Interpreted in the context of a larger framework, older individuals are allowed a greater autonomy over choices and roles than are the young, who are offered a unitary, society-driven, sex-role orientation. Gutmann (1987) argued in a similar vein, claiming that the biosocial imperatives of parenting in young adulthood lead to an exaggeration of gender-specific personality characteristics. Consequently, younger men tend to identify themselves as providers and protectors, whereas younger women emphasize dependent and nurturing features in their self-definition. However, once individuals have passed the stage of parenting and have moved into the stage of middle age, these definitions become obsolete and are abandoned, giving room for a more balanced, androgynous view of self, more in line with the gender-neutral tasks predominant at middle adulthood. Indeed, there is evidence that gender identities are more closely linked with the stage in family cycle (e.g., prepartnership, preparenthood, parenthood, grandparenthood) than with age, per se (as Jung would suggest; see also Feldman, Biringen, & Nash, 1981). In addition, it certainly has to be taken into account that trajectories of masculinity/femininity are also related to age-related changes in endocrinal levels (e.g., Rossi, 1988, 1994). Certainly, it is an interesting question to which degree sociohistorical circumstances may influence such patterns. For instance, what happens in a society with a very low reproduction rate and rising androgyny?

There appears to be yet another interpretation for converging gender-related self-definitions. Given the pervasiveness of masculine ideals such as assertiveness, competitiveness, and independence in modern culture (e.g., Hofstede, 1998), the effect could be also explained by women's increasingly positive and self-assertive view of themselves. Thus, instead of a mutual rapprochement of both men and women, the convergence of gender-related characteristics could be due to a shift on the women's side in the direction of masculine characteristics based on heightened self-esteem.

Let us take a look at the empirical side of the issue: Is it true that both men and women become more androgynous during midlife? Most of these studies assess femininity and masculinity by using self-report questionnaires. This implies the problem of social desirability. Indeed, the feminine characteristics are often negative (e.g., dependence, abasement). High femininity on the frequently used California Psychological Inventory scale femininity (CPI; Gough & Bradley, 1996), for instance, is also called "vulnerability." Low femininity on this scale means being skeptical, aspiring, and autonomy-seeking—traditional masculine characteristics.

An early study by Neugarten and Gutmann (1968) employed a projective measure to assess feminine and masculine characteristics. They found that during middle age and the transition to old age (40–70 years), women became more tolerant of their own aggressive, egocentric impulses, whereas men learned to accept their nurturing and affiliative impulses. A more recent longitudinal study also made use of a projective method to investigate motivational structure (Franz, 1994; see also Gutmann, 1975). These studies showed that although on average, men decreased in achievement and increased in affiliation over time, women did so, too. Franz (1994) concluded that this pattern of results might be a cohort effect due to "the cultural constraints of the generation of midlife men and women" at the time of measurement (p. 234).

These studies, however, are the only ones reporting increasing femininity in men. In a cross-sectional study, Lowenthal, Thurnher, and Chiriboga (1975) found no significant changes in masculinity or femininity (as measured by separate masculine and feminine attributes) in men from high school age to preretirement, although masculinity decreased slightly. For women, there was a significant drop in femininity during middle age. It is notable that social desirability ratings of the feminine and masculine attributes in this study indicate again that femininity is indeed less socially desirable than masculinity: Ten of 13 masculine adjectives, but only 5 of 11 feminine adjectives, were perceived as socially desirable.

More recent studies on femininity and masculinity predominantly draw on the sample of the Mills longitudinal study (e.g., Helson et al.,

1984; Helson & Wink, 1992; Roberts, Helson, & Klohnen, 2002) and have only investigated women. Apart from reporting the development of femininity and masculinity over the life span, researchers have been interested in exploring variables that influence and moderate these changes. Findings show that femininity increased and dominance decreased during young adulthood, but femininity dropped between the measurement points of 27 and at 43 (Helson et al., 1984). This trend continued up to age 52 (Helson & Wink, 1992; Roberts et al., 2002). The initial increase in feminine attributes is significantly related to motherhood: Young women who became mothers between 21 and 27 increased more in femininity during that time than those who did not have children (Helson et al., 1984). Similarly, those who experienced motherhood after 27, when femininity of the whole sample dropped, stayed the same in their femininity rating (Roberts et al., 2002). Women, who, at age 52, had partners and children at home scored higher on femininity than others in the years before (43–52 years; Helson & Wink, 1992). It seems, therefore, that motherhood, the role of being a mother, or both has a femininity-promoting impact. Participation in the labor force, on the other hand, seems to raise masculinity. Working women experienced a stronger increase in dominance (27–43 years) than those without a job (Helson et al., 1984; Roberts et al., 2002). They were also higher in masculine attributes, such as capacity for status, self-acceptance, and independence (Helson et al., 1984). However, they also scored higher in sociability, social presence, and empathy—characteristics that could be called positive feminine attributes. Combining male and female strengths seems to be a characteristic of midlife women participating in the labor force.

To summarize, evidence that men become more androgynous in midlife is scarce and mainly draws on studies that employed projective methods (or studies that examined motives rather than traits; see, e.g., Franz, 1994; Levinson, 1986). For women—especially women of more recent generations—there seems to be a trend toward decreasing femininity and increasing dominance and independence, beginning in middle age. This change seems closely linked with life experiences and social roles (such as motherhood or work). Therefore, it seems questionable whether the label "masculinity/femininity" is appropriate to categorizing these changes. It seems more adequate to consider these changes as a consequence of adjustment to age-graded societal demands, combined with age-related biological changes. Thus, certain contexts are necessary to develop these competences, and these have not always been accessible for women.

Empirical Results on Personality-Related Adjustment and Growth in Midlife

In the following section, we will review empirical evidence on the development of the self in midlife. When talking about the self in midlife, we assume a broad frame of reference, comprising two distinct and—at least functionally—interrelated areas that are usually addressed in clearly separated literatures (Staudinger & Pasupathi, 2000): (a) trait personality and (b) self-concept, self-definition, or identity.[1]

Under the trait approach to the study of personality, we subsume efforts to characterize individuals in terms of attributes and behavioral dispositions, a line of research that originated primarily in the psychometric tradition. Research in this area focuses on the identification of the structure of personality, interindividual differences, and the extent of longitudinal stability (e.g., Costa & McCrae, 1994a, 1997; Goldberg, 1993; John, 1990). Of primary interest from a lifespan perspective are the conditions and factors that account for constancy and change in personality as well as inter- and intraindividual variability in development.

When speaking of self-concept, self-definition, and identity, we subsume lines of work that highlight the "inside" view on personality (see Ryff, 1984; Singer, 1984). Persons have a relative stable picture of who they are, what they like, how they would react to certain events, how they appear to others, and so forth. In any given situation, only a part of this picture is accessible to the persons themselves (e.g., Markus, 1977; Markus & Wurf, 1987). In addition to these "seasonal" dynamics—which do not really present changes but rather express fluctuating saliencies—there are also "macro"-dynamics: A person might truly change with regard to his or her self-concept. Again, a lifespan perspective aims at identifying normative and idiosyncratic trajectories of self-concept development in the attempt to uncover the reasons for, and consequences of, changes and continuity of the self-concept.

To get a picture of changes in the self that take place during midlife, we inspect indicators of personality adjustment (some of the Big Five dimensions and some self-concept assessments) as well as of personal growth (such as generativity, inward vs. outward orientation, personal wisdom, and self-concept maturity).

Empirical Evidence on Adjustment During Midlife

The Big Five in Midlife: Development Toward Adjustment?

Most studies examining the relationship of personality and age have studied the Big Five personality factors: Extraversion, Neuroticism, Openness to Experience, Agreeableness, and Conscientiousness (e.g., Costa & McCrae, 1988a). There are two facets to the study of personality and age: rank-order stability and mean-level stability. Rank-order stability means, for example, that those high in openness maintain their high level relative to others. However, this does not preclude that the overall level of openness might decrease over the years (mean-level change).

Much of the empirical work in this area shows high rank-order stability across time (e.g., Costa & McCrae, 1989). According to Costa and McCrae (e.g., 1980, 1989, 1994a, 1994b, 1997), trait consistency should be reached by the age of 30. This implies that in midlife, people do not change their position relative to others. However, the findings from several empirical studies cast doubt on this position, and many longitudinal studies reveal changes in trait dimensions during middle and later adulthood (e.g., Helson, Kwan, John, & Jones, 2002; Helson & Wink, 1992; Roberts, 1997). A meta-analysis of 124 longitudinal studies by Roberts and DelVecchio (2000) examined rank-order consistency on personality trait dimensions over time. The study demonstrated that trait consistency increased in a stepwise manner. Looking specifically at the period of middle age, there is a slight drop in consistency in the first decade of middle age (40–49 years) compared to the previous decade. In the second decade of middle age (50–59 years), consistency increases dramatically to .72, where it peaks. Overall, these results indicate that during adulthood, personality rank orders become more and more stable, reaching a peak in late midlife. Early midlife, in contrast, might potentially be a time conducive of more change than during the decade before and the decade afterwards (Roberts & DelVecchio, 2000). According to Roberts and DelVecchio, the late midlife peak in personality consistency is due to the prominence of *identity certainty* (qtd. in Stewart & Ostrove, 1998) and the "executive personality" (Neugarten, 1968) of middle age. The authors argue that as persons become secure about who they are, they tend to change their outside environment rather than their "inside"—their personality—in order to attain an ideal fit between themselves and their life circumstances. Thus, again there is evidence that supports the usefulness of the distinction between early and late midlife.

Costa and McCrae (e.g., 1994a) expected that there would be no changes in mean levels of the Big Five personality factors after age 30, or that changes would slow down after that point (McCrae & Costa, 1990). However, a number of recent studies have demonstrated that there are still significant changes after this point (e.g., McCrae et al., 2000; Srivastava, John, Gosling, & Potter, 2003). Thus, there is reason to expect mean-level changes in personality during midlife. Results on mean-level changes in the Big Five personality factors are quite consistent. *Extraversion* does not demonstrate a clear pattern of mean-level changes unless we consider two constituent elements separately: Social Dominance and Social Vitality (Helson & Kwan, 2000). Social Dominance, reflecting characteristics such as dominance, independence, and self-confidence in social contexts, increases with age. Social Vitality, corresponding to features like sociability, positive affect, gregariousness, and energy level, decreases with age (for an overview, see Roberts, Robins, Caspi, & Trzesniewski, 2003).

Agreeableness, that is, the propensity to be altruistic, trusting, modest, and warm (John & Srivastava, 1999), has been shown to increase with age in several cross-sectional studies (Johnson et al., 1983; McCrae et al., 1999), very rapidly through the 30s and slowing down in middle adulthood (Srivastava et al., 2003). Longitudinal studies focusing on middle age found increases in affiliation from age 27 to 52 (Wink & Helson, 1993), in warmth from 40 to 54 (Haan, Millsap, & Hartka, 1986), and in nurturance from 40 to 70 (Dudek & Hall, 1991).

Conscientiousness, which reflects the tendency to be self-controlled, task- and goal-directed, planful, and rule-following (John & Srivastava, 1999), shows increases with age, just like agreeableness (e.g., Helson & Kwan, 2000; Johnson et al., 1983; McCrae et al., 1999; Srivastava et al., 2003). Although some longitudinal data seem to indicate that conscientiousness plateaus in middle age (Costa, Herbst, McCrae, & Siegler, 2000), the majority of results point toward a continuing increase throughout middle age: It has been found that socialization, self-control, responsibility, norm orientation, and achievement via conformance increase from age 33 to 75 (Helson & Kwan, 2000), from 43 to 52 (Helson & Wink, 1992), and from 31 to 46 (Cartwright & Wink, 1994).

Neuroticism, contrasting even-temperedness and emotional stability with the experience of anxiety, worry, anger, and depression (John & Srivastava, 1999), shows slight decreases with age in cross-sectional studies (Johnson et al., 1983; McCrae et al., 2000). Studies focusing specifically on midlife have found decreases in neuroticism (Costa et al., 2000) and negative affect (Charles, Reynolds, & Gatz, 2001). However, others have found no changes in emotional stability during middle age (Costa & McCrae, 1988b, 1989; Dudek & Hall, 1991), and that increase of positive and decrease of negative emotions only took place after middle age (Mroczek, 2004, as cited in Lachman, 2004). There is a lack of further decrease of neuroticism in old age (Field & Millsap, 1991; Pedersen & Reynolds, 1998). Emotional stability seems to peak around age 60 and remains on a high level for a few years before decreasing again. Overall then, middle age seems to be characterized by a steady decrease in neuroticism, which is stronger for women than for men, leading to its all-time low in early old age.

Finally, *Openness for Experience*, the disposition to be original, complex, creative, and open to new ideas (John & Srivastava, 1999), has been shown to decrease with age in cross-sectional studies (McCrae et al., 1999; Srivastava et al., 2003). However, related aspects like intellect (Goldberg, Sweeney, Merenda, & Hughes, 1998) and complexity (Helson & Kwan, 2000) are not correlated with age. Longitudinal studies have shown that openness decreases in midlife, a trend that continues into old age (Costa et al., 2000; Field & Millsap, 1991).

We can conclude that midlife seems to be a time when interindividual differences in personality stabilize. Nevertheless, there are age-related changes in mean-levels during that period. People become more socially dominant and less socially active (extraversion) and, at the same, more altruistic, trusting, and warm (agreeableness). They become more self-controlled, planful, and rule-following (conscientiousness) and less open for new experience. Emotional stability reaches its height at the end of midlife. The picture emerges of an increasingly calm, planful, and focused person, feeling more in command, with regard to social situations, and less stressed, but also less exuberant, creative, and outgoing. In short, according to the Big Five pattern, midlife can be characterized by reaching psychosocial adjustment (see Staudinger, in press).

Self-Concept Development in Midlife: Does It Support Adjustment and/or Growth?

As we explained earlier the notion of self-concept focuses on the way individuals view themselves. A study by Cross and Markus (1991), conducted in the framework of the possible selves theory, provides some evidence on the self-concept of middle-aged adults. The possible selves theory (Markus & Nurius, 1986) suggests that the self-concept of individuals contains subjective evaluations of what they could become (possible selves), what they would like to become (hoped-for-selves), and what they are afraid of becoming (feared selves). Cross and Markus (1991) tested the possible selves model among adults between the ages of 18 and 86. Midlife adults (i.e., ages 40–59) reported less hope for expansive changes (e.g., new beginnings or drastic changes), but more hope for enjoyment and achievement in current roles and responsibilities (e.g., work, current partnership, children); family-hoped-for-selves in midlife, for example, focus on children, and not on marriage. Similarly, occupational selves are concerned with moving up the career ladder rather than with different job options. Cross and Markus (1991) view these changes as a result of a change in time perspective. Middle-aged adults may no longer see the future as full of opportunities to explore; instead, they may focus on accomplishing their goals in the remaining time that they have left. Which are the life domains that attract the hopes and aspirations of midlifers? The six most frequently mentioned areas of hoped-for-selves of middle-aged adults are (starting with the most frequent one): family (concerned with children), personal (e.g., ways of growing old), physical (health and appearance), occupation (career, success), leisure (e.g., travel), and material (financial concerns). Here, the most striking difference between middle-aged and young adults is the increase in importance of the family domain, which in the latter group is ranked sixth. Occupation and leisure are less important for the middle-aged than for young adults. After middle age, family loses its importance again in favor of personal (e.g., ability to be active) and physical (health) hoped-for-selves.

Possible selves are closely related to another important part of the self-concept, that is, personal goals. The difference between possible selves and goals, however, is that possible selves do not imply a commitment to a certain goal but rather reflect wishes that are not necessarily grounded in reality. When comparing the importance of different goal domains across the life span, it is found that young adults are most interested in goals concerning future education and family; goals named by middle-aged adults are mostly related to their children's welfare, their occupation, their health, and their property; older adults are most concerned with health, retirement, leisure activities, and general world issues (e.g., peace, the environment; Nurmi, 1992). Similar results emerged in a recent study on life investment over the life span that investigated how people distribute their time and energy across different life domains (Staudinger & Schindler, 2005). Middle-aged adults reported that their highest investment was in family, and this investment was still stronger in old age. The second most important investment area in midlife was occupation, which attracted lower investment after retirement.

In sum, we can describe middle-aged adults' self-concept and goals as firmly grounded in reality and centered mainly around family, specifically children. Other important themes are occupation, mental and physical self-improvement, and property. All in all, the research on the self-concept seems to confirm the hypothesis that middle-aged adults are very much involved with everyday life and the mastery of their manifold responsibilities.

Empirical Evidence on Growth in Midlife

Evidence From Studies on Generativity

Generativity can be summarized as "the concern for and commitment to promoting future generations through parenting, teaching, mentoring, and generating products and outcomes that aim to benefit youth and foster the well-being and development of individuals and social systems that will outlive the self" (McAdams, 2001, p. 396). We have also pointed out the twofold character of the concept of generativity, which brings together "power and love, agency and communion, self-expansion and self-surrender" (McAdams, 2001, p. 405). When it comes to generativity in midlife, further theoretical specifications have been made. Following Erikson, the most obvious hypothesis is that generativity should peak at midlife (see also McAdams, 2001). Or rather should we assume that it takes a different form at different ages? Erikson described generativity in midlife as including "procreativity as well as productivity and creativity" (Erikson, Erikson, & Kivnick, 1986, p. 285). The dominance of the agentic, as opposed to the communal, facet of generativity as expressed in this statement seems to be in line with other theories contrasting midlife and old age. This reminds us of the emphasis on agency and executive functions that Neugarten found in her interviews with middle-aged adults. Furthermore, the "gender cross-over" posited by Gutmann (1987), and mentioned earlier in this chapter, would imply that men move from an active, assertive mode to a more yielding and nurturing mode of generativity, whereas women might become prone to realizing more of the agentic side of generativity at midlife (cf. MacDermid, Franz, & De Reus, 1998).

Empirical evidence on the role and expression of generativity and its facets in middle adulthood is extremely incongruent (see McAdams, 2001, for an overview). Sheldon and Kasser (2001) examined the occurrence of Eriksonian themes in goal statements of four groups of adults (20 and younger, 21–39, 40–59, and 60-plus years). They found a linear and significant increase of themes mirroring generative concerns. Middle-aged adults ranked second highest after older adults in referring to generative topics, such as creating something, giving of oneself to others, purposeful and positive interaction with the younger generation, or symbolic immortality. Similarly, a study tracing the course of generativity by comparing 20-, 40-, and 60-year-olds, as well as assessing one cohort longitudinally at three ages, found linear increases of generativity with age. However, the increase was clearly more pronounced in individuals between the ages of 20 and 40 years (Zucker, Ostrove, & Stewart, 2002). A linear trend of generativity was also uncovered in a cohort-sequential study (Whitbourne, Zuschlag, Elliot, & Waterman, 1992). Using the Inventory of Psychosocial Development (Constantinople, 1969), these researchers found generativity to be significantly higher at age 42 as compared with younger control groups. Since the oldest age group in this study was middle aged, it is not possible to make inferences about the key question whether or not generativity increases beyond middle age. All in all, when only the level of generativity was compared across age groups, most studies yielded linear rather than quadratic age-graded trends, implying that older, and not middle-aged, adults rank highest in terms of generativity.

Using a multidimensional assessment instrument of generativity that distinguishes between care and nurturing (Communion scale), efficacy and productivity (Agency scale), and self-insight, MacDermid et al. (1998) found that overall generativity increased from 31 to age 54. The subscale communion, however, exhibited a significant decrease for male participants between the ages of 31 and 42 years (which, in fact, provides strong negative evidence against the gender cross-over hypothesis). In contrast, no significant changes were observed in generativity or one of its subscales from the fifth to the sixth decade of life (MacDermid et al., 1998). With regard to gender differences, women scored higher in overall generativity and in communion at all ages. Follow-up analyses concerning the gender difference showed that for males, increases in generativity were associated with the adoption of the conventional masculine role of being an adequate provider (e.g., having children, being the only earner in their family, being employed). This was not the case for women, where both conventional (e.g., being a homemaker, being a mother) and unconventional behavior patterns (e.g., being divorced, being remarried, having an unemployed spouse) correlated with being generative.

Finally, there is yet another model of generativity that differentiates three components that each follow a different developmental trajectory (Stewart & Vandewater, 1998). First, there is a *desire for generativity* that is most distinct in early adulthood and declines thereafter. Secondly, there is *generative accomplishment*, which is the product of desire and increases linearly throughout adulthood. Third is *generative capacity*, that is, expecting one's future generative achievements to exceed present generative efforts. Felt generative capacity is supposedly most distinct in midlife and shows lower levels in early and late adulthood. This differentiation was confirmed in two longitudinal studies (both reported in Stewart & Vandewater, 1998). Thus, according to this model, midlife is characterized by maximal generative capacity, combined with steadily increasing generative accomplishment and a decreasing desire to act in generative ways. On the one hand, generative accomplishment in midlife gives rise to a heightened sense of self-efficacy and self-esteem and, thus, enhances subjective well-being. On the other hand, a high amount of generative desire in midlife is significantly related to lower subjective well-being. According to this model then, the age-appropriate expression of generativity seems to play a key role when it comes to the functionality of generativity.

All in all, a tentative interpretation of these different results points toward a linear rather than a curvilinear trend for generativity, with the highest levels being reached in late adulthood. Therefore, it seems useful to further differentiate, as Stewart and Vandewater (1998) did, between desire, accomplishment, and capacity. These three aspects have to be crossed with the agency and communion facets of generativity (McAdams, 2001). The difference between generativity in midlife and generativity in old age may then lie in the weights assigned to desire, accomplishment, and capacity, respectively, combined with the fact that the agency facet plays a more prominent role in midlife than in old age.

Turning Inward or Outward?

It remains an open question whether middle age is indeed a time of turning inward in an attempt to rethink one's priorities and values (as suggested by Jung, Bühler, and Levinson), or whether it is a time of heightened outward orientation in the sense of manifesting social power and harvesting the fruits of earlier investments (e.g., Erikson, Havighurst, Neugarten). To answer this question, it may be helpful to look at studies that allow for the differentiation between an outward orientation, including the interest in succeeding generations, and an inward orientation.

If the assumption of an outward orientation were confirmed, we would see increases in environmental mastery and social competence during adulthood. Conversely, if the assumption of a beginning inward orientation were correct, increases on dimensions, such as self-insight and integrated self-complexity, would be observed.

A measurement instrument that seems apt to uncover age trends in outward versus inward orientation is Carol Ryff's scale of psychological well-being. The subscales "personal growth" and "purpose in life" capture the inward orientation. In contrast, the subscales "positive relations" and "environmental mastery" index outward orientation. What are the developmental trajectories of these scales? Whereas environmental mastery clearly increases with age, especially until midlife, personal growth and purpose in life show age-related decreases, especially from midlife to old age. There were no significant age differences for "positive relations with others" (Ryff, 1995). These findings were replicated in other studies (e.g., Ryff, 1995). Only the age trend of positive relations with others varied across studies between no differences and increases with age. Thus, at least as measured by the Ryff scales, there seems to be evidence for both orientations in midlife.

Ryff's measure of psychological well-being, however, is a self-report measure, which may involve problems of social desirability when positive aspects of development are assessed. A measurement approach suggested by Labouvie-Vief (2003) may complement the picture. Building on her earlier work on cognitive-emotional integration, Gisela Labouvie-Vief has recently focused on the development and/or maturation of self-regulation (Labouvie-Vief & Medler, 2002). In this approach, she has developed a notion of personality development that combines Affect Optimization, "the tendency to constrain affect to positive values," with Affect Complexity, "the amplification of affect in the search for differentiation and objectivity" (2002, p. 571).

The two styles parallel our distinction between inward and outward orientation, or growth and adjustment. Affect Optimization is related to living in an integrated and well-functioning social climate (outward), whereas Affect Complexity is the result of social-cognitive and internal processes (inward). Indeed, it was found that a high degree of Affect Optimization, although being closely associated with positivity of affect, simultaneously goes along with repressive coping styles and lower intellectual ability. Social relationships, however, are especially positive for those individuals high on Affect Optimization. Conversely, high levels of

Affect Complexity are related to higher intelligence, as well as to a high degree of openness and objectivity.

What are the levels of Affect Optimization and Affect Complexity observed among middle-aged adults? Of all possible combinations of the two scales, a combination of high levels on both Affect Optimization and Affect Complexity, was most frequently found among middle-aged adults (40%) as opposed to younger and older age groups. Equal percentages (around 20%) of the middle-aged sample showed high Affect Optimization but low Affect Complexity and, conversely, low Affect Optimization and high Affect Complexity (Labouvie-Vief & Zhang, 2003). Thus, according to this study, inward and outward orientation are well represented among middle-aged adults. Again, we find that midlife has a Janus face looking inward as well as outward. This pattern of results underscores that midlife is a phase characterized by a rich supply of resources.

In the following section, we will introduce two more measures of personality growth in adulthood. Both measures are performance-based, or unobtrusive, measures rather than self-report scales and were developed based on theoretical conceptions of personal growth.

Personal Wisdom

An obvious candidate for the definition of personal growth is wisdom. However, the wisdom literature shows that a clear distinction between personal and general wisdom is lacking (see Staudinger et al., in press). Wisdom usually is referred to as sound judgment and good advice in uncertain and important matters of life (Baltes & Staudinger, 2000). This does not take into account that it may infer very different criteria for judging one's own problems, as compared with the problems of others. We aimed to fill this gap and assumed that it may be useful to develop independent operationalizations of both types of wisdom. That way, we obtain the opportunity to empirically test the relationship between personal and general wisdom. By personal wisdom, we mean individuals' insight into their own lives; that is, what do people know about themselves and their lives? General wisdom, in contrast, is concerned with insights into life in general. What do individuals know about life from an observer's point of view, that is, when they are not personally concerned? For instance, your general wisdom is tapped if a friend comes to you because his or her marriage is in a deep crisis and he or she is considering divorce. But it takes your personal wisdom if you search for a solution because your own marriage is in a deep crisis and you are considering divorce. The hypothesis is that different, yet overlapping, self-regulatory processes are necessary to achieve one or the other form of wisdom.

To compare personal and general wisdom without much methodological confusion, we developed a measure of personal wisdom that was modeled after the Berlin wisdom paradigm for general wisdom (Staudinger et al., in press). The Berlin wisdom paradigm produces a well-established and validated performance measure of (general) wisdom. Next, we systematically reviewed different approaches to the conceptualization of personality growth from the developmental, clinical, and personality literature, with regard to the characteristics of a mature person in the areas of cognition, emotion, motivation, and volition (e.g., Allport, 1961; Bühler, 1959; Cloninger, 2003; Erikson, 1959; Freud, 1917/1993; Jung, 1934/2001; Labouvie-Vief, 1982; Loevinger, 1976; Maslow, 1968; Rogers, 1961). These aspects of personality growth were then checked against the five criteria of the Berlin wisdom paradigm (for a detailed explanation, see Staudinger, Smith, & Baltes, 1994). Consequently, self-related specifications were identified, and five new criteria of personal wisdom were developed (for a detailed explanation, see Mickler & Staudinger, 2005).

The first criterion is *rich self-knowledge*, that is, deep insight into oneself. Self-wise persons are aware of their own strengths and weaknesses, emotions and goals, and meaning of life. The second criterion requires self-wise persons to have available *heuristics for growth and self-regulation* (e.g., how to express and regulate emotions or how to develop and maintain deep social relations). Humor is an example of an important heuristic that helps persons to cope with various difficult and challenging situations. *Interrelating the self*, the third criterion, refers to the ability to reflect on, and have insight into, the possible causes of one's behavior, feelings, and motives. Such causes can be age related, situational, or linked to personal characteristics. Interrelating the self also implies that there is an awareness about one's own dependency on others. The fourth criterion is called *self-relativism*. People high on self-relativism are able to evaluate themselves as well as others from a distance. They critically appraise their own behavior, but at the same time, they display a basic acceptance of themselves. They also show tolerance for others' values and lifestyles, as long as they are not damaging to self or others. Finally, *tolerance of ambiguity* involves the ability to recognize and manage the uncertainties in one's own life and one's own development. It is reflected in the awareness that one's life is full of uncontrollable and unpredictable events, including death and illness. At the same time, tolerance for ambiguity includes the availability of strategies to manage this uncertainty through openness to experience, basic trust, and flexible solutions. Personal wisdom is measured by using a thinking-aloud procedure, followed by a rating procedure, developed after the Berlin (general) wisdom paradigm.

In a first study, the measure of personal wisdom showed good convergent validity (Mickler & Staudinger, 2005). It is positively correlated with other measures of personality growth, such as Ryff's personal growth and purpose in life (from the inventory of Psychological Well-Being; Ryff, 1989), Loevinger's ego development (Loevinger, 1976; see also Hy & Loevinger, 1996), and benevolent values (Mickler & Staudinger, 2005; Schwartz, 1992). With regard to discriminant validity, it has been demonstrated that personal wisdom, as to be expected for a measure of personal growth, is uncorrelated with notions of subjective well-being and adjustment, such as life satisfaction, negative or positive emotions, and adaptive motives such as power, achievement, and hedonism. Personal wisdom certainly cannot be reduced to a person's intelligence. As far as the relationship with personality variables is concerned, openness to experience is the most important predictor; of the other Big Five variables, none showed significant correlations. Psychological mindedness, a concept that measures interest in thoughts and feelings of other people, was also significantly correlated. The first time the measure of self-related wisdom was employed, we used a sample of 169 adults aged 20 to 40 years and 60 to 80 years. Subsequent studies with a middle-aged population will have to validate the emerging age trends and confirm whether relations to age are linear or curvilinear. As for the comparison between younger and older adults, we found that younger adults scored significantly higher on the measure of self-related wisdom, which was particularly due to lower performance levels of the older participants on the scales "interrelating the self" and "self-relativism." No significant difference was left, however, when controlling for length of response and tendency for self-disclosure. Both seemed to be confounding variables that may follow their own cohort logic. In essence, this result suggests that there are no age differences in terms of self-related wisdom when comparing young and older adults. Thus, we may conclude that we do not find any age differences between young and old adulthood. It is unclear whether the middle group would show a peak in between or whether the age trajectory of personal wisdom is flat, as suggested by evidence from the realm of general wisdom (e.g., Staudinger, 1999).

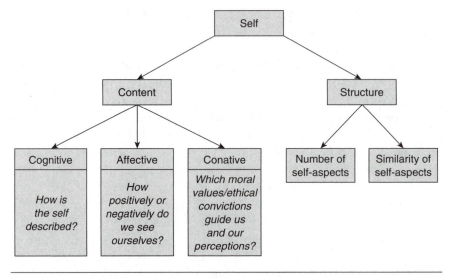

Figure 9.1   A Conceptualization of the Self-Concept

The Mature Self

Unlike most other theories of maturity, growth, or wisdom, self-maturity theory is grounded not in cognitive or personality theories but in the self-concept literature (for more detail, see Dörner & Staudinger, 2005). In this literature, content and structural dimensions of the self-concept are usually distinguished. Figure 9.1 illustrates how these two basic dimensions are further differentiated. Based on the self-concept and the personality growth literature, we first defined self-esteem as a necessary, but not sufficient, precondition of personality growth. Second, self-complexity, integration, and value orientation are indicators of the mature self (e.g., Linville, 1985, 1987; Noam & Röper, 1999; Staudinger & Baltes, 1994; Sternberg, 1998). In the following paragraphs, these four facets of the mature self are introduced in more detail.

(1) *Self-esteem.* We believe that the basic precondition for any self-growth to occur is an intermediate level of self-esteem. Clinicians have never failed to stress that personality growth is not possible without a certain amount of self-esteem (e.g., Maslow, 1968; Noam, 1998; Rogers, 1961). A basic degree of self-esteem is necessary to pursue the often challenging route of self-exploration. Very high self-esteem, however, undermines

questioning and re-defining oneself and, as a consequence, hinders personality growth.

(2) *Self-complexity.* Although self-complexity is one of the most often cited and studied characteristics of self-concept development, empirical investigations regarding self-complexity and its relations to personality growth rather than psychosocial adjustment are scarce. A study by Labouvie-Vief, Chiodo, Goguen, and Diehl (1995), showing a relation between affect complexity of written self-descriptions and higher ego levels, is one of the few exceptions (see Evans & Seaman, 2000, for another example). In our understanding, self-complexity can refer to content as well as affect (see Figure 9.1). Thus, a self-complex person is characterized by a self-description that covers a wide array of self-relevant domains (Linville, 1985, 1987) as well as self-related feelings.

(3) *Integration.* Even though a mature self should be complex, this complexity also needs to be integrated. A mature self also needs a common self-descriptive core that cuts across different self-aspects. It is this common core that allows the experience of a consistent self across different self-aspects, that is, situations. Without this integration, the person lacks a sense of identity or "self-sameness" (Erikson, 1959), which has been demonstrated to be a vital antecedent of psychological health and maturity (e.g., Campbell, Assanand, & Di Paula, 2003; Diehl et al., 2001). However, the degree of integration should not be such that no differentiation is left; that is, the self-concept should remain the same, irrespective of situational demands. Such a poorly integrated individual behaves uniformly in all situations, disregarding the different responsibilities different circumstances may impose. Obviously then, this kind of self-concept should not be called mature. Although the self-concept of a mature person should provide a sense of self-sameness (Erikson, 1950/1995), or continuity, it nevertheless should also respond to the opposite demand, namely to affirm the person's capacity to adapt and accommodate to different surroundings. As a consequence, for a mature person, the task would be to find the proper balance between role rigidity and role confusion (see Block, 1961). Therefore, we would expect a medium degree of self-concept integration, or self-concept differentiation.

(4) *Value orientation.* Even integrated complexity does not make a mature self. Integrated complexity can be applied to achieve many things, for example, to commit the perfect crime. It is obvious, therefore, that

a fourth facet needs to be added, which is the value orientation that characterizes a person (e.g., Allport, 1961; Orwoll & Perlmutter, 1990). A mature person is driven by self-transcending values and by the attempt to balance self-centered and altruistic goals (e.g., Kunzmann & Baltes, 2003; Sternberg, 1998).

In sum, the four facets need to be considered in combination when defining the mature self. This combination, however, cannot be achieved by using a linear combination of the four indicators because some of them show a curvilinear relationship with self-growth. Thus, we defined the profile of an ideally self-mature person across the four indicators and then computed for each person the correlation with this ideal profile. The profile of an ideally self-mature person is characterized by an intermediate level of self-esteem, a maximum level of self-complexity (in terms of content and affect), an intermediate level of integration, and high levels of an altruistic, self-transcendent value orientation.

As expected, this indicator of maturity is related to other measures of personality growth, such as openness to experience, Ryff's scales of personal growth and purpose in life (Ryff, 1989), Loevinger's ego development (Loevinger, 1976; see also Hy & Loevinger, 1996), and the measure of personal wisdom (see previous section; Mickler & Staudinger, 2005). It is not associated, however, with indicators of adjustment and hedonism (Dörner & Staudinger, 2005). As for age trends, again, the age composition of our sample (20–40 and 60–80 years) does not allow for explicit statements about middle age. When comparing younger and older adults, however, no significant differences were found. Thus, for both measures, personal wisdom and self-concept growth, we do not find normative age-related increases.

Conclusion

In traditional conceptions, the human life course is often depicted as a staircase following an inverted u-shape. This implies that the middle-aged person thrones in solitary splendor over the other life phases. This image brings together two somewhat divergent notions about midlife mentioned in this chapter. First, it explains the awe and anxiousness toward midlife as perceived by younger persons: Will this stage truly bring the desired culmination of their lives? Second, it accounts for the mixed feelings reported by middle-aged adults: Who could indulge in a peak experience without reservations when knowing that decline is approaching?

Of course, we do not argue for this simplistic, inverted u-shaped model of human development. On the contrary, our selective review of studies has provided once again clear evidence of the multidimensionality and multidirectionality of development. For instance, psychosocial adjustment seems to continue to increase after midlife into old age, defying the idea of a midlife peak. In contrast, growth—depending on the measure—either peaks in midlife or shows a stable trajectory throughout adulthood.

We reviewed some of the classical approaches to the study of midlife, and two somewhat diverging viewpoints emerged: Jung, Levinson, and Bühler suggested that midlife is a time of reconsidering familiar patterns and priorities, turning inward, and increasingly assuming a more passive, observant role. In contrast, Erikson, Havighurst, and Neugarten deemed middle-aged adults at the peak of their competencies and their powers, actively involved in and committed to social and societal tasks, with a firm grounding in the here and now.

The differentiation of midlife into early and late midlife (Staudinger & Bluck, 2001; Dittmann-Kohli, Chapter 10, this volume) turned out to be useful with regard to integrating diverging evidence. We may be able to identify greater convergence between studies when treating earlier (40–50 years) and later midlife (50–60 years) separately. This distinction accommodates the two perspectives on midlife just described. It is early midlife that follows the notion of agency and social impact, and it is late midlife that brings in some of the turning inward that Jung had suggested. Another indicator for the difference between the years before and after age 50 is the change in rank-order consistency of personality traits (see paragraph summarizing Big Five trajectories during midlife). While experiencing a considerable drop in the 40s as compared to the decade before, during the 50s, rank-order consistency increases up to its maximum, suggesting that the 40s might entail a greater variety of possible life paths than the subsequent years (Roberts & DelVecchio, 2000). Further, our review of the empirical evidence on generativity showed that the relative weight of the agentic, as compared with the communal, facet of generativity seems to shift between early and late midlife. Yet, so far, there are only a few studies considering the two decades of midlife separately (e.g., Hooker & Kaus, 1994; Lachman & Weaver, 1998; cf. also Staudinger & Bluck, 2001). Hence, the usefulness of this subdivision needs further support.

The research on the role of social norms for adjustment and growth at midlife suggests that adhering to social norms, while resulting in relatively high levels of adjustment, does not foster personality growth. Facing challenges, in contrast, seems to be much more conducive to growth. Compared with younger age, on average, midlife is characterized by increased levels of psychosocial adjustment. When it comes to personal growth, the empirical evidence is not unequivocal. Depending on the measurement approach chosen (self-report or performance), personal growth peaks in midlife or stays stable, respectively.

In sum, we conclude that throughout midlife, we improve in our capacity to manage the challenges of everyday life. However, when choosing the developmental goal of personal growth as well, it seems that we need to—literally—go out of our way to make progress on that trajectory through midlife. Dealing with the usual, in the sense of average, biological and societal tasks does not suffice for personal growth to occur.

Note

1. We are aware that by dissolving this distinction, we are violating conventions that draw a clear line between the two topics. Our intention here is not to question the usefulness of this commonly found separation, but rather to arrive at a comprehensive view on the development of the self in midlife. Thus, it seems adequate to regard these two streams of research jointly.

References

Allport, G. W. (1961). *Patterns and growth in personality.* New York: Holt, Rinehart & Winston.

Baltes, P. B. (1968). Longitudinal and cross-sectional sequences in the study of age and generation effects. *Human Development, 11,* 145–171.

Baltes, P. B., Lindenberger, U., & Staudinger, U. M. (1998). Life-span theory in developmental psychology. In R. M. Lerner (Ed.), *Theoretical models of human development* (Handbook of Child Psychology, 5th ed., Vol. 1, pp. 1029–1143). New York: Wiley.

Baltes, P. B., Reese, H. W., & Lipsitt, L. P. (1980). Life-span developmental psychology. *Annual Review of Psychology, 31,* 65–110.

Baltes, P. B., Reese, H. W., & Nesselroade, J. R. (1988). *Life-span developmental psychology: Introduction to research methods.* Hillsdale, NJ: Erlbaum. (Originally published 1977)

Baltes, P. B., & Staudinger, U. M. (2000). Wisdom: A metaheuristic to orchestrate mind and virtue towards excellence. *American Psychologist, 55,* 122–136.

Block, J. (1961). Ego identity, role variability, and adjustment. *Journal of Consulting Psychology, 25,* 392–397.

Brandtstädter, J., Renner, G., & Baltes-Götz, B. (1989). Entwicklung von Wertorientierungen im Erwachsenenalter: Quersequentielle Analysen [Development of value orientation in adulthood: Cross-sectional analyses]. *Zeitschrift für Entwicklungpsychologie und Pädagogische Psychologie, 21,* 3–23.

Bühler, C. (1935). The curve of life as studied in biographies. *Journal of Applied Psychology, 19,* 405–409.

Bühler, C. (1959). *Der menschliche Lebenslauf als psychologisches Problem* [The human life course as a psychological problem]. Göttingen, Germany: Dieterichsche Universitäts-Buchdruckerei.

Bühler, C. (1968). The general structure of the human life cycle. In C. Bühler & F. Massarik (Eds.), *The course of human life: A study of goals in the humanistic perspective* (pp. 12–26). New York: Springer.

Campbell, J. D., Assanand, S., & Di Paula, A. (2003). The structure of the self-concept and its relation to psychological adjustment. *Journal of Personality, 71,* 115–140.

Cartwright, L. K., & Wink, P. (1994). Personality change in women physicians from medical student years to mid-40s. *Psychology of Women Quarterly, 18,* 291–308.

Caspi, A. (1987). Personality in the life course. *Journal of Personality and Social Psychology, 53,* 1203–1213.

Charles, S. T., Reynolds, C. A., & Gatz, M. (2001). Age-related differences and change in positive and negative affect over twenty-three years. *Journal of Personality and Social Psychology, 80,* 136–151.

Clark-Plaskie, M., & Lachman, M. E. (1999). The sense of control in midlife. In S. L. Willis & J. D. Reid (Eds.), *Life in the middle: Psychological and social development in middle age* (pp. 181–208). San Diego, CA: Academic Press.

Cloninger, C. R. (2003). Completing the psychobiological architecture of human personality development: Temperament, character, and coherence. In U. M. Staudinger & U. Lindenberger (Eds.), *Understanding human development: Dialogues with lifespan psychology* (pp. 159–181). Boston: Kluwer Academic.

Constantinople, A. (1969). An Eriksonian measure of personality development in college students. *Developmental Psychology, 1,* 357–372.

Costa, P. T., Herbst, J. H., McCrae, R. R., & Siegler, I. C. (2000). Personality at midlife: Stability, intrinsic maturation, and response to life events. *Assessment, 7,* 365–378.

Costa, P. T., & McCrae, R. R. (1980). Still stable after all these years: Personality as a key to some issues in adulthood and old age. In P. B. Baltes & O. G. Brim, Jr. (Eds.), *Life-span development and behavior* (Vol. 3, pp. 66–102). New York: Academic Press.

Costa, P. T., & McCrae, R. R. (1988a). *The NEO personality inventory manual.* Odessa, FL: Psychological Assessment Resources.

Costa, P. T., & McCrae, R. R. (1988b). Personality in adulthood: A six-year longitudinal study of self-reports and spouse ratings on the NEO personality inventory. *Journal of Personality and Social Psychology, 54,* 853–863.

Costa, P. T., & McCrae, R. R. (1989). Personality continuity and the changes of adult life. In M. Storandt & G. R. VandenBos (Eds.), *The adult years: Continuity and change* (pp. 41–77). Washington, DC: American Psychological Association.

Costa, P. T., & McCrae, R. R. (1994a). Set like plaster? Evidence for the stability of adult personality. In T. F. Heatherton & J. L. Weinberger (Eds.), *Can personality change?* (pp. 21–40). Washington, DC: American Psychological Association.

Costa, P. T., & McCrae, R. R. (1994b). Stability and change in personality from adolescence through adulthood. In C. F. Halverson, G. A. Kohnstamm, & R. P. Martin (Eds.), *The developing structure of temperament and personality from infancy to adulthood* (pp. 139–150). Hillsdale, NJ: Erlbaum.

Costa, P. T., & McCrae, R. R. (1997). Longitudinal stability of adult personality. In R. Hogan, J. Johnson, & S. Briggs (Eds.), *Handbook of personality psychology* (pp. 269–290). San Diego, CA: Academic Press.

Cross, S. E., & Markus, H. R. (1991). Possible selves across the life span. *Human Development, 34,* 230–255.

Crowley, B. J., Hayslip, B. J., & Hobdy, J. (2003). Psychological hardiness and adjustment to life events in adulthood. *Journal of Adult Development, 10,* 237–248.

Diehl, M., Hastings, C. T., & Stanton, J. M. (2001). Self-concept differentiation across the adult life span. *Psychology and Aging, 16,* 643–654.

Dörner, J., & Staudinger, U. M. (2005). *The mature self: The meaning of the self-concept beyond well-being.* Manuscript in preparation.

Dudek, S. Z., & Hall, W. B. (1991). Personality consistency: Eminent architects 25 years later. *Creativity Research Journal, 4,* 213–231.

Elder, G. H., Jr. (1998). The life course and human development. In R. M. Lerner (Ed.), *Theoretical models of human development* (Handbook of Child Psychology, 5th ed., Vol. 1, pp. 939–991). New York: Wiley.

Erikson, E. H. (1959). *Identity and the life cycle.* New York: International University Press.

Erikson, E. H. (1995). *Childhood and society.* London: Vintage. (Original work published 1950)

Erikson, E. H., Erikson, J. M., & Kivnick, H. (1986). *Vital involvement in old age: The experience of old age in our time.* London: Norton.

Evans, D. W., & Seaman, J. L. (2000). Developmental aspects of psychological defenses: Their relation to self-complexity, self-perception and symptomatology in adolescents. *Child Psychiatry and Human Development, 30,* 237–254.

Feldman, S. S., Biringen, Z. C., & Nash, S. C. (1981). Fluctuations of sex-related self-attributions as a function of stage of family life cycle. *Developmental Psychology, 17,* 24–35.

Field, D., & Millsap, R. E. (1991). Personality in advanced old age: Continuity or change? *Journals of Gerontology, 46*, 299–308.

Franz, C. E. (1994). Does thought content change as individuals age? A longitudinal study of midlife adults. In T. F. Heatherton & J. L. Weinberger (Eds.), *Can personality change?* (pp. 227–249). Washington, DC: American Psychological Association.

Freud, S. (1993). *Vorlesungen zur Einführung in die Psychoanalyse* [Lectures. Introduction to psychoanalysis]. Frankfurt, Germany: Fischer. (Original work published 1917)

Goldberg, L. R. (1993). "The structure of phenotypic personality traits": Author's reactions to the six comments. *American Psychologist, 48*, 1303–1304.

Goldberg, L. R., Sweeney, D., Merenda, P. F., & Hughes, J. E. J. (1998). Demographic variables and personality: The effects of gender, age, education, and ethnic/racial status on self-descriptions of personality attributes. *Personality & Individual Differences, 24*, 393–403.

Gough, H. G., & Bradley, P. (1996). *CPI Manual* (3rd ed.). Palo Alto, CA: Consulting Psychology Press.

Gutmann, D. L. (1975). Parenthood: A key to the comparative study of the life-cycle. In N. Datan & L. Ginsberg (Eds.), *Life-span developmental psychology: Normative life crises* (pp. 167–184). San Diego, CA: Academic Press.

Gutmann, D. L. (1987). *Reclaimed powers: Toward a new psychology of men and women in later life*. New York: Basic Books.

Haan, N., Millsap, R., & Hartka, E. (1986). As time goes by: Change and stability in personality over fifty years. *Psychology and Aging, 1*, 220–232.

Havighurst, R. J. (1972). *Developmental tasks and education* (3rd ed.). New York: McKay.

Heckhausen, J. (1999). *Developmental regulation in adulthood. Age-normative and sociostructural constraints as adaptive challenges.* Cambridge, UK: Cambridge University Press.

Helson, R., & Kwan, V. S. Y. (2000). Personality development in adulthood: The broad picture and processes in one longitudinal sample. In S. Hampson (Ed.), *Advances in personality psychology* (Vol. 1, pp. 77–106). London: Routledge.

Helson, R., Kwan, V. S. Y., John, O. P., & Jones, C. (2002). The growing evidence for personality change in adulthood: Findings from research with personality inventories. *Journal of Research in Personality, 36*, 287–306.

Helson, R., Mitchell, V., & Moane, G. (1984). Personality and patterns of adherence and nonadherence to the social clock. *Journal of Personality and Social Psychology, 46*, 1079–1096.

Helson, R., & Picano, J. (1990). Is the traditional role bad for women? *Journal of Personality and Social Psychology, 59*, 311–320.

Helson, R., & Roberts, B. W. (1994). Ego development and personality change in adulthood. *Journal of Personality and Social Psychology, 66*, 911–920.

Helson, R., & Wink, P. (1987). Two conceptions of maturity examined in the findings of a longitudinal study. *Journal of Personality and Social Psychology, 53,* 531–541.

Helson, R., & Wink, P. (1992). Personality change in women from early 40s to the early 50s. *Psychology and Aging, 7,* 46–55.

Hofstede, G. (1998). *Masculinity and femininity. The taboo dimension of national culture.* Thousand Oaks, CA: Sage.

Hooker, K., & Kaus, C. R. (1994). Health-related possible selves in young and middle adulthood. *Psychology and Aging, 9,* 126–133.

Huyck, M. H. (1999). Gender roles and gender identity in midlife. In S. L. Willis & J. D. Reid (Eds.), *Life in the middle: Psychological and social development in middle age* (pp. 209–232). San Diego, CA: Academic Press.

Hy, L. X., & Loevinger, J. (1996). *Measuring ego development* (2nd ed.). Mahwah, NJ: Erlbaum.

John, O. P. (1990). The "Big Five" factor taxonomy: Dimensions of personality in the natural language and in questionnaires. In L. A. Pervin (Ed.), *Handbook of personality* (pp. 66–100). New York: Guilford Press.

John, O. P., & Srivastava, S. (1999). The Big Five trait taxonomy: History, measurement, and theoretical perspectives. In L. A. Pervin & O. P. John (Eds.), *Handbook of personality theory and research* (Vol. 2, pp. 102–138). New York: Guilford Press.

Johnson, R. C., Nagoshi, C. T., Ahern, F. M., Wilson, J. R., McClearn, G. E., & Vandenberg, S. G. (1983). Age and cohort effects on personality factor scores across sexes and racial/ethnic groups. *Personality and Individual Differences, 6,* 709–713.

Jung, C. G. (2001; first edited: 1934). *Modern man in search of a soul.* London: Routledge.

Keyes, C. L. M., Shmotkin, D., & Ryff, C. D. (2002). Optimizing well-being: The empirical encounter of two traditions. *Journal of Personality and Social Psychology, 82,* 1007–1022.

Klohnen, E. A., Vandewater, E. A., & Young, A. (1996). Negotiating the middle years: Ego-resiliency and successful midlife adjustment in women. *Psychology and Aging, 11,* 431–442.

Kotre, J. (1984). *Outliving the self: Generativity and the interpretation of lives.* Baltimore: Johns Hopkins University Press.

Krueger, J., Heckhausen, J., & Hundertmark, J. (1995). Perceiving middle-aged adults: Effects of stereotype-congruent and incongruent information. *Journal of Gerontology, Series B, 50,* 83–93.

Kunzmann, U., & Baltes, P. B. (2003). Wisdom-related knowledge: Emotional, motivational, and interpersonal correlates. *Personality and Social Psychology Bulletin, 29,* 1104–1119.

Labouvie-Vief, G. (1982). Dynamic development and mature autonomy: A theoretical prologue. *Human Development, 25,* 161–191.

Labouvie-Vief, G. (1994). *Psyche and Eros: Mind and gender in the life course.* New York: Cambridge University Press.

Labouvie-Vief, G. (2003). Dynamic integration: Affect, cognition, and the self in adulthood. *Current Directions in Psychological Science, 12,* 201–206.

Labouvie-Vief, G., Chiodo, L. M., Goguen, L. A., & Diehl, M. (1995). Representations of self across the life span. *Psychology and Aging, 10,* 404–415.

Labouvie-Vief, G., & Medler, M. (2002). Affect optimization and affect complexity: Modes and styles of regulation in adulthood. *Psychology and Aging, 17,* 571–587.

Labouvie-Vief, G., & Zhang, F. (2003, August). *Dynamic integration: Affect, cognition, and the organization of the self.* Paper presented at the 111th annual convention of the American Psychological Association, Toronto, Ontario, Canada.

Lachman, M. E. (2004). Development in midlife. *Annual Review of Psychology, 55,* 305–331.

Lachman, M. E., & Weaver, L. (1998). Sociodemographic variations in the sense of control by domain: Findings from the MacArthur Studies of Midlife. *Psychology and Aging, 13,* 553–562.

Lansford, J. E., Sherman, A. M., & Antonucci, T. C. (1998). Satisfaction with the social networks: An examination of socioemotional selectivity theory across cohorts. *Psychology and Aging, 13,* 544–552.

Levinson, D. J. (1986). A conception of adult development. *American Psychologist, 41,* 3–13.

Linville, P. W. (1985). Self-complexity and affective extremity: Don't put all of your eggs in one cognitive basket. *Social Cognition, 3,* 94–120.

Linville, P. W. (1987). Self-complexity as a cognitive buffer against stress-related illness and depression. *Journal of Personality and Social Psychology, 52,* 663–676.

Loevinger, J. (1976). *Ego development: Conception and theory.* San Francisco: Jossey-Bass.

Lowenthal, M. F., Thurnher, M., & Chiriboga, D. (1975). *Four stages of life: A comparative study of women and men facing transition.* San Francisco: Jossey-Bass.

MacDermid, S., Franz, C. E., & De Reus, L. A. (1998). Adult character: Agency, communion, insight, and the expression of generativity in mid-life adults. In A. Colby, J. B. James, & D. Hart (Eds.), *Competence and character through life* (pp. 208–229). Chicago: University of Chicago Press.

Markus, H. (1977). Self-schemata and processing information about the self. *Journal of Personality and Social Psychology, 35,* 63–78.

Markus, H., & Nurius, P. (1986). Possible selves. *American Psychologist, 41,* 954–969.

Markus, H., & Wurf, E. (1987). The dynamic self-concept: A social psychological perspective. *Annual Review of Psychology, 38,* 299–337.

Maslow, A. H. (1968). *Toward a psychology of being.* New York: Van Nostrand Reinhold.

McAdams, D. P. (2001). Generativity in midlife. In M. E. Lachman (Ed.), *Handbook of midlife development* (pp. 395–443). New York: Wiley.

McAdams, D. P., & de St. Aubin, E. (Eds.). (1998). *Generativity and adult development. How and why we care for the next generation.* Washington, DC: American Psychological Association.

McAdams, D. P., Diamond, A., de St. Aubin, E., & Mansfield, E. (1997). Stories of commitment: The psychosocial construction of generative lives. *Journal of Personality and Social Psychology, 72,* 678–694.

McCrae, R. R., & Costa, P. T. (1990). *Personality in adulthood.* New York: Guilford Press.

McCrae, R. R., Costa, P. T., Ostendorf, F., Angleitner, A., Hrebickova, M., Avia, M. D., et al. (2000). Nature over nurture: Temperament, personality, and life span development. *Journal of Personality and Social Psychology, 78,* 173–186.

McCrae, R. R., Costa, P. T., Pedroso de Lima, M., Simoes, A., Ostendorf, F., Angleitner, A., et al. (1999). Age differences in personality across the adult life span: Parallels in five cultures. *Developmental Psychology, 35,* 466–477.

Mickler, C., & Staudinger, U. M. (2005). *Self-insight: Definition and measurement of self-related wisdom.* Manuscript in preparation.

Moen, P., & Wethington, E. (1999). Midlife development in a life course context. In S. L. Willis & J. D. Reid (Eds.), *Life in the middle: Psychological and social development in middle age* (pp. 3–23). San Diego, CA: Academic Press.

Morfei, M. Z., Hooker, K., Carpenter, J., Mix, C., & Blakeley, E. (2004). Agentic and communal generative behavior in four areas of adult life: Implications for psychological well-being. *Journal of Adult Development, 11,* 55–58.

Mroczek, D. K. (2004). Positive and negative affect at midlife. In O. G. Brim, C. D. Ryff, & R. Kessler (Eds.), *How healthy are we: A national study of well-being in midlife* (pp. 205–226). Chicago: University of Chicago Press.

Neugarten, B. L. (1968). The awareness of middle age. In B. L. Neugarten (Ed.), *Middle age and aging* (pp. 88–92). Chicago: University of Chicago Press.

Neugarten, B. L., & Gutmann, D. L. (1968). Age-sex roles and personality in middle age: A thematic apperception study. In B. L. Neugarten (Ed.), *Middle age and aging* (pp. 58–71). Chicago: University of Chicago Press.

Neugarten, B. L., Moore, J. W., & Lowe, J. C. (1965). Age norms, age constraints, and adult socialization. *The American Journal of Sociology, 70,* 710–717.

Noam, G. (1998). Solving the ego development–mental health riddle. In P. M. Westenberg, A. Blasi, & L. D. Cohn (Eds.), *Personality development: Theoretical, empirical, and clinical investigations of Loevinger's conception of ego development* (pp. 271–295). Mahwah, NJ: Erlbaum.

Noam, G., & Röper, G. (1999). Auf dem Weg zur entwicklungspsychologisch differentiellen Intervention [On the way to a differential developmental intervention]. In R. Oerter (Ed.), *Klinische Entwicklunspsychologie. Ein Lehrbuch*

[Clinical developmental psychology. A handbook] (pp. 478–511). Weinheim, Germany: Beltz Psychologie.

Nurmi, J.-E. (1992). Age differences in adult life goals, concerns, and their temporal extension: A life course approach to future-oriented motivation. *International Journal of Behavioral Development, 15,* 487–508.

Orwoll, L., & Perlmutter, M. (1990). The study of wise persons: Integrating a personality perspective. In R. J. Sternberg (Ed.), *Wisdom: Its nature, origins, and development* (pp. 160–177). New York: Cambridge University Press.

Peck, R. (1956). Psychological development in the second half of life. In J. E. Anderson (Ed.), *Psychological aspects of aging* (pp. 42–53). Washington, DC: American Psychological Association.

Peck, R. C. (1968). Psychological developments in the second half of life. In B. L. Neugarten (Ed.), *Middle age and aging* (pp. 88–92). Chicago: University of Chicago Press.

Pedersen, N. L., & Reynolds, C. A. (1998). Stability and change in adult personality: Genetic and environmental components. *European Journal of Personality, 12,* 365–386.

Riegel, K. F. (1972). Time and change in the development of the individual and society. In H. W. Reese (Ed.), *Advances in child development and behavior* (Vol. 7, pp. 81–113). New York: Academic Press.

Riley, M. W., Kahn, R. L., Foner, A., & Mack, K. A. (1994). *Age and structural lag: Society's failure to provide meaningful opportunities in work, family, and leisure.* Oxford, UK: Wiley.

Roberts, B. W. (1997). Plaster or plasticity: Are work experiences associated with personality change in women? *Journal of Personality, 65,* 202–232.

Roberts, B. W., & DelVecchio, W. F. (2000). The rank-order consistency of personality traits from childhood to old age: A quantitative review of longitudinal studies. *Psychological Bulletin, 126,* 3–25.

Roberts, B. W., & Friend, W. (1998). Career momentum in midlife women: Life context, identity, and personality correlates. *Journal of Occupational Health Psychology, 3,* 195–208.

Roberts, B. W., Helson, R., & Klohnen, E. C. (2002). Personality development and growth in women across 30 years: Three perspectives. *Journal of Personality, 70,* 79–102.

Roberts, B. W., Robins, R. W., Caspi, A., & Trzesniewski, K. H. (2003). Personality trait development in adulthood. In J. L. Mortimer & M. Shanahan (Eds.), *Handbook of the life course* (pp. 579–598). New York: Kluwer Academic.

Robins, R. W., Trzesniewski, K. H., Tracy, J. L., Gosling, S. D., & Potter, J. (2002). Global self-esteem across the life span. *Psychology and Aging, 17,* 423–434.

Rogers, C. R. (1961). *On becoming a person.* Boston: Houghton Mifflin.

Rosenberg, S. D., Rosenberg, J. H., & Farrell, M. P. (1999). The midlife crisis revisited. In S. L. Willis & J. D. Reid (Eds.), *Life in the middle. Psychological and social development in middle age* (pp. 47–73). San Diego, CA: Academic Press.

Rossi, A. S. (1988). Growing up and older in sociology: 1940–1990. In M. W. Riley (Ed.), *Social change and the life course* (Sociological Lives, Vol. 2, pp. 43–64). Thousand Oaks, CA: Sage.

Rossi, A. S. (1994). Eros and caritas: A biopsychosocial approach to human sexuality and reproduction. In A. S. Rossi (Ed.), *Sexuality across the life course* (Series on Mental Health and Development, Studies on Successful Midlife Development, pp. 3–36). Chicago: University of Chicago Press.

Ryff, C. D. (1979). Value transition and adult development in women: The instrumentality-terminality sequence hypothesis. In M. Rokeach (Ed.), *Understanding human values* (pp. 148–153). New York: Free Press.

Ryff, C. D. (1982). Self-perceived personality change in adulthood and aging. *Journal of Personality and Social Psychology, 42,* 108–115.

Ryff, C. D. (1984). Personality development from the inside: The subjective experience of change in adulthood and aging. In P. B. Baltes & O. G. Brim, Jr. (Eds.), *Life-span development and behavior* (Vol. 6, pp. 249–279). New York: Academic Press.

Ryff, C. D. (1989). Happiness is everything, or is it? Explorations on the meaning of psychological well-being. *Journal of Personality and Social Psychology, 57,* 1069–1081.

Ryff, C. D. (1995). Psychological well-being in adult life. *Current Directions in Psychological Science, 4,* 99–104.

Ryff, C. D., & Baltes, P. B. (1976). Value transitions and adult development in women: The instrumentality-terminality hypothesis. *Developmental Psychology, 12,* 567–568.

Schaie, K. W. (1965). A general model for the study of developmental problems. *Psychological Bulletin, 64,* 92–107.

Schwartz, S. H. (1992). Universals in the content and structure of values: Theoretical advances and empirical tests in 20 countries. In M. P. Zanna (Ed.), *Advances in experimental social psychology* (Vol. 25, pp. 1–65). San Diego, CA: Academic Press.

Settersten, R. A., Jr., & Mayer, K. U. (1997). The measurement of age, age structuring, and the life course. *Annual Review of Sociology, 23,* 233–261.

Sheldon, K. M., & Kasser, T. (2001). Getting older, getting better? Personal strivings and psychological maturity across the life span. *Developmental Psychology, 37,* 491–501.

Singer, J. L. (1984). The private personality. *Personality and Social Psychology Bulletin, 10,* 7–30.

Srivastava, S., John, O. P., Gosling, S., & Potter, J. (2003). Development of personality in early and middle adulthood: Set like plaster or persistent change? *Journal of Personality and Social Psychology, 84,* 1041–1053.

Staudinger, U. M. (1999). Social cognition and a psychological approach to an art of life. In F. Blanchard-Fields & T. Hess (Eds.), *Social cognition and aging* (pp. 343–375). San Diego, CA: Academic Press.

Staudinger, U. M. (2001). Life reflection: A social-cognitive analysis of life review. *Review of General Psychology, 5,* 148–160.

Staudinger, U. M., & Baltes, P. B. (1994). The psychology of wisdom. In R. J. Sternberg (Ed.), *Encyclopedia of intelligence* (pp. 1143–1152). New York: Macmillan.

Staudinger, U. M., & Bluck, S. (2001). A view on midlife development from life-span theory. In M. E. Lachman (Ed.), *Handbook of midlife development* (pp. 3–39). New York: Wiley.

Staudinger, U. M., Dörner, J., & Mickler, C. (in press). Wisdom and personality. In R. J. Sternberg & J. Jordan (Eds.), *Handbook of wisdom.* New York: Cambridge University Press.

Staudinger, U. M., & Kunzmann, U. (2005). *Adult personality development: Adjustment and/or growth?* Manuscript submitted for publication.

Staudinger, U. M., & Pasupathi, M. (2000). Life-span perspectives on self, personality, and social cognition. In F. I. Craik & T. A. Salthouse (Eds.), *The handbook of aging and cognition* (2nd ed., pp. 633–688). Mahwah, NJ: Erlbaum.

Staudinger, U. M., & Schindler, I. (2005). *Personal life investment: A window on developmental tasks and adaptation.* Manuscript in preparation.

Staudinger, U. M., Smith, J., & Baltes, P. B. (1994). *Manual for the assessment of wisdom-related knowledge.* Berlin, Germany: Max-Planck-Institut für Bildungsforschung.

Sternberg, R. J. (1998). A balance theory of wisdom. *Review of General Psychology, 2,* 347–365.

Stewart, A. J., & Ostrove, J. M. (1998). Women's personality in middle age. Gender, history, and midcourse corrections. *American Psychologist, 53,* 1185–1194.

Stewart, A. J., & Vandewater, E. A. (1998). The course of generativity. In D. P. McAdams & E. de St. Aubin (Eds.), *Generativity and adult development. How and why we care for the next generation* (pp. 75–100). Washington, DC: American Psychological Association.

Triandis, H. C. (2004). Dimensions of culture beyond Hofstede. In H. Vinken, J. Soerters, & P. Ester (Eds.), *Comparing cultures. Dimensions of culture in a comparative perspective* (pp. 28–42). Leide, Netherlands: Koninklijke Brill NV.

Whitbourne, S. K., Zuschlag, M. K., Elliot, L. B., & Waterman, A. S. (1992). Psychosocial development in adulthood: A 22-year sequential study. *Journal of Personality and Social Psychology, 63,* 260–271.

Wink, P., & Helson, R. (1993). Personality change in women and their partners. *Journal of Personality and Social Psychology, 65,* 597–605.

Zucker, A. N., Ostrove, J. M., & Stewart, A. J. (2002). College-educated women's personality development in adulthood: Perceptions and age differences. *Psychology and Aging, 17,* 236–244.

Ten

Middle Age and Identity in a Cultural and Lifespan Perspective

Freya Dittmann-Kohli

M idlife research requires a multilevel and a multidisciplinary approach. The multilevel perspective implies the integration of concepts and findings from various interfaced and embedded disciplines. They reach from the neurological science and biology to the ecological approach of viewing individuals in a microsystem environment being part of mesosystems and macrosystems. The macrosystems on a national level are part of larger cultural and more global systems up to the planetary system and the historical context of individual and social evolution. The cognitive framework used to look at midlife is in this perspective necessarily also interdisciplinary, because social, cultural, behavioral, natural, and medical research covers phenomena on different levels. Sociology overlaps with the psychological sphere; psychology overlaps with sociology and anthropology, as well as with biological, medical, and neurological issues. The individual as an organism and member of society can be seen to be situated on the middle level, being determined by component and environmental factors, processes, and structures (see Settersten, 1999).

Using these and other scientific approaches, a particular position concerning the nature and problem of middle age will figure as the blueprint behind the various themes and observations presented in the following paragraphs.

Staudinger and Bluck (2001; see also many other lifespan publications they cite) have presented a lifespan approach for middle age that incorporates the multiple factors and approaches sketched above. The main point they make is the dependence of the nature and meaning of middle age on its location in space and time. In other words, types of life in the middle years, as well as the subjective meaning of self and life in middle age, depend on its context. This context dependence also holds for the individuals' identity and self-understanding, because self-conceptualizations reflect the individual's understanding of body and mind, as well as the individual's understanding of person-context interactions. This process of understanding occurs through the filter of categories and models adopted from the environment starting at birth (or earlier). Cultural categories provide filters and programs for overt behavior, cognition, feelings, and evaluation. Cultural categories and the social environment direct the process of applying sociocultural learning to our own individual case. The above observations must remain cursory because their function is to activate more or less general knowledge on the topic.

The implications of these observations are quite specific for middle age. In spite of their stress on context dependence, Staudinger and Bluck maintain that gains start to decline in the beginning of the midlife phase at around 40 years. However, whether gains or losses, or a mix of both, characterize this period, depends on the cultural patterns for the life course. It has been rather common, and still is in some parts of the world, that adolescence and young adulthood are a time of deficit, because it is considered as incomplete, as inferior to the mature adult, and as subject to the wishes and commands of those who are older. Young women in particular are subjected to extensive suffering first and get their rewards in midlife.

I shall report some anthropological examples where the sequences of gains and losses are in reverse of our Western ones. Even in the Western sphere, late midlife and early old age may be more gainful than earlier life periods, depending on individual fate and historical events. Sometimes, even a loss of resources may be beneficial, depending on whether resources are perceived as objective control over socially valued materials and goods, or as control over immaterial, subjectively valued goods, such as time, a very simple and modest life, and freedom from obligations. The perception of what constitutes a satisfactory life may vary strongly between cultures.

The implication from the context dependency of the nature and meaning of middle age is therefore that psychological findings from one culture cannot be easily generalized. Research done in the Western world cannot be generalized to traditional life in India or Africa; neither can observations from tribal Africa, from traditional Afghanistan, Iraq, Iran, or other non-Westernized countries in the world be interpreted based on findings about the Western world. How far generalizations of findings in the United States can be applied to European countries, or to countries in North, East, Middle, and Southern Europe, is also unclear. The new task for psychological theory and research will be the development of conceptualizations for the region of validity and the boundaries of our findings. Unfortunately, the cultural limits of our psychological theories are not clear-cut and simple, are not the same for different kinds of variables, and do not simply coincide with countries, cultures, or continents in their historical times. This seemingly unending variability is a problem for research, of course. Therefore, new concepts and models have to be developed in order to avoid the conclusion that everything can vary always and no generalizations are possible. Because of our changing global world, we must start to gain insight into the laws of cultural assimilation and global exchange and influences. About three decades ago, for instance, the cultural and psychological differences between modern Western and developing countries attracted research that has since become more or less unknown. In the future, the culture clash between the Western and the Islamic worlds will probably attract much attention.

In spite of all that cultural relativism, it is necessary to use our own Western scientific framework and our own experiential worlds if we want to be able to talk about middle age. It is necessary to use our own cultural categories and scientific language to encode what is to be said. In this code, we can describe conceptualizations (social constructions) and findings from various cultural regions, including our own, and from various temporal "spaces" in the past, the present, and the future. That does not keep us from striving to be open and preventing ethnocentrism. Of course, we also have to use our Western type of middle age as a point of departure in thinking about the lives of people in middle age elsewhere in space and time. This Western type of middle age is what we experience or observe ourselves.

Psychological findings on the life span periods have been heavily influenced by conditions, conceptualizations, and scientific results from the United States. Unless there is comparative research on the differences and similarities between Europe and North America on all levels and variables, we have only impressionistic sensations about what these differences might be. One such impression is that the consumerism, education, technology, knowledge society, and other communalities of the modern world make more similarities than differences. Intra-European comparisons between East and West Germany and the Netherlands revealed significant differences in the general decline of the basic orientations of individuality and relatedness, but few differences were found in a broad category of "physical integrity" (Bode, 2003; Dittmann-Kohli, Bode, & Westerhof, 2001; Mahler, 2004). Only on a second, more differentiated level of response categories were significant differences found in physical integrity (i.e., health and general functioning).

In this chapter, the concentration on American data will be balanced by a stronger focus on European research, and also to a greater extent than is usual, non-Western research will be cited. In the latter case, psychological but mostly anthropological materials and perspectives will obtain attention. Middle age is the period that anthropologists have most often attended to when they want to characterize a culture, so the database is relatively rich.

The Midlife Period in Western and Global Perspective

Definitions of midlife depend on particular historical and social settings. Therefore, distant cultural, historical, and societal settings regarding midlife, as well as our own modern Western version, will be mentioned. Of course, psychological theory and empirical research are a response to and a part of our own social-cultural characteristics, produced to a large extent by middle-aged scientists in their own middle-aged worlds, and influencing the younger scientists by their own self- and world-understanding.

From a lifespan theory perspective, it is important to tie features of life stages to their context. For instance, lack of survival resources (through war, climate, subsistence-level economy, AIDS) can render middle age, as we understand it at present, very short or even non-existent in large groups of individuals. In prehistoric times, few people survived our present young adulthood.

From a Western scientific and everyday understanding, middle age is defined and delineated as an age period following young (and mature) adulthood and preceding (very) old age. A stage of life is thought to have comparatively similar life circumstances (or at least a regular change) for the average person, so that coping and life management are similar for those within the same age group. Our present Western life-course concept includes infancy, childhood and adolescence, youth, young and mature adulthood, middle age, and old age.

There are no clear biological or functional factors enforcing a particular delimitation of the midlife period. For practical purposes, middle age is here defined as the period from age 40 to age 70. The choice of these ages reflects the practical decision made by two research teams in relation to a sociopsychological and sociocultural conceptualization of middle age in Germany and the Netherlands. This decision had to be made with regard to the planning and implementation of the German Aging Survey, which was carried out by a sociological research group in Berlin Forschungsgruppe Altern und Lebenslauf (FALL; Research Group on Aging and the Life Course) and a psychological research team in Nijmegen.

Independent from our modern age definitions, midlife can be generally thought of as a taking-off point for late life and as the end point of being young or of being in early adulthood. In a mundane perspective, the term "middle age" is a friendly expression for being not young anymore but not really very old yet, since "old" will include some frailty. Frailty is defined as the Fourth Age, the time when we need increased support from others in order to survive in style. Middle age (or midlife) is the Third Age when people in the Western world are living autonomously and self-determined. This Third Age is separated into two periods because of the characteristics of the "institutionalization of the life course" in Western countries (Kohli, 1985). In the case of middle age, the division of this period derives from the regulations of the work life in national economies. In all the modern Western countries, retirement is regulated by national laws, varying around the age of 65. At present, early retirement schemes and other regulations also allow early retirement or part-time work until the legal retirement age of 65 years. Because of economic problems with the welfare state, the discussion about having to work beyond the age of 65 is underway in many European countries. Until they retire, employed and self-employed people have to function as "active adults"; they have middle adult roles in work, family, community, and organized activities on a regional, national, or international level. With retirement, some roles are lost, but there is more freedom of choice for other tasks and roles, at least until one becomes severely limited through illness or other malfunctions. Some persons stay "middle-aged" much longer than 70 and seem to age only in their late 80s or early 90s. Thus, we shall differentiate between early and later middle age, because the life structure and the functional characteristics of these periods are separated by a slow or sudden transition from work to retirement.

It is evident that intrasocietal variations in the character and shape of life in middle age are common. In particular, gender plays a role here, so that in many respects early and late middle-aged men and women have different life circumstances and concerns. In addition, regional differences and economic status are of importance in Europe, and urban-rural and other factors also affect lifestyle. Parallel to the differences in life context and midlife lifestyle within societies, intrapersonal differences in the natural aging trajectories are well known to gerontologists and life span psychologists. This is the reason for the existence of an intrapersonal differentiation in functions of middle-aged men and women. In particular, physical aging can limit sportive activities while mental potentials unfold and grow.

Non-Western and Traditional Perspectives on Middle Age

The middle-age period in modern industrialized societies comprises the great majority of people in adulthood; historically, longevity is a recent phenomenon. Before modern civilization, medicine, and the welfare state, the midlife period was often the end of life, and many women, soldiers, and unlucky young men died in young adulthood. Those who survived and could accumulate material resources and social power tended to be on top of the hierarchy. Social power tended to rest with males (Borscheid, 1987). Nevertheless, midlife and old age were well represented in ideas about the life course even in the early Middle Ages (Dittmann-Kohli, 1987). The medieval conceptions of the cycle of the seasons, of the staircase of life, and so forth, drew on the cultural basis of ancient Greece and Rome, where life stages were also recognized (Burrow, 1986).

The status and well-being of the rich and powerful, on the one hand, and the old and frail, on the other, were very different in the European historical past and in many traditional societies. A historical study of aging in Europe gives ample evidence for the disadvantaged status of poor and powerless elderly. From the 14th to the 16th centuries, middle age was always located on the highest step of the staircase of life, while (very) old age was put on the same level as powerless and vulnerable children. Only with the mental development in the beginning of the era of Enlightenment, did empathy and care as an attitude toward the frail become more widespread in the general population. In the 18th and 19th centuries, civilization would include the conviction of the necessity of general support for the weakest. Middle age, however, was the time when resources had been accumulated, and respect and power in material, familial, and societal domains were highest.

From these observations it is legitimate to ask: Does middle age exist in all societies where people live beyond the onset and predominance of biological maturity? How common are psychological characteristics of middle-aged adults, such as superior knowledge, mental and emotional maturity, social status and responsibility? Are large parts or even the majority of the population in societies regularly excluded from having a normal midlife?

The richly documented ancient civilizations and democracies in Greek and Roman times show that middle-aged adults were similar in mental and motivational potential to modern Westerners. However, it is also clear that these persons represented a minority, while the majority were slaves and poor people who had no right to participate in civil society functions and often not even in family functions.

Costa et al. (2000) maintain that there are anthropological constants for middle age in societies who are beyond the barest subsistence level. In their view, middle age has (near-) universal developmental and psychosocial tasks: completing procreation, caring for the young adult children and grandchildren, continuing work as seniors and possibly as experts, representing personhood and lifestyles after the romantic and early career period. The accumulation of power and means of production allows this age group to acquire and entertain a (large) family and homestead. In their cross-cultural research, Costa et al. find evidence of changes in the mean level of personality traits. The authors think that these are in line with the requirements of societies and the functions their members fulfill while they have needed biological capacities (e.g., as warrior, for child bearing).

In traditional non-industrialized societies, our modern midlife equals the group usually called the "elderly." This group had passed young adulthood, had wives, and usually had grown-up children. Power and leadership usually correlated with authority and wealth. Religious and ritual power was mostly associated, and often competence and character made them the natural people to turn to. In traditional tribal societies, social, cultural, and religious tasks and roles were defined according to biological developmental states of individuals and in line with ecological preconditions. The rules for conduct, tasks, and roles centered on physical and mental potentials of gender, age, birth order, and age-related biological states.

The tribal society of the Luo (Dittmann, 1973, 1974) was made up of semi-nomadic herders and resided originally in southern Sudan before entering Kenya and settling around Lake Victoria. Their social structure and life course followed a pattern quite typical in traditional Africa. Middle adulthood was characterized, in the case of men with wives, children, and grandchildren, by leadership of the extended family. The authority was coupled with seniority; in childhood and adulthood, younger members were obliged to show deference and obedience to older ones. The extended family lived together in a compound where each woman and her children had their own hut. There were no possibilities in adulthood for self-determined behavior. Instead, behavior was regulated by tradition, social control, and fear of punishment from the elderly or magic.

The leading elder was bound by religion and tradition to direct the seasonal activities needed for their subsistence economy, and his task was to solve the many social conflicts. The middle-aged men under him had to do certain types of work that allowed their women to feed their families. Beyond that, they were busy with political and interpersonal networking and religious duties. Women had to work the land and bear children and were visited by their husbands. Everybody was completely dependent on proper integration into the clan and family; any action needed the consent of the group. Non-married men had a low status in the compound, and an even lower one when they joined other families. In modern Africa, many of the traditional structures of identity and society have been destroyed by urbanization, economic modernization, education, Christianization, or AIDS. Nevertheless, some of the older ideas on the life span and the meaning of time had been preserved in young people at least until the 1970s (Dittmann, 1973).

Findings from anthropological research are complemented by current public media reports on midlife and other age groups. Examples from the daily news and television documentaries abound: Muslim women, refugees in Darfur and other African regions, fighters in Palestine, asylum seekers in Europe, and so forth. These examples demonstrate that normal midlife functions and life conditions are denied to many; they are denied chances to grow and to acquire ability for functioning at higher levels of competence. Two additional examples of how midlife is conceptualized in non-Western cultures, and how this affects middle adult identity, are presented below.

Samoa

Shore (1998, p. 132) collected empirical data in Samoa in order to determine the characteristics of different stages of life. His data are based on questionnaires and other instruments used with a cross-section of male and female villagers. Associations with adult life were similar in two surveys. Middle-aged Samoans were seen as hard-working, respected, self-controlled, responsible, and active. "In middle age, people are both politically powerful and physically active. It is in middle age that the two axes of power come together for Samoans in a way that is true for no other status. From a cultural perspective, Samoan life suggests no crisis; rather it offers an intersection of 'powers' that no other stage of life unites in the same way" (Shore, 1998, p. 132). Of course, as in other traditional societies, there were gender differences. The male status was that of active power; the female status was connected to passive power. Furthermore, Samoan aging is not simply understood as a trajectory of physical aging and the loss of young adult vitality. Rather, in Samoa, middle adulthood is the period where activity and passive power converge, which is seen as a privileged place in society. Aging as a loss of youth is not given any importance in cultural representations and models in Samoa. Shore also points out, however, that through the process of modernization and emigration, the relative position of power and social respect have been changing toward the Western patterns.

India

Kakar (1998) presents his findings about middle age in Hindu India. In the standard Hindu dictionary, the term *adher* for middle age stands for declining years (Kakar, p. 76). In religious images, a decisive break in the mode of life can be found. The main component of the religious ideas for lifestyle is a withdrawal from family ties and family affairs that were typical of the previous stage, that of the "householder." Also, the renunciation of worldly concerns and pleasures is seen as desirable. This, however, is not without conflict, in particular for the rich and powerful. Kakar even suggests that there is a "midlife crisis" of renunciation versus worldly involvement.

Today, the middle-aged woman's role is defined by her role as mother-in-law, while the young married woman is the inferior to everybody in the family, especially to her mother-in-law. When a young woman marries, she passes from her parents to the house of her parents-in-law, where she is in the lowest position in her new family. Obedience and compliance with the wishes of the older women are imperative. Thus, marriage as a young adult is not a period of gains for these women, but rather a loss compared to her situation in her parents' house. As she becomes older, this situation changes gradually, but only when her adult children give birth to their own children will the status of the woman completely change (Menon & Shweder, 1998). The weak and vulnerable position of the young woman is in fact widespread in traditional societies. In Islamic and African societies, the place of a woman often becomes uncomfortable and disadvantaged when further wives are taken by the men. While men are gone from home because they work in distant places, the mother-in-law has control and may thoroughly restrict the freedom of her sons' wives.

There is a certain regularity in the former traditional societies and in the present-day traditional groups of societies that women only rise to their full adult status when they have reached a middle-aged status, and under bad conditions they never do. In that case, they are never given adult roles, autonomy, decision powers, knowledge, education, or the material resources to lead an independent life. Traditional religions tend to keep this power differential of men and women in place.

One other feature of the relationship between society and the midlife period needs to be stressed. Highly developed civilizations such as China, India, Japan, ancient Egypt, Greece, and Rome have known social structures providing for many differentiated social positions for middle-aged adults. Middle-aged adults filled many or most of the main roles of those societies. While military service required muscle strength, military and political strategies demanded intelligence, experience, authority, and leadership of a certain type. There were young leaders, but more often they must have been middle-aged. Corresponding to a system's stability, traditional civilizations put a premium on conventional identities and institutionalized selves, transmitted over many generations, as in the case of collective and rule-oriented civil servants in ancient Egypt. In times of turmoil and rapid change, the orderly transmission of identities may have been interrupted as well, and the role of corruption and Machiavellianism was also recognized. Middle adulthood has been strongly tied to the roles defined within a system, but individual personalities could also unfold. In this respect, the difference between old and new civilization is not so strong. In regard to middle adulthood, the discrepancy between modern Western and ancient civilizations lies perhaps in the extent of democracy and equality among the members of society. The interindividual differences in living standards, hardship, mental potentials, personal freedom, lifestyle, and so forth, of the poor and rich are not as extreme in modern as in traditional civilizations.

Modern Societies and Late Midlife Personhood

It is admittedly not comfortable to make sweeping generalizations about tribal societies, ancient civilizations, and modern Western countries, but it is the only way to direct the reader's attention to the societal frameworks and cultural factors that are so important in defining middle age. In speaking about modern society, I have in mind the countries of Europe and North America, and, in a way, the prototypical middle adult person. The borders are fuzzy, and the generalizations are "typifications" (Holstein & Gubrium, 2000). However, the differences in lifestyle, role embeddedness, and identity in early and late middle adulthood are well documented, mainly because the idea of a relative retreat from some roles and activities is widespread. This discrimination was already known and practiced in older societies that had no modern pension system and had to organize a shift in the leadership of households and the larger cultural and economic groups. In the modern context, this is leadership and decision-making in family and paid work. Late middle adulthood is thus characterized by a certain amount of detachment from societal duties while still having access to external resources, a comfortable life, a certain amount of power, and mental and physical potentials.

In our present, relatively rich economic situation, many persons with adequate educational, financial, and social resources, as well as good health and expertise, are entering late middle adulthood without much knowledge about how to use their internal and external resources for something other than their own enjoyment. In the last half century, historical conditions were such that many men and women could develop their intelligence and acquire extensive knowledge as well as emotional-affective resources, creative and productive abilities, and motivational energy. "Psycho-talk" has spread, so that conscious knowledge about inner functioning, such as how to combine productive activities with rewards and satisfaction, is available for the intentional planning of new activities. Here, knowledge about aging processes is also helpful in order to take the onset of physical and cognitive limitations into account, while taking maximum advantage of the rich potentials accumulating throughout life. These are mature emotional and social behaviors, intelligence and expertise in certain domains, a heightened level of general world knowledge and of private life management knowledge. Globalization and higher education make late middle age into a new period of life, filled with potential for life fulfillment and new meaning, beyond the ties of work and family roles enforced by early chosen pathways. For many, late life freedom has become an additional, new stage of life that calls for a new design for the self and its role in the world. It is also a new life task, compared to the earlier generation, and it is a social and political task for the future, where lifespan psychologists have a central role in understanding human resources and in "social design."

Such a social-design function is a correlate and an outcome, not only of the individualized and global culture, but also more directly of the growth in psychological knowledge about abilities for intentional self-development and intentional action, which in turn is dependent on the type of personhood defined as being mature and ideal in a culture. Openness and flexibility of self to ideas and change are factors in self-development. However, there is also useful knowledge about the workings of the brain in relation to emotion, behavior, thinking, and self-awareness, in order to understand how one can change oneself and how not. For instance, Goschke (2004), in a synthesis of many research areas, describes the levels and aspects of free will and intentionality. Insight into neurological and psychological mechanisms may prevent us from investing much effort on self-change where it is hardly possible, and concentrate instead on those aspects of thought and action where success is more likely.

Another area of useful knowledge for late middle adulthood is private life management. Such knowledge would include understanding of causes, consequences, and situations, as well as procedural knowledge, involving lines and sequences of (inductive) thinking, problem solving, decision-making, strategies, and tactics. Understanding situations covers knowing about the important features of important settings and devices for life management activities and resources, such as societal requirements and regulations for dealing with money, marriage, transportation, and other things about our way of life. These requirements for life management are rather complex in our modern world. For early middle adulthood, complexity for personal life management often is high for those who want to combine work and family, as well as strive for social success and security. When the goals and tasks attempted by individuals in late middle adulthood are too demanding, and are coupled with high ambitions regarding the social, professional, artistic, or political value of the output or the problem solved, the resources of the organism and its changing potential may be overtaxed. Prolonged stress may be the result, with the consequences of heart attacks or other threatening conditions.

Thus it would seem that there are two sides of knowledge and understanding for successful self- and life management. As I shall demonstrate, self-knowledge in the narrower sense and self-in-world knowledge are both part of what people have in mind when they are asked to describe themselves.

In modern societies, there is often high developmental potential in the second part of middle adulthood, but only few settings that allow use of the increased, cumulated knowledge, such as emotional and social intelligence, interpersonal skills, occupational wisdom and knowledge, familiarity with books and documents from past and present, or global insights and humanistic orientation, cultures, the human factor, and the combination of inner understanding and universal context.

Another important point is that social role structures activities and social participation. Knowledge and skills without a setting for their application may be fulfilling for its owner but cannot be transmitted or applied. As was proposed before, society is a major factor in the "formatting" of adults' ways of life, as well as of their knowledge and dispositions. Midlife persons have specialized fields of work and other activities, embedded in particular work environments and social settings, on particular socioeconomic levels, within certain cultural and subcultural systems. They have acquired and accumulated knowledge and expertise during their first half of life to enact their roles in their second half of life during early middle adulthood. In their 40s and 50s, they have reached their final pathways in work organizations and communal systems. In their 60s, however, these old pathways become closed. Most people realize that toward the end of their own or their husbands' or wives' working lives, a period of mental orientation occurs that allows for thoughts about possible selves in a stage following the end of the regulation of daily life through work. It involves the realization that late middle adulthood is arriving with a change of lifestyle: a new beginning that will require a reorganization of everyday life and a new exploration of settings that allow for personal expression of needs, goals, and desires.

One of the major societal tasks for the future of a society whose members live ever-longer lives is to provide fields of activity and settings to use acquired potentials. The size of this task has not been recognized by scientists, politicians, the media, and the economic system. Unemployment of midlife persons, or forced early retirement, is robbing society of the creativity and productivity of a human potential of great worth.

The Modern Self

Is the human self a potential of the human brain that is largely genetically determined in its structure and content, or is there a modern self that is completely different from that of prehistoric people, early historic people, or tribal, traditional, or conventional selves or identities?

The term "self" refers to a being that has ego awareness, but this ego awareness is part of an organism that has many features of which there is no awareness. The latter comprise not only the workings of the body, but also the working of our minds and many aspects of our personalities (Goschke, 2004; Roth, 2001). At the same time, a number of brain structures create the possibility of certain types of self-conceptualizations to develop in human beings. For instance, feedback systems for body movement, location, temperature, physical stresses, and so forth, allow for a rudimentary self-concept, as well as the possibility of our autonoetic and autobiographical memories, which create the experience of an enduring person with both stability and change. Biological evolution has slowly shaped our animal brain, and self-awareness is said to be closely related to social functioning (Sedikides & Skowronski, 1997). The earliest date at which artistic production is known to have taken place is 70,000 years ago. On the other hand, it is also clear that the rudimentary genetic features of the brain determining the direction of self-development can be shaped by learning in very different ways, and that thousands of years of cultural development and social learning have preceded the "formatting" of the modern self in modern men and women (for details, see Dittmann-Kohli, in press-a, in press-b). The cultural and historical evolution of the basic cognitive-affective structures of modern selfhood has certainly been different in different parts of the world. The Western modern self can be delineated back to the ancient Greek and Roman culture and seems to have been established around the time of early Christianity (Vroon, 1978). Authors such as Augustine and Seneca have provided us with texts of elaborate personal individuality (in relation to God) and of sophisticated reflections about the lifestyle of (rich) elderly citizens striving for continued self-realization. Further historical evolution of the mind has resulted from the cultural transmission of ideas during the last two millennia, but a decisive increase in this development of cultural knowledge has occurred in the last few centuries. What has been discovered and accumulated on inner experiences and reflections on personhood has been disseminated through writing, verbal communication, pictures, cross-cultural assimilation, and so forth. There were formations and discoveries related to Christian practices in the sense of a self-technology, but there were also periods of decline of reflexive self-awareness, for example, when survival was more important during times of war.

Turning back to ontogenetic development, neurological research has established that cultural and environmental learning does create enduring neurological structures in an organism, and that these structures are the foundations (and provide the limitations) for later learning and change in (middle) adulthood. These foundations may, in the case of traditional societies and groups, and in the case of fundamentalist religions, prevent much change in self-awareness and in self-directed change in early and late middle adulthood. In other cases, growing up under other conditions, it may just result in a flexible self ready to try out and take on all sorts of different self-ways.

Veroff (1983; see also Veroff & Smith, 1985) has provided important empirical evidence about the considerable amount of change in personal meanings, needs, aspirations and standards in work motivation, self-evaluation, and the openness toward and handling of personal difficulties. Using the same questionnaires 20 years apart, he and his colleagues established this evidence through representative national surveys. They found that mental outlook and motivational cognitions changed thoroughly in the U.S. within 20 years, quite in contrast to earlier assumptions about the stability of the achievement and affiliation motive. The amount of social change and change in mentality may be similar in Europe, but it may be very different in different regions and historical periods. Thus, while West Germany followed its established direction of change, East Germans had to reorient after reunification. At present, students in Southern Europe are in the course of changing from traditional rural Catholic identity to modern urban, mundane, and flexible selves. In two or three generations, women changed from uneducated, dependent marriage partners to independent, productive career women with modern outlooks, for instance regarding equality between men and women.

Determinants and Features of Modern Selves and Identities

Can we use psychological knowledge about development of body and mind in middle adulthood to make certain assumptions about the modern self during that period of life? Self-awareness has been defined as "self-focus and identity recognition" (Hart & Fegley, 1997). The experience of getting older should produce a sediment of self-awareness that internalizes one's cultural models and social representations about this and use it to code (new) individual self-observations and accumulated self-understanding.

Because identity includes adult roles, and self-focus may be stimulated through some kinds of life events, self-awareness and self-knowledge should have a different content in midlife than that in childhood and young adulthood. For instance, certain types of frustrations and failures in work and family must produce something different in the adult identity than in youth and, by this definition, are specific to middle adulthood. Also, social comparisons of achievement with one's own children and younger colleagues are not typical for young adulthood but for the middle-age period. Certain biological changes of aging around midlife affect competencies and potentials that interfere directly with the execution of plans and duties. This creates the difficult task of identity reconstruction. It demands much attention and effort to establish a new self-concept of one's abilities and to redefine personal goals and aspirations.

Models of lifespan adaptation and aging, such as Selective Optimization with Compensation (SOC), and the shift from primary to secondary control, do predict the occurrence of such changes, but do not specify the experience of change and adaptation. To derive hypotheses about how self-reports should differ between age groups, it is easier to look at life tasks and life situations in a country or group.

Cultures that stress chronological age as markers of life periods have a different effect on self-construction as a lifespan construct than cultures that have largely age-indifferent regulations of the adult life course. The latter implies that age plays only a minor role in the allocation of roles, duties, rights, and expectations toward the individual's behavior. In cultures in which social roles instead of age norms define women's personhood and selfhood, the consequences for identity are that the self-concept is not centered on chronological age and fears about looking old in midlife but on the life tasks, social relations, and obligations connected to their designated roles. Because biological aging within the hormonal system is accompanied by decline in aggression and sexuality, mental maturity and religious achievement was thought to be an easy task of midlife in medieval monks (Burrow, 1986; Dittmann-Kohli, 1986). Even today in Western countries, mental development—wisdom, maturity, full deployment of awareness, and individuality in midlife—is expected to be associated more with the second half of life (Dittmann-Kohli, 1984).

Within modern, Western societies, there are certain sociostructural differences in the life course related to social class, education, occupation, and gender (Dittmann-Kohli, Bode, & Westerhof, 2001). The social identities (roles and group memberships) in midlife are bound to what sociologists call "the active age" regarding work and family, where gender roles and activities are devised by society and biology. Modern society has dissolved age-related expectations and has strongly influenced the definition of these roles especially for women. Though the obligation to have children is no longer felt, the orientation of women toward social relations and partnership is still different from that of men (Bode, 2003). Apart from the role identities and interpersonal aspects of self-conceptualization, there is also the experience of ongoing daily life, of the appearance and sensations of the body, and of the mind's stream-of-consciousness. In spite of its change with aging, the body is also a continual and central part of experiencing oneself, so that it should enter one's self-knowledge and identity more strongly when more is experienced with it.

McAdams (1996) has delineated a conceptualization of narrative identity that is suited to determine a method as well as a scientific construct of the self, incorporating the experiences of body and mind, environment and change. All of these are constructed and interpreted within a culturally formatted narrative identity. Narrative identity is the representation of the story of the self, the ordered story lines of events and processes representing selfhood in a temporal perspective of the life span. Method and results of empirical research on the modern self using a specific instrument to assess the narrative self are described as follows.

* * *

Empirical Findings

In the following sections, results from various studies on aspects of identity will be presented. These studies use narrative data collected with low-structured sentence stems, allowing for self-reports and statements similar to everyday communications. This type of data is different from questionnaires that provide reactive judgments, but there is a specific profile of divergence and similarities in findings (Dittmann-Kohli, Bode, & Westerhof, 2001). Most of the studies cited in the following have been part of the research program on identity and personal meaning representing the psychological part of the German Aging Survey (Dittmann-Kohli et al., 2001). An earlier study (Dittmann-Kohli, 1995) comparing 300 young (17–25 years) and 300 elderly (60–90, average 74) adults and several smaller (cross-cultural) studies with the same instrument (and fewer items) provided the point of departure for planning the psychological part of the German Aging Survey, which investigates in detail the second half of life. Spontaneous responses and standardized instruments about self and life of nearly 3,000 men and women from East and West Germany provided us with their own view of selfhood and its relation to other psychological and demographic variables.

Features of Narrative
Self-Reports and Life Reports

The Growth of the Existential Self

One characteristic of midlife is the emerging perception of oneself as having a temporary existence and being dependent on one's body. From early to late midlife, these physical and temporal aspects of identity (i.e., the existential self) are growing in personal significance; that is, these aspects become more frequent in thoughts, feeling content, and self-narratives.

The Physical Self

Two of the five dimensions Améry (1968) used in his essay on the experience of aging in present society deal with these aspects of identity in early and late midlife. The first dimension subsumes time-bound existence and the passing of time. The second dimension deals with observations about how physical aging leads to gradual estrangement from the body and its appearance.

Empirical data in age-comparative studies (young and elderly adults) and in a national representative survey (age 40–85) show large differences in frequencies of spontaneous self-reports on health, illness, and psychophysical functioning in early and late adulthood and between three age groups over the second half of life (Kuin, Westerhof, Dittmann-Kohli, & Gerritsen, 2001; Westerhof, Kuin, & Dittmann-Kohli, 1998). These findings are in line with other studies in Europe and North America and are paralleled by biological and medical findings. The physical self is related to the task of adaptation to biological aging. Bode (2001b) found consistent age-related changes of responses to the loss of competence showing that the two middle-aged groups (40–54, 55–69 years) reported more active coping strategies than the elderly from 70 to 85 years. Compensation potentials in case of ability decline were viewed differently by men and women.

From the beginning to the end of the midlife period, biological aging is experienced more strongly and more frequently. Cross-sectional studies show that health-related hopes and concerns increase steadily with age. This suggests that cohort differences regarding the physical self are not a prominent factor in the last half century. Our research on self-narratives shows that hope for good and prolonged health, fear of illness, and many specific features of psychophysical functioning are strong in early middle age and increase in late middle age. They continue to become an even more central facet of personal identity in late old age (70–85). In contrast to the second half of life, the meaning of the body seems radically different for young adults (Dittmann-Kohli, 1995), both in the aspects, functions, and assets mentioned and in the frequency and tone of references to physical integrity. The vast qualitative and quantitative differences in the experience of the body and its needs and functions found between young adulthood and old age, however, are largely reduced quantitative differences between early and late middle age. The difference between midlife and old age is again mostly quantitative.

Sex and romantic events are of great importance in late adolescence and young adulthood but are hardly mentioned in midlife and old age self-narratives. This probably does not mean that sex and love have disappeared but indicates the operation of social norms. Soekar (2000) coded the answers to one sentence stem reading "My body. . . ." She compared the answers of 450 young adults (18–25 years) with a middle-aged group

(40–60 years, N = 470) and 483 late middle-aged and elderly (61–85 years). She found that the main shift in the quality of body identity takes place in the period between young and early middle adulthood. Young and middle-aged adults differed significantly on six categories that indicated more concern over health and physical functioning in the middle-aged group and on statements of satisfaction with and importance of the body in the young adult group. We can thus ascertain that the radical qualitative differences in body identity observed between young and elderly adults do start before the age of 40 and continue to gain in centrality at least until age 85. From further analyses within the German Aging Survey, we also know that hopes and concerns for physical integrity (the content categories of health, illness, and psychophysical functioning) are not concentrated in only a few individuals and one or two items, but are spread out over people as well as over type of semantic reference of the sentence stem as well as in instruments with closed answers.

Biological aging affecting appearance and good looks is a theme for middle-aged adults but refers to different standards of evaluation and comparison groups. The social representations and cultural models for the body in Western culture are strongly affected by the market economy (Biggs, 1999), and the stress of looking young is more problematic for middle-aged women than men, who tend to be more satisfied with their looks. There is no sex difference, though, in concerns for health and functioning. In late old age, the question of not looking young any more is usually decided, but between age 40 and 60, or longer, women may be torn between still feeling and looking young or not (Dittmann-Kohli, 1995; Jaeggi, 1996). In the world of mass media, women are mostly in their first half of life, while middle-aged men are seen as "interesting" and attractive because of social status and other resources. Body appearance is thus an aspect of physical and social identity.

That physical integrity and its threat from biological aging is considered the main component of the process of individual aging is also corroborated by the content analysis of close to 6,000 statements responding to two sentence stems on what is positive and negative about aging. The frequencies for the category "physical integrity" are much higher than those for any other type of response to the item "what I do not like about aging . . . ," while it does not occur in the case of what is liked about aging. What is mainly liked about aging is freedom, own decision-making, and lack of unrest. Steverink and Timmer (2001) present further proof of the strong role of physical aspects of identity in middle and late adulthood by means of a closed instrument on the personal meaning of aging. They found three dimensions of aging; psychophysical decline and personal growth in abilities and activities had the highest scores, socioemotional disadvantages had somewhat lower scores. Over six age groups, the scores of psychophysical decline and socioemotional drawbacks increased in regular steps from age 40 to 85, while the opposite was true for personal growth.

References to Self-Concept Composition and Lifestyle Characteristics

Many aging-related variables concerning the body increase continuously from early midlife to late adulthood, but no salient, sudden turns were observed. Rather, in using different variables and combinations of variables, as well as different sections of age groups, all point to a gradual increase in centrality of body awareness and awareness of biological change. The contrary finding was made in regard to other meaning domains of the self, for instance, the psychological self and life satisfaction. Gerritsen, Bode, and Dittmann-Kohli (2001) found a decrease in the amount of personality traits mentioned in the super-category of the "psychological self," as well as a shift in the emotions and dispositions attributed to the self. In parallel to lifestyle preferences, the preferred quality of mood and emotion was found to be different in midlife and old age. The change in category frequency goes toward less agitated and more sedate, as evidenced by the frequent assertions of being content and satisfied. In her analysis of future personal projects, possible selves, and expectation of events, Timmer (2000) also found that rest and relaxation were significant goals. There were very few self-narrative statements about intention or desire for organized, voluntary activities after the early-midlife period, and even within this period the frequency dropped. Intended personal projects involved activities offering freedom of choice and self-enjoyment.

Qualitative lifestyle preferences were also observed in an investigation of self-reported well-being and life satisfaction (Westerhof, Dittmann-Kohli, & Bode, 2003). The level of well-being did not differ between early and late middle age and was not found to be lower in the oldest age group. However, the content of the judgment criteria changed significantly. In a similar way, the criteria of self-evaluation showed qualitative age-dependent shifts in response to a social comparison item. Thus, the preferred type of lifestyle and the criteria of self-evaluation were different between middle and old age but also between early and late middle age.

The Temporal Self

In this section, findings associated with the temporal aspects of identity and self are presented. One part of this section deals with linguistic expressions of temporal references within accounts about varied aspects of self and life. A second part will deal with findings about the amount and content of statements about past life and future-directed anticipations of self and life. Both of these types of categories of narrative self-accounts can figure as markers or indicators of what Whitbourne (1985) termed "life span construct," which is similar to the "life span construct" studied by Holstein and Gubrium (2000) within their sociological constructivist approach. Another concept of relevance from the cognitive psychology tradition is "autonoetic memory" (Welzer & Markowitsch, 2001), which comprises the personal past and future perspective. Temporal identity (Dittmann-Kohli, in press-a, in press-b) is connected to the experience of moving through the life cycle and the knowledge of getting closer to frailty and death.

The findings reported so far derive from categories for self-narrative statements containing semantic content about the personal self and the self in relation to events or elements within the environment. In addition to these, time references appear within such statements. Temporal adverbs and other temporal terms (marking periods, age, etc.) locate situations, relationships, persons, and events within a dimension of time and change, such as continuation and non-continuation, decline or growth, time structures, and ordering of periods (Dittmann-Kohli, in press-a). Spontaneous time references were so far rarely used in research on self-narratives and identity because of the dominance of closed questionnaires. The latter provide conscious opinions, beliefs, and attitudes toward life time and time perspective, but are of questionable validity for the assessment of temporal aspects of identity. Open-ended instruments, however, show the inadvertent use of linguistic means indicating a person's implicit temporal frame of reference for (aspects of) self and life, so that the self-location on the life line, the direction of change, and the expectation of stability come to the fore.

Extensive analysis of time references found in young, middle-aged, and elderly adults shows that the second half of life is characterized by a steady increase in the use of linguistic temporal references, and that young adults use few of the markers of life period (being old, being of a certain age) and change typical of middle-aged and elderly adults, such as limited continuation, maintenance, and decline (Dittmann-Kohli, 2004). These markers appear in very large numbers and can be seen as indicators of an increasing time and change consciousness, such as self-awareness of position on the life line, of the time left to live, and of the past and future changes accompanying aging. In addition to the most numerous time concepts referring to limited continuity, continued gains, and decline, temporal terms referring to the loss of consciousness and other references to finitude were also found in late middle-age and old-age groups.

Autobiographical Memories and Reminiscence

The past self comprises all thoughts relating clearly to the biographical past of a person (Dittmann-Kohli, 1995; Dittmann-Kohli, in press-a). Midlife is the time when one's past is long, and a considerable part of life has materialized. Knowledge about what old age will be like also increases, as does the awareness that time and other resources for reaching important goals are shrinking faster. The findings comparing young adults and young old age show a lack of spontaneous references to the past life in young people but are very numerous in persons from 60 to 90 years (Dittmann-Kohli, in press-a). This is evidence for the significance of past identity in later life; that is, the self-concept includes the past events and processes of life. These events and processes can be understood as the remembered context and conditions to the development of present identity and selfhood. A separate analysis of the sentence stem "What I resent about my past life . . ." was performed on responses of nearly 4,000 people in Germany and the Netherlands in order to analyze retrospective cognitions about the perceived faults and the uncontrollable critical life events in former life (Timmer, Westerhof, & Dittmann-Kohli, in press). The early middle-aged adults used internal attributions as reasons for regrets three times more often, whereas the older persons gave external attributions three times more often. Women and persons from East Germany were also found to be more external in their regrets. This pattern of regret may reflect objective differences in freedom of choice in the war and postwar cohorts, in women, and in those who lived in Eastern Germany. Classified according to specific themes, the early middle-aged group specified by far the most regrets about their own faults and bad decisions, whereas the elderly (70–85) spoke more often about the hard times in their life than the other two groups. The two middle-aged groups more often reported missed educational opportunities, but there was no age difference for the category regrets about (missed) social relationships. The latter category appeared more often in responses from women, but the faults and wrong decisions appeared more in men's responses. In the Netherlands, social relationships and missed education are mentioned more often than in Germany.

Future Perspective

The future perspective is an important motivational and behavioral factor throughout the life span. In a separate analysis, Timmer (2000) investigated the content of the future goals and expectations of men and women in the German Aging Survey. Using six future-directed sentence stems, Timmer analyzed the answers to the SELE instrument in the German Aging Survey. It concerned somewhat less than 3,000 men and women from age 40 to 85. For purposes of more detailed analysis, not three but six age groups were compared.

The six future-directed sentence stems were coded in categories classifying the direction of motivational cognitions and the content within these directions. The frequencies were studied in relation to age group, demographic variables, and psychological scores. The answers in these six sentence stems uncovered a wide range of personal projects, possible selves, expectation of events, fears, hopes, and so forth with varying content. Age differences were found within and between early and late middle age, and between age groups older than that.

The frequencies of future-oriented cognitions of the lower (40–46) and the higher (47–54) subgroup of the early middle-age period indicate a shift from "very active middle age" (as would be expected for persons younger than 40) to characteristics of people somewhat closer to retirement. The youngest group (40–46) preferred statements in categories such as generativity and concerns with work and family, about needing some rest, about goals involving personal growth, and about external gains or change. Group two (47–54) mentioned retirement, traveling and future hobbies, physiological aging, and early death more often than the first group, but they also mentioned "young-profile themes" such as self-expansion and self-realization, interest in new experiences and learning, and desire for more awareness. Groups three (55–61) and four (62–69), both in the late middle-age period, provided even more characteristics related to desires and concerns about aging, such as plans for free time and retirement, worries about loneliness, old-age homes, dependency, possible decline, and hopes for preservation of health and psychophysical functioning. Few persons in Group four mentioned continuation of work, and a considerable number of people looked forward to the pleasures and projects open to the Third Age, such as travel. The 62 to 69 group voiced more fears about loneliness than any other of the six groups. Regarding late middle age, the adoption of meaning components representing an "old-age profile" of self and life progresses further toward the old age pattern.

From the age of 70 on, there seems to be a more outspoken differentiation in the "rate of aging." While a comparatively small group of elderly describe themselves in ways revealing vitality, there are many reflections of decline in bodily potentials. The elderly men and women of Group five (70–76 years) expected more aging problems and had fewer positive plans except for travel than Group four. Hopes and intentions to maintain personal features, lifestyle, and behavior were the highest of all groups; many elderly just want to continue life as it is at present. The oldest group (77–85 years) mentioned no thoughts about losses and few about old-age homes and aging problems but also gave the smallest number of goals and projects except understanding and living with full awareness. They expressed few expectations of positive events but satisfaction with the present and few fears except of mental decline and possibly needing full-time care. Overall, the future-directed self-reports show gradual increases in anticipating the process of aging from Group two to Group five. Only the youngest participants report themselves being "purely midlife," tending toward the "young age profile." After 45, thoughts about aging intrude more and more. Persons in the oldest group reflect a state of "being old" instead of getting old; they seem to have "renounced active life," as one would say in the Hindu world.

Context-Directed Meaning Domains

In contrast to interpersonal relations, the world of work has been neglected by psychologists; for that reason, I shall report more topics related to work identity and life at work than for interpersonal and social identity. Both topics, however, are dealt with extensively in Dittmann-Kohli et al. (2001).

Work Identity

For the majority of modern Western women and for nearly all men, work identity is a central aspect of life. It is generally observed that the second part of work life, for instance from age 40 to 65, is characterized by higher work satisfaction, positive work motivation, social and professional expertise, mature social work relations, and responsibility at work. The general adaptability, however, is seen as somewhat lower compared to that of younger workers (Dittmann-Kohli & van der Heijden, 1996; Dittmann-Kohli, Sowarka, & Timmer, 1997).

For men as well as women, work and career should provide the possibility to be productive and creative. This expectation emerged from a series of interviews students from Southern and Eastern European countries carried out on the topic of creativity and productivity of their middle-aged parents. It became also apparent how much young women in Southern European countries gained from their upward mobility compared to their mothers or grandmothers. In Eastern and Southern European countries, gender differences in the type of work identity were also evident, even if educational and professional levels were the same. In the students' extensive interviews, mothers' career identities were coupled with a strong family identity comprising their children and husbands. Men followed their career paths from a much greater psychological distance to the family.

People's sense of work identity (Gollwitzer & Kirchhof, 1998) may become threatened in early and late middle adulthood. On the one hand, competition for the best positions gets very intense in midlife when the chances for career success become fewer. In case of economic pressures, people in early middle age feel urged to get rid of or marginalize successful late middle-aged women and men in order to obtain higher positions. In addition, there is the threat of obsolescence to self-perceived competence in early and late middle age. Finally, innovations (e.g., new information technology) can be more quickly absorbed by younger than by older adults, and training often goes only to the young employees. Fierce competition may render the work environment full of stress, as is now the case in many European university systems and large firms. Late middle-aged men and women will rarely find a new position of a comparable quality (Dittmann-Kohli et al., 1997).

Under such circumstances, and because they are connected to private goals, self-definitional goals in the domain of work will affect self-esteem and life satisfaction. The threat of identity loss can thus be serious at a time when under different (better) circumstances one's feeling of competence, expertise, experience, social knowledge, and self-knowledge should be highest, and productivity could be high as well. Problems of work identity and productivity are expected to become a central focus of interest when older employees or self-employed professionals are expected to work longer than they do now. At present, the pre-pension system keeps relatively few people at work until 65 years.

Untrained workers versus professionals differ with respect to the time of their career peak and derive different kind of rewards. However, from skilled work upwards, people are generally proud of and identify with their work. This is especially underlined by the spontaneous reports of unemployed men and women; they experience their non-working status as being undesirable, even if the financial problems are not overriding (Westerhof, 2001a, 2001b; Westerhof & Dittmann-Kohli, 2000).

Van Selm (1998) conducted an interview study with workers of a Dutch truck company after they had become unemployed because of business reduction. The average age was 53 (range 37–60), and the level of education varied from lower to higher vocational training. Some employees had made their careers within the company and had reached higher positions. The work domains included technical jobs, public relations, and export managers. Nine of the 25 workers had found new jobs; the others were still unemployed. The great majority was married. Before the in-depth interview, the SELE instrument was applied and, as expected, meaninglessness could be detected with both methods. The workers expressed feelings of dejection and agitation, a negative or unclear future perspective, and a lack of goals within the affective and motivational aspects of meaninglessness. Cultural alienation and estrangement, lack of control, lack of reaching work aspirations, and lack of social support were also expressed in the interviews. In terms of self-evaluation it became evident that the workers experienced threats to their self-esteem, feelings of inferiority, and doubts about the reasons for job loss. Several workers also blamed themselves for having been too idealistic. The overall results clearly showed that the loss of work in midlife is a very critical life event in terms of identity and selfhood.

The same conclusion can be drawn from data from the German Aging Survey. Unemployment was seen as definitely negative, to have work as beneficial and desirable (Westerhof, 2001a). The features of identity regarding the work role were regularly found in middle-aged men and women, and even in retired people a considerable amount of past work-role identity appeared. In East Germany, work identity of women was stronger than that in the West. This became manifest in the finding that none of the unemployed East German women identified themselves as housewives; all of them defined themselves as "unemployed." Only in West Germany, being a housewife was chosen as a self-descriptive category within the questionnaire.

Gender differences have their greatest impact in middle age, that is, in late career. Middle-aged women with high career aspirations meet the barriers for entering high positions in greater numbers. The "glass ceiling" is a term describing this process of declining female promotion rates (Dittmann-Kohli et al., 1997). In the last two decades, the number of women in high academic and managerial positions has not really increased (Valian, 1999).

In her study on 300 middle-aged and elderly women and men, Weingart (1997) found no gender differences between the groups in early and late middle age in regard to several work-related categories. In the group of elderly men and women, significantly more men than women referred to their former work and occupations, though a considerable number of these women had worked. In respect to housework activities, of course, it was the women and not the men who reported them. Weingart interprets this as pointing toward more traditional work versus family identities in the oldest group.

Work identity and personality issues are the topics of a conceptual study by Axelrod (1999). In his treatment of adult development, a woman in her 30s must direct her attention to how she is seen and respected by others if her life goal includes a career in the domain of work. For men the same is the case. The 30s prepare the way for the early and late middle-age periods at work; career paths usually represent a sequence of steps building on each other. Axelrod (1999) perceives the midlife transition in the world of work as passing from the "heroic illusion" (p. 29) to a new sense of purpose, because this sense of purpose will animate work life through middle adulthood. Work goals will often become more personal and less conventional. Men and women obtain a clearer sense of what they are able to do and to achieve, where their problems and deficits may lie, and what rewards they can expect within the world of work before they reorient themselves to face a new role identity, that of the retired man or woman. The midlife period is frequently seen as the phase of reappraisal of work life. Work involvement, especially as it relates to one's goals and ideals, is reflected upon. Also, early midlife is often the time for the last possibility of fundamental change in the type and direction of work involvement.

The Social Self in Interpersonal and Social Context

In her probability sample of 300 men and women from German Aging Survey, Weingart (1997) also found the expected gender differences in respect to the interpersonal categories of the social self. As expected from the literature, women offered more self-statements about social contacts with other people and about getting and giving help and support from/to others. This was true for all three age groups. Also, women described themselves significantly more often in terms of loneliness and concerns about independence. In view of the fact that women live longer and are widowed or single more frequently and for a much longer time, their more frequent statements about these concerns were expected.

During the early and late-midlife period, the significance of the social self is stable in terms of the number of thoughts and feelings constituting it. However, corresponding to social structural features of Western life stages, the type of persons nominated as well as the content interpersonal relations mentioned varied in the self-reports between the three age groups (Bode, 2001a). The differences in the biological life cycle of the family are reflected in statements of women and men in different age groups.

In several aspects, the expected stronger social attachments of women were reflected in many types of narrative self-statements. Women referred to other persons more often than men did, especially in the midlife period. Statements classified as referring to interpersonal relations were found significantly more often in women than men. Surprisingly, this female surplus was accounted for by more frequent negative and ambivalent statements about interpersonal relationships (Bode, 2003). This indicates that middle-aged and elderly women are less content and probably less detached than men. Within the basic orientations toward relatedness and individuality as twin aspects of identity, women are stronger on the former than the latter, as expected. Both of these orientations were lower in old age than in the midlife period, but individuality decreased much more in old age, while themes of relatedness stayed comparatively higher until the age of 85. While the frequencies for individuality decreased regularly over the six age groups from 40 to 85 years, the frequencies of relatedness were higher in Group one (40–48 years) than in Group two (49–57 years), but increased for Group three (58–66 years), and then decreased again until old age. As in other studies within the German Aging Survey research program, the categories within relatedness shifted somewhat in content, especially those about the quality of relationships and common projects. All in all, social identity and relatedness stay relatively central over the life course, but change very much in content (Bode, 2003; Dittmann-Kohli, 1995).

Conclusion

From a global perspective, non-Western and traditional patterns of the adult life course could be cited that render the middle-age period the time of gain and full personhood. Conversely, conditions of suppression, war, and illness rob large groups from experiencing or attaining midlife at all. Psychological models of life span development that take such factors into account cannot predict the form of midlife identity under conditions at variance with our own average conditions. Highly general models of behavior tendencies and fate tendencies (such as gains and losses) need specification regarding their meaning and implications for different cultures. Gains and losses, for instance, can be the reverse sequence of that in the West. If we continue to collect, interpret, and integrate psychological and other social science research about Western countries, we must further our understanding of the psychological and macrosystem factors that may allow us to generalize or not generalize our findings.

Specific data on specific cultural regions in modern Western countries can be used to promote personal growth and productive lives in midlife, however. Feedback about the way average persons and specific groups think about themselves and their context can enhance self-understanding and facilitate readjustment of possible selves. This is a relevant field of learning for those who want to undertake intentional self-development (Brandtstädter, 1999). Furthermore, understanding the way middle-aged adults think and feel about themselves and their lives would also benefit those who are involved in helping others to age successfully, namely psychotherapists, trainers, and designers of training schedules and curriculum development. This applies also to decision-makers on all levels, in educational institutions, work organizations, in local communities, and at regional or national levels. In addition to the acquisition of knowledge about the status quo of the relevant population and demographic group, understanding of the relevant fundamentals of self-change and self-regulation should be disseminated. Otherwise, there is danger of effort without success. Furthermore, a range of facts and principles relevant for goal selection is of importance, because it does not make sense to strive for unattainable goals. "Sensible" new goals must meet all sorts of criteria from motivational relevance, to fitting of important values, to availability of external social, material, and cultural resources. In addition, internal psychological potential like abilities and motivation are important. The type of self-knowledge of particular relevance for self-development in middle age includes the role and amount of automaticity, the limits of free will, and the conditions of psychological change, including the role of context. It could also be important to learn about the laws of creative thinking and productivity (see Simonton, 1998). In order to promote midlife flexibility and productivity, the media can promote facilitative images of midlife personhood that elaborate the poetic, attractive, and intriguing aspects of that life period, much as is done with the romantic and desirable aspects of youth. For instance, the late-midlife freedom and the possibility for exquisite sensations, powerful thought, productive use of available internal and external resources, and responsible understanding of obligations toward coming generations and global problems can be offered as goals for selfhood in the Third Age.

Apart from any individual or group efforts for change, unintentional changes in the cultural models of personhood and selfhood could occur through social change already underway. For instance, women may become less different from men in their preferences for self-assertiveness, individuality, and relatedness because of their participation in male work role levels. Extensive further dissemination of findings from brain research in the mass media and models of personality and change may increasingly include the role of brain functions, which are then included in the psychological and physical self-concept. Future cultural changes may not come in a regular pace, however, but occur in fast typification shifts (Holstein & Gubrium, 2000) alternating with more stable periods.

References

Améry, J. (1968). *Über das Altern*. Stuttgart, Germany: Klett.

Axelrod, S. D. (1999). *Work and the evolving self*. Hillsdale, NJ: Analytic Press.

Biggs, S. (1999). *The mature imagination. Dynamics of identity in midlife and beyond*. Buckingham, UK: Open University Press.

Bode, C. (2001a). Das soziale Selbst [The social self]. In F. Dittmann-Kohli, C. Bode, & G. J. Westerhof (Eds.), *Die zweite Lebenshälfte–Psychologische Perspektiven. Ergebnisse des Alters-Survey* (Vol. 195, pp. 279–339). Stuttgart, Germany: Kohlhammer.

Bode, C. (2001b). "Wenn ich bestimmte Dinge nicht mehr kann . . .": Der antizipierte Umgang mit Einbußen im Kompetenz-und Fähigkeitsbereich. In F. Dittmann-Kohli, C. Bode, & G. J. Westerhof (Eds.), *Die zweite Lebenshälfte– Psychologische Perspektiven. Ergebnisse des Alters-Survey* (Vol. 195, pp. 169–191). Stuttgart, Germany: Kohlhammer.

Bode, C. (2003). *Individuality and relatedness in middle and late adulthood. A study of women and men in the Netherlands, East and West Germany.* Enschede, Netherlands: Printpartners Ipskamp.

Borscheid, P. (1987). *Geschichte des Alters.* Münster, Germany: Coppenrath Verlag.

Brandtstädter, J. (1999). The self in action and development: Cultural, biosocial, and ontogenetic bases of intentional self-development. In J. Brandtstädter & R. M. Lerner (Eds.), *Action and self-development* (pp. 37–65). Thousand Oaks, CA: Sage.

Burrow, J. A. (1986). *The ages of man. A study of medieval writing and thought.* Oxford, UK: Clarendon Press.

Costa, P. T., McCrae, R. R., Martin, T. A., et al. (2000). Personality development from adolescence through adulthood: Further cross-cultural comparisons of age differences. In V. J. Molfese & D. L. Molfese (Eds.), *Temperament and personality across the life span* (pp. 235–252). Mahwah, NJ: Erlbaum.

Dittmann, F. (1973). *Kultur und Leistung. Zur Frage der Leistungsdispositionen bei Luo und Indern in Kenia.* Saarbrücken, Germany: Verlag der SSIP-Schriften Breitenbach.

Dittmann, F. (1974). *Cultural constraints on the acquisition of achievement motivation* (Research Note 18). Menlo Park, CA: Stanford Research Institute, Educational Policy Research Center.

Dittmann-Kohli, F. (1984). Weisheit als mögliches Ergebnis der Intelligenzentwicklung im Erwachsenenalter [Wisdom as a possible consequence of cognitive development in adulthood]. *Sprache und Kognition, 2,* 112–132.

Dittmann-Kohli, F. (1986). Problem identification and definition as important aspects of adolescents' coping with normative life tasks. In R. K. Silbereisen (Ed.), *Development as action in context* (pp. 19–37). Berlin, Germany: Springer.

Dittmann-Kohli, F. (1987). Medieval life-span psychology. *Ageing and Society, 7,* 105–108.

Dittmann-Kohli, F. (1995). *Persönliche Sinngebung in frühen und späten Erwachsenenalter* [Personal meaning system in early and late adulthood]. Göttingen, Germany: Hogrefe.

Dittmann-Kohli, F. (2004, July). *Temporal aspects of identity in a life-span perspective.* Paper presented at the Third International Biennal SELF Research Conference, Berlin, Germany.

Dittmann-Kohli, F. (in press-a). Self and identity. In M. L. Johnson & V. L. Bengtson (Eds.), *Cambridge handbook on age and ageing.* Cambridge, UK: Cambridge University Press.

Dittmann-Kohli, F. (in press-b). Time and identity in a life span perspective. In J. Baars & P. Visser (Eds.), *Interdisciplinary research on the concepts of time and aging.* Amityville, NY: Baywood.

Dittmann-Kohli, F., Bode, C., & Westerhof, G. J. (Eds.). (2001). *Die zweite Lebenshälfte–Psychologische Perspektiven. Ergebnisse des Alters-Survey.* Stuttgart, Germany: Kohlhammer.

Dittmann-Kohli, F., Sowarka, D., & Timmer, E. (1997). Beruf und Alltag: Leistungsprobleme und Lernaufgaben im mittleren und höheren Erwachsenenalter [Work and daily life: Achievement problems and learning tasks in middle and late adulthood]. In F. E. Weinert & H. Mandl (Eds.), *Psychologie der Erwachsenenbildung: Psychologie der Erwachsenenbildung* (Enzyklopädie der Psychologie, Vol. 4, pp. 179–235). Göttingen, Germany: Hogrefe.

Dittmann-Kohli, F., & van der Heijden, B. (1996). Leistungsfähigkeit älterer Arbeitnehmer–interne und externe Einflussfaktoren. *Zeitschrift für Gerontologie und Geriatrie, 29,* 323–327.

Gerritsen, D., Bode, C., & Dittmann-Kohli, F. (2001). Das psychische Selbst. In F. Dittmann-Kohli, C. Bode, & G. J. Westerhof (Eds.), *Die zweite Lebenshälfte–Psychologische Perspektiven. Ergebnisse des Alters-Survey* (Vol. 195, pp. 401–447). Stuttgart, Germany: Kohlhammer.

Gollwitzer, P. M., & Kirchhof, O. (1998). The willful pursuit of identity. In J. Heckhausen & C. S. Dweck (Eds.), *Motivation and self-regulation across the life span* (pp. 389–423). Cambridge, UK: Cambridge University Press.

Goschke, T. (2004). Vom freien Willen zur Selbstdetermination. Kognitive und volitionale Mechanismen der intentionalen Handlungssteuerung [From free will to self determination. Cognitive and volitional mechanisms of intentional action control]. *Psychologische Rundschau, 55,* 186–197.

Hart, S., & Fegley, S. (1997). Children's self-awareness and self-understanding in cultural context. In U. Neisser & D. A. Joplin (Eds.), *The conceptual self in context.* Cambridge, MA: Cambridge University Press.

Holstein, J. A., & Gubrium, J. F. (2000). *Constructing the life course* (2nd ed.). Dix Hills, NY: General Hall.

Jaeggi, E. (1996). *Viel zu jung um alt zu sein. Das neue Lebensgefühl ab sechzig* [Much too young to be old. The feeling of new life starting at age sixty]. Reinbeck bei Hamburg, Germany: Rowohlt.

Kakar, S. (1998). The search for middle age in India. In R. A. Shweder (Ed.), *Welcome to middle age! And other cultural fictions* (pp. 75–98). Chicago: University of Chicago Press.

Kohli, M. (1985). Die Institutionalisierung des Lebenslauf [The institutionalization of the life course]. *Kölner Zeitschrift für Soziologie und Sozialpsychologie, 37,* 1–29.

Kuin, Y., Westerhof, G. J., Dittmann-Kohli, F., & Gerritsen, D. (2001). Psychophysische Integrität und Gesundheitserleben. In F. Dittmann-Kohli, C. Bode, & G. J. Westerhof (Eds.), *Die zweite Lebenshälfte–Psychologische Perspektiven. Ergebnisse des Alters-Survey* (Vol. 195, pp. 343–450). Stuttgart, Germany: Kohlhammer.

Mahler, M. (2004). *Verschillen in de beleving van gezondheid tussen ouderen in Duitsland and Nederland.* Unpublished thesis, University Nijmegen, Psychogerontology Center, Nijmegen, Netherlands.

McAdams, D. P. (1996). Personality, modernity, and the storied self: A contemporary framework for studying persons. *Psychological Inquiry, 7,* 295–321.

Menon, U., & Shweder, R. A. (1998). The return of the "White man's burden": The moral discourse of anthropology and the domestic life of Hindu women. In R. A. Shweder (Ed.), *Welcome to middle age! And other cultural fictions* (pp. 139–188). Chicago: University of Chicago Press.

Roth, G. (2001). *Fühlen, Denken, Handeln* [Feeling, thinking, acting]. Frankfurt, Germany: Suhrkamp.

Sedikides, C., & Skowronski, J. J. (1997). The symbolic self in evolutionary context. *Personality and Social Psychology Review, 1,* 80–102.

Settersten, R. A. (1999). *Lives in time and place.* Amityville, NY: Baywood.

Shore, B. (1998). Status reversal: The coming of aging in Samoa. In R. A. Shweder (Ed.), *Welcome to middle age! And other cultural fictions* (pp. 101–137). Chicago: University of Chicago Press.

Simonton, D. K. (1998). Career paths and creative lives: A theoretical perspective on late life potential. In C. E. Adams-Price (Ed.), *Creativity and successful aging. Theoretical and empirical approaches* (pp. 3–18). New York: Springer.

Soekar, S. (2000). *'Mijn lichaam wordt ouder': Relatie tussen zelf and lichaam vergeleken bij drie leeftijdsgroepen* ["My body ages": Self and body relations compared in three age groups]. Predoctoral thesis, University of Nijmegen, Nijmegen, Netherlands.

Staudinger, U., & Bluck, S. (2001). A view on midlife development from life-span theory. In M. E. Lachman (Ed.), *Handbook on midlife development* (pp. 3–39). New York: Wiley.

Steverink, N., & Timmer, E. (2001). Das subjektive Alterserleben. In F. Dittmann-Kohli, C. Bode, & G. J. Westerhof (Eds.), *Die zweite Lebenshälfte–Psychologische Perspektiven. Ergebnisse des Alters-Survey* (Vol. 195, pp. 451–484). Stuttgart, Germany: Kohlhammer.

Timmer, E. (2000). *Antizipation von Gewinn, Fortsetzung des Status Quo und Verlust. Eine Untersuchung über persönliche Zukunftsbezüge in der zweiten Lebenshälfte* [Anticipations of gains, maintenance of the status quo, and loss in the second half of life]. Nijmegen, Netherlands: Nijmegen University Press.

Timmer, E., Westerhof, G. J., & Dittmann-Kohli, F. (in press). When looking back on my past life I regret . . . Retrospective regret in the second half of life. *Death Studies.*

Valian, V. (1999). *Why so slow? The advancement of women.* Cambridge: MIT Press.

van Selm, M. (1998). *Meaninglessness in the second half of life.* Nijmegen, Netherlands: Nijmegen University Press.

Veroff, J. (1983). Contextual determinants of personality. *Personality and Social Psychology Bulletin, 9,* 331–343.

Veroff, J., & Smith, D. A. (1985). Motives and values over the adult years. In D. A. Kleiber & M. Maehr (Eds.), *Advances in motivation and achievement* (Vol. 4, pp. 1–53). Greenwich, CT: JAI.

Vroon, P. (1978). *Stemmen van vroeger. Ontstaan en ontwikkeling van het zelfbewustzijn* [Voices of the past. Emergence and development of self-awareness]. Baarn, Netherlands: Ambo.

Weingart, G. (1997). *Gender differences in the personal meaning systems of adults in the second half of life.* Unpublished diploma thesis, University of Bielefeld, Bielefeld, Germany.

Welzer, H., & Markowitsch, H. J. (2001). Ausgangspunkte und Möglichkeiten interdisziplinärer Gedächtnisforschung [Starting points and possibilities of interdisciplinary memory research]. In Kulturwissenschaftliches Institut Essen (Ed.), *Jahrbuch 2000/2001* (pp. 460–482). Essen, Germany: Kulturwissenschaftliches Institut.

Westerhof, G. (2001a). Arbeit und Beruf im persönlichen Sinnsystem. In F. Dittmann-Kohli, C. Bode, & G. J. Westerhof (Eds.), *Die zweite Lebenshälfte–Psychologische Perspektiven. Ergebnisse des Alters-Survey* (Vol. 195, pp. 195–246). Stuttgart, Germany: Kohlhammer.

Westerhof, G. (2001b). Lebensevaluierung: Bewertungsdimensionen und Vergleichsprozesse. In F. Dittmann-Kohli, C. Bode, & G. J. Westerhof (Eds.), *Die zweite Lebenshälfte–Psychologische Perspektiven. Ergebnisse des Alters-Survey* (Vol. 195, pp. 129–168). Stuttgart, Germany: Kohlhammer.

Westerhof, G. J., & Dittmann-Kohli, F. (2000). Work status and the construction of work-related selves. In K. W. Schaie & J. Hendricks (Eds.), *Evolution of the aging self* (pp. 123–157). New York: Springer.

Westerhof, G., Dittmann-Kohli, F., & Bode, C. (2003). The paradox of aging: Toward personal meaning in gerontology. In S. Biggs, A. Lowenstein, & J. Hendricks (Eds.), *The need for theory* (pp. 145–159). Amityville, NY: Baywood.

Westerhof, G. J., Kuin, Y., & Dittmann-Kohli, F. (1998). Gesundheit als Lebensthema [Health as a life topic]. *Zeitschrift für Klinische Psychologie, 27,* 136–142.

Whitbourne, S. K. (1985). The psychological construction of the life span. In J. E. Birren & K. W. Schaie (Eds.), *Handbook on the psychology of aging* (pp. 549–618). New York: Van Nostrand Reinhold.

Eleven

Metacognition in Midlife

Christopher Hertzog and Roger A. Dixon

Metacognition is a relatively new concept in cognitive and developmental psychology, its origins being traceable to writings by John Flavell and others in the early 1970s (e.g., Flavell, 1979; Perlmutter, 1978). However, the issues addressed by contemporary research on metacognition have historical roots that long predate the creation of the term *metacognition* in the scientific literature, including such issues as whether conscious monitoring is required to achieve effective cognitive self-regulation (Nelson, 1996).

Metacognition can be defined as cognition about cognition, and as such, this broad conceptual definition implies, in turn, many subordinate categories of metacognitive constructs. Elsewhere (e.g., Hertzog & Dixon, 1994; Hertzog & Hultsch, 2000) we have argued that metacognition is appropriately framed as consisting of (a) declarative knowledge about cognition—that is, knowledge about the cognitive processes and mechanisms that are

Research described in this chapter was supported by grants from the National Institute on Aging, one of the National Institutes of Health, to C. Hertzog (R37 AG13148) and to R. A. Dixon (R01 AG08325).

relevant to thinking, learning, and remembering, as well as how a person's behavior influences goal attainment that requires cognition; (b) beliefs about self and others as cognitive agents—that is, whether specific persons (including most especially oneself) are able to accomplish certain tasks when relying on cognition; and (c) monitoring internal cognitive states.

Developmental psychologists focusing on children have tended to emphasize research on the development of knowledge about the efficacy of different strategies and the development of effective strategy use as children grow older. Metacognitive knowledge (e.g., which strategies are more effective than others, for oneself, or in general; e.g., Kuhn, 2000) is seen as an important factor contributing to children's use of more sophisticated organizational strategies, such as relational processing between different words when studying a word list in a free recall task. Modern cognitive psychology frames metacognition in an architecture of executive control over behavior (Hertzog & Robinson, 2005; Sternberg, 1985). From this perspective, accurate monitoring of internal cognitive states is a key component of achieving control in cognitively demanding situations (Nelson, 1996). For example, when a student is studying for a test, monitoring is needed to determine whether material is comprehended, whether it has been sufficiently memorized, and whether additional study effort would be fruitful. Thus, in both these traditions, metacognition is construed as having close links to effective strategy use and related constructs. However, strategy use itself would be construed as implementation of cognitive control, a behavior that is linked to metacognition but not part of it.

In lifespan developmental psychology, metacognitive research has focused on (a) the interplay between knowledge and strategies in adulthood (e.g., Dunlosky & Hertzog, 2000), (b) the relationship between monitoring and strategic behavior (e.g., Dunlosky & Connor, 1997; Lovelace, 1990; Murphy, Schmitt, Caruso, & Sanders, 1987), (c) several types of beliefs (or implicit theories) about aging and cognition (Cavanaugh, Feldman, & Hertzog, 1998), (d) individualized beliefs about one's own cognition and cognitive self-efficacy (Bandura, 1997; Berry, 1999), and (e) how knowledge, general beliefs, and individual beliefs influence (directly or interactively) cognitive performance on laboratory tasks and in everyday life.

Although metacognition in childhood and adulthood (aging) is voluminously researched, relatively little is known about metacognitive phenomena in midlife, per se. Certainly, we know of no research that focuses specifically on how metacognition in midlife differs from metacognition at other points in the adult life span. A similar phenomenon was observed earlier in the case of memory in midlife (Dixon, de Frias, & Maitland, 2001). In writing this chapter, we have concentrated on aspects of metacognition where there is at least some data available on middle-aged adults. Almost without exception, such studies involve evaluation of beliefs about memory over the life course, as measured by questionnaires such as the Metamemory In Adulthood scale (MIA; see Dixon, 1989). In contrast, studies of metacognitive monitoring in adulthood have tended to compare young adults and older adults in extreme age group designs, in which a group of young adults (often students) are compared to a group of older adults (Hertzog, 1996). These studies typically use experimental tasks that enable measurement of monitoring for specific items during encoding, retention, and retrieval. The dominant finding in this literature is that elementary monitoring processes are unimpaired by aging (e.g., Hertzog, Kidder, Powell-Moman, & Dunlosky, 2002; Robinson, Hertzog, & Dunlosky, in press; see also Hertzog & Hultsch, 2000, for a review), although some complex types of monitoring (e.g., source monitoring) and achievement of effective control through utilization of monitoring (e.g., allocation of study time during multiple trial learning; Dunlosky & Connor, 1997) may be impaired.

Despite the evidence that older adults are often as accurate in their monitoring of encoding and retrieval, it is preliminary to assume that nothing unique occurs during midlife. It could be the case that middle-aged adults have superior monitoring accuracy to either younger adults or older adults because the experience they gain in using cognition in everyday life is used effectively, without the negative consequences of age-related changes in cognitive mechanisms and resources that might act to constrain monitoring accuracy in older adults (e.g., Bieman-Copland & Charness, 1994). It could be the case that metacognition in domains of cognitive expertise reaches its peak at midlife but is only applied to (and exercised in) specific and well-practiced leisure or professional pursuits. We simply do not know.

Given this state of affairs, this chapter focuses on beliefs about cognition in middle-aged adults and how these beliefs may affect cognitive task performance, within and outside the laboratory. We differentiate between two classes of beliefs: (a) general beliefs about how cognition is affected by aging during adulthood, for self and others; and (b) self-referent beliefs about cognition, as exemplified by the self-efficacy construct. The two classes of beliefs are undoubtedly interrelated, as we discuss later in the chapter, but the distinction is conceptually useful.

An important backdrop for a theoretical account of metacognition in midlife is the fact that normative age-related decline in cognition is relatively modest in magnitude through the 50s and 60s after which age-related declines begin to accelerate (Dixon, de Frias, & Maitland, 2001; Hultsch, Hertzog, Dixon, & Small, 1998; Martin & Zimprich, Chapter 6, this volume; Schaie, 1996). Certainly, these modest normative changes are accompanied by individual differences in rates of change, with some persons maintaining or improving functioning and others declining to a meaningful and substantial degree (e.g., Schaie, 1996). At the same time, middle-aged adults observe enough physical changes associated with aging (e.g., graying hair, loss of flexibility, weight gain in themselves and others) to become concerned about the effects of aging (Lynch, 2000). Furthermore, early signs of cognitive aging may be manifested in midlife, including an increased incidence rate of retrieval blocks, failures in name finding, or losing one's train of thought (see, e.g., Cohen & Faulkner, 1986). Moreover, landmark events (e.g., one's 40th, 50th, and 60th birthdays; an emptying nest; or the death of one's parents) serve as reminders to middle-aged adults of the progression of life and the inevitability of death (Pyszczynski, Greenberg, & Solomon, 2004), threatening self-esteem and heightening concern about integrity of cognitive function as an important prerequisite for both longevity and a high quality of life in old age. Finally, the growing industry of "antiaging" products for sale on the commercial market ensures that problems associated with aging are continually front and center in the media and public discourse.

Given this constellation of events, there is good reason to suspect that middle-aged adults' implicit theories about aging and cognition, and their beliefs about their own cognitive function, may undergo major transformations at the same time that cognition itself is relatively stable. Given that metacognitive beliefs are often inaccurate (see Hertzog & Hultsch, 2000), it is possible that developmental changes in cognition will be dissociated from beliefs about cognitive development and changes in those beliefs. Moreover, beliefs about cognition may play a more important role in explaining the behavior of middle-aged adults than cognitive status itself. For example, some middle-aged adults may become vigilant about preventing cognitive decline through lifestyle changes, given their belief that cognitive decline is normative but potentially preventable, whereas other middle-aged adults may engage in compensatory behaviors to adjust for perceived cognitive decline even when it doesn't exist or is of only marginal practical consequence (Dixon, de Frias, & Maitland, 2001).

Finally, to the extent that a healthy lifestyle in midlife promotes successful aging (Rowe & Kahn, 1998), then beliefs about causes and manifestations of cognitive development may actually alter the course of cognitive development itself through instantiation and reinforcement of behaviors promoting physical and psychological health and cognitive stimulation (e.g., Schooler, Mulatu, & Oates, 1999). For all these reasons, understanding metacognitive beliefs in midlife may be an important part of understanding adult development in general, and cognition in midlife and beyond, in particular.

General Beliefs About Cognition and Aging

General beliefs about cognition and aging can be treated as propositions about how aging processes influence cognition for everyone, or perhaps, for different clusters of individuals. The beliefs of interest include lay theories about types of cognition and intelligence (e.g., Berg & Sternberg, 1985) and beliefs about how different types of cognition change over the adult life course (e.g., Heckhausen, Dixon, & Baltes, 1989; Ryan & Kwong See, 1993). The latter type of general beliefs may be closely related to stereotypes about adulthood and aging, in which older adults are viewed as lacking certain cognitive attributes (e.g., speed of processing) and, perhaps, gaining others (e.g., wisdom). These attributes may, in turn, be part of larger person schemas seen as typifying classes of older adults, such as the John Wayne conservative or the activist volunteer (Hummert, 1990). Not all stereotypes about aging and cognitive functioning are negative, so one cannot assume that activated stereotypes universally have deleterious effects (e.g., Chasteen, Schwarz, & Park, 2002).

Ellen Ryan (1992; Ryan & Kwong See, 1993) adapted existing metamemory questionnaires to measure beliefs about aging and memory, asking individuals to complete the questionnaires as if they were the average person of different ages (i.e., age 20, 50, and 70). The results indicated that people anticipated self-reported declines in memory functioning during adulthood. Lineweaver and Hertzog (1998) developed an alternative method for scaling implicit theories about memory development in adulthood, the General Beliefs about Memory Instrument (GBMI). Figure 11.1 shows a sample item. Individuals rate on a vertical visual analog scale the memory of an adult of a target age (e.g., age 20). Multiple age targets are arranged in a row, from youngest to oldest (see Guilford, 1932, for a

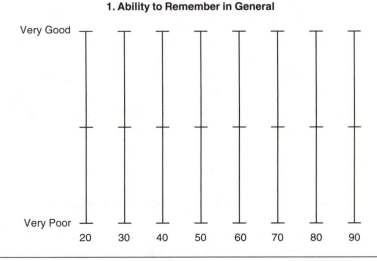

1. Ability to Remember in General

Very Good

Very Poor

20   30   40   50   60   70   80   90

Figure 11.1   Sample Item Measuring Implicit Developmental Theory About Changes in Memory

SOURCE: From Lineweaver and Hertzog's (1998) GBMI.

NOTE: Individuals make a perpendicular mark to each vertical rating scale (for ages 20-90) to indicate expected level of memory functioning.

We would like to know how good you think the memory of average adults is. This question is asking about the ability of each adult to remember in general.
Please read the item carefully and mark your answers on a range from "Very Good" to "Very Poor."

rationale in favor of this type of scaling). One advantage of this approach in developmental applications is that individuals construct their subjective curve for the target construct over the adult life span. Thus, it is possible to compare the curves of people of different ages in a variety of ways, such as in the slopes of their subjective curves.

Figure 11.2 shows rating data for adult lifespan changes in memory collected by Lineweaver and Hertzog (1998) in a sample including younger, middle-aged, and older adults. Note that middle-aged adults and older adults are somewhat more alike than younger adults, in that they both tend to rate memory decline as starting later in the life course. However, all three age groups view memory as declining after age 40 for the average adult. These data seem to reinforce Ryan's (1992) findings that there are only minor age differences in beliefs about memory development in

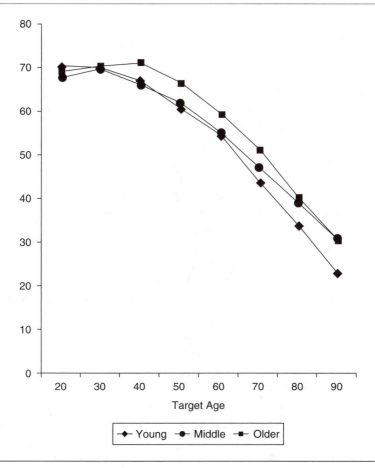

Figure 11.2   Perceived Developmental Functions for Memory (Implicit
Theories) for Three Age Groups, Ages 20–90

SOURCE: From Lineweaver, T. T., & Hertzog, C. (1998). Adults' efficacy and control beliefs
regarding memory and aging: Separating general from personal beliefs in *Aging, Neuropsychology, and Cognition*, 5, 264-296. Copyright © 1998. Reprinted with permission.

adulthood. Middle-aged adults, like older adults, believe that memory
declines during midlife.

There are three reasons why one should be cautious in generalizing
from such findings to conclude that there are only minor age-related
changes in beliefs about memory development in adulthood. First,
Lineweaver and Hertzog (1998) asked individuals to rate different kinds

of memory and found some differences between ratings of specific memory attributes. For example, people rated memory for faces as declining less than memory for names, and they tended to perceive smaller effects of aging on remote memory (things learned long ago) than on recent memory. Thus, in principle, ratings of other aspects of cognition, or of cognition in everyday contexts, could show smaller perceived age effects, or perhaps, different patterns for middle-aged adults.

Second, Lineweaver and Hertzog (1998) asked people to rate the average person of a given age. Individuals might believe that it is possible to improve memory over the life course but that such improvements are relatively rare. In fact, Hertzog, Baldi, and York (2001) reported results from a different type of scale inspired by the GBMI. People were shown hypothetical developmental curves that could have been drawn by people responding to the GBMI. Multiple shapes were rated, including patterns of stability, continuous increment, or continuous decrement. Study participants were asked to rate the typicality of such developmental functions and to estimate the percentage of persons in the population showing that type of function. Older adults tended to rate incremental profiles as being slightly more typical and applying to a larger percentage of the population. Hence, there may be an evolution of beliefs regarding possibilities of maintenance or improvement as people grow older.

Third, individual differences in memory beliefs may have stronger relationships to outcome variables, such as memory task performance, in middle-aged and older adults. Similar beliefs may have disparate consequences at different points in the life span.

Generally, one can imagine that an implicit theory of memory decline would have larger potential consequences in persons later in life than persons early in life. Indeed, there is good reason to believe that similar decline beliefs would result in different reactions for persons of different ages. Consider Figure 11.3. A 20-year-old person and a 70-year-old person may have roughly equivalent beliefs about the development of memory, producing essentially parallel developmental curves on the GBMI. We have only separated the curves, by differing the initial level of perceived memory functioning, to enhance the illustration. The point we make would also apply if the curves were completely overlapping. The figure shows each person's own age as a point on his or her perceived developmental function. Note that, despite the similar curves, the 70-year-old person is likely to perceive lower levels of performance, due to age-related memory decline, at his or her own age, despite the fact that in Figure 11.3, the

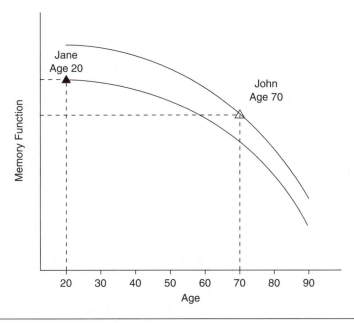

Figure 11.3   How Implicit Theories for Two Adults Translate Into Expected Memory Functioning for an Individual of One's Own Age

NOTE: Projection of the function onto the y-axis (corresponding to memory function) represents perception of level of function for a person of a given age.

70-year-old person believes memory functioning is better (at all ages) than the 20-year-old person. Now extrapolate either curve to a person in midlife (say, age 50). Note that persons in midlife are likely to perceive both lower levels of current functioning and decline from previous status. Thus, if the 50-year-old person's implicit theory holds that decline starts at age 40, then he or she is likely to experience concern about the memory decline that is believed to already have begun. It is far less likely that a 20-year-old person would have similar concerns.

Of course, implicit theories about memory and aging are broader than representations of developmental changes in memory performance. Individuals may also differ substantially in perceived causes of memory decline. Dweck and colleagues (e.g., Dweck & Leggett, 1988) have argued that children differ in whether they view their school performance as deriving from inherent ability (an entity theory) or from practice and effort (a skill theory). Elliott and Lachman (1989) suggested that these beliefs carry forward into adulthood, and are also related to implicit theories of aging and cognitive decline. From this perspective, it is important to account for individual differences in beliefs as a potential explanation for individual differences in cognition within an age range, such as midlife.

Certainly, older adults differ from younger adults in causal attributions about memory performance, with older adults more likely to attribute poor memory performance by themselves and others to age and ability rather than poor utilization of strategies or low levels of memory skills (Hertzog, Lineweaver, & McGuire, 1999; Lachman, Steinberg, & Trotter, 1987). Older adults also differ in implicit theories about the inherent controllability of memory. Lineweaver and Hertzog (1998) showed that GBMI measures of perceived control over memory show a similar developmental trajectory to memory ability (as in Figure 11.2). Similarly, Lachman and her colleagues (e.g., Elliott & Lachman, 1989) have emphasized how implicit theories about the inherent controllability or uncontrollability of age-related cognitive changes (deriving from implicit theories about cognition as endowed ability vs. realized skill) can influence cognitive performance.

There are also other pathways by which general beliefs or implicit theories could affect the memory performance of middle-aged adults (see Cavanaugh et al., 1998, for a review). Levy (1996), for example, has claimed that implicit activation of aging stereotypes, without conscious awareness, impairs the memory performance of older adults. The mechanisms for this possible effect are unknown but can include evoked performance anxiety or unconscious adoption (mimicry) of trait attributes contained in a stereotype of aging (Langer, 1989). Hummert, Garstka, O'Brien, Greenwald, and Mellott (2003) used a memory-specific version of the Implicit Attitudes Test (see Greenwald & Banaji, 1995, for a review of literature on implicit attitudes and their measurement) to show that like younger adults, older adults have negatively valenced implicit attitudes about memory in old age. Activation of these implicit attitudes may help to explain memory-related stereotype threat in older adults (Hess, Auman, Colcombe, & Rahhal, 2003). Originally studied in the context of racial stereotypes (e.g., Steele & Aaronson, 1995), stereotype threat refers to the emotional experience of threat when achievement of a desired goal (i.e., good memory performance) is perceived to be at risk due to personal attributes contained in a person stereotype. If a performance context activates stereotypes about aging, individuals may experience a threat of failure if they are motivated to perform well and have beliefs suggesting the cognitive skills of persons their own age may have eroded to the point that cognitive performance will be impaired. Once the person is threatened, the associated emotional and cognitive reactions can impair their performance. To date, there has been no evaluation of whether these effects can be observed in middle adulthood. Given the data in Figure 11.2, it is plausible to think they might be operating earlier in the life span.

Self-Referent Beliefs About Cognition

Types of Questionnaires

There is a long history of research using questionnaires to measure beliefs about one's own cognition during adulthood (Dixon, 1989; Hertzog & Hultsch, 2000). Although the vast majority of these questionnaires measure beliefs about memory and related variables in everyday life, measures have also been created to examine other cognitive constructs, such as intellectual ability (Schaie, Willis, & O'Hanlon, 1994) and attention (Tun & Wingfield, 1995). Specific research questions have also tended to encourage specialized metacognition questionnaires. For example, Johnson and colleagues developed a questionnaire focused on self-reported source monitoring (e.g., Henkel, Johnson, & De Leonardis, 1998), and Crawford, Smith, and Maylor (2003) created a questionnaire designed to focus on the distinction between prospective and retrospective memory. Given that most of the available literature (especially on beliefs during middle adulthood) concerns self-ratings of memory, we will focus on this domain, restricting ourselves to reviewing results from the more broadly constructed metamemory questionnaires.

Questionnaires about memory often focus on perceived memory problems or memory complaints (see Gilewski & Zelinski, 1986), asking individuals to rate how frequently they have problems remembering different kinds of information. Often, these types of questionnaires derive from an interest in clinical memory assessment (Crook & Larrabee, 1990). The best-known measure of memory complaints is probably the Memory Functioning Questionnaire (MFQ; Gilewski, Zelinski, & Schaie, 1990). Other questionnaires focus on obtaining ratings of memory ability or capacity. The most widely used questionnaire measuring perceived memory ability is probably the MIA (Dixon & Hultsch, 1983). The MIA Capacity scale measures perceived memory ability. Although there are conceptual differences between memory complaints and beliefs about memory ability, the two constructs are closely related, showing strong convergent validity (Hertzog, Dixon, & Hultsch, 1990; Hertzog, Hultsch, & Dixon, 1989) in samples of middle-aged and older adults.

Another important approach to measuring ratings of one's own memory involves task-specific measures of memory self-efficacy (e.g., the Memory Self-Efficacy Questionnaire [MSEQ]; Berry, West, & Dennehey, 1989), in which individuals are asked to rate whether they can achieve a given level of performance (e.g., number of words recalled on a free recall task), using methods for scaling self-efficacy strength and confidence advocated by Bandura (1989). Whereas self-efficacy measures focus on self-efficacy in a particular task context, the typical metamemory questionnaire is more decontextualized, measuring self-rated memory ability (or complaints) for types of everyday memory tasks (e.g., remembering information read in a newspaper), but not those in a particular context (i.e., the newspaper I am reading now). To avoid confusion, we shall refer to the convergent, higher-order construct measured by the MIA and MFQ as "memory self-concept" and the construct measured by the MSEQ as "memory self-efficacy." Baldi and Hertzog (2000) showed that the MSEQ correlates with other measures of memory self-concept but that both memory self-efficacy and memory self-concept independently predict memory performance in older adults. These results suggest that (a) the two constructs are not identical, and (b) contrary to the self-efficacy perspective (e.g., Berry, 1999; Berry & West, 1993), task-specific memory self-efficacy is not a complete mediator of the relations between memory self-concept and memory performance.

The MIA and MFQ are also multidimensional, in that they also ask respondents to rate other attributes, including measurement of perceived change in memory ability over time and use of external aids in everyday life. The MIA also measures perceived locus of control over memory, anxiety about memory performance, and achievement motivation for memory. Perceived control over memory may be more important than memory self-concept as a predictor of use of strategic skills for enhancing memory (Hertzog et al., 1999; Lachman, Bandura, Weaver, & Elliott, 1995). Although most research has focused on measures of memory self-concept and perceived change in memory, memory anxiety and achievement motivation for memory have recently been evaluated as predictors of stereotype threat (Hess et al., 2003).

As noted, a perennial challenge for metacognitive research has been to elucidate the relationships among aging, metacognition, and cognitive performance. Regarding memory, this challenge may be put in terms of a question: To what extent does memory-related awareness, beliefs, or knowledge have an effect on actual memory-related behaviors during adulthood (e.g., Intons-Peterson & Fournier, 1986)? How do people seek to prevent the consequences of memory failures and adapt to age-related memory decline? Some recent efforts have adapted metacognition questionnaires to the challenge of exploring the relationships of aging to strategy use in everyday memory. The Memory Compensation Questionnaire (MCQ; Dixon, de Frias, & Bäckman, 2001) was designed to evaluate the extent to which middle-aged and older adults report using strategies or techniques to maintain or improve their everyday memory functioning. This research was founded on the following three assumptions:

1. Early signs of normal, gradual memory changes may occur in midlife.

2. Abrupt changes associated with preclinical conditions of neurodegenerative diseases may reach back as early as midlife.

3. In this period of heightened awareness, even the most innocuous instance of benign memory failure may be endorsed and interpreted as indicative of (1) or (2).

Research with the MCQ has shown that many middle-aged and older adults are indeed aware of the challenge of age-related memory changes, are committed to maintaining or even enhancing everyday memory abilities, and select and implement effective mechanisms of memory compensation (e.g., de Frias, Dixon, & Bäckman, 2003; Dixon, de Frias, & Bäckman, 2001; Dixon & de Frias, 2004). Like the MIA and MFQ, the MCQ is a multidimensional instrument, tapping five relatively independent (statistically and theoretically) compensatory techniques (de Frias & Dixon, in press). These five common forms of everyday memory compensation include use of (a) external aids, (b) increased recall-related effort, (c) internal mnemonic techniques, (d) investing extra time, and (e) recruiting human collaborative assistance.

Lineweaver and Hertzog (1998) created a measure of memory self-concept and perceived change in memory, the Personal Beliefs About Memory Instrument (PBMI). This scale uses items that are similar to those in the MIA, but it uses a visual analog rating scale rather than a discrete

Likert rating format (as used in the MIA and MFQ). It also measures perceived change in memory from the past to the present (retrospective change), predicted changes in memory from the present to the future (prospective change), and ratings of personal control over memory in the present and the future.

Memory Self-Concept in Midlife

Cross-sectional studies of memory self-concept typically find that there are age differences in memory self-concept and perceived change in memory. Hertzog et al. (1989) used polynomial regression to plot age functions for the MIA and MFQ questionnaires in cross-sectional samples ranging from early adulthood to old age. Memory complaints, as measured by the MFQ Frequency of Forgetting subscale, showed no reliable age trends, but memory self-concept, as measured by the MIA Capacity scale, showed reliable linear age effects. The MIA Locus scale, which measures a sense of internal control over memory, also showed reliable age effects. These data can be interpreted as indicating that middle-aged adults have lower memory self-concept than younger adults, a finding confirmed by Lineweaver and Hertzog (1998). A recent longitudinal study by Lane and Zelinski (2003) also indicates reliable age changes in memory complaints in a sample including middle-aged adults. Although these effects are reliable, it should be emphasized that the age differences (or age changes) in memory self-concept are relatively small in magnitude over the entire adult life course. The largest differences between middle-aged and younger adults have been found for measures of perceived change (Hertzog et al., 1989; Lineweaver & Hertzog, 1998). There are competing explanations for why perceptions of memory change should be more strongly related to age than measures of memory self-concept.

Memory self-concept is apparently quite stable over the adult life course, based on the limited longitudinal data that are available. McDonald-Miszczak, Hertzog, and Hultsch (1995) found high 3-year test-retest correlations for the MIA Capacity and Change scales from the Victoria Longitudinal Study in a sample ranging from middle adulthood to old age. In fact, correcting for attenuation due to measurement error led to the conclusion that stability of individual differences in MIA Capacity was nearly perfect, implying that only small amounts of variance are due to individual differences in change. Lane and Zelinski (2003) used a latent growth curve approach to assess this issue. They found reliable variance in estimated slopes for their Frequency of Forgetting scale from the MFQ (indicating some individual differences in change in memory complaint), but the effect size was very small. Thus, individual differences in change in memory self-concept do exist, but the predominant theme is one of stable individual differences.

Although some diagnostic systems use subjective memory complaint as a criterion for inferring actual (or objective) mild cognitive impairment, it is clear that memory beliefs are not closely related to individual differences in memory (see Hertzog & Hultsch, 2000; Rabbitt, Maylor, McInnes, Bent, & Moore, 1995), even in longitudinal data (e.g., McDonald-Miszczak et al., 1995; Lane & Zelinksi, 2003; Smith, Petersen, Ivnik, Malec, & Tangalos, 1996). For the most part, measures of memory self-concept correlate between .2 and .3 with memory performance, and a number of studies have suggested that memory complaints may be more closely tied to neuroticism, depression, conscientiousness, or other personality factors than they are to objective memory status (e.g., Niederehe & Yoder, 1989; Pearman & Storandt, 2004). Failures to detect memory self-concept correlations with memory performance may also reflect problems due to reliability, low statistical power, and selection of criterion tasks (see Rabbitt et al., 1995, for other potential explanations). Given that there is some evidence that neuroticism and depressive affect decrease in magnitude from young adulthood through middle age (Helson, Jones, & Kwan, 2002; Newmann, 1989; Rothermund & Brandstädter, 2003), yet another explanation for low relations of age to memory self-concept is that developmental changes in facets of neuroticism suppress some of the relationship between memory and memory self-concept.

Hertzog, Park, Morrell, and Martin (2000) examined relationships of the MFQ and self-reported problems taking medications to actual medication adherence behavior, using data from a sample of rheumatoid arthritis patients ranging in age from early middle age through old age. Age was associated with improvements in medication adherence, despite age-related changes in cognition that were positively associated with adherence. Instead, middle-aged adults were at risk for forgetting to take medications, and self-reports of busyness in everyday life correlated with adherence errors (see Park et al., 1999). These results reinforce the idea that strategies for managing everyday memory tasks (e.g., Dixon, de Frias, & Bäckman, 2001) may be more important than memory ability (as measured by cognitive tasks) for ensuring success in memory use in everyday life. In this sense, middle-aged adults who do not use external aids and strategies to cope with memory demands may be most at risk for everyday cognitive failures.

Hertzog et al. (2000) found that the MFQ Frequency of Forgetting scale predicted laboratory memory task performance independent of depressive affect. Furthermore, specific reports of difficulties in taking medications (gleaned from an interview about each medication the person was taking) prospectively predicted medication adherence but not memory task performance; conversely, the MFQ scale did not predict actual medication adherence, even though it was related to laboratory memory performance. Such findings suggest that middle-aged and older adults can give valid self-reports of specific memory problems in everyday life. However, metamemory questionnaires may be too broad and decontextualized in their questions about everyday memory problems, thereby diluting predictive validity to specific memory behaviors in everyday life.

In summary, memory self-concept does appear to change over the adult life span, although these changes are small in magnitude. In contrast, perceptions of memory change begin to show reliable age differences even in midlife. Memory self-concept measures do predict memory performance, but the relationship is modest. The distinction between memory beliefs and actual memory suggests that memory self-concept is a distinct construct from actual memory and points to the possibility that it is determined by factors other than accurate monitoring of one's own memory status. Finally, memory self-concept seems to be relatively stable, in terms of individual differences, during adulthood, including midlife.

Self-Reported Strategy Use

Questionnaire measures of use of internal strategies and external aids also show age-related trends, with older adults more likely than younger adults to report use of external aids to support memory (e.g., Hertzog et al., 1989; Loewen, Shaw, & Craik, 1990). This age-related increase may be compensatory in nature, with individuals attempting to compensate for the perception of an increasing incidence of everyday memory failures (de Frias et al., 2003). For example, among healthy middle-aged and older adults in the initial study (Dixon, de Frias, & Bäckman, 2001), the most frequently reported everyday strategy was use of external memory aids, a strategy often recognized as powerfully generalizable. Many adults also reported trying harder to manage and execute memory tasks, and some reported using mnemonic strategies, such as rehearsal. One notable finding of later studies was that as adults became more vulnerable to serious memory decline or impairment, they reported an increased use of human collaborative memory assistance (e.g., Dixon, Hopp, Cohen, de Frias, & Bäckman, 2003). In general, research on reports of compensatory strategy use in midlife to later adulthood has suggested that it may be one form of cognitive resilience, perhaps buffering late-life cognitive decline.

Relations Between General Beliefs and Self-Referent Beliefs

Given that there are age-related stereotypes about cognitive capacity and change, and that individuals appear to have implicit theories about cognition and its development in adulthood, an important question is how these general beliefs relate to personal beliefs. Are implicit theories about cognitive development an important influence on personal beliefs? Do these belief systems exist in parallel, with little interaction between each other? And how do these processes play out in midlife?

Ellen Langer argued that individuals internalize stereotypes of age-related decline in youth, at a point in the life span when they have no reason to question the validity of their decline beliefs for themselves or for others (e.g., Langer, 1989). There is some evidence in the literature consistent with this view. Cutler and Hodgson (1996) have described an interesting phenomenon that occurs in the middle-aged children of older adults with familial Alzheimer's disease. These children are more likely than others to assume that they, too, will begin experiencing dementia at some point. Indeed, they tend to report that their memory has already started changing, even though they are still in their 40s; normatively speaking, it is unlikely that they are experiencing preclinical decline due to neurodegenerative cognitive pathology. In effect, these individuals may become vigilant about the possibility of memory decline, interpreting everyday memory failure as a sign of impending onset of an outcome they fear and wish to avoid (Hodgson & Cutler, 2003).

Lineweaver and Hertzog (1998) examined the hypothesis that personal beliefs (memory self-concept and personal control over memory) are closely tied to individuals' general memory beliefs. Given that the individuals in their sample produced GBMI rating curves (as in Figure 11.2), it was possible to estimate polynomial regression functions for all individuals, capturing their perceived developmental function for memory and control over memory. Lineweaver and Hertzog then substituted each respondent's age into the age function estimated from the GBMI ratings, thereby computing an age-equivalent rating (i.e., how well an individual thinks a person of his or her own age functions, on average). Indeed, the points on the two curves in Figure 11.3 are the predicted scores in question. Age-equivalent ratings were reliably correlated with personal ratings from the PBMI for all three age groups, including middle-aged adults. In the aggregate, age-equivalent ratings of memory correlated about .5 with measures of memory self-concept. Age-equivalent ratings for control correlated between .4 and .5 with personal control ratings. Lineweaver and Hertzog (1998) found much lower correlations of personal beliefs with GBMI slopes and intercepts. This pattern is consistent with the hypothesis that internalized general beliefs influence personal beliefs, although it is certainly not definitive evidence of a causal linkage.

Unpublished data from that project also suggest a strong relationship between perceived (retrospective) change in one's own memory and age-equivalent ratings. Several retrospective change questions asked individuals about changes over the last 10 years in their lives. Hence, we computed 10-year changes in age-equivalent ratings, estimating the amount of perceived memory decline from 10 years before the person's current age to the present. Regression analysis revealed a reliable relationship of change in a person's GBMI function and perceived change in memory, controlling on current level of perceived memory functioning (which correlated substantially with perceived change; see also Dixon & Hultsch, 1983; Hertzog et al., 1989). The level of prediction accuracy was comparable for ratings of both retrospective and prospective change.

Such findings are relevant to competing hypotheses about why there are robust age differences in perceived change, for example, the implicit theory hypothesis and the accurate monitoring hypothesis (see McDonald-Miszczak et al., 1995). The implicit theory hypothesis states that individuals perceive memory decline when it is consistent with their implicit theory about age change in or around their current age. Ross and colleagues (McFarland, Ross, & Giltrow, 1992; Ross, 1989) have suggested that individuals evaluate retrospective change by using their beliefs about current status, combined with an implicit theory about change in a given attribute, to construct an estimate of perceived change that is merely an extrapolation of their implicit theory. The accurate monitoring hypothesis states that individuals monitor memory successes and failures and perceive change in memory status when there is an increased prevalence of difficulties in using memory. Thus, the implicit theory hypothesis states that middle-aged adults will perceive memory change if they believe it occurs, in general, during this period of the life span. By this account, age differences in perceived change are merely a manifestation of the implicit theory.

McDonald-Miszczak et al. (1995) identified several patterns in longitudinal data on the MIA Change and Capacity scales that appeared to be more consistent with the implicit theory hypothesis. For example, perceived change (i.e., as measured by the MIA Change scale) was more highly related to concurrent ratings of memory self-concept (i.e., MIA Capacity) than to longitudinal changes in memory self-concept. However, there were small but reliable correlations of longitudinal changes in memory with MIA Change, consistent with the accurate monitoring hypothesis (see also Lane & Zelinski, 2003). Hence, both kinds of influences may be operating, but several patterns in the data suggest that people do access implicit theories about change when perceiving personal change in memory (see McFarland et al., 1992).

These findings imply that middle-aged adults may perceive personal change in memory even when there has been none, using their implicit theory of change as a filter to make attributions about memory failures in everyday life. Such failures occur for every human being, regardless of age. Like the children of Alzheimer's disease patients referred to earlier, middle-aged adults in general may use their beliefs about aging to interpret normal memory failures as evidence of decline. It is conceivable that these beliefs cause psychological distress and trigger coping and compensatory behaviors even for individuals who have not yet experienced meaningful cognitive change. Thus, we would argue that it is important to study these belief systems about memory and cognition in middle-aged adults, even when it is the case that there is little evidence of age-related changes in cognition itself during that age period.

Conclusion

As in other areas of research on midlife, there is much that is unknown about how metacognition changes during adulthood. As noted earlier, virtually nothing is currently known about middle-aged adults' capability of monitoring ongoing cognitive processes and adapting strategies on the basis of that monitoring. The research to date on memory beliefs indicates that middle-aged adults are vulnerable to everyday cognitive failures if they do not use effective support strategies, and they are also vulnerable to interpreting everyday cognitive failures as evidence of irreversible cognitive decline. The work to date has been promising, and there is reason to be optimistic that new research focusing on the relationships between implicit theories, self-referent beliefs such as memory self-concept, and everyday cognitive performance will yield new insights about mechanisms that may have important practical implications for quality of life in midlife and older adulthood (e.g., Hertzog, 2002).

References

Baldi, R., & Hertzog, C. (2000). *Memory self-concept and memory self-efficacy: Independent influences on memory task performance?* Unpublished manuscript.

Bandura, A. (1997). *Self-efficacy: The exercise of control.* New York: Freeman.

Bandura, A. (1989). Regulation of cognitive processes through perceived self-efficacy. *Developmental Psychology, 25,* 729–735.

Berg, C. A., & Sternberg, R. J. (1985). A triarchic theory of intellectual development during adulthood. *Developmental Review, 5,* 334–370.

Berry, J. M. (1999). Memory self-efficacy in its social cognitive context. In T. M. Hess (Ed.), *Social cognition and aging* (pp. 69–96). San Diego, CA: Academic Press.

Berry, J. M., & West, R. L. (1993). Cognitive self-efficacy in relation to personal mastery and goal setting across the life span. *International Journal of Behavioral Development, 16,* 351–379.

Berry, J. M., West, R. L., & Dennehey, D. M. (1989). Reliability and validity of the Memory Self-Efficacy Questionnaire. *Developmental Psychology, 5,* 701–713.

Bieman-Copland, S., & Charness, N. (1994). Memory knowledge and memory monitoring in adulthood. *Psychology & Aging, 9,* 287–302.

Cavanaugh, J. C., Feldman, J., & Hertzog, C. (1998). Memory beliefs as social cognition: A reconceptualization of what memory questionnaires assess. *Review of General Psychology, 2,* 48–65.

Chasteen, A. L., Schwarz, N., & Park, D. C. (2002). The activation of aging stereotypes in younger and older adults. *Journal of Gerontology: Psychological Sciences, 57B,* P540–P547.

Cohen, G., & Faulkner, D. (1986). Memory for proper names: Age differences in retrieval. *British Journal of Developmental Psychology, 4,* 187–197.

Crawford, J. R., Smith, G., & Maylor, E. A. (2003). The prospective and retrospective memory questionnaire (PRMQ): Normative data and latent structure in a large nonclinical sample. *Memory, 11,* 261–275.

Crook, T. H., III, & Larrabee, G. J. (1990). A self-rating scale for evaluating memory in everyday life. *Psychology and Aging, 5,* 48–57.

Cutler, S. J., & Hodgson, L. G. (1996). Anticipatory dementia: A link between memory appraisals and concerns about developing Alzheimer's disease. *The Gerontologist, 36*, 657–664.

de Frias, C. M., & Dixon, R. A. (in press). Confirmatory factor structure and measurement invariance of the Memory Compensation Questionnaire. *Psychological Assessment.*

de Frias, C. M., Dixon, R. A., & Bäckman, L. (2003). Use of memory compensation strategies is related to psychosocial and health indicators. *Journal of Gerontology: Psychological Sciences, 58B*, P12–P22.

Dixon, R. A. (1989). Questionnaire research on metamemory and aging: Issues of structure and function. In L. W. Poon, D. C. Rubin, & B. A. Wilson (Eds.), *Everyday cognition in adulthood and old age* (pp. 394–415). New York: Cambridge University Press.

Dixon, R. A., & de Frias, C. M. (2004). The Victoria Longitudinal Study: From characterizing cognitive aging to illustrating changes in memory compensation. *Aging, Neuropsychology, and Cognition, 11*, 346–376.

Dixon, R. A., de Frias, C. M., & Bäckman, L. (2001). Characteristics of self-reported memory compensation in late life. *Journal of Clinical and Experimental Neuropsychology, 23*, 650–661.

Dixon, R. A., de Frias, C. M., & Maitland, S. B. (2001). Memory in midlife. In M. E. Lachman (Ed.), *Handbook of midlife development* (pp. 248–278). New York: Wiley.

Dixon, R. A., Hopp, G. A., Cohen, A.-L., de Frias, C. M., & Bäckman, L. (2003). Self-reported memory compensation: Similar patterns in Alzheimer's disease and very old adult samples. *Journal of Clinical and Experimental Neuropsychology, 25*, 382–390.

Dixon, R. A., & Hultsch, D. F. (1983). Structure and development of metamemory in adulthood. *Journal of Gerontology, 38*, 682–688.

Dunlosky, J., & Connor, L. T. (1997). Age differences in the allocation of study time account for age differences in memory performance. *Memory & Cognition, 25*, 691–700.

Dunlosky, J., & Hertzog, C. (2000). Updating knowledge about strategy effectiveness: A componential analysis of learning about strategy effectiveness from task experience. *Psychology and Aging, 15*, 462–474.

Dweck, C. S., & Leggett, E. L. (1988). A social-cognitive approach to motivation and personality. *Psychological Review, 95*, 256–273.

Elliott, E., & Lachman, M. E. (1989). Enhancing memory by modifying control beliefs, attributions, and performance goals in the elderly. In P. S. Fry (Ed.), *Psychological perspectives of helplessness and control in the elderly* (pp. 339–367). Amsterdam: North-Holland.

Flavell, J. H. (1979). Metacognition and cognitive monitoring: A new area of cognitive-developmental inquiry. *American Psychologist, 34*, 906–911.

Gilewski, M. J., & Zelinski, E. M. (1986). Questionnaire assessment of memory complaints. In L. W. Poon, T. Crook, K. L. Davis, C. Eisdorfer, B. J. Gurland,

A. W. Kaszniak, et al. (Eds.), *Handbook for clinical memory assessment of older adults* (pp. 93–107). Washington, DC: American Psychological Association.

Gilewski, M. J., Zelinski, E. M., & Schaie, K. W. (1990). The Memory Functioning Questionnaire for assessment of memory complaints in adulthood and old age. *Psychology and Aging, 5*, 482–490.

Greenwald, A. G., & Banaji, M. R. (1995). Implicit social cognition: Attitudes, self-esteem, and stereotypes. *Psychological Review, 102*, 4–27.

Guilford, J. P. (1932). *Psychometric theory.* New York: McGraw-Hill.

Heckhausen, J., Dixon, R. A., & Baltes, P. B. (1989). Gains and losses in development throughout adulthood as perceived by different adult age groups. *Developmental Psychology, 25*, 109–121.

Helson, R., Jones, C., & Kwan, V. S. Y. (2002). Personality change over 40 years of adulthood: Hierarchical linear modeling analyses of two longitudinal samples. *Journal of Personality and Social Psychology, 83*, 752–766.

Henkel, L. A., Johnson, M. K., & De Leonardis, D. M. (1998). Aging and source monitorings: Cognitive processes and neuropsychological correlates. *Journal of Experimental Psychology: General, 127*, 251–268.

Hertzog, C. (1996). Research design in studies of aging and cognition. In J. E. Birren & K. W. Schaie (Eds.), *Handbook of the psychology of aging* (4th ed., pp. 24–37). New York: Academic Press.

Hertzog, C. (2002). Metacognition in older adults: Implications for application. In T. J. Perfect & B. L. Schwartz (Eds.), *Applied metacognition* (pp. 169–196). Cambridge, UK: Cambridge University Press.

Hertzog, C., Baldi, R. A., & York, A. R. (2001, June). *New measures of implicit theories about memory and aging.* Paper presented at the 13th Annual American Psychological Society Conference, Toronto, Ontario, Canada.

Hertzog, C., & Dixon, R. A. (1994). Metacognition and memory development in adulthood and old age. In J. Metcalfe & A. P. Shimamura (Eds.), *Metacognition* (pp. 225–251). Boston: MIT Press.

Hertzog, C., Dixon, R. A., & Hultsch, D. F. (1990). Relationships between meta-memory, memory predictions, and memory task performance in adults. *Psychology and Aging, 5*, 215–227.

Hertzog, C., & Hultsch, D. F. (2000). Metacognition in adulthood and aging. In T. Salthouse & F. I. M. Craik (Eds.), *Handbook of aging and cognition* (2nd ed., pp. 417–466). Mahwah, NJ: Erlbaum.

Hertzog, C., Hultsch, D. F., & Dixon, R. A. (1989). Evidence for the convergent validity of two self-report metamemory questionnaires. *Developmental Psychology, 25*, 687–700.

Hertzog, C., Kidder, D. P., Powell-Moman, A., & Dunlosky, J. (2002). Aging and monitoring associative learning: Is monitoring accuracy spared or impaired? *Psychology and Aging, 17*, 209–225.

Hertzog, C., Lineweaver, T. T., & McGuire, C. L. (1999). Beliefs about memory and aging. In F. Blanchard-Fields & T. M. Hess (Eds.), *Social cognition and aging* (pp. 43–68). New York: Academic Press.

Hertzog, C., Park, D. C., Morrell, R. W., & Martin, M. (2000). Ask and ye shall receive: Behavioral specificity in the accuracy of subjective memory complaints. *Applied Cognitive Psychology, 14*, 257–275.

Hertzog, C., & Robinson, A. E. (2005). Metacognition and intelligence. In O. Wilhelm & R. W. Engle (Eds.), *Handbook of understanding and measuring intelligence* (pp. 101–124). Thousand Oaks, CA: Sage.

Hess, T. M., Auman, C., Colcombe, S. J., & Rahhal, T. A. (2003). The impact of stereotype threat on age differences in memory performance. *Journal of Gerontology: Psychological Sciences, 58B*, P3–P11.

Hodgson, L. G., & Cutler, S. J. (2003). Looking for signs of Alzheimer's disease. *International Journal of Aging & Human Development, 56*, 323–343.

Hultsch, D. F., Hertzog, C., Dixon, R. A., & Small, B. J. (1998). *Memory change in the aged.* New York: Cambridge University Press.

Hummert, M. L. (1990). Multiple stereotypes of elderly and young adults: A comparison of structure and evaluations. *Psychology and Aging, 5*, 183–193.

Hummert, M. L., Garstka, T. A., O'Brien, L. T., Greenwald, A. G., & Mellott, D. S. (2003). Using the Implicit Association Test to measure age differences in implicit social cognitions. *Psychology and Aging, 17*, 482–495.

Intons-Peterson, M. J., & Fournier, J. (1986). External and internal memory aids: When and how often do we use them? *Journal of Experimental Psychology: General, 115*, 267–280.

Kuhn, D. (2000). Metacognitive development. *Current Directions in Psychological Science, 9*, 178–181.

Lachman, M. E., Bandura, M., Weaver, S. L., & Elliott, E. (1995). Assessing memory control beliefs: The Memory Controllability Inventory. *Aging and Cognition, 2*, 67–84.

Lachman, M. E., Steinberg, E. S., & Trotter, S. D. (1987). Effects of control beliefs and attributions on memory self-assessments and performance. *Psychology and Aging, 2*, 266–271.

Lane, C. J., & Zelinski, E. M. (2003). Longitudinal hierarchical linear models of the Memory Functioning Questionnaire. *Psychology and Aging, 18*, 38–53.

Langer, E. J. (1989). *Mindfulness.* Reading, MA: Addison-Wesley.

Levy, B. (1996). Improving memory in old age through implicit self-stereotyping. *Journal of Personality and Social Psychology, 71*, 1092–1107.

Lineweaver, T. T., & Hertzog, C. (1998). Adults' efficacy and control beliefs regarding memory and aging: Separating general from personal beliefs. *Aging, Neuropsychology, and Cognition, 5*, 264–296.

Loewen, E. R., Shaw, R. J., & Craik, F. I. M. (1990). Age differences in components of metamemory. *Experimental Aging Research, 16,* 43–48.

Lovelace, E. A. (1990). Aging and metacognition concerning memory function. In E. A. Lovelace (Ed.), *Aging and cognition: Mental processes, self-awareness, and interventions* (pp. 157–188). Amsterdam: North-Holland.

Lynch, S. M. (2000). Measurement and prediction of aging anxiety. *Research on Aging, 22,* 533–558.

McDonald-Miszczak, L., Hertzog, C., & Hultsch, D. F. (1995). Stability and accuracy of metamemory in adulthood and aging. *Psychology and Aging, 10,* 553–564.

McFarland, C., Ross, M., & Giltrow, M. (1992). Biased recollections in older adults: The role of implicit theories of aging. *Journal of Personality and Social Psychology, 62,* 837–850.

Murphy, M. D., Schmitt, E. A., Caruso, M. J., & Sanders, R. E. (1987). Metamemory in older adults: The role of monitoring in serial recall. *Psychology and Aging, 2,* 331–339.

Nelson, T. O. (1996). Consciousness and metacognition. *American Psychologist, 51,* 102–116.

Newmann, J. P. (1989). Aging and depression. *Psychology and Aging, 4,* 150–165.

Niederehe, G., & Yoder, C. (1989). Metamemory perceptions in depressions of older and younger adults. *Journal of Nervous and Mental Disease, 177,* 4–14.

Park, D. C., Hertzog, C., Leventhal, H., Morrell, R. W., Leventhal, E., Birchmore, D., et al. (1999). Medication adherence in rheumatoid arthritis patients: Older is wiser. *Journal of the American Geriatric Society, 47,* 172–183.

Pearman, A., & Storandt, M. (2004). Predictors of subjective memory in older adults. *Journal of Gerontology: Psychological Sciences, 59B,* P4–P6.

Perlmutter, M. (1978). What is memory aging the aging of? *Developmental Psychology, 14,* 330–345.

Pyszczynski, T., Greenberg, J., & Solomon, S. (2004). Why do people need self-esteem? A theoretical and empirical review. *Psychological Bulletin, 130,* 435–468.

Rabbitt, P., Maylor, E., McInnes, L., Bent, N., & Moore, B. (1995). What goods can self-assessment questionnaires deliver for cognitive gerontology? *Applied Cognitive Psychology, 9,* S127–S152.

Robinson, A. E., Hertzog, C., & Dunlosky, J. (in press). Aging, encoding fluency, and metacognitive monitoring. *Aging, Neuropsychology, and Cognition.*

Ross, M. (1989). Relation of implicit theories to the construction of personal histories. *Psychological Review, 96,* 341–357.

Rothermund, K., & Brandstädter, J. (2003). Depression in later life: Cross-sequential patterns and possible determinants. *Psychology and Aging, 18,* 80–90.

Rowe, J. W., & Kahn, R. L. (1998). *Successful aging.* New York: Pantheon.

Ryan, E. B. (1992). Beliefs about memory changes across the adult life span. *Journal of Gerontology: Psychological Sciences, 47,* P41–P46.

Ryan, E. B., & Kwong See, S. T. (1993). Age-based beliefs about memory changes for self and others across adulthood. *Journal of Gerontology: Psychological Sciences, 48*, P108–P118.

Schaie, K. W. (1996). *Intellectual development in adulthood: The Seattle Longitudinal Study.* New York: Cambridge University Press.

Schaie, K. W., Willis, S. L., & O'Hanlon, A. M. (1994). Perceived intellectual performance change over seven years. *Journal of Gerontology: Psychological Sciences, 49*, P108–P118.

Schooler, C., Mulatu, M. S., & Oates, G. (1999). The continuing effects of substantively complex work on the intellectual functioning of older workers. *Psychology and Aging, 14*, 483–506.

Smith, G. E., Petersen, R. C., Ivnik, R. J., Malec, J. F., & Tangalos, E. G. (1996). Subjective memory complaints, psychological distress, and longitudinal change in objective memory performance. *Psychology and Aging, 11*, 272–279.

Steele, C. M., & Aaronson, J. (1995). Contending with a stereotype: African-American intellectual test performance and stereotype threat. *Journal of Personality and Social Psychology, 69*, 797–811.

Sternberg, R. J. (1985). *Beyond IQ: A triarchic theory of human intelligence.* New York: Cambridge University Press.

Tun, P. A., & Wingfield, A. (1995). Does dividing attention become harder with age? Findings from the Divided Attention Questionnaire. *Aging and Cognition, 2*, 39–66.

PART IV

Summary and Future Directions

Twelve

Midlife Development

Past, Present, and Future Directions

Mike Martin and Sherry L. Willis

We believe there are important reasons to study aging processes across middle age:

1. Ways of coping with tasks and stressors are learned in middle age, and how or if persons cope in later life depends on expectations of being successful built in earlier phases of the life span (Ruth & Coleman, 1996).

2. An accumulation of risk factors or risky health behaviors in midlife might show effects only in late life (Rabbitt, Bent, & McInness, 1997; Wang & Snyder, 1998).

3. Individual skills are at a maximum level in midlife (Mirowski & Ross, 1999).

4. The importance of family and job factors is largest in midlife and may influence further development in individually quite different ways (Rossi, 2001).

5. In midlife, it is possible to detect the first indications of developmental decline (Schaie, 2000).

6. Middle age is characterized by a high level of plasticity and of the potential to effectively use a variety of personal and contextual resources (Titov & Knight, 1997).

In addition, in comparison to earlier cohorts, middle-aged adults are better educated, have higher incomes, and show higher levels of health and competence. Due to these differences, prognoses about aging processes lack a sufficiently current data basis (Robison & Moen, 2000).

As the chapters in this volume amply demonstrate, the group of middle-aged adults between the ages of roughly 40 to 65 years has consequently attracted a lot of interest from longitudinal developmental researchers. Research covers aspects of the biology, physiology, psychology, and sociology of aging, paying tribute to the fact that middle-aged adults currently represent one of the largest age groups in Europe and the United States. A better understanding of their development and factors related to the developmental trajectories in midlife will become increasingly important as these cohorts reach old age. Consequently, the focus of the chapters in this book is on longitudinal changes in aspects of development that can be considered among the key competencies needed in young and old age to meet the challenges of education, job demands, and everyday life (see Martin & Zimprich, Chapter 6, this volume).

Studies of development in midlife can be characterized by two main approaches. On the one hand, the decline of particular cognitive, social, or financial resources is a main concern for persons from middle age onward (e.g., Lawton et al., 1999). Thus, studies on midlife cognition have focused on the question of whether groups at risk for decline in early old age can be identified. The timely identification of at-risk individuals would permit preventive measures targeted at early stages of decline (cf. Schaie, 2000). In addition, even though declines in performance are from a high starting level, these first signs of decline might be salient enough to motivate persons to participate in interventions. On the other hand, midlife might be characterized by a wealth of demanding activities and relatively high levels of performance. Thus, there is an interest in examining if and how demanding activities and a wide spectrum of interests in middle age may protect individuals from decline or may at least provide compensatory potential for the later years of life.

This volume covers middle adulthood development in a four-step fashion. In a first step, the conceptual foundations of research in the area are spelled out. In a second step, the genetic bases and the societal conditions limiting development and providing opportunity structures for individual decisions concerning lifestyles and behaviors are laid out. In a third step, the developmental changes of the interactions between individual resources (such as cognition, personality, or mental health) and the environment (e.g., stressors and life events) are presented. In a fourth step, the bases for individual decision making, such as processes of metacognition, identity, and the self, are discussed as they inform the developmental goals persons set for themselves.

Together, the volume highlights international efforts to study and understand the key factors involved in development across middle adulthood. The chapters emphasize that middle adulthood is characterized by stability in some aspects of development, but also change in many other aspects of development. Several chapters have also highlighted the importance of differentiating between different developmental phases within the middle adulthood range (e.g., early and late middle adulthood), thus focusing on quantitative and qualitative differences and changes within this age group. This suggests that regulatory efforts and skills across domains of functioning play a decisive role in understanding midlife development and that more effort needs to be directed toward examining the regulatory mechanisms that help persons to achieve and maintain high levels of functioning throughout adulthood and well into old age.

Future Directions

Before discussing future directions, we should emphasize the contributions made by the chapters in this book. First, the data from a number of international longitudinal studies focusing on different aspects of development in middle age all demonstrate that there are substantial differences in the types, direction, and size of change between early and late middle age. For example, the relation between individual differences in 4-year longitudinal speed and memory changes is minimal in early middle age and in the range of 25% in old age (e.g., Martin & Zimprich, Chapter 6, this volume). Hence, future research on middle adulthood may profit from taking a closer look at the age differences in the factors influencing development in early and late middle adulthood. The development of persons between the ages of 50 and 65, the "older workers," is much more likely influenced by the opportunity structure of the sociostructural environment, whereas the change in abilities, skills, or fitness plays a much smaller role for the achieved level of well-being.

Second, from a methodological point of view, there are differences in the reported longitudinal findings due to differences in the length of the longitudinal measurement interval. The use of measurement-intensive designs with repeated measures within each measurement occasion could be an aspect of change that, in the future, could provide more insights into the processes responsible for the empirical relations between functioning in different domains, such as cognitive, social, emotional, or affective development (e.g., Martin & Hofer, 2004). This would allow examining a process-oriented account of longitudinal change in functioning, such as compensatory processes in which declines in particular functions or differing levels of environmental stress lead to increases in other domains of functioning. Within the same person, the burst design enables researchers to examine to what degree the individual differences in one domain of functioning can be accounted for by environmental influences such as stress, and it may determine the relations between variability of earlier, current, and later stress and cognition or health variables. In fact, the focus on individual differences in different aspects of change in functioning across middle adulthood highlights that despite relatively high mean levels of performance, a large amount of developmental change occurs in midlife. Focusing on these aspects of change clearly suggests a need for more data and more specific change theories on development across middle adulthood.

Third, although differing in many ways, both Europe and the United States are experiencing major changes in the sociostructural conditions under which middle adult development occurs. Working conditions (legal and financial aspects of work, retirement), family life (lifestyles in terms of partnerships, children, and family), social interactions, behaviors (diets, everyday and leisure activities), housing conditions, and health care are all changing in the wake of the aging of our societies. Hence, the aging process itself and the developmental tasks going along with it are changing. Thus, it is extremely important to use research to accompany the middle-aged adults and their adaptation to the ongoing changes, because not only will this help now to predict their future needs for successful aging, but it will also inform younger as well as older generations about the interventions that might help them to prepare for old age across the whole life span. Perrig-Chiello and Perren (Chapter 5) addressed this point by focusing on factors from early life influencing the responses to stressful situations in midlife. In a similar way, one may conceive that lifestyle factors in midlife, such as treatments for illnesses, might affect the course of aging in old age, as demonstrated in Deeg (Chapter 7) on mental health. In general, the view and empirical examination of middle age needs to become more contextualized to include the short- and long-term effects of environmental influences and stressors.

Fourth, the identification of persons at risk for problematic development is one challenge research is facing; the development and evaluation of interventions designed as preventive measures to protect individuals from risky developmental trajectories is a major challenge, in particular when considering that the positive effects of such interventions might show only in decades to come. This would, on the one hand, address the concern of the present-day middle-aged who ask what they could be doing to positively affect the development of resources across the rest of their life span. Processes of recovering from the impact of stress or illness is one area of study, but it is also worthwhile to more strongly emphasize the examination of those individuals characterized as gainers across middle age. Research on processes of adaptation should thus be complemented by research on processes of growth and profiting from developmental gains, such as factors contributing to the accumulation of knowledge or strategy repertoires or experiences of growth, meaningfulness, sense of coherence, personality, intergenerational and social exchange, and emotion regulation.

Fifth, based on the now existing longitudinal data suggesting particular regulatory mechanisms aimed at stabilizing well-being and the achievement of personal goals, it would now be interesting to see more experimental data examining middle adult developmental processes. The experimental examination of developmental processes across middle age does, however, also point to the need for specific theories about the processes involved in midlife development. For instance, once researchers specify which regulatory skills affect cross-domain interactions of available resources (e.g., affect and cognition or emotion and health) and which differ between early and late middle adulthood, we might see more experimental studies in this area. We believe this would complement the longitudinal studies by more quickly improving our understanding of adaptive processes across midlife.

On a more general note, theories on lifespan development might profit from including middle adulthood and the knowledge accumulated about individual differences in intraindividual change across middle adulthood. The theories need to include explanations of mean level stability in particular outcomes while at the same time allowing for adaptational and anticipatory processes to vary in order to maintain this level of stability. One possibility for midlife developmental theories is to focus more strongly on the regulatory behaviors persons engage in across the life span, that is, which resources from different domains of functioning individuals engage in to achieve particular individual and meaningful goals. The focus on individual goals can help to reflect one of the important aspects of how aging itself has changed and is changing: The majority of the members of current cohorts of middle-aged adults can practically count on becoming 80 years and older. Different from life expectations only a few decades ago, this might influence the type of goals persons set for themselves and how they are related to expectations that refer to individuals' life spans. This could help to explain the somewhat lower relationships between levels of available resources and aspects of well-being in middle age, but it might also provide a new approach for examining development in old age. Overall, the focus of theories thus needs to include environmental pressures and changes, that is, the sociostructural environments and interactions of individual goals related to a person's identity across the whole life span (see Dittmann-Kohli, Chapter 10, this volume; Dörner, Mickler, & Staudinger, Chapter 9, this volume). This would make the theories flexible enough to describe, explain, and predict midlife development in existing and future cohorts in different cultural and sociostructural contexts. In addition, these types of theories would also guide the examination of particular aspects of the aging process in middle age. They would include regulatory behaviors within and across domains of functioning, anticipatory and planful behavior foreshadowing the expectation of a long life left to live, the time perspectives of individuals as they get older but still have many years to live, and choices persons make with respect to which domain to invest their emotional, cognitive, social, and financial resources. Theories would also look at how persons perceive and respond to stress and, in general, how individuals go through life after not having had to respond to normed expectations about the life course as in earlier-born cohorts. Instead, the middle-aged have become lifespan entrepreneurs, that is, individuals defining their own goals, creating sense of what they make of their lives, shaping their own development, and becoming more and more different from each other.

References

Lawton, M. P., Moss, M., Hoffman, C., Grant, R., Ten Have, T., & Kleban, M. H. (1999). Health, valuation of life, and the wish to live. *The Gerontologist, 39*, 406–416.

Martin, M., & Hofer, S. M. (2004). Intraindividual variability, change, and aging: Conceptual and analytical issues. *Gerontology, 50,* 7–11.

Mirowski, J., & Ross, C. E. (1999). Well-being across the life course. In A. V. Horwitz & T. L. Scheid (Eds.), *A handbook for the study of mental health: Social contexts, theories, and systems* (pp. 328–347). New York: Cambridge University Press.

Rabbitt, P., Bent, N., & McInness, L. (1997). Health, age and mental ability. *Irish Journal of Psychology, 18,* 104–131.

Robison, J. T., & Moen, P. T. (2000). Future housing expectations in late midlife: The role of retirement, gender, and social integration. In K. Pillemer, P. Moen, E. Wethington, & N. Glasgow (Eds.), *Social integration in the second half of life* (pp. 158–189). Baltimore: Johns Hopkins University Press.

Rossi, A. (Ed.). (2001). *Caring and doing for others: Social responsibility in the domains of family, work, and community.* Chicago: University of Chicago Press.

Ruth, J. E., & Coleman, P. (1996). Personality and aging: Coping and management of the self in later life. In J. E. Birren & K. W. Schaie (Eds.), *Handbook of the psychology of aging* (4th ed., pp. 308–322). San Diego, CA: Academic Press.

Schaie, K. W. (2000). The impact of longitudinal studies on understanding development from young adulthood to old age. *International Journal of Behavioral Development, 24,* 257–266.

Titov, N., & Knight, R. G. (1997). Adult age differences in controlled and automatic memory processing. *Psychology and Aging, 12,* 565–573.

Wang, E., & Snyder, D. S. (Eds.). (1998). *Handbook of the aging brain.* San Diego, CA: Academic Press.

Author Index

Subject Index

About the Editors

Sherry L. Willis is Professor of Human Development at The Pennsylvania State University. She received her PhD in Educational Psychology from the University of Texas at Austin. Her research interests include adult cognitive development with a focus on middle age, cognitive training in later adulthood, and everyday problem solving in adulthood. She is a codirector of the Seattle Longitudinal Study with K. Warner Schaie and has coauthored the textbook *Adult Development and Aging* (5th ed.). She is coeditor of two other books on midlife: *Life in the Middle,* coedited with J. Reid, and *The Baby Boomers,* coedited with S. Whitbourne.

Mike Martin is Professor of Gerontopsychology and Director of the Center of Gerontology at The University of Zurich, Switzerland. He received an MA at the University of Georgia, a PhD in developmental psychology at The University of Mainz, Germany, and his habilitation at The German Center for Research on Aging, The University of Heidelberg, Germany. His research focuses on longitudinal and experimental studies of cognitive and social development across the life span, including studies examining predictors of development in childhood, middle adulthood, old age, and extreme old age. His recent publications include an encyclopedia of gerontology and a textbook on the psychological foundations of aging.

About the Contributors

Dorly J. H. Deeg is Professor of the Epidemiology of Aging at the Institute for Research in Extramural Medicine and the Department of Psychiatry, Free University Medical Center, Amsterdam. Since 1991, she has been the scientific director of the ongoing Longitudinal Aging Study Amsterdam (LASA). By education a methodologist, she has worked mainly in the areas of public health and gerontology. To date, publications include studies of longevity, chronic conditions, functional limitations, cognitive impairment, depression, personal competence, social support, and methodology of longitudinal research. Current interests include cross-national comparison and time trends.

Freya Dittmann-Kohli is Professor and Director of the Center for Psychogerontology at the University of Nijmegen, Netherlands, where research and teaching on various aspects of normal and pathological development in adulthood and aging is carried out. Under her direction, a long-term research program on content and contextual determinants of identity and personal meaning has been conducted, based on data from two representative national surveys and other national and cross-cultural investigations. In addition, she has led many other projects using self-narratives (low-structured sentence stems), psychological scales, and demographic data. Her earlier research includes studies on work and aging, intelligence and wisdom, adolescent life tasks, learning and curriculum development, and culture and personality.

Roger A. Dixon is Canada Research Chair and Professor of Psychology at the University of Alberta. He is Director of the Victoria Longitudinal Study (VLS), a long-term, multicohort epidemiological investigation of cognitive, neurocognitive, biological, social-personality, and health aspects of human aging. The VLS is funded by grants from the U.S. National Institute on Aging.

Jessica Dörner is a doctoral student at the Jacobs Center for Lifelong Learning and Institutional Development, International University Bremen, Germany. She received her MA in psychology from the University of Goettingen, Germany, in 2001. During her studies, she also spent one year at the University of California, Santa Cruz. Her current research centers on the development of a new instrument for assessing personality growth via the self-concept. Subsidiary research interests include analysis and assessment of change in personality, identity and self-definitions over the life span, the importance of self-reflection and life review for personality development, and positive conceptions of lifespan development in general.

Taru Feldt received her MA in 1991 and PhD (in psychology) in 2000 at the University of Jyväskylä, Finland. Her doctoral thesis concerned the structure, stability, and health-promoting role of a sense of coherence in the working life. She is currently working as a postdoc in the Human Development and Its Risk Factors program in the Department of Psychology at the University of Jyväskylä.

Christopher Hertzog is Professor of Psychology at the Georgia Institute of Technology in Atlanta. He joined the faculty at Georgia Tech in 1985, after being an Assistant Professor in the Human Development and Family Studies at The Pennsylvania State University. His research focuses on individual differences in adult cognitive development, with an emphasis on application of quantitative methods to developmental research. He is currently the principal investigator on two research grants from the U.S. National Institute on Aging.

Kenji Kato received a PhD in health science from Osaka University in Japan, and is currently working toward another PhD at Karolinska Institutet in Sweden. He started working with Swedish twin studies in 2002, primarily focusing on the relationship between stress, personality, and health problems. As a registered nurse and public health nurse in Japan, he is particularly interested in the application of behavior–genetic approaches to prevention and intervention for lifelong health promotion.

Martin Kohli is Professor of Sociology at the European University Institute in Florence, Italy, on leave from the Free University of Berlin where he has been a professor since 1977. He is a member of both the Berlin-Brandenburg and the Austrian Academy of Sciences, and from

1997 to 1999 was President of the European Sociological Association (ESA). In Berlin, he directs the Research Group on Aging and the Life Course (*Forschungsgruppe Altern und Lebenslauf [FALL]*). He has published extensively on the sociology of the life course; generations and aging; family, labor markets, and social policy; and more recently on the emergence of a European society.

Katja Kokko received her MA degree in 1996 and PhD degree (in Psychology) in 2001 at the University of Jyväskylä, Finland. Her doctoral thesis was on the antecedents and consequences of long-term unemployment. She is currently working as a postdoc in the Human Development and Its Risk Factors program, at the University of Jyväskylä. She analyzes data based on the Jyväskylä Longitudinal Study of Personality and Social Development (JYLS), led by Professor Lea Pulkkinen. She has also conducted postdoctoral studies at the University of Montreal.

Andreas Kruse is Director of the Gerontological Institute of the University of Heidelberg, Germany. Formerly, he was Foundation Director, Professor, and Chair of Lifespan Psychology and Pedagogical Psychology at the Psychological Institute of the University of Greifswald, Germany. Kruse received his PhD in psychology at the University of Bonn, Germany, and his habilitation in psychology at the University of Heidelberg, Germany. His research focuses on competence in old age, productive aging, consequences of demographic change, rehabilitation, intervention research, palliative medicine and palliative care, and ethical questions. He received the First International Presidential Award of the International Association of Gerontology and is a member of numerous international and national expert comissions. He is editor and author of several textbooks on psychological and medical aspects of aging across the life span.

Harald Künemund is Assistant Professor at the Institute for Sociology, member of the Research Group on Aging and the Life Course (FALL) at the Free University of Berlin, and Deputy Professor for Methods of Empirical Research and Statistics at the University of Erfurt, Germany. He was involved in several research projects and, together with Martin Kohli, he has designed and realized the sociological part of the German Aging Survey. He specializes in research design and methods and studies social participation and generational relations, with a focus on elderly people (e.g., productive aging, social networks and support, intergenerational transfers).

Charlotte Mickler is a doctoral student at the Jacobs Center for Lifelong Learning and Institutional Development, International University Bremen, Germany. She received her MA in psychology from the Free University Berlin in 2001. During her studies, she spent one year at the University of North London, London, UK. Her current research focuses on the development of a conception of self-related wisdom as a form of maturity and on the distinction between growth and functionality.

Nancy L. Pedersen received her training as a behavioral geneticist at the University of Colorado in Boulder. She has been in Sweden at the Karolinska Institutet since the late 1970s, where she is currently the Director of the Swedish Twin Registry and Professor of Genetic Epidemiology in the Department of Medical Epidemiology and Biostatistics. She is also Research Professor of Psychology at the University of Southern California, Los Angeles. Her research interests have focused on gerontological genetics through longitudinal studies of aging such as the Swedish Adoption/Twin Study of Aging (SATSA), GENDER, and OCTO twin studies, neurodegenerative disorders (Alzheimer's and Parkinson's diseases), depression, and chronic fatigue.

Sonja Perren is a developmental psychologist, Assistant Professor in the Department of Psychology (Social and Health Psychology) at the University of Zurich, and senior researcher at the Department of Child and Adolescent Psychiatry at the University of Basel, Switzerland. Her research and teaching interests include various life course transitions ranging from kindergarten entry to transition to parenthood to caregiving in old age. Her main research question concerns the significance of social relationships for adjustment and well-being.

Pasqualina Perrig-Chiello is Professor of Developmental Psychology at the University of Bern, Switzerland. Her teaching and major research interests focus on lifespan developmental psychology (especially well-being, personality, and gender roles), developmental health psychology, and familial intergenerational relations. She has held teaching appointments at the Universities of Saarbrücken (Germany), Frankfurt (Germany), and Basel (Switzerland). She co-organized the Fifteenth Meeting of the International Society for the Study of Behavioral Development (ISSBD) in 1998, at the University of Bern. She is a member of the Swiss National Research Council, and she chairs the Directory Board of the National Research Program 52 on "Intergenerational Relations."

Lea Pulkkinen is Professor of Psychology at the University of Jyväskylä, Finland, and Director of the Program on Human Development and Its Risk Factors (approved as the Center of Excellence in 1997). She received her PhD at the University of Jyväskylä in 1969 and did her postdoctoral studies at Sussex University, UK. She was the President of the International Society for the Study of Behavioral Development (ISSBD) from 1991 to 1996. She received the Finnish Science Prize in 2001, and in 2003, she was awarded the Aristotle Prize by the European Federation of Psychologists Association (EFPA).

K. Warner Schaie, the Evan Pugh Professor of Human Development and Psychology at The Pennsylvania State University, is regarded as one of the foremost scholars in the field of adult development and aging. He holds a PhD in psychology from the University of Washington, Seattle. Since 1956, he has directed the Seattle Longitudinal Study (SLS), a major study of intellectual performance in older adults. He received an honorary PhD from Friedrich-Schiller University, Jena, Germany, in 1997; the Mensa Education and Research Foundation Lifetime Achievement Award in 2000; and an honorary ScD from West Virginia University in 2002.

Erica L. Spotts is Assistant Research Professor in the Department of Psychiatry and Behavioral Sciences at the George Washington University in Washington, DC. After receiving her PhD in 2001, she went on to a postdoctoral fellowship at the Department of Medical Epidemiology and Biostatistics at the Karolinska Institutet in Sweden. Her research interests focus on better understanding the genetic and environmental underpinnings of the links between interpersonal relationships and mental health across the life span, with particular emphasis on romantic relationships and depression.

Ursula M. Staudinger is Professor of Psychology, Academic Dean, and Vice President at the International University Bremen, Germany. She received her PhD in 1988 and her Habilitation in 1997 from the Free University of Berlin. Among her research interests are the study of plasticity and resilience in lifespan development, the interaction between cognition, emotion, and motivation across the life span, and the social-interactive nature of human functioning. She is a Fellow of the American Psychological Association and a member of the German Academy of Natural Scientists Leopoldina and of the Heidelberg Academy of Sciences.

Hans-Werner Wahl is Professor of Social and Environmental Gerontology and Chair of the Department of Social and Environmental Gerontology at the German Center for Research on Aging at the University of Heidelberg. He received his PhD in psychology from the Free University of Berlin. His current research interests cover conceptual and empirical issues of environmental gerontology, the psychosocial consequences of age-related vision loss, everyday competence of older adults and related intervention strategies, and the history of gerontology. He was awarded the "Max-Bürger-Preis" for outstanding research in gerontology from the German Society of Gerontology and Geriatrics.

Daniel Zimprich is Assistant Professor in the Department of Psychology at The University of Zurich, Switzerland. Zimprich received his MA (Diplom) at the University of Mannheim, Germany, and his PhD in psychology at The Institute of Gerontology of The University of Heidelberg, Germany. His current research focuses on methods of longitudinal research, intellectual development across the life span, and experimental studies of learning, cognition, and metacognitive skills. He is part of an international network of researchers on longitudinal research and has worked with numerous longitudinal data sets covering development from childhood and adolescence to middle age and old age.